THERAPEUTIC STRATEGIES
FOR TREATING ADDICTION

LIBRARY OF SUBSTANCE ABUSE AND ADDICTION TREATMENT

A Series of Books Edited by
Jerome David Levin, Ph.D.

Substance abuse and addiction are the third most common cause of mortality in the United States. They are among the most prevalent mental illnesses, not only in the United States, but throughout the world. They are also notoriously difficult to treat. Mental health professionals see few patients whose lives or illnesses have not been profoundly affected by their own use or that of their families or peers. Addiction is not peripheral but central to the human condition and research into it is illuminating our understanding of self.

The *Library of Substance Abuse and Addiction Treatment* is dedicated to providing mental health professionals with the tools they need to treat these scourges—tools ranging from scientific knowledge to clinical technique. Nonideological, it is equally open to behavioral, cognitive, disease model, psychodynamic, and least harm perspectives. An overdetermined disorder affecting millions of people requires multiple viewpoints if it is to be successfully treated. The *Library* provides those multiple perspectives for clinicians, students, and laypeople as articulated by the most insightful workers in the field. Practical, utilitarian, scholarly, and state-of-the-art, these books are addressed to all who wish to deepen their understanding of and increase their clinical efficacy in treating addiction.

THERAPEUTIC STRATEGIES FOR TREATING ADDICTION

From Slavery to Freedom

JEROME DAVID LEVIN, PH.D.

JASON ARONSON INC.
Northvale, New Jersey
London

This book was set in 11 pt. Berling by Alpha Graphics of Pittsfield, NH, and printed and bound by Book-mart Press, Inc. of North Bergen, NJ.

Bob Dylan quotation on p. 18 "It's All Right Ma (I'm Only Bleeding)"
Copyright © 1965 by Warner Bros. Inc. Copyright renewed 1993 by
Special Rider Music.

Library of Congress Cataloging-in-Publication Data

Levin, Jerome D. (Jerome David)
    Therapeutic strategies for treating addiction: from slavery to freedom / Jerome David Levin.
        p. cm.
    Includes bibliographical references and index.
    ISBN 0-7657-0287-8
    1. Compulsive behavior—Patients—Rehabilitation. 2. Psychotherapy. 3. Psychoanalysis. 4. Addicts—Rehabilitation. I. Title.
RC533.L488 2000
616.86'0651—dc21   00-038967

Printed in the United States of America on acid-free paper. For information and catalog write to Jason Aronson Inc., 230 Livingston Street, Northvale, NJ 07647-1726, or visit our website: www.aronson.com

In memory of Lila Rosenblum,

who accompanied so many on their

journeys to freedom

Be drunk, always. Nothing else matters; this is our sole concern. To ease the pain as Time's dread burden weighs down upon your shoulders and crushes you to earth, you must be drunk without respite.

Drunk with what? With wine, with poetry, or with virtue, as you please. But be drunk.

And if sometimes, on the steps of palaces, on the green grass in a ditch, in the dreary solitude of your room, you should wake and find your drunkenness half over or fully gone, ask of wind or wave, of star or bird or clock, ask of all that flies, of all that sighs, moves, sings, or speaks, ask them what time it is; and wind, wave, star, bird, or clock will answer: "It is time to be drunk! To throw off the chains and martyrdom of Time, be drunk; be drunk eternally! With wine, with poetry, or with virtue, as you please."

Baudelaire, *Be Drunk*

❖ CONTENTS ❖

Introduction

The epigraph from Baudelaire's *Be Drunk* can be read in two ways—as a comment on the intolerability of sober insight, which ineluctably and insistently calls attention to the grim realities of life, in particular the devastating effect of time; or as an endorsement of a Dionysian ecstatic approach to life, as opposed to an Apollonian calm, rational, and steady approach. Eugene O'Neill (1946), maintains something similar to the first way in his play *The Iceman Cometh*, in which a group of skid-row rummies try to give up their pipe dreams, their delusions, and fail, returning to their alcohol-reinforced fantasies. O'Neill seems to be saying that human life is intolerable when faced in all of its horror, and that delusion of one sort or another, chemical or otherwise, is necessary even to endure. This is a view shared, consciously or unconsciously, by most addicts, and we therapists should not reject it out of hand as a rationalization in service of the addiction. Freedom is complex; freedom is dialectical. Paradoxically, the very journey from slavery to freedom involves the relinquishing of a certain kind of freedom, however delusional, and the patient's sorrow at this loss should be acknowledged and indeed the therapist should enable a mourning process for this loss. The move from the Dionysian to the Apollonian, from the ecstatic to the rational, that sobriety entails also constitutes a loss, albeit there is much gained, and this, too, must be acknowledged by the therapist and mourned by the patient.

Much of the material in this book has previously appeared elsewhere, generally in a somewhat or even radically different form. So in some sense this book is a variant on the collected (or selected) papers format. I've chosen the materials I have because I believe it is useful to have them available in a single format, and that that format gives them the shape and meaning they would otherwise lack. Finally, they are united by and belong together because of their thematic unity. Each chapter in its own way is either about the journey from addiction to recovery, from slavery to freedom, or it is about how to take patients on that journey. In bringing together these works something new has emerged for me. For the first time I came to see my work as about enabling freedom, and by extension, came to view all addiction work, if not all therapy, through this lens and illuminated by this light. The acquisition of this perspective has changed my take on the entire process of addiction treatment and of the nature of the disorder itself.

Although united thematically, the chapters elucidate the theme in a radically different way. Some are how-to chapters, others are narratives, some are dramatizations, and yet others adumbrate theoretical models and are predominantly didactic in nature. Just as treatment requires a multimodal approach, understanding addiction, elucidating is phenomenology and dynamics, and developing and conveying treatment approaches similarly require multiple perspectives. It is my hope that this book provides just such a polymorphous perverse—to use Freud's wonderful phrase for the ubiquity of Eros in the body—approach to addiction, giving the reader multiple perspectives conveyed by literarily diverse styles and genres. Such diversity runs the risk of incoherence, while opening up possibilities for playfulness and pleasure in this rather grim subject matter. I hope that the reader finds more fun than confusion in the seemingly random compilation, which actually has a method behind its eclecticism of content, genre, and style. It is a method that necessarily entails some redundancy, but I believe that such redundancy is minimal and may even serve a pedagogical purpose of clarifying difficult concepts.

Chapter 1 introduces the concept of freedom as a goal of therapy, particularly in the therapy of addicted patients. Chapter 2 is didactic in nature. It briefly highlights the salient assumptions of the major schools of therapy and elucidates their understandings of human nature and the human condition. It then goes on to show how their therapeutic strategies are grounded in those understandings. Although this exposition is basic, and its content may be familiar to readers of this book, I believe it nevertheless serves a useful purpose as a prolegomenon to making explicit how the insights and technical procedures of the various schools can be adapted to work with addicted populations. Both their utility in addiction therapy and the way in which they are not applicable to this work are made explicit, as are the necessary modifications of their theoretical assumptions and characteristic ways of working in order to derive the maximum benefit from their adaptation to work with substance abusers and behavioral addicts.

The second part of Chapter 2 does for therapeutic techniques such as reflection, confrontation, and interpretation what the first part does for the schools. Since considerable modification and adaptation of technique is necessary in addiction work, this section, both in its expository and in its creative reshaping of received methodology, has direct, unmediated, immediate implications for working with the addicted, and should be of great utility in doing that work.

Chapter 3 focuses on theory, and uses the work of Heinz Kohut, the founder of the psychoanalytic school of self psychology, to suggest ways of understanding and empathizing with the inner world, the subjective experience, of the addicted. Although this chapter draws on the sometimes awkward and often off-putting terminology Kohut developed in elucidating the model, its intention is to move the therapist closer to the patient's lived life so that communication becomes possible and the therapist speaks to the patient where he or she is at. As with any metapsychological formulation, the intent is to bring coherence to widely variegated clinical and research observations. This integration not only illuminates the addicted patient's inner experience, but also predicts his or her characteristic behavior, including behavior toward the therapist. The chapter ends with a set of explicit treatment recommendations, which however theory- and model-based, are highly practical. They are tips for moving the patient toward liberation.

The case history chapters that follow are intended to vivify the process by which addicted patients are facilitated in making their journey from slavery to freedom. The success of the process and the length of the distance transversed varies from case to case as it does in actual clinical practice. Some barely get their bags packed; others arrive. The cases also vary in the degree to which they are straight narratives and the degree to which they adumbrate theory and explicitly illustrate technique. However, regardless of the balance between narrative and didactic exposition, it is my hope that the process comes alive. The first case is the story of a severely traumatized borderline patient who was treated psychodynamically (Chapter 4). The next case is different, in that the patient, a tormented clergyman, is in recovery when he comes to treatment (Chapter 5). Although no longer chemically dependent, he is far from free. His motivation for seeking treatment is fear of slipping, and the case makes clear the necessity of dealing with underlying emotional issues once stable sobriety is established. It also deals with countertransferential issues and working with difficult, provocative, addicted patients, which is more the rule than the exception.

The next case is that of a man I never saw face to face. It is a case of a behavioral rather than chemical addiction, and the "patient" is someone of considerable influence; in fact, a man who was the most powerful man on earth—the president of the United States. My analysis of President Clinton's seemingly irrational behavior in the Monica Lewinsky scenario and my conclusion that he is best understood as sex addicted is drawn from my 1998 book, *The Clinton Syndrome: The President and the Self-Destructive Nature of Sexual Addiction*, but it is here modified to put a greater emphasis on treatment possibilities. Clinton's "case" is an opportunity to elucidate diagnostic criteria for a controversial nosological category—sexual addiction—and to make some recommendations for treating it. So Chapter 6 turns out to be as much about sexual addiction and its treatment as about Bill Clinton.

Technology influences every aspect of life including psychotherapy and its delivery. I address one aspect of the impact of technology, that of the telephone, on therapy in Chapter 7. Since Monica Lewinsky and Bill Clinton are reported to have practiced telephone sex, it is perhaps fitting that this chapter follows my discussion of the president and his sexual vicissitudes.

Although the telephone is hardly a new invention—Sigmund Freud had one of the first telephones in Vienna—and there are already Internet therapeutic websites, telephone therapy has been relatively rare until recently. Its practice raises all sorts of questions about ethics, about technique, and about transference and countertransference in telephone therapy. Chapter 7 addresses these issues as manifest in the telephone therapy of addiction, which raises special problems that are not present in other telephone therapies, and I try to deal with these special problems as well.

In this era of short-term, issue-oriented, increasingly mechanistic psychotherapy, it is all too easy to forget about the patient's inner world of fantasy, unconscious conflict, and repressed emotion. Since this forgetting is exactly what the patient has been doing, especially if the patient is addicted, this is a form of collusion. Fortunately, there is a strong antidote to temptation to move toward this socially reinforced superficiality, namely the magnificent contribution of the psychodynamic tradition to the understanding of human nature. Chapter 8 is an exposition of the insights of this tradition into substance abuse and addiction. It shows how these insights can be used therapeutically.

Moving away from the theoretical, Chapter 9 dramatizes the countertransferential ensnarlments, the entrapments awaiting the therapist, particularly the addictions therapist. In their own way, therapists are just as subject to—in danger of—enslavement as patients are. They get sucked into the vortex of irrationality, primitive passion, and behavior that their patients bring to the table—or should I say couch? Additionally, therapists starting with Freud have been anything but immune to addictions of their own. Therapists are an at-risk group for chemical and behavioral addictions, not to mention other psychopathologies. Since a sizable part of my practice consists of treating manifestly impaired professionals, I am all too aware of the human vulnerability of high achievers, including psychotherapists. Since I also do a good deal of supervision, I also see nonaddicted therapists struggling to maintain their autonomy and freedom while working day in and day out with highly disturbed addicted patients fighting tenaciously to defend their addictions—not infrequently through the use of projective identification, the inducement of unacceptable feelings in the therapist, as a way of getting rid of them. Such projective identification does indeed not infrequently succeed in the inducement of states of being in the therapist. Since these feelings and states are being externalized in the first place because they are intolerable, it is not surprising that therapists do not always succeed in maintaining their autonomy and freedom. They too become enslaved and must transverse a steep and treacherous path if they are to regain their lost freedom.

I struggled with how to present such dilemmas, and came to the conclusion that because issues of confidentiality are more acute and salient when working with professionals, particularly mental health professionals, some of whom are publicly prominent, it would not be salutary to do a straight case history of either treatment or supervision. Instead, the possibility of dramatization dawned on me and I took that route. Although Dr. Sonnenshein is fictional, he is a composite of real persons and his difficulties are drawn from real situations, albeit heightened for dramatic and literary purposes. In creating him, I have drawn not only on experiences with patients and supervisees, but on my own feelings of exasperation with my patients, fears of merging with them and getting lost in their misery, and fears of losing such freedom as I possess. These dangers to the therapist doing addiction work are very real. Sonnenshein's vicissitudes, however magnified, even exaggerated, are one with the experience of all of us in the field. They are exemplary and will, I hope, serve as warnings and alert us to the need to take protective measures and live our lives with sufficient balance to serve as a counterforce to the addictive potential of therapy itself—not only for patients but also for therapists. Addiction to work, something I see all the time in therapists, is no less enslaving than any other behavioral addiction, while carrying the additional danger that comes with working with demons on an ongoing basis.

Sonnenshein and his vicissitudes are intended not only to serve a pedagogical purpose but also to entertain, a purpose given the frequently grave nature of our subject matter that is by no means counterindicated. Tales of Dr. Sonnenshein were written for this book.

Many types of people get addicted to various substances and behaviors. It has been said that addiction is an equal-opportunity destroyer. These people vary not only in terms of socioeconomic status, race, gender, sexual orientation, and social class, but also, and perhaps more saliently, in terms of their inner worlds—of where they are coming from and what drives their addictions. In Chapter 10 I look at some alcoholics who vary in terms of what is driving their addiction, and try and convey this subjective experience through interior monologue while at the same time objectively analyzing it in terms of the four factors that drive any chemical addiction: the pharmacology of the drug, constitutional predisposition (genetic endowment), personality, and environment. Each of our monologists is considering whether or not he or she drinks too much, and in eavesdropping on them we gain insight into the intense ambivalence that characterizes any recovery. Each session ends with some thoughts on how to move these folks—who are at least wondering if they have a problem—toward recovery and toward freedom.

Chapter 11 is an attempt to harness the wisdom of one of the West's greatest philosophers for therapeutic purposes. Spinoza was a metaphysician, not a therapist. Nevertheless, his work was never merely abstract. It always had an ethical and practical purpose. His goal was nothing less than to release from bondage the few people he thought capable of it. This most radical of determinists is nevertheless the philosopher par excellence of freedom. But a strange freedom it is since he defines freedom as "the acceptance of necessity." No other thinker I know of struggled so hard with the paradox inherent in the very notion of freedom and felt so deeply into the lived experience of illusionary, even delusional beliefs that man is free, while unceasingly searching for genuine freedom that indeed releases from bondage. Not only did he discover a path to freedom, in the sense of release from bondage, or as he called it a path to blessedness, but he grounded his ethical vision in a metaphysical vision, in an understanding of reality itself, of the universe and man's place in it.

Spinoza developed very specific directions for entering into the journey from slavery to freedom, directions austere and forbidding that nevertheless constitute a cognitive therapy, a cognitive therapy in need of explication to make it accessible and a cognitive therapy in its accessible guise directly applicable to addiction treatment. How to make intelligible and applicable the dialectical tension between freedom and necessity in Spinoza's philosophy is the question I had to answer in writing Chapter 11. And there is yet another dialectical tension in his work between the cognitive and affective. This most intellectual of thinkers turns in the end to Eros as the source of transformation, the energy that permits man to reach a state of blessedness. In what is perhaps an oxymoronic phrase he calls this energy "intellectual love." But for him intellectual love is not an oxymoron; it is a creative tension, the tension of paired antinomies that can open new vistas. To bring the discussion down to earth, we might say that Spinoza's approach is, to steal a phrase from Albert Ellis, a rational-emotive therapy. But again, how to bring in Spinoza's thought, which I am convinced can be used therapeutically in addiction treatment, without turning a book on psychotherapy into a philosophy lecture, remained a dilemma. Then a solution occurred to me. His was the most dramatic of lives, lived in a time and a place itself filled with conflict, tension, danger, and a clash of armies and ideologies. So why not dramatize Spinoza's life, time, and thought as an alternative to straight exposition and in so doing use Freud, Nietzsche, and William James as foils to make real the complexity and depth of conflict in the man and his work. I've done so. But they are not only foils; they also embody conceptualizations of the dialectical tension between freedom and necessity.

My dramatization tries to make clear the human cost and the emotional source of Spinoza's therapy. It does so largely through the agency of a character called the Chorus, who articulates Spinoza's unspoken and unconscious conflicts. It is for the reader to judge the success of this dramatization. After this indirect exposition of Spinoza's philosophy, I spell out the therapeutic implications of it and try to elucidate what a Spinozaistic cognitive therapy would look like. Finally, I give a case history of a Spinozaistic treatment of an addict.

After this rather extended side trip to the imaginary, the book returns to the more conventional and clinically therapeutic, this time centering on the family therapy approach to addiction treatment in Chapter 12. Addiction has been rightly described as a family disease, and the loss of freedom, the enslavement, we attributed to the addicted themselves is no less true of those intimately, sometimes all too intimately, involved with addicts. Perhaps their enslavement is less total, although not necessarily so. Nevertheless, they, too, desperately need help in achieving their own releases. Codependency can be as addictive as heroin—and just as enslaving.

As I have pointed out elsewhere (Levin 1998b), addiction is a family disease in at least three senses. It runs in families; each and every family member has an impact on the identified patient, the active addict. They do so not only individually, but collectively, and their collective influence is greater than the sum of their parts. That is, the family has a life and dynamics of its own. Families often, either intentionally and consciously or unwittingly and unconsciously, perpetuate not only their own unfreedom but that of the addicted family member.

Finally, the addict and the addicted behavior have a profound effect on each and every family member and on the family dynamics as a whole. This effect is almost always overwhelmingly deleterious, especially in its impact on children. Another way of looking at the three senses in which addiction is a family disease is temporally. The past, both in terms of genetically transmitted vulnerability and in terms of model, cultural pattern, and trauma, contributes to addictive potential; the present is an interlocking system, a mutually reinforcing enslavement between family members, and the future is poisoned and compromised by the addictive behavior in the present. A mess indeed. What has to be done?

Essentially, two things can be done. The family members, or the subset that is available for treatment, are worked on and with individually. If possible, that subset includes the addict. All the family is seen as a dynamic entity, which is something different from the sum of its components and their interaction, and the family as a whole becomes the patient. When that happens we have family therapy, a modality widely and wisely used in substance abuse and behavioral addiction treatment.

There are many schools of family therapy and many approaches to practicing it. In the first part of the Baker case, I briefly explain the sources, underlying assumptions, and ways of working of each school. I also touch on the personalities and professional backgrounds of the founders of the various schools, and how who they were influenced what they did and how they did it. The rest of the chapter is devoted to the Baker case itself. The Bakers are a family with a teenage son who is a relapsing pot addict. In the case presentation the Bakers are treated by therapists from each of the schools and by a substance abuse family therapist, who comes closest to my way of working with families with an addictive member. This gives you a chance to see many ways, not only my own, of working with addicted families. The therapist's goal in this family work can be conceptualized in exactly the same way as it is in individual therapy as facilitating a journey, or in this case journeys, from slavery to freedom.

Chapter 13 presents a long monologue spoken by a recovering substance abuser in the course of his therapy sessions. Set in a mental hospital, it gives the reader a glimpse into the inner world of an addict at the end of his rope and a sense of the forces that allowed him to snap the chains of addiction and move from slavery to freedom.

In his conclusion to his great Midrash (commentary) on the book of Exodus and the interpretive uses to which it has been put by men and women struggling for liberation in sundry times and places, Michael Walzer (1985) tells us that we are always in Egypt, that there is always a Canaan that is simply a better place and not an ideal one, and that "there is no way to get from here to there except by joining hands and marching" (p. 149). Substance abusers are always and most certainly in bondage in Egypt; sobriety or recovery is assuredly a better place, albeit and significantly not a perfect one, and just as assuredly, the only way to get there is to join together and march, join together in alliance with therapist, group, spouse, family, and Twelve-Step meeting, and to march through, work through, the wilderness of denial, conflict, and emotional arrest. And we therapists are privileged to go on our patient's march from slavery to freedom, from Egypt to Canaan, from the darkness of addiction to the light of the better place of sobriety. But we too are in our Egypts and we too need to join together and march to a better place. And if we do it right, it is not only that we march with them, they march with us, and both patient and therapist arrive at a better place.

Therapists Are in the Freedom Business

All psychotherapy is about increasing freedom, loosening the bonds that hold the patient enthralled and enmeshed. The psychotic who suffers from command hallucinations that tell him to kill, the obsessive who can't stop the squirrel running in his head, the compulsive who can't stop washing his hands or checking the stove, and the hysteric who can't stop emoting without feeling are all unfree, are all enslaved. Whether such enslavement is understood as the effect of genetically determined neurochemistry, or the effect of acute and chronic trauma, or the result of unconscious conflict, or the effect of some interaction of all the above, the result is the same—compulsion. Symptoms and symptomatic behavior imprison. And even in cases in which the prisoner is reasonably seen as being his own jailer, the patient has no idea of where to find the key. Indeed, it has not even occurred to the prisoner that the key exists. Life outside of the cell remains incomprehensible if envisioned or thought of at all. The job of the therapist is to provide a vision that encompasses life outside of the cell; to inculcate a notion of freedom, a life beyond the compulsion of the symptom or disease.

Patients lack such a vision. Habituation, familiarity, what Freud called the "conservatism of the instincts," the repetition-compulsion, fear of the novel and unknown, and not infrequently, the presence of very real jailers who benefit from the prisoner's enslavement, all prevent this. Therefore, therapists must be in the freedom business. They must be guides, mentors, and facilitators on the journey from slavery to freedom.

Plato (375 B.C.) caught all this poignantly in his myth of the cave in book six of *The Republic*. In the myth, the prisoners are chained to a wall that they face; behind them is a fire that casts shadows on the wall. The prisoners, who know no other reality, mistake the play of shadows for reality. They are released and leave the cave. Blinded by the unfamiliar sun, bringer of illumination-insight as well as freedom, if the two are separable, since insight leads to freedom or, at the very least, is a precondition of it, the prisoners are bewildered and return to the cave. The insight that is perhaps the most crucial is the insight that freedom exists, that it is desirable, and that it is possible; such insight is not possible for the prisoners of the cave. Immured to the shadows in the darkness, they flee the light of the sun back into the darkness of the cave. Although their fetters have been removed, they remain prisoners of their own fear. Sound familiar? Hasn't Plato described the course of every psychotherapy?

What is true of every therapy is true a fortiori of the psychotherapy of addiction. Few patients are as enslaved as the addicted, few patients so totally mistake the fleeting shadows for reality, few patients live in deeper darkness, and few patients are more prone to run back into the cave, to flee sobriety and recovery, as the addicted. They do so essentially because they are afraid. If every successful therapy is in some sense a journey from slavery to freedom, and I believe that it is, then successful therapy of addiction is a journey from the very lowest, darkest, coldest, most miserable cell with the heaviest most rusty chains to what must ineluctably, by virtue of the starkness of the contrast, seem to be particularly blinding light and agoraphobia-inducing spaciousness. It is no accident that Sigmund Freud identified, however grandiosely, with Moses, the great liberator. As any reader of the book of Exodus knows, the liberated slaves yearned for the "fleshpots of Egypt." The addictions therapist can hear his patients in the newly liberated slaves' question, "Aren't there enough graves in Egypt that you had to bring us into the wilderness to die?" Newly recovering substance abusers not only yearn for their fleshpots, they experience themselves as lost in the wilderness of a bewildering state of being—sobriety—and not infrequently feel that they are going to die. There is no more trapped feeling than the deep-down conviction that drinking is no longer possible, that life cannot continue if the drinking continues, while being just as sure that life is not possible without it. The same applies to drugging or compulsive gambling or compulsive sexing. Such a state of being is total enslavement.

The now-free slaves are continually backsliding. They are stiff-necked and not amenable to reason or persuasion. Any leader, political, spiritual, or therapeutic, who has tried to take anyone toward freedom understands backsliding and stiff-neckedness. Those damn patients are always backsliding and they are stubborn as mules. Dostoevsky (1880) makes the same point—that freedom, however cherished, is equally feared in his "Myth of the Grand Inquisitor" in *The Brothers Karamazov*. In the myth, Christ returns to earth to be sent away by the Grand Inquisitor who tells him that men are not equal to fully experiencing reality and gaining knowledge of the truth, nor of handling the freedom that is the concomitant of insight. So the Inquisitor and his confederates will bear the burden of such insight and protect mankind from the truth and from the responsibility that they cannot stand. Instead the Inquisitor will provide them with comforting myths. Of course, the trade-off is social control by the Inquisitor.

Eric Fromm (1941) makes exactly the same point in his classic *Escape from Freedom*, in which, much like Dostoevsky, he sees as a central dynamic driving totalitarianism at the political level, and neurosis and addiction at the personal level, fear of freedom and the radical contingency and responsibility for self that comes with it. Men throw away their freedom, indeed flee it, into abasement and submission to a strong leader and his ideology, a consuming neurosis, or a drug. It is not merely that the strong man, or the ideology, or the neurosis, or the drug enslaves; rather, it is the escape from freedom that motivates the submission to the power of the leader, the party, the compulsion, or the addiction. It is the inability to tolerate what

Søren Kierkegaard (1849) called, the "dizziness of freedom" that enslaves. The dizziness of freedom has set off many a slip (relapse) among recovering addicts. Therefore, the therapist must articulate the inchoate fear that having so many choices engenders in the patient. This freedom induces more anxiety than can be sustained, and the therapist in his very capacity as one in the freedom business must paradoxically help the patient avoid the dizziness of freedom by demonstrating to the patient that choices can be postponed until sobriety solidifies and the patient's capacity to endure sobriety is augmented. What Exodus's Moses calls backsliding and Plato calls the regressive pull of the cave, Freud calls resistance. It is resistance, along with ignorance, and external oppression that maintains enslavement. From the beginning, Freud recognized that there were forces in the patient that militated against cure, that fought to maintain the illness and the unfreedom that goes with it. Over the years of his long career he repeatedly speculated about the nature of the forces that lead patients not only to resist moving toward health, but also to tenaciously fight to remain sick. In his last major clinical monograph, *Inhibitions, Symptoms, and Anxiety* (1926), he systematizes his understanding of resistance using his structural model (Freud 1923) to categorize resistances. In the structural model Freud postulated that mental and emotional life can be understood as a dynamic struggle among three agencies of the mind—id, ego, and superego—defined by their functions. The id, literally the "it," is the repository of instinctual energy, of drives pressing for discharge. The id is the biologically given, soma not psyche, and it is its mental representations or derivatives that allow us to have knowledge of the id, just as we "know" the electron through its effects. By definition this seething cauldron of pure energy is unconscious.

The ego is the rational part of the mind, the weak executive who tries to mediate between biological imperatives, internalized cultural standards, and external reality so that a modicum of satisfaction can be gleaned from life. There are many ego functions, among them defense. The ego operates on both conscious and unconscious levels. It is usually unconscious of its defensive maneuvers, and making the characteristic defenses and the ways the patient uses them conscious is a major part of modern psychodynamic treatment. The superego is the internalized parental prohibitions and restrictions. Freud tells us that it is the heir of the Oedipus complex; the child, realizing that he or she can't win the oedipal struggle, identifies with and internalizes the same-sex parent. If you can't beat 'em, join 'em; or better yet have them join you. The superego constitutes both the conscience and the ego ideal—what we want to be.

Freud (1926) uses this model to categorize resistance, discussing resistance from each of the agencies of the mind. The resistance from the id is twofold: the conservatism of the instincts and the adhesion of the libido. By conservatism of the instincts Freud meant the built-in tendency of the psyche to stay with what it knows, its tendency to maintain homeostasis and not risk upsetting the apple cart (no matter how rotten the apples) by trying something new. In health there are other forces seeking growth and development, but these are unfortunately in abeyance, or fettered, as is the patient, in illness. It is this inertial conservatism that drives the repetition-compulsion, the built-in tendency to go around and around the same circle in a dynamic stasis, which is a simulacrum of the stasis of death. The conservatism of the instincts fights liberation and maintains enslavement. Insofar as this eternal—unless an outside force acts on it—repetition, this stuckness in the known and familiar, is a form of death, death at least of psychic growth, it can be seen as a manifestation of Thanatos, Freud's death instinct, the entropy of every living thing that seeks the quietus of the inorganic. In *Beyond the Pleasure Principle* (1920) Freud presents us with a metaphysical vision of the eternal struggle between Eros, the force of growth, differentiation, and integration, and Thanatos, the force of regression, dedifferentiation, symbiosis, and disintegration. Those of us in the freedom business need to be on the side of Eros.

Less metaphysically, the Twelve-Step, Alcoholics Anonymous (AA)-type programs define insanity as doing the same thing over and over again while expecting a different result. They too point to the conservatism of the instincts. Whether one buys Freud's metapsychology (abstract theorizing) or not, there is no doubt that phenomenologically, that is, descriptively, he is right. Human beings are indeed conservative in the sense that at least part of them will not change easily or gladly. This is particularly true, beyond the typical strength of this innate tendency, of substance abusers and other addicts. Theirs is indeed a built-in inertia. The clinical implication of all this is that powerful counterforces must be brought to bear on this intrinsic conservatism. For that reason, I favor multimodal treatment of substance abuse and addiction. Such multimodal treatment includes detoxification; inpatient rehabilitation, if needed; individual, group, and family therapy, as indicated; participation in Twelve-Step programs, if desirable; and such ancillary interventions as vocational counseling and educational remediation.

The second id resistance Freud calls the adhesion of the libido. The notion here is that once people love something, they love it forever, or at least it is very difficult to relinquish love objects, particularly archaic ones. Our first loves, our attachments to our parents, persist over a lifetime. Few are loved as passionately, as devotedly, or as faithfully as substances are loved by substance abusers. And insofar as these substances are symbolic representations of the parents of early childhood and fantasized as omnipotent providers, that love is all the stronger. The same is true of behavioral addictions such as compulsive gambling, in which the addict loves the activity with all the avidity with which the cocaine devotee loves the stimulant. These are loves that imprison, loves from which it is all too difficult to break free.

There are three ego resistances: repression, transference, and secondary gain. Freud used the term *repression* to mean psychological defenses in general. It is generic rather than specific. Repression includes "repression proper" and the characteristic defenses of substance abusers and addicts: denial, projection, splitting, rationalization, and intellectualization. These defenses do their work tenaciously. They defend not only the ego but also the illness. Maladaptive defenses can be compared to autoimmune diseases; just as the body needs immune reactions, the psyche needs defenses. But when the immune process goes awry, it attacks that which it is meant to defend. Such maladaptive defenses always imprison insofar as they hold the ego in enthronement to the symptom or symptomatic behavior, in our case to the addiction. But defenses are there for a reason and they are clung to so tenaciously out of fear, indeed terror. The therapist needs to speak to the fear, rather than interpret the defenses, although one can do both: call attention to the projection or denial while empathizing with the fear driving it. Addicted patients repress, that is, defend, so desperately and self-defeatingly because they believe, consciously or unconsciously, that they literally cannot survive without the addiction. No other coping mechanism is available, or at least so the patient believes. Ironically, this attempt to stave off death may, and indeed not infrequently does, kill. The enslavement is a "lesser" death.

Freud tells us that the second ego resistance is the transference, the patient's intensely emotional returning to early experience—love and hate for parents and siblings—in his or her relationship to the analyst. In early analysis (Freud and Breuer 1895) the "cure" was held to be the abreaction of strangulated affect. What is needed is derepression, freeing of the strangulated affect in primal screaming. Further, the patient was seen as suffering from reminiscences, that is, from repressed traumatic memories. The "cure" lies in the recovery of these traumatic memories in all their affective intensity. The two formulations—strangulated affect and repressed memory of trauma—are intrinsically intertwined. Freud (1912a) saw the transference as a resistance because the patient "acted instead of remembering"; that is, the emotion attached to the traumatic memory is drained off by being redirected to the analyst or therapist instead of being experienced as the trauma is remembered. Of course, Freud largely and famously changed his mind about this, coming to see the transference as analyzable and a very real opportunity for emotional insight. Nevertheless, the transference can be a diversion and a smokescreen, as when an addict focuses on his or her feelings for the therapist to the exclusion of focusing on the addiction. Enthrallment to the therapist, that which classical analysts called the "transference neurosis," can most certainly be used therapeutically, but that is rarely the case in substance abuse treatment. Here the focus must be on the patient's addictive behavior, not on the patient's feelings for the therapist. Not that these should be ignored. The transference as a resistance maintains the enslavement and the therapist needs to comment on the resistance aspect of the transference. This is particularly true of what is sometimes called the malignant erotic transference, in which love of the therapist is all-consuming. Having said this, it is also true that transference can be a vehicle of recovery, a force moving the patient from slavery to freedom. Plato noted long ago that the pupil learns to please the teacher, that indeed it is Eros, the love of the pupil for the teacher, that is the driving force that allows some to leave and stay out of the cave. Freud was on to the same idea when he said, "Love is the great educator." So the transference is complex, a force that is in the service of resistance and the perpetuation of enslavement *and* a force that liberates, a force that provides the fuel for the journey toward freedom. The therapist must be in touch with both faces of the Janus-like transference.

The third resistance of ego is secondary gain. Here Freud is right on the money, at least when it comes to the maintenance of addiction. Many a substance abuser has died of the "fringe benefits" of that abuse: attention, power, control of others, avoidance of adulthood and its responsibilities, being taken care of by others, indirect expression of hostility—the possibilities for secondary gain are legion. The price of secondary gain(s) is not usually physical death, although that is a distinct possibility; rather, it is emotional and spiritual death, the perpetuation of self-impoverishment and self-imprisonment. It is highly therapeutic to point out the secondary gains derived from addiction and their cost. However transparent this may be to the therapist, it is not to the addicted patient.

Freud said that the resistance from the superego, the patient's feeling that he or she doesn't deserve to get well, or, even worse, the use of the illness as self-punishment, is the hardest resistance to overcome. Freud was right, guilt is a killer, and shame even more so. Addicts are often viewed as sociopathic, but this is inaccurate. Empirical studies show that approximately 20 percent of alcoholics and 30 percent of other substance dependents are sociopathic, while the rest are not. On the contrary, they suffer from harsh, primitively punitive superegos, and the substance use is often what Leon Wurmser (1978) calls "a flight from conscience." This is not to say that the addicted don't commit antisocial acts—they frequently do—in the service of their addiction and in their quest for supplies, and they suffer deep guilt, however anesthetized by drugs or defended by repression for this antisocial behavior. Antisocial behavior secondary to addiction largely dissipates in recovery.

Needless to say, the guilty are unworthy of freedom, a conviction subscribed to and enacted by the guilty themselves. Therefore, the management of guilt is central in the psychotherapeutic treatment of addiction.

Every therapy is a struggle between the forces of regression and the forces of progression; between the resistance and the drive for health; between Thanatos and Eros, the forces of death and the forces of life as Freud (1920) mythologizes them in his great metaphysical vision adumbrated in *Beyond the Pleasure Principle*. Nowhere is this more true than in the treatment of addiction. The therapist must articulate, must make manifest both sides of the struggle, which is, at the least, not clearly in the patient's consciousness, and more usually is not in consciousness at all. In bringing both sides of the conflict into awareness, the therapist is not neutral; rather he or she must communicate understanding of the patient's emersion in both sides of the struggle, while simultaneously taking a strong stand for individualization, differentiation, integration, growth, and freedom, conditions only possible if the addiction is arrested.

No cultural hero took a stronger stand for freedom than Beethoven. In his opera *Fidelio*, the heroine, Leonora, disguised as a man, descends into the deepest, darkest recess of a dungeon in search of her unjustly imprisoned husband, Florestan. Accompanied by the jailer, who has been ordered to dig a grave for the prisoner, Leonora looks into the gloom and dimly sights the prisoner who is to be killed, but in the near dark she cannot be sure that he is her husband. Singing to music of ineffable beauty, she says that she will rescue the prisoner no matter who he is, whether he is her husband or not, for no human being should be treated this way. No human being should be enslaved; all are worthy of freedom. In a thrilling denunciation, Leonora reveals her identity, draws a pistol, confronts the tyrant, and frees the prisoner. The addiction therapist could do worse than identify with Leonora, thereby conveying through his or her very presence, very being, rather than by preaching, exhorting, or being didactic, his or her inalienable belief that every human being is deserving of freedom. This attitudinal component of the therapeutic enterprise is vital because our patients don't believe that they are worthy of freedom, just as much as they don't believe that they can deal with that freedom. Paradoxically, the patients who are the most defiant, most sullen, and most capricious are the most unfree, and at an unconscious level the most convinced that they are undeserving of freedom and most afraid of that freedom. Therefore, we must, in everything we are and can do, convey our profound disagreement with these unconscious beliefs, these chains that sustain the addiction and maintain the bondage.

Oh, you say, all this highfalutin stuff is very impressive, but in the final analysis, who is free? Addicts may be a little less free than most, but it is a distinction without a difference. We are all caught in the coils of necessity, not to mention being in bondage to boss, spouse, family, society, and government. To which I reply that no matter what the ultimate truth about free will and determinism, no human being actually lives believing that he or she is not in some sense a free, autonomous agent. The philosopher who argues most vehemently that all is determined and that freedom is an illusion does not actually act on that premise, nor does he act as if his life or his choices are meaningless, as such a belief in the absence of volition would entail. Radical determinism is not a belief that is livable, even if it is the case. Such philosophical debates are mandarin games that have little to do with life as lived. Everyone assumes, rightfully or wrongfully, that they have some degree of volition, and this recitation of the restrictions all of us live with has little to do with the unfreedom of the addicted, just as the conditions of the chattel slave have little similarity to the restraints on the master. Clearly there are degrees of freedom, even if necessity rules in some ultimate sense, and the addicted are among those with the fewest degrees of freedom.

There is a paradox and mystery here. Science, including psychology and psychodynamic theory, is deterministic, yet the very purpose of psychodynamic treatment is the maximization of freedom. Some of the best minds in history have struggled with this mystery and paradox. Immanuel Kant (1781), the great eighteenth century rationalist philosopher, concluded that "Man as phenomenon is part of the causal chain of nature, while man as noumenon is free." What he meant by this is that human actions are explainable by the same sort of scientific theorizing that the physicist uses to explain natural phenomenon because they are similarly part of the ineluctable chain of causality that characterizes nature. This makes possible a scientific psychology. Yet the inner experience of freedom, experienced by all human beings, is no less empirical and makes possible moral choice. A mystery it may be, but according to Kant, any adequate account of reality must make a place for both necessity and freedom.

William James, America's preeminent philosopher and psychologist, approaches the problem from a different angle, a far more personal one. James suffered a severe depressive breakdown in his late twenties and early thirties. He attributed at least part of it to the overwhelming depression he experienced when he became convinced that his life was utterly meaningless because it was completely determined, a notion he had become obsessed with as he absorbed the scientific Weltanschauung of his day in the course of his studies of anatomy, chemistry, and medicine. James spent several years studying the arguments for and against free will and for and against determinism. He concluded that none of the philosophical arguments was convincing and that therefore he was entitled, as a rational man, to believe as he chose on this question. Having arrived at this point after great effort and in deep pain, he wrote, "I concluded that my first act of free will will be to believe in free will" (James 1902), and starting with that act of affirmation, which was intrinsically an act of self-efficacy, he worked his way out of his depression. James's cure was what was then called a "mind cure." We would now call this a form of self-administered cognitive therapy. Interestingly, James is the only professor of philosophy cited in the AA literature. It is noteworthy that people who suffer depression or manic depression, as well as other forms of mental illness, and are diagnosed with these conditions and are told that their mental and emotional state is caused by biochemical imbalances, which implies that they are completely unfree in the sense that they are determined by their abhorrent neurochemistry, which is then treated with drugs to alter that neurochemistry, do not experience themselves as unfree. On the contrary, what they seem to do is to redefine the very boundaries of self, the area of freedom, as something apart from the disease. This is particularly significant in light of James's linking depression with lack of freedom and meaninglessness.

The disease, deterministic as it is, is something that attacks that island of freedom, the self. So the chemical treatments are not seen as diminishing freedom, but as attacking an outsider, an invader, a force seeking to enslave the inner core of freedom. This gets even more paradoxical when we consider that many forms of talk therapy, not necessarily psychodynamic in approach, take the very opposite stand and urge the patient to "own" his or her depression, or whatever the symptom is, and by incorporating the symptom into the self to come to terms with it. Both approaches somehow preserve an island of volition, the one by redefining the boundaries of self and of volition, and the other by taking on that which seems to be the other and making it the self.

No philosopher is more rigorously deterministic than Baruch Spinoza (1677), yet the most famous chapters in his masterpiece, *Ethics Demonstrated by the Geometric Method*, are entitled, "Of Human Bondage" and "Of Human Freedom." They are about liberation and the acquisition of such freedom as humans are capable of. Spinoza has much to say that is of relevance to our topic, and he makes a major appearance in this book. In the Buddhist scriptures, the tale is told of Buddha's disciple Ajunta going to the master and asking, "Does the world have a beginning in time, or was it always here?" "Does the universe have a boundary or does it extend forever?" and "Are we free or determined?" The master remained silent. The Ajunta asked his questions again and yet again, but the master remained as impassive as ever. Finally, Ajunta asked, "Master, why do you not answer my questions?" The Buddha replied, "My son, I do not answer your questions because the answers make not for salvation." Similarly, our philosophical ruminations on freedom and necessity set off by the question, "Who is free?" makes not for salvation.

There is yet another aspect of freedom. I learned about this dialectical wrinkle almost forty years ago from Raymond Klibansky, professor of philosophy at McGill University. Klib, as he was known, was a renaissance scholar as well as a scholar of the Renaissance who wore elegantly tailored double-breasted suits, carried a walking stick with a gold-plated head, and sight-translated classical Greek, Latin, rabbinical and talmudic Hebrew, as well as half a dozen modern European languages. I was in his ethics and political philosophy seminar. Like most of his students I felt something akin to love in my admiration of Klib. It wasn't so much his erudition or brilliance, as impressive as those were, that elicited these emotions; it was his passion, his transcendent conviction that philosophy mattered, in fact mattered more than anything else. In a sense he was a therapist treating what Paul Tillich called one of the basic ontological, that is, intrinsic to being human, anxieties—the anxiety arising from the threat of meaninglessness.

The nature of freedom was a recurring theme whether we were talking about Plato, Hegel, or Marx. But one day the usually playful and debonair, albeit conveying a sense of high seriousness, Professor Klibansky grew still and contemplative, looking about as if he were engaged in prayer. After a prolonged silence he returned from his abstraction, looked up, and said in his inimitable accent, "Freedom is not capriciousness; it is not contingency. No, it is relational. Freedom is always in relation to; freedom always entails commitment to that which it is in relation to." Klib's voice trailed off. He became silent again as a barely perceptible tear half escaped from the peripheral margin of his eyelid. He began speaking again: "My friend and I both escaped from Nazi Europe and were safe in England. I spent the rest of the war teaching at Oxford, but not my friend. He returned to France to join the resistance. He was captured by the Gestapo, tortured, and killed. Who was more free, me or my friend?" Another barely perceptible tear appeared at the corner of his eye as he paused to let his question, "Who is more free?" reverberate before turning to an exposition of Hegel's *Philosophy of History*.

Who indeed was more free? I don't think anyone in that seminar ever forgot that lecture. As our patients move on in their journeys from slavery to freedom, they must struggle with this dimension of freedom also. Few have so mistaken caprice for freedom as the addicted, and few would find the notion of freedom as relational, as in relation to that to which one is committed, as incomprehensible or even nonsensical as the newly recovered. We are in the territory of profound mystery here, filled with paradox and dialectical reversal: freedom is the acceptance of necessity; freedom is commitment. Some of the greatest minds the human race has produced have struggled with these mysteries and paradoxes and none of their answers is wholly satisfying, so how can we expect those bewildered souls just emerging from the befuddlement and grossly manifest imprisonment of addiction to come up with livable answers to these questions? Of course we cannot, any more than we can expect ourselves to do so. But that is not the point. The point is to be cognizant that freedom and its vicissitudes is a clinical issue in sobriety and that how it is understood and how that understanding, however unconscious and unarticulated, is enacted is crucial, indeed is central, to the maintenance of sobriety.

Therefore, the therapist's meditation must be, among other things, a meditation on freedom. You cannot lead others to freedom if you yourself are not free. Professor Klibansky's question reminds us that freedom and its opposite, slavery, are always a dialectic between the inner and the outer, between the restraints within and the chains without. Every victory of freedom over slavery is a victory over *both* the tyrants within and the tyrants without. As therapists concerned with the inner world, we easily forget that tyrants abound and that some people are toxic and neglect to support our patients in their struggle with those who would, consciously or unconsciously, perpetuate their servitude. Many addicted patients have to struggle not only against inward restraints and enslavement to chemicals and compulsive activities, but also against very real oppressors in the external world. Often those oppressors, however unaware of what they are doing, have a vested interest in the patient remaining addicted.

The fight wherever fought against external tyranny has always moved me. I suspect that most therapists share my sentiments about that kind of freedom, freedom from oppression. Those sentiments are part of the Weltanschauung of dynamic psychotherapy correlative to its stock in trade—facilitating inner liberation.

To return to Professor Klibansky's central point, there is always a tension between freedom as self-expression and self-liberation, and freedom as relational and entailing commitment. Each human being must resolve this dilemma or exist in its tension, in his or her own way. Therefore, the therapist must be simultaneously fully there for and with the patient *and* neutral once the patient is free of the bond of addiction as the patient seeks his or her own way in this ontological dilemma. This seemingly abstract and philosophical question is in reality a highly practical matter since what the patient does with his or her hard-won freedom from compulsion is fateful for not only the quality but also the very maintenance of recovery.

Therapeutic Strategies in the Treatment of Addiction

The great romantic poet William Blake wrote, "The road of excess leads to the palace of wisdom." Unfortunately, it more often leads to the cemetery. The job of the therapist treating addiction is to direct as many as possible of those on the road of excess to the palace of wisdom rather than to the cemetery. This chapter is about how to direct them there.

It focuses on substance abuse counseling and addiction psychotherapy. Although the therapy techniques and approaches discussed are used in treating all sorts of conditions, they must be modified and fitted to the particularity of the substance abusing or otherwise addicted patient.

Chemical dependency counseling and addiction psychotherapy are unique; they have their own way of helping people recover from chemical dependency. Nevertheless, they draw upon and build on already existing schools and their techniques. Over the last century a number of ways of going about counseling and therapy have been elaborated. They all work. That is, they all help the populations their advocates treat, but they all have their limitations. Most counselors and therapists evolve a style that suits their personalities, their training, their knowledge, their temperament, and their patient population, which selectively makes use of elements drawn from each of the counseling schools. Such an approach is called eclectic, that is, it utilizes multiple approaches. An eclectic style should not be a grab bag of unrelated tricks; rather, it should be an integrated way of counseling in which the elements borrowed from diverse sources fit together in a more or less harmonious way. Over time, therapists, regardless of theoretical orientation, do more of what works for them and their patients and less of what doesn't work. Therapeutic styles are shaped by experience. Letting your experience shape your approach to counseling or therapy is both pragmatic—that is, what you choose to do will be determined by its "cash value," as William James, the father of the philosophical school of pragmatism, put it—and rational in the sense that it is determined by the requirements of the situation.

Not all counselors and therapists take an eclectic approach. Some become advocates and practitioners of one school of counseling or therapy. I respect those therapists who find that a particular way of working is best for them. The practitioners of each of the schools do indeed help people. Nevertheless I believe that in treating substance abusers and behavioral addicts, a borrowing from each of the major therapy traditions, when integrated both with other borrowings and with techniques belonging to substance abuse counseling alone, gives the counselor or therapist the best chance at helping clients. Most therapists not only evolve their own style, they will go on evolving in an ongoing dialectic of working and learning. As knowledge and experience increase, ways of working with patients change to keep pace with professional growth. As Bob Dylan put it, "he not busy being born/Is busy dying."

Each of the major schools is more than a set of techniques. Rather each set of techniques is based on an understanding of human nature, a body of more or less empirically derived knowledge, and a theory about how human beings learn, grow, and change. People are so complex, and those who study people have such diverse perspectives and beliefs about how to best go about studying people, that it is hardly surprising that the various schools do not see human beings in the same way or come up with the same understandings of human nature. Perhaps that will always be so, or perhaps increased knowledge will result in an integrated understanding. Be that as it may, for the moment there is a philosophical as well as a scientific aspect to each of the schools. Since each has a history and has developed over time, I prefer to regard them as traditions. Each of these traditions was originally applied to individual counseling and therapy, but now the theories and the recommended techniques are also applied to couple, family, and group work, as well as to individual therapy. However, in this chapter the focus is on individual counseling. The counseling and psychotherapeutic traditions discussed are client-centered, directive, psychodynamic, Gestalt, behavioral, cognitive, and existential.

COUNSELING AND THERAPY TECHNIQUES

Each of the schools utilizes one or more of the basic counseling techniques. The schools or traditions are complex ways of viewing human beings and their behavior that have evolved into treatment strategies—broad-based ways of going about counseling and therapy. They are like scripts with plots, characters, acts, and finales, while the various counseling and therapy techniques characterize particular lines in the script. Techniques include active listening, establishing rapport, exploration, clarification, confrontation, reflection, guidance or direction, education, interpretation, affect labeling, modeling, reinforcement, shaping, making drink/drug signals conscious, relaxation training, guided imagery, assertiveness training, and hypnosis.

Not every school uses every technique, and each school has its favorite—often trademark—techniques. But in the real world of substance abuse counseling and addiction psychotherapy, most practitioners find all of the techniques useful.

In counseling in general and in psychotherapy, the term *intervention* refers to anything the counselor or therapist does—the application of any of the techniques discussed here. But in substance abuse counseling, *intervention* has a special meaning—the planned confrontation of a substance abuser with the intention of pressuring the abuser into entering treatment. This chapter uses the first meaning—intervention as psychological technique manifest in a particular verbalization by the counselor or therapist. Although each technique is unique and has its own procedures, rationale, and tradition of use, there is some overlap. For example, the technique called "affect labeling" involves interpretation and is a form of reflection. Nevertheless it is its own thing. As I define and elaborate each technique and cite the schools that use it most frequently, it is important to remember that technique in and of itself does not cure. Relationship does. Technique—the tools of the trade—must be embedded in the context of a therapeutic attitude and a viable connection with the patient.

Active Listening

Active listening means avidly taking in as much of the patient's communication as possible without straining or trying too hard, *and* conveying by attitude, body language, and appropriate reference to the patient's words and nonverbal communications that you are attending in a very special nonjudgmental way to all that is happening in the session. Active listening is listening at many different levels for manifest content and latent meaning, conscious communication, and unconscious communication. Of course, no one can take it all in, and this description of active listening is intended as an ideal to be striven for, not a standard for the counselor or therapist to literally reach. It is not intended as a stick for therapists to beat themselves with for not reaching the ideal.

Freud (1913a) recommended that the analyst have an "evenly hovering attention," that is, that in a substance abuse treatment context the therapist or counselor not pay more attention to one thing than to another, and not have preconceived ideas about what is important or what is not. Rather, he or she lets the order of importance emerge from the patient's communication itself. Too much theory, too self-consciously used, gets in the way. Theories guide observation, but they are themselves generalizations from experience. Therapists need to try not to let them screen the living reality of what is going on in the treatment room. Of course, there is a place for selective attention, and therapists always make choices about what to respond to, based on what they consider relevant to the therapeutic task. Both evenly hovering attention and selective attention have their place in substance abuse counseling and addiction psychotherapy, and both have their place in active listening.

Active listening is, at bottom, attitudinal; it means attending to and caring and being open to the patient's feelings, thoughts, beliefs, struggles, pain, and joy. Without it no counseling or therapy can occur.

Establishing Rapport

The first thing a counselor or therapist must do is establish rapport. How is this done? Essentially, simply by being there. If the therapist is actively listening, truly nonjudgmental, there to meet the patient's needs rather than his or her own, and has something to offer the patient (knowledge and skill), rapport will come about by indirection. There is no technique to establish rapport; it is therapeutic attitude, everything the therapist does and is, that facilitates establishment of rapport. Of course there are patients (in some settings the majority of patients) whose life experience make them suspicious and even paranoid. Additionally, substance abusers and behavioral addicts are commonly filled with shame and guilt, and are highly invested in protecting and defending their addictions. All of these factors make it difficult to establish rapport, and all that the therapist can do is to maintain a therapeutic attitude and hope that his or her patient stays long enough so that the two of them establish a history of going through things together, which builds rapport so that the patient is able to move from being "alone alone" to being "alone together." Aloneness is inherent in human life. We are all ultimately alone. But that aloneness can be shared. When there is rapport both patient and therapist are alone together and that togetherness is curative in and of itself.

Exploration

Exploration is a technique that helps people open up and learn more about themselves. Counselors and therapists sometimes explore by asking questions, for example, "What were you thinking before you walked into the liquor store?" Or they may explore by encouraging the patient to do so, for example, "Tell me more about that." If the imperative, "Tell me," feels too bossy, controlling, or pressuring, then the therapist might say, "Can you tell me more about that?" Or "How do you know that when your mother exposed herself she was stoned?" Generally speaking, using interrogatories is the better approach, but sometimes therapists need to put pressure on patients by using the imperative voice. Exploration can be very open-ended: "Just say whatever comes to mind." Or it can be very focused: "When did you realize that the hook would pull out of the ceiling when you tried to hang yourself from it?" Exploration may be about the patient's inner world: "Can you go deeper into your anxiety and tell me how your body feels when the anxiety wells up in you?" Or about the environment: "Is there a way to get home from work without passing the corner where you used to cop drugs?" Exploration is one of the most useful counseling techniques; addiction therapists use it often. But they should always use it with discretion. Exploration is called for when the patient needs to learn more about self or situation, not when the therapist is merely curious for his or her own reasons. As with any intervention, in deciding whether or not to use exploration as a technique, ask yourself, "What does the patient need to learn or experience now?" If exploration facilitates that learning or experience, then use it; if not, don't.

Generally speaking, exploration opens things up. But in substance abuse counseling and addiction psychotherapy, the therapist also has to focus to keep the patient's attention on the substance use or addiction and its consequences. Don't ask open-ended exploratory questions when they take the patient away from the central problem—chemical dependence or behavioral addiction. Use them when you believe that the patient needs more self-knowledge, or when it is important, to you as therapist, to know more about some aspect of the patient's life or situation that is not easily brought forth by a direct question.

Clarification

An intervention may be a therapist's request for clarification: "Your comment that you only smoked 'because the crowd did, but that I didn't want to' confused me. Can you clarify?" Or it may be a clarification by the therapist: "When you said your father only beat you when he was sober, you were saying that your father's drunkenness was better for you than his sobriety." Clarification highlights and pinpoints. It also intensifies. A clarification focuses and concentrates; it is the therapist's equivalent of underlining. So clarifications not only clear up confusions and ambiguity, they put the spotlight on whatever is being clarified.

Beginning (and sometimes not so novice) therapists are often afraid to say, "I don't understand that." Or "I'm confused by what you said." Or "I can't make much sense of that." They are afraid of looking stupid, of offending the patient or of hurting his or her feelings. Don't be afraid to ask for clarification or to offer it if that will facilitate the work you are doing with the patient at the moment. Substance abusers and behavioral addicts are prone to use confusion and ambiguity as defenses, as places to hide—particularly hide their substance abuse or addiction. They are also not infrequently genuinely confused. Therefore, clarifying interventions, especially those requiring clarification by the patient, are extremely useful in substance abuse counseling and addiction psychotherapy.

Confrontation

Depending on their temperaments, some therapists find confrontation of patients hostile and unempathic, while others regard it as a welcome opportunity to unleash their aggression in the patient's "interest." Confrontation as a psychological intervention is neither. There is nothing unempathic about confronting, for example, self-destructive behavior or a maladaptive defense such as denial. On the contrary, to not confront is the unempathic response. On the other hand, confrontation is not an opportunity to "duke it out" with a patient, however welcome that can sometimes seem. Nevertheless, it does take a certain amount of aggression to confront. And the release of energy in so aggressing may feel good, yet the motivation of the confrontation should not be retaliation, humiliation, or expression of the therapist's anger. Of course, patients sometimes make therapists angry, and it is good that they feel and be aware of that anger. Nevertheless, being angry and experiencing it is not the same as expressing it in inappropriate, hostile confrontation with a patient.

It is my experience that far more counselors and therapists, especially novices in addiction treatment, inhibit themselves and do not confront appropriately, than confront to express their own frustration, whether such confrontation is therapeutic or not. For the therapist who never confronts, confrontation is a punch. Since confrontation is so crucial in treatment, therapists who have difficulty confronting would be well advised to get help in therapy and/or supervision.

Confrontation is essential to substance abuse counseling and addiction psychotherapy. For example, the patient's denial must be confronted in situations like the following: "Mr. Smith, being arrested for DWI (driving while intoxicated) for the fourth time can't possibly be the result of your taillight being out. If you weren't drunk, all the mechanical defects in the world won't get you arrested for DWI." Or "Mary, your father beating you with his belt until you had welts all over your body wasn't strict discipline, it was child abuse." Or "John, it just isn't true that you don't want to smoke weed any more; you dream about getting high every night." Or "Sally, do you realize that your shouting, 'Like hell I'm angry, you SOB' proves that you are angry?" Or "Your missing appointments violates your probation contract." Or "If you treat people so callously, you aren't going to have many friends."

All of the above are confrontations. Some confront the substance abuse itself, some confront denial, some confront the client's repudiated emotions, some confront unacceptable behavior. The latter shades into *limit setting*, which is an implicit confrontation of transgression of boundaries or rules. Limit setting is an important part of substance abuse counseling. It does not necessarily involve confrontation, as in the example of the counselor who said to the client; "If you commit suicide, I will refuse to see you any more." Nevertheless, I subsume limit setting under confrontation in this discussion of interventions. Limit setting is part of the contract and includes understandings about missed appointments, fees, being sober at the session, not being violent to self and others, and in some cases attendance at AA or another Twelve-Step program.

Confrontation is an absolutely necessary tool in the armamentarium of the substance abuse counselor and addiction therapist. If you sense that your patient needs something brought to his or her attention, such as a feeling, a false belief, a behavior, then confront. Try to use therapeutic tact—your sense of what the patient can hear and can stand at a given time—in deciding if a necessary confrontation should take place now or later. If the resistance is too high, the patient too unable to deal with the insight confrontation would bring about, then store away your observation for future use. The patient will give you many other chances to confront whatever the issue is. On the other hand, remember that confront you must.

Reflection

Reflection means reflecting back to the client or patient his or her feelings, thoughts, and behavior. In using reflection as an intervention, the counselor or therapist refrains from making directive statements, giving interpretations as to why or as to meaning, and most certainly from judgment. Rather, the therapist acts as a mirror—one that distorts as little as possible. For example, the patient is talking about her struggle with her desire to "do a line" at a party Saturday night. The therapist reflects: "You felt deeply torn." Note that in reflecting the therapist doesn't comment on the patient's putting herself in jeopardy by going to a party where cocaine was available, or strategize with her about how to handle the situation, or confront her active craving for the drug, or do anything but reflect back the intense conflict the patient has told the therapist she has experienced.

In substance abuse counseling and addiction psychotherapy, reflecting feelings and conflicts is a frequently used technique. It is highly useful to the patient because it heightens awareness of the feeling or conflict. Nevertheless, the strictly hands-off nature of reflection, especially when used singularly or predominantly as a technique, makes such use untenable in substance abuse counseling. It is too nondirective when it is used as the dominant technique. Most often addiction therapists first reflect, and then, if there is danger, comment on the danger or suggest an alternate behavior. In spite of this caveat, I am well aware that reflection is an extremely powerful technique. It is seemingly simple, but to do it well is a true art form and it takes lots of practice to gain proficiency at reflection. Use reflection to increase awareness and intensify emotion. Sometimes reflection seems too simpleminded; for example, the patient says: "I'm really pissed off," and the therapist says: "You're enraged." Simple or foolish as it may seem, this reflection increases the patient's awareness of his emotional state and may lead him to question it. If it serves a therapeutic purpose don't hesitate to make "simpleminded" reflective interventions.

Guidance or Direction

Guidance or direction is a technique many forms of counseling and psychotherapy shy away from. This is especially true of dynamic approaches, yet it is necessarily and inevitably a component of substance abuse counseling technique. "Go to a meeting tonight," (meaning a Twelve-Step meeting) is the most common directive intervention in substance abuse counseling and addiction therapy. When someone is stepping in front of a speeding truck it is empathic to call out: "Stop!" Substance abusers are forever stepping in front of speeding trucks.

While it is true that therapists neither can nor should live their patient's lives for them, it is equally true that many addicted patients (especially in early treatment) have poor judgment and impaired reality testing, so that they really need guidance and direction. The therapist's judgment is better than that of a patient suffering from the effects of prolonged substance abuse on his or her brain, and the therapist should not let false modesty or fear of being bossy inhibit him or her from giving appropriate direction and guidance. Direction overlaps with limit-setting, discussed above under confrontation, with which it also overlaps. Don't be afraid to be directive or to set limits. Impaired early recovering patients need that, and this is just as true if the patient is recovering from compulsive overeating, compulsive gambling, or compulsive sexual behavior as it is if the patient is recovering from heroin addiction. Mere advice-giving may not feel like professional work, and that is the main reason that therapists are reluctant to do it. There is some truth in this, but patients aren't there to increase therapists' sense of professional pride. "You need to stop running and stand still," "This isn't the time to quit your job," and "Go late and leave early" (referring to a mandatory social occasion in which drugs and/or alcohol will be present) are all helpful directives if appropriate.

On the other hand, if temperamentally therapists are on the bossy or controlling side, they should be aware of it and limit their use of directive interventions. As clients become more stably sober and consolidate their recovery, therapists should use less and less directive technique. However, clients are not going to get to that point if they step in front of those trucks. So make use of directives early and then back off.

Needless to say, directives aren't always heeded and advice isn't always taken even if solicited. That can be very upsetting to novice addiction therapists, who will find it helpful to remember that they can't step aside from the truck for patients, but can only warn them that it is about to hit.

Education

There is a sense in which every counseling and therapy intervention is educational, and every counseling and therapy technique an educational tool. All counseling and psychotherapy involves and facilitates learning, particularly affective (emotional) learning. Freud (1912b) spoke of psychoanalysis, the grandfather of talk therapies, as "re-education," the purpose of which is to correct faulty or miseducation.

One of the most famous accounts by a patient of her therapy was written by the American poet Hilda Doolittle (known as H.D.). In *Tribute to Freud* (H.D. 1956), she speaks of being at school with Freud.

Psychotherapy (and counseling) existed long before Freud's invention of psychoanalysis in the late nineteenth century. Humans have always had some institutionally sanctioned means of talking things out and of getting in contact with feelings and expressing them. It just wasn't called counseling or therapy. At the beginning of the Western philosophical tradition, Socrates taught that evil (dysfunction) was ignorance and that "to know the good was to do the good." Accordingly, he derived a method that we call Socratic inquiry, in which the philosopher (counselor) helps the pupil (patient) discover the truth within. The Socratic therapist brought to conscious awareness that which was latent in the patient, and that awareness was held to be transforming. Socrates's method remains a model for most of what modern therapists do, and they too believe that *Wissen Macht Frei* (knowledge liberates), as nineteenth century German thinkers put it. So all counseling and psychotherapy is in a sense educational.

However, the Socratic method educates in its root meaning of educing—drawing-out—rather than teaching in a more didactic sense. When I speak of educational interventions in this chapter, I am talking not about the drawing-out function of all counseling and therapy, but rather that component of counseling and therapy that is explicitly teaching—the conveying of information. You may say that nobody has ever gotten sober by listening to a lecture, and in a sense that is true. Emotional resistance, denial, physiological dependence, and a host of other factors militate against it. This is so, yet it is also true that being sane entails knowing how to be sane. Knowledge is a necessary, if not sufficient, condition of human transformation (or in this case of recovery). The great seventeenth-century rationalist philosopher Baruch Spinoza (1677) spoke, in the final section, "Of Human Freedom," of his masterpiece *The Ethics* of "intellectual love," and of the passion to understand and to know the truth, which integrates reason and affect into a transfiguring experience, and brings about radical change. Spinoza also said that only an affect can change an affect, so emotion is always intrinsic to understanding and insight that moves human beings to a better place. But so is knowledge, which brings me to educational interventions per se.

Substance abuse counselors and addiction therapists educate in the strict sense of imparting knowledge. In fact, one quality that distinguishes substance abuse counseling and addiction therapy from other forms of counseling and therapy is the major role of didactic intervention in that work. One can't teach what one doesn't know; therefore, mastery of the factual basis of substance abuse counseling and addiction psychotherapy, mastery of what scientists and addiction specialists have learned about what drugs and compulsive behavior do to body, mind, and spirit, is absolutely vital if one is going to be an effective substance abuse counselor or addiction therapist. The following are examples of educational/didactic interventions.

"Mr. Smith, do you know that alcohol, although it may give you some temporary relief because it is an anesthetic, actually makes your depression worse? As we said yesterday, your drinking is really self-medication—you're trying to treat your depression. I think I can understand that. Your depression is so painful you will do anything to get some relief. Unfortunately, the medication you are using—martinis—is making you even more depressed. That is because alcohol depresses the central nervous system—your brain and spinal cord. The pharmacology is all wrong and works against you. There are medications that *do* help depression and I want you to talk to our psychiatrist about them."

That is a long intervention and it may be more than poor Mr. Smith can take in. In that case, start with the first sentence of this intervention and discuss it with Mr. Smith. There is plenty of time to complete Mr. Smith's education on the effects of alcohol on depression. Give him bite-size pieces and then sum up and repeat. Addiction therapists need to be simple, clear, and redundant because their patients have trouble taking in what they say *both* because their brains are poisoned by their drug use and they aren't playing with a full deck *and* because resistance and denial are defending them against hearing more than they want to hear.

Another example: "Ms. Brown, you thought the police were looking in your window because you free-based last night. Free-basing hits
you a lot harder than snorting a line so you had lots of cocaine in your
bloodstream. Cocaine raises the level of a chemical called dopamine
in your brain. People who have the terrible mental illness called paranoid schizophrenia have too much dopamine working in certain parts
of their brain. That's what happened to you. You got paranoid because your free-basing threw off the chemical balance in your brain.
For a few hours your brain was working the same way a paranoid
schizophrenic's does."

If Ms. Brown is in no shape to take all that in, the therapist can
simply say: "Ms. Brown, free-basing poisoned your brain and made
you paranoid." A fuller explanation can wait for later.

Mr. Lott had an intensely paranoid episode on coke which was far
worse than Ms. Brown's. He was terrified. When he came down he
entered into a passionate discussion with the therapist in which he
insisted the therapist validate his experience by agreeing that the FBI
was after him. The therapist refused to be drawn into a futile debate.
Instead he said, "Mr. Lott, if the FBI really has you staked out and
has wired your apartment, you will have to give up coke or you will
be arrested and go to jail. But if the FBI isn't there, then your coke
use is making you paranoid and crazy so you will have to stop if you
don't want to go out of your mind. So it doesn't matter what I think
about the reality of the FBI being there. Either way, you will have
to stop because if you keep using you're heading for even deeper
trouble—you're either heading for jail or for the nuthouse." Mr. Lott
actually did stop using cocaine, although unfortunately not other
drugs.

The more the therapist knows, the better he or she can educate.
Therefore, professional life should be one of continuous growth—
new learning and integration of that new learning with what is already known. The ideal therapist, like Chaucer's clerk in the *Canter-
bury Tales*, will "gladly learn and gladly teach."

Educational interventions are not only about specifics like the depressive effects of alcohol and the paranoia induced by cocaine use.

They are also about larger, more conceptual issues like the disease concept of addiction and the nature of the Twelve-Step programs.

Most substance abuse counselors subscribe to the disease model of addiction, as do I. That is, I believe that addiction is best accounted for by regarding it as disease much like high blood pressure with a complex, multifaceted etiology, and a predictable deteriorating course if not treated. That treatment importantly focuses on behavioral change and modification of lifestyle. However, I am aware that there are cogent and powerful arguments against the disease model as an explanation of addiction, and that there are respected workers in the field who have concluded that the disease model is not the best mode of explanation of addiction. Models are not realities, they are ways of understanding realities. It is a question of goodness of fit, of which model gives the best explanation of the phenomenon. And choice of model is a pragmatic question of which model provides the best map to recovery and which is the most useful in treatment. With a phenomenon as complex as addiction, it may be the case that multiple models are needed—one perspective best explains one thing and other perspectives other things. In fact, it is helpful to think of models as perspectives, not dogmas.

As therapists gain clinical experience with substance abuse and addiction, they sometimes conclude that the disease model is off-base or that it really doesn't explain much, or that it lacks empirical support. Perhaps you have had that experience and have reached that conclusion. In that case, you cannot in good conscience, and should not, teach the disease model to your patients. But that is not very likely. Far more probably, the disease model will make theoretical sense and make sense of the clinical data as you learn more about addiction. Clinical experience tends to give the disease model empirical support. If that is your case, you should, indeed must, educate your addicted clients by teaching them the disease model.

Why, you ask, do addicted patients need to be taught a theory? The answer is that doing so strongly enhances the chances of recovery. At least that is my experience. The reasons that this is so are multiple. Addiction is chaos; it is bewilderment; it is confusion; it is desperation; it is pain; it is the continuing experience of awful things happening for no apparent reason. The disease model makes sense of that chaos. Suddenly the patient has an explanation of why his or her life has gone downhill so precipitously. The disease concept offers a cognitive structure that makes the irrational rational and reduces anxiety, which is helpful because anxiety makes for slips (relapses). Suddenly the patient realizes, "It's the booze, stupid!" and that is highly therapeutic. "That's an oversimplification," you say. Yes it is, but the fine-tuning and caveats can and should come later. Right now the patient needs some bedrock to stand on while he or she rebuilds a life. The insight enabled in part by exposure to the disease model, "It's my addiction that's destroying me," provides that bedrock.

Aristotle (330 B.C.) wrote in his *Metaphysics*, "All men by nature desire knowledge," and the sixteenth-century English philosopher Francis Bacon wrote, "Knowledge is power." Exposure to the disease model gratifies the desire to know—to understand—even as it provides fuel to power recovery. The disease model also reduces guilt and guilt is a killer. What substance abusers and other addicts do with guilt is to punish themselves by "slipping," an act of self-punishment that simultaneously anesthetizes the guilt. Anything that reduces guilt—which is not the same as diminishing responsibility—is therapeutic. So this is yet another reason to teach the disease model.

How is the disease model taught? Sometimes very simply, "Did you know that addiction is a disease?" Other times more elaborately, as for example using Jellinek's (1960) chart on the progression of the disease as a teaching aid, or explaining in simple terms the genetic vulnerability toward addiction. Frequently, exposition of the disease model takes place in more or less formal lectures in rehabilitation unit settings. The stages of progression and recovery are usually depicted in a U-shaped curve for educational purposes. But most counselors and therapists do not work in such settings, and even if they do such lectures need reinforcement in therapy sessions. Here is an example of a disease model educational intervention: "Mr. Billings, as you heard during last night's lecture, there's a genetic component to many addictions and here we are talking about all four of your grandparents being alcoholic. With that kind of heredity your chances of returning to social drinking are nil."

Jellinek thought that one form of alcoholism, which he called *gamma alcoholism*, was characterized by *progression* and *loss of control*. He thought progression was invariant (which probably isn't the case, although the general deterioration predicted by his model does occur). By loss of control, Jellinek meant that the consequences of taking a drink became unpredictable, not that the drinker passed out every time. It is important that the therapist make this distinction because addicted patients use incidents when they didn't lose control in the service of denial.

With the clients who just can't be sold on the disease model, and virtually all clients (and most counselors and therapists) have moments when they repudiate the disease model and disown it as a cop out, the therapist shouldn't force the issue. Share what you know and believe, but don't indoctrinate, bully, or insist that the patient adopt your perspective. No particular belief is necessary for recovery including belief in the disease model, although some beliefs about the nature of addiction are more conducive to recovery than others. Therefore, be as convincing as you can, but respect the patient's conclusions.

Counselors and therapists also teach clients about the Twelve-Step programs. Every addicted patient should be exposed to the Twelve-Step movement and have a chance to be educated about it and to ask questions about it. Some patients take other routes to recovery—Twelve-Step is just not for them—and their values should be respected. However, the majority of recovering addicts do wind up in Twelve-Step programs. The combination of counseling or therapy and Twelve-Step participation during the first year of recovery undoubtedly gives the patient the very best chance to succeed. In introducing recovering persons to the Twelve-Step programs, it is well to remember that there are clients who don't have the least interest in the spiritual growth emphasized by those programs or in the rest of the Twelve-Step "stuff"; they just want not to get high and to learn some tricks for handling drug signals and the like. They should be met where they are and given what they request. I tell such patients to go to

Twelve-Step meetings and regard them as smorgasbords from which they can take what appeals to and seems useful to them. I am aware that Twelve-Step members, for the most part, would not agree with this advice. But I am a therapist, not a Twelve-Step sponsor, so I have a different point of view and a different responsibility.

After all these qualifications, it must be said that teaching about Twelve-Step groups and their ideologies is a central part of substance abuse counseling and addiction psychotherapy. The addiction therapist must have knowledge of the Twelve-Step program, its history, its ideology, the steps themselves, the sponsor–sponsee relationship, and idiosyncrasies of local meetings. Therapists have ample opportunity to talk about all of these things as they come up naturally in the course of treatment without forcing the issue.

An example of an educational intervention about the Twelve-Step movement is as follows:

PATIENT: They said at the meeting I should have a sponsor. But I have you, so why do I need a sponsor?

THERAPIST: A sponsor does different things than a therapist. You need both. I help you with professional knowledge, while your sponsor helps you by sharing his experience. Your group is right—getting a sponsor would be helpful.

Another example:

PATIENT: I'm having trouble with the third step, the one about turning our will and our lives over to God as we understand him. I'm a nonbeliever and I'm not comfortable with that.

THERAPIST: There are NA (Narcotics Anonymous) members with all sorts of beliefs and they are all able to benefit from participating in the program. If it makes you more comfortable, you can secularize the third step into "Let it happen," or "Go with the flow," or "Get out of your own way." The third step is about relaxing the need to control, relinquishing the need to run the show, which no one can really do anyway—it just sets you up for frustration. So try going more with the flow.

Related to teaching the Twelve-Step approach is the issue of abstinence. I espouse the position that abstinence is necessary for recovery from full-blown addiction (as opposed to problem drinking or drugging). Nevertheless, therapists inevitably have to deal with patients who do not accept abstinence as a goal. In those cases, therapists need to make *least-harm* interventions. For example, for a therapist not to tell an active intravenous drug user who has no intention of stopping about his city's needle exchange program is not only cruel, it is criminal. Nor should therapists fail to tell pregnant teenagers who have no intention of giving up drinking and drugging long-term about the fetal alcohol syndrome in the hope (not infrequently justified) that they will remain abstinent until delivery. Such simple least-harm educational interventions save lives. The therapist should never put ideology above the patient's needs. That does not mean that therapists have to go on treating patients who have no intention of stopping their drug use if they are working from an abstinence model stance.

Interpretation

Interpretation is an explanation of why. It explains something, such as the patient's behavior, thoughts, or feelings. The use of interpretation as a technique is most characteristic of the psychodynamic school. In fact, classical (Freudian) psychoanalysis relies on it almost entirely. On the other hand, substance abuse counseling and addiction psychotherapy are chary of interpretation. They tend to offer few interpretations and rely more on reflection, direction and education. The type of interpretation they most often make relates something that is happening to the patient to his or her substance use or compulsive behavior. Yet selectively and wisely used interpretation is one of the most therapeutic of interventions. An accurate interpretation resonates. The patient not only hears it but also feels it, and feels it deep down where it counts. Interpretation cures not only because of content (what the therapist actually says, which enables insight) but also by giving the patient the feeling of being understood. That strengthens rapport, feels supportive, and deepens the bond between patient and therapist, even if the content of the interpretation is painful.

Therapists use interpretation to increase insight, that is, to raise the patient's self-awareness. To do that, the interpretation must not only be accurate—it must be timely. An interpretation given before the patient is ready to hear it grates, strengthens the patient's resistance, and more generally backfires. Knowing when to interpret requires therapeutic tact, which comes with experience and the kind of sensitivity therapists develop as they work with patients. This is especially true with addicted patients, who tend to be hypersensitive and to use their hypersensitivity in defense of their addictions. There is simply no substitute for working with addicts for developing a sense of therapeutic tact attuned to their inner worlds. There is no cookbook recipe for knowing when; rather, it is something therapists develop as they gain experience and with which they need to get help in clinical supervision.

The real danger of overusing interpretation is that the therapy becomes too intellectual. Interpretations can also engender resentment over what feels like being understood "from above," that is, condescendingly. It is generally better to let the patient have an experience, to be in a feeling state, before offering an interpretation— affect first, then an understanding of the affect. When Freud and Josef Breuer (1895) wrote the first book on psychodynamic psychotherapy, *Studies on Hysteria*, they concluded that their patients suffered from *strangulated affect*, or what we would call "stuffed feelings," and recommended what they called *abreaction*, de-repression and expressive release of the strangulated affect, which they believed was associated with repressed traumatic memories. As they put it, hysterics (and by extension substance abusers and compulsives) suffer from *reminiscences*. The modern form of abreaction is primal scream therapy (Janov 1970). Abreaction is also called *catharsis*. Whatever it is called, release of repressed emotion plays a central part in all counseling and psychotherapy including substance abuse counseling. As Freud gained experience he concluded that abreaction or catharsis was not enough; insight was also needed, and he shifted the emphasis of his therapeutic technique to interpretation. Modern substance abuse counselors and addiction therapists rely on both catharsis to express feelings and interpretation to increase understanding and insight. So use interpretation when you want to deepen patients' understanding of themselves and you sense that they are ready to hear what you have to say. If you can (and it fits), make a connection with the substance abuse or behavioral addiction as part of your interpretation.

There is an interpretive aspect to all interventions, if only in their selectivity, in the therapist's implied selection of one thing rather than another as being the most relevant and important for the patient to hear at that moment. Although addictions therapists do so sparingly, they definitely interpret. If you think you see something that the addicted patient doesn't that will help the patient, don't hesitate to verbalize your insight.

There are two main types of interpretation: here and now, and then and there. The first makes some connection between current events; the second connects the present with the past. They make the patient aware that his or her current feelings (or behavior) are being driven by a "blast from the past." This type of interpretation is called *genetic interpretation* (because it reveals the genesis, the source of something) or *historical interpretation*. In substance abuse counseling and addiction therapy, therapists mainly use here-and-now interpretations. Interpretations that refer to the relationship with the counselor or therapist are called *transference interpretations*. Transference interpretations can be here and now or they can connect the patient's reaction to the therapist to the patient's past. In substance abuse counseling and addiction psychotherapy, here-and-now transference interpretations are preferred, although there are occasions to connect present reactions in the session with past experience.

All of this must be pretty abstract. Some examples should make interpretation come alive. "Mr. Adams, you are angry at your wife because she doesn't like you to get high," is an interpretation. Mr. Adams thinks he is angry at his wife because she's a "bitch." "Mr. Adams, you are depressed because booze isn't working for you anymore," makes a connection of which Mr. Adams is oblivious. "You're enraged with me because I confronted you on missing meetings" is a here-and-now transference interpretation. Mr. Adams thinks he is angry at the therapist for being an idiot, and doesn't see the connection between his anger and the discussion about missed meetings. "You're enraged at me because my confrontation about your missing the meeting reminded you of your hated father's beating you when you disobeyed him," is a genetic transference interpretation. All of the above can be helpful. "It's a good thing that you are expressing your anger at me instead of drinking over it," is both interpretive and supportive. The possibilities for interpretation are infinite, limited only by the therapist's creativity and by the patient's needs. Deeper insight into self gained through personal psychotherapy makes people better interpreters.

Affect Labeling

Affect labeling simply means highlighting the patient's feelings by giving them a name. It is one of the most helpful things that substance abuse counselors and addiction therapists do. Affect labeling is a form of interpretation—interpretation of what the patient is feeling. That sounds tricky and even presumptuous. In a way that is true. How can the therapist know more about what the patient is feeling than the patient? In some basic ultimate sense we are each alone in our experience and nobody can know what we are feeling better than we can. Our experience is our experience and no one else's. Yet there are factors that mitigate this intuitive conclusion. Substance abuse muddies and confuses, so addicted patients literally don't know what they are feeling. Repression and suppression, conscious and unconscious stuffing, makes feelings unavailable to immediate awareness. Patients may not have labels for the inchoate feelings seething around within them—they cannot effectively put words to what they are feeling. Also their early experience may have been so traumatic or deficient that they never learned to label feelings accurately in the first place. For all of these reasons, substance abuse patients badly need their therapists to give them names for what they are experiencing.

The therapist's own experience, the patient's presentation and body language, the therapist's understanding of what is going on within him- or herself during the session, and the therapist's empathy make it surprisingly easy for therapists to accurately label affects. Of course, they make mistakes and sometimes even their most strongly felt intuitions about what the patient is feeling are off. But that happens rarely if the therapist is attuned to the patient, and when it does the patient corrects the therapist, so little or no damage is done. Don't be afraid to label feelings, or to stick to your guns if you think the patient is blocking or repressing in his or her denial of your affective interpretation. Affect labeling really helps. There is a technical word for not being able to put feelings into words: *alexithymia*. It is a good word to know. It is used a good bit in the technical literature, and it characterizes a number of the more severe mental illnesses.

There is an important theory about the development of affect that casts light on why affect labeling is so vital in substance abuse counseling. Krystal and Raskin (1970), who worked extensively with substance abuse, hypothesized that at the beginning of life infants and toddlers experience their feelings as global, massive, somatized (that is, experienced as bodily states), undifferentiated, overwhelming, and unverbalized. As children grow and mature, their feelings become more fine-tuned, more differentiated, less one big ball of wax, more manageable, and de-somatized (that is, less experienced as bodily states), and they come to have names so they can be verbalized. This developmental sequence doesn't happen automatically. It happens in the context of interaction with loving caregivers. Mom or Dad says, "Janice, you're crying because you are (sad), (angry), (hurt) because your dolly broke." And Janice learns a name for a feeling. In highly dysfunctional families, like the ones many substance abusers and behavioral addicts grow up in, this process doesn't take place in the way it does in healthy development, and the child is left vulnerable to alexithymia. He or she is likely to experience feelings as bodily states and to be vulnerable to psychosomatic illness, to experience feelings as massive, undifferentiated, and overwhelming, and be deficient in the ability to verbalize feelings. That is a set up for substance abuse and other addiction.

To make matters worse, Krystal and Raskin hypothesized that trauma, including the trauma of substance abuse itself, causes *affect regression*, characterized in their somewhat forbidding technical language by de-differentiation, re-somatization, and de-verbalization. In spite of the awkward technical language, Krystal and Raskin know what they are talking about; and they have lots of clinical evidence to support their hypothesis. The substance abuse counselor's and addiction therapist's job is to reverse this regression by giving names to feelings, and the more of this they do the better.

Modeling

Modeling is usually not so much a technique as something that just happens. Clients model on counselors, and patients on therapists, whether or not their counselors or therapists want this or are aware of it. Better to be aware that you are a model. What is it that the therapist should be modeling? Tolerance, self-acceptance, openness, contact with feelings, sobriety in the sense of avoiding excess, honesty, empathy, and compassion for self and others head the list. It is especially important to model the exploration of powerful feelings and experiences. Therapists are usually uncomfortable with this instant canonization, and they should be. Of course, no therapist is all of these things consistently or reliably. Rather, these are ideals that therapists strive for. Nevertheless, therapists incarnate some characteristics and values their patients lack, and patients' identification with some aspects of their therapists and their internalization of them as a model is extremely helpful. Therapists should not go out of their way to disillusion their patients, who find out their flaws soon enough in any case.

In addition to this unself-conscious modeling by the therapist, and conscious and unconscious identification with the therapist by the patient, there is the deliberate, consciously crafted use of modeling as a teaching device. This occurs, for example, when the therapist role-plays, let us say, assertiveness or sorrow. In the first case, the therapist illustrates or models assertiveness by role-playing sending the soup with the fly in it back to the restaurant kitchen. In the second case, the therapist models the feeling by experiencing and expressing the feeling, as when the patient's disclosure of, let us say, childhood abuse makes the therapist feel sad and the therapist shares the feeling: "Listening to you I feel so sad, I'm almost crying." Therapists consciously model (role-play) many things, from refusing a drink, to setting limits with children. Patients are often unable to do particular things, and modeling is often the best technique for teaching them how. Here modeling is an educational intervention. Don't be afraid to model if you sense that your patient will learn from it. Modeling is a very helpful technique that is much made use of in substance abuse counseling and addiction therapy.

Reinforcement

There are nondirective techniques, such as mirroring, and their opposite, such as direct guidance. Reinforcement is directive. It is telling the client that some behaviors are desirable by reinforcing them, and some undesirable by not reinforcing or actively disapproving of them. In psychodynamic psychotherapy and counseling, reinforcement is rarely if ever used. Rather, the therapist tries to maintain an attitude of *technical neutrality*, which means that the therapist deliberately doesn't take one side or another in dealing with the patient's inner conflicts or struggles with the world. Technical neutrality is a powerful technique; it suspends judgment and facilitates the patient's opening up to self as well as to the therapist. It helps the unconscious become conscious. Yet therapists generally don't assume the attitude of technical neutrality in substance abuse work. Here they have a definite goal. They want to lead the patient toward recovery. They are advocates of sobriety, and not neutral at all. That does not mean that there aren't times in substance abuse counseling and addiction therapy when it isn't useful for the counselor or therapist to remain neutral. On the contrary, there are many such moments and situations. Nevertheless, addiction therapists are advocates, not neutral observers. How do they advocate? In many ways, especially in their educational interventions, but primarily by reinforcing some behaviors and not others.

The way therapists reinforce is by verbal approval. "I'm delighted you went to a meeting when you realized how upset you were."

"Turning down that job after you realized it was so stressful that it might threaten your sobriety was a wise and mature decision." "Pouring all the liquor in the house down the drain was really a good move." Sometimes the reinforcements are more tangible, such as the granting of privileges in an inpatient setting. But for the most part they are verbal. Don't underestimate their efficaciousness because they are merely verbal. If your patient has established a therapeutic alliance with you, your approval is of the greatest significance. Don't be afraid to use that leverage to promote recovery, health, and growth.

Shaping

Shaping means reinforcing approximations to the desired behavior. In that way the client is gradually moved toward the goal. The counselor continues to reinforce each step along the way until the client has secured mastery, then stops reinforcing that step and begins to reinforce the next step on the path, and so on until the goal is reached. For example, the client's rages have been getting him in trouble. In the past he was frequently physically violent and this had led to substance abuse among other difficulties. Mr. Smith has been working on anger management. He comes in and relates how he abstained from punching out an associate who irritated him by trivial trespass on his feelings. Mr. Smith tells the counselor, "I really wanted to put out his lights, but I controlled myself and told him to go fuck himself." The counselor says, "I'm really proud of you, Mr. Smith." The counselor doesn't think blowing up and cursing someone out for a trivial offense is a desirable behavior, but he does think that it is an improvement over physical violence, so he reinforces it. This is shaping. Once Mr. Smith is securely beyond punching people's lights out, cursing them out will no longer be reinforced. Now tolerating minor offenses (real or imagined) will be reinforced and so on until the goal of anger management has been reached. Substance abuse counselors and addictions therapists do a good deal of shaping, sometimes carefully planning and strategizing their course, and sometimes shaping more intuitively.

Making Drink/Drug Signals Conscious

Substance abuse counselors and addictions therapists work hard to make patients aware of their "triggers"—the places, people, things, and feelings that set off relapses. This involves a combination of exploration, education, and interpretation. Once the patient is aware of the trigger, he or she is in less danger of acting on it. The danger is further reduced if the therapist can suggest or help the patient to find an alternate coping mechanism, such as rewarding herself with a milkshake instead of a double scotch for surviving the workday. Both gaining awareness of triggers (in this case the end of the workday) and learning alternate responses to the trigger are of the essence in optimizing the patient's chances of maintaining recovery. This is part of what is called *relapse prevention*. It is one of the most helpful things substance abuse counselors and addictions therapists do.

Relaxation Training

In many settings counselors do relaxation training, although traditionally this was psychologists' turf. Substance abusing clients and behavioral addicts typically have few resources to induce relaxation besides substance use or compulsive behaviors. They tend to be tense and uptight. There are many relaxation techniques, the most popular of which is called *progressive relaxation training* (Jacobson 1938). This is a technique of first increasing tension and then relaxing body parts until all parts of the body are relaxed. "Feel the tension in your fingers. They are getting tenser and tenser. Feel how tight they are. Now let the tension go. You can feel the tension leaving your fingers. They are getting more and more relaxed. More and more relaxed. Feel the difference between the tension and relaxation in your fingers." And so on throughout the entire body. By the time the exercise is over, the client is in a deep state of relaxation and after a time the client begins to self-induce relaxation. Relaxation training is most often done in a group setting, but it can also be used in individual work.

Guided Imagery

Relaxation can also be induced through guided imagery. "Imagine yourself on the beach on a glorious midsummer day, the sand is warming your back, the gentle waves fall back and forth, back and forth. You are becoming more and more relaxed." And so on. The best image for inducing relaxation for a particular patient is elicited by exploration before the guided imagery exercise begins. Obviously my example wouldn't work for a patient who had been bitten by a shark.

Guided imagery can be used for many purposes including getting in contact with the unconscious. But in substance abuse counseling and addiction therapy it is generally used as a relaxation technique. This is an area where the therapist can let creativity flow freely. Guided imagery is intrinsic to many meditation practices and traditions. Meditation techniques ranging from Zen to transcendental meditation are all helpful to recovering persons, and if you are familiar with one and it seems appropriate to teach it to your patient, do so.

Assertiveness Training

Substance abusers and other addicts are usually rambunctious, surly, rageful, and generally hard to be around, but they are rarely effectively assertive. It is not just the angry, blustering type of substance abuser who is deficient in assertiveness skills and angry, among other reasons, because he doesn't know how to get what he wants; so too is the quiet depressive type of substance abuser (mouse-like and miserable). Therefore, assertiveness training is useful for almost all substance abusing clients. Most rehabs make it part of their treatment protocol.

Assertiveness training involves role playing, shaping, and homework. Positive reinforcement by group and therapist is generously disbursed. Usually done in a group, the therapist and group members role-play assertiveness starting with easy situations and then progress to more difficult ones. Assertiveness is distinguished from aggression. There is no hostility behind assertiveness—it is just getting your due. The connection between lack of assertiveness and low self-esteem is made by the therapist so that the lack is understood by the patient as both an emotional problem and a skill deficit. The assertiveness training concentrates on ameliorating the skill deficit. First the therapist models, then the patient role-plays, and finally the patient is given homework so that he or she can try out new skills in the real world. Patients are instructed to report back how they have done, and they are reinforced (encouraged) and, if necessary, shaped. All of this can be done in individual therapy as well as in group.

This is another place to be creative. Besides improving your role playing skills by practice, try exploring areas where your patients are having difficulties with assertion and developing scenarios related to those situations. There are a number of excellent books on assertiveness that can be assigned as homework.

Hypnosis

Hypnosis requires special training. It is an extension of relaxation, guided imagery, and meditation techniques. There are many techniques to induce hypnotic state, but all move the patient from ordinary consciousness to another state closer to the unconscious.

Hypnosis is used in substance abuse and addiction therapy for two purposes: (1) to put the patient in contact with unconscious material, particularly with repressed traumatic memories, and (2) to help the patient control behavioral excess. My experience with hypnosis for behavioral excess (for example, smoke cessation) is that it is a valuable adjunct, but not a cure in itself. For the patient who sincerely wants to stop smoking but is having trouble with impulse control, hypnosis will help, but not if the willingness and desire is not there.

The use of hypnosis to facilitate recovering traumatic memories has come under strong attack in recent years, its critics maintaining that the recovered memories are the fruit of suggestion. Hypnosis is not widely used in substance abuse treatment, but if it is, the therapist should avoid putting thoughts in the patient's head, and instead allow the patient to explore his or her state of altered consciousness.

SCHOOLS OF PSYCHOTHERAPY

Client Centered, Nondirective

Client centered, also known as nondirective, counseling is strongly associated with its originator, Carl Rogers. Rogers, who started out as a clergyman, was one of the founding fathers of clinical psychology. He was the one who brought nonmedical professionals into talk therapy, so most mental health professionals owe him a debt of gratitude.

Rogers's (1961) research established the absolute centrality of counselor traits to successful counseling. The traits—or perhaps attitudinal stance—that makes for counseling success are nonjudgment, unconditional positive regard, and genuineness, along with the capacity for empathy. Subsequent research has demonstrated that Rogers was absolutely right—no matter what the counselor's or therapist's theoretical orientation or the "school" to which he or she gives allegiance, it is the presence or absence of these traits that makes for therapeutic success. Nondirective or client-centered counseling is an outgrowth of Rogers's belief that counselor attitude in and of itself heals and of his belief that human beings have an inherent, intrinsic, innate drive for health and for growth. The "cure" already lies within the client, and what the counselor must do is to provide the right environment for the natural healing forces within to manifest themselves. It is very much a "provide the plants with sun, water, and nutrients and they will grow and flourish" model. So the client-centered counselor does two basic things: stays out of the way by being nondirective, and waters the plants attitudinally by being who he or she is. But it is not quite so simple. The client-centered counselor also provides sunlight by reflecting the light—the emotional awareness—back to the client. That is why reflection is the principal technique used in nondirective counseling.

As the client opens up in the safety of the counseling relationship and has feelings reflected back, his or her self-concept expands and enriches. More and more of self becomes available to the client, and the gap between the client's ideal self (what the client would like to be) and the client's real self (what the client thinks he or she is) narrows. Another way to say this is that client-centered counseling raises self-esteem while lowering unrealistic grandiose expectations. This has obvious applicability to substance abuse counseling.

Nevertheless, substance abuse counseling, which wholeheartedly subscribes to Rogers's views of the overriding importance of the nonspecific, attitudinal components of counseling technique for counselor effectiveness, and makes use of reflection as a technique when appropriate, is not a client-centered, nondirective counseling.

Rogers would have acknowledged that his approach does not quite fit the situation of the substance abusing or otherwise addicted client. Rogers, who worked mostly with what he called "normal neurotics," often in educational settings such as college counseling services, did research on the applicability of his approach to more seriously disturbed patients. He concluded that it wasn't particularly effective.

There is the joke about the client who goes to the nondirective counselor and says, "I am desperate." The counselor reflects, "You feel desperate." The client continues, "I feel like killing myself." The counselor reflects, "You feel so desperate you want to end it." To which the client replies, "I feel like jumping out the window" (they are on the twentieth floor); to which the counselor reflects, "You are feeling so desperate you want to end it now." The client lets out a blood-curdling scream as he goes out the window. The counselor gets up out of his chair, goes over to the window, listens, and says, "Splat!" This rather nasty parody is hardly fair to Rogers or to client-centered, nondirective therapy, but it makes a valid point.

Rogers's contribution to our understanding of human nature and how to facilitate growth is magnificent. Nevertheless, too many substance abusers and other addicts are in the process of going out of the window for the nondirective approach to play much of a role in substance abuse counseling. Rather, addiction therapists borrow aspects of it—especially the use of reflection—and assume a nondirective approach in situations where it is appropriate. It becomes increasingly appropriate and useful after the patient achieves sobriety.

Directive (Reality) Counseling

Although there is no one name associated with the directive approach, Glasser (1965) has developed an approach called *reality therapy*, which is essentially directive. Directive counseling is the essence of substance abuse therapy. Addiction therapists direct patients toward abstinence, sobriety, Twelve-Step participation, appropriate psychopharmacological help (for example, referral to a psychiatrist for Antabuse [a drug that reacts with the first metabolite of alcohol to make the drinker ill] or antidepressant medication), a healthier social system, and continuing involvement in treatment. Addiction therapists give a good deal of guidance and advice. Of course, that is not all they do. If all therapists had to do was to tell the stubborn donkeys to straighten up, they would all be out of jobs in short order. Fortunately or unfortunately, things don't work that way. Yet the use of the directive approach is a necessary if not sufficient component of substance abuse counseling and addiction therapy. Without it, few would become sober and enter recovery.

The characteristic techniques of the directive approach are confrontation, direct guidance, and education. Direction is most effective when it takes place in the context of rapport, therapeutic alliance, and unconditional positive regard.

Psychodynamic Therapy

The oldest of the therapy traditions is the psychodynamic—"psycho" comes from the Greek word *psyche*, meaning mind or soul, and "dynamic" refers to the contending forces struggling within the psyche. The psychodynamic approach highlights conflict within the patient. For example, the conflict between the desire to stay sober and the desire to get high. Many if not most schools of therapy recognize that human beings are conflicted. The contending forces within them pull them in many ways, and not infrequently in diametrically opposite directions. What makes the psychodynamic tradition unique is its postulation that *unconscious* forces—aspects of ourselves of which we have no awareness—determine much of our lives. As Freud put it, "We are not masters in our own houses."

Sigmund Freud (1856–1939), himself afflicted with two substance dependencies—to cocaine (which he overcame) and to nicotine (which killed him)—is the father of the psychodynamic tradition and the author of a vast, complex, and beautifully written body of work. But it is difficult to know what Freud taught or believed. His ideas evolved over more than half a century and he changed his mind about many things. Nevertheless, there is a core set of hypotheses about the human mind and its operations that are central to Freud's thought. These hypotheses are present in nascent form from the beginning in his writings and remain part of his final work. Further, they have been elaborated and refined by many workers over the past century.

Freud's core beliefs are the following: the importance of childhood and infancy in shaping adult character and behavior; the continuing living influence of the past on the present; the revival of old relationships through unconscious projection onto present relationships, which he called *transference*; the power of unconscious thoughts, feelings, beliefs, and fantasies over our lives; the continuity of disease and health; the centrality of conflict—the war within—in human life and behavior; and the meaningfulness of dreams, slips of the tongue, and psychological symptoms. Yet another Freudian contribution was his elaboration of the mechanisms of psychic defense. These largely unconscious *defense mechanisms* include repression, regression, denial, minimization, introjection, projection, rationalization, splitting into all good and all bad, intellectualization, rationalization, turning against the self, and isolation of affect (separating thought from feeling). Substance abusers and other addicts, in common with all human beings, make use of each and every one of these defense mechanisms; yet the predominant use of the defenses of denial, projection, and rationalization is so characteristic of substance abuse that reliance on these defenses is said to be *pathognomonic*, that is defining, of the disease. Although people with other problems sometimes use these mechanisms as their predominant defenses, their predominance strongly suggests the presence of substance abuse or behavorial addiction.

Freud developed a number of models of the mind, the best known of which is the *structural model*, in which he (1923) postulated that there were three agencies of the mind defined by their function: id, ego, and superego. This is a conflict model. Each of the mental agencies struggles for dominance with the others and with the external world. The id is a repository of the biological drives: sexual, aggressive, dependent. In Freud's original German, the id was simply the "it"—the impersonal biological, the nonself aspect of the self. The superego (literally the "over-I") consists of the internalized parents and cultural standards. It is the product of identification with the parents. The superego contains the conscience and the ego-ideal (what I would like to be.) The ego (or "I") is the personal part of self. It is a sort of weak executive who tries hard to mediate between the demands of the id, the prohibitions of the superego, and the demands and restrictions of recalcitrant reality so that some modicum of satisfaction can be achieved. The id demands it—whatever "it" happens to be—yesterday. The superego says, "Never"; external reality says, "Try to get it"; and the poor beleaguered ego says, "Maybe I can get some of it without getting in trouble." Freud's structural model is a powerful depiction of weak, conflicted humans trying to manage the seething biological forces within, the massive cultural forces both within and without, and the slim pickings in the fields around to gain some satisfaction in life. It is sometimes useful for the substance abuse counselor or addiction therapist to conceptualize his or her patient's conflicts and struggles in terms of Freud's agencies of the mind.

Resistance

Another Freudian notion substance abuse counselors and addictions therapists borrow from the psychodynamic tradition is resistance. Resistance comes from internal conflict. There is a part of the patient that wants to stay sick, just as there is a part of the patient that wants to get well. Without a desire for health, however flickering the spark may be, therapy can do nothing. The therapist can facilitate the spark bursting into flame, but he or she can't put the spark there. Learning to deal with the resistance—and there's always resistance— is a vital part of therapeutic technique. Freud (1926) had some very shrewd things to say about resistance. He used his structural model to classify categories of resistance. I discussed these categories from the point of view of their contribution to enslavement in the previous chapter. Here I want to discuss them from the point of view of the therapeutic process.

According to Freud, the resistance arising from the id is twofold: the "adhesion of the libido," and the "conservatism of the instincts." What Freud meant by this is that once we love something we love it forever. We hold on to things tenaciously and give them up only with the greatest reluctance. That's the adhesion of the libido part. The conservatism of the instincts refers to our reluctance to change, which Freud put in biological terms. One doesn't have to agree with his assertion that these things are the results of instincts to realize that it is indeed true that human beings don't change readily or easily. All of this applies directly to work with substance abusers and behavioral addicts. They love their substances or compulsive activities and cling to them tenaciously, and that is the major source of their resistance. Substance abusers and other addicts are like other human beings only more so in that they don't change easily or gladly even if the change is one for the better. People tend to stay with what they know (Freud's conservatism of the instincts), no matter how bad the familiar may be. Better a known evil than an unknown one.

Addicts are often unaware of how attached they are, how much they love their addictions and the chemicals or activities they are addicted to, just as they are unaware of how afraid they are to change. It is helpful for the therapist to make this conscious by saying such things as, "You love coke more than you love your family." "You are so loyal to your beloved, heroin, that your love may kill you." "No matter how horrible your life is, it is familiar and you are afraid to change." Clinging to the familiar helps to explain why people get themselves into terrible relationships, including their relationship with drugs. They are all too familiar repetitions of pathological, dysfunctional relationships of the past, particularly with parents, and therapists can and should talk about that, too.

Freud wrote that there are three resistances from the ego: the transference, repression (or defense), and secondary gain. Transference is so important in life and in therapy that it warrants further discussion.

Transference and Countertransference

Transference is perhaps the most important of Freud's discoveries. Transference is the unconscious reenactment of early relationships in present ones. It is a new edition of an old book, so to speak. Transference always involves distortion and projection, and it may include behavioral manipulation to induce behavior in the people in the present relationship that is similar to the behavior of people in the old relationship. This is called *projective identification*. The example of a child of an angry father who provokes anger in male authority figures and then reacts to them as if they were his father is a clear illustration of a transference reaction utilizing this mechanism.

Transference is part of all human relationships. We never experience others in their full reality, but rather through the lens of our own perception, which is heavily influenced by our past—especially very early—experience. As William Wordsworth (1850) put it in his great autobiographical poem *The Prelude*, "The world is half created and half perceived" (p. 646). However, in healthy relationships transference distortion is at a minimum. In therapy the transference—the projection of experience with parents and siblings onto the therapist—is inevitable. But in therapy the situation is different from that in life because the therapist tries to be aware of the transference and to use it as a therapeutic tool.

When Freud (1912a) first discovered the transference, he regarded it as a resistance. As he put it, "The patient acts instead of remembers." Freud was then working from a therapeutic model that held that repressed memories of early trauma were the cause of psychopathology, the treatment being the recovery of those memories. But the patient acted out the memories by re-creating the traumatic situation with the therapist. Freud saw that as a resistance to the affective, deeply felt, experience of the repressed trauma, an experience he thought would be curative. Later he realized that the transference was a therapeutic opportunity bringing the repressed trauma into the treatment room. Freud then arranged his treatment modality, psychoanalysis, to maximize the transference by having the patient lie on a couch with no eye contact with the analyst and free-associate, that is, say whatever came to mind. The job of the analyst became to interpret the transference by relating the patient's behavior with the analyst to past experience. It is a technique of great emotional power, but it is unsuitable to the treatment of active substance abuse and early recovery substance abusers. Psychoanalysis works too much with fantasy and projection to be helpful to people with more severe reality problems. (There are analysts who would rigorously dispute this, but I think it is true for patients who are seriously addicted.) However, analysis *is* helpful after stable recovery has been achieved and the former active addict now has the emotional strength to safely regress and work through early trauma. Although few recovering substance abusers become classical analytic patients, most do, in one way or another, return to the past to work through underlying trauma, and this is a vital part of addiction psychotherapy.

In substance abuse counseling and addict therapy, the transference is noted and occasionally interpreted. For example, "You're angry with me for interfering with your pleasures just like your mother did." Generally speaking the substance abuse counselor or addictions therapist leaves off the last phrase, "just like your mother." Rather, he or she interprets the here and now of the relationship, "You're angry at me because I threaten your drinking." Commenting on the relationship and on what is going on between therapist and patient is almost always helpful. Such comments on the here-and-now goings on in the relationship are considered transference interpretations, although they differ from those interpretations that relate the present to the past, which are called "genetic" (for genesis or origin) or "historical" transference interpretations. These are seldom used in substance abuse counseling or addictions therapy.

Transference is sometimes broken down into *positive transference*, where the therapist is warmly regarded by the patient and early experiences of loving and being loved are revived, and the *negative transference*, where the therapist is hated, envied, devalued, and so forth, and early experiences of anger and hatred are revived.

There can be no therapeutic relationship without rapport—the feeling of being connected, understood, and cared about from a stance of nonjudgment and unconditional positive regard. Rapport makes for connection, and feelings of being connected make therapy possible. Related to rapport is the development of the *therapeutic alliance*, the partnership of the therapist and patient in the therapeutic task. In substance abuse counseling and addictions psychotherapy (and perhaps in all therapy), the development of the therapeutic alliance takes precedence over all else. It is the sine qua non, the necessary condition, for therapy to occur. The therapeutic alliance, unlike the transference, is reality based and does not involve projection or distortion. Some analysts disagree with this and do not distinguish between positive transference and therapeutic alliance, but I believe that the distinction is valid and useful.

It is well for the therapist to remember that substance abusers and behavioral addicts have transferences to the substance abuse or compulsive activity that may be experienced, for example, as the all-loving mother who will give everything. It is useful for the counselor to *explore* with the client the various meanings that the substance has for him or her.

Countertransference is the therapist's projection of his or her past experience onto the patient. There are patients a particular therapist just can't work with because the patient is too reminiscent of his or her Uncle Bob, who beat his kids before he committed suicide. But generally speaking, countertransference is not disabling; rather it is the inevitable result of being human. The most important thing about countertransference is to be aware that it is always present to some degree and to use that self-awareness to not let it interfere with the work. One of the best ways to do this is to increase your self-awareness through personal psychotherapy or analysis, and to discuss countertransferential feelings in supervision.

The term *countertransference* is also used to denote the therapist's feelings in general, not only those that are his or her own stuff projected onto the patient. Countertransference in this sense includes feelings induced by the patient. The therapist's feelings of sadness, despair, futility, anger, or joy during the session are important data about what the patient is experiencing and about what the patient is inducing in the therapist. These days *countertransference* is more usually used in this latter sense. Therapists need to remember that their feelings in the session are partly their stuff and partly induced by the patient, and they must try to be as aware as possible of what belongs where.

To return to Freud's analysis of the resistance from the ego, the second resistance from the ego Freud called *repression*, by which he meant all of the defense mechanisms that the patient uses to avoid experiencing painful or otherwise unwelcome feelings, memories, or awarenesses. Defense is an ego function in Freud's structural model. Psychological defenses are necessary to protect people from things they can't handle at the moment. So defenses may contribute to health and a sense of well-being. But defenses can also be pathological, and then they become part of the problem. Think of the body's immune system—when it works well it protects from disease. But it can fail in either of two ways. It can be too weak, then it fails to defend; but if it is working overtime and inappropriately, it can bring on autoimmune diseases such as rheumatoid arthritis.

Similarly, psychological defenses can be weak, in which case the therapist has to support whatever defenses the patient has and help him or her build new and stronger ones. Or the psychological defenses can turn into enemies and destroy that which they were meant to protect, exactly like the body's immune system can turn against the very body it was meant to defend. When psychological defenses become too rigid, too impermeable, and too at variance with reality, they become pathological. The therapist must then confront the pathological defenses, for example, denial of the negative consequences of the substance abuse. Denial, projection, and splitting are characteristic defenses of very young children. Hence they are considered primitive defenses. Overreliance on such primitive defenses works against the person using them, and an important part of substance abuse counseling and addiction psychotherapy consists of bringing to awareness patients' overuse or maladaptive use of these defense mechanisms through confrontation and interpretation. Opportunities to do so arise when the patient is talking about his or her relationships with other people, when the patient is talking about the substance abuse or compulsive activity itself, and in the patient's relationship with the therapist.

Defense Mechanisms

It may be helpful to review the more common defense mechanisms. *Repression* is stuffing it, pushing down unwelcome, painful, or unmanageable feelings, memories, thoughts, and fantasies. True repression is an unconscious process, while *suppression* is a more conscious form of stuffing. Substance abusers not only repress psychologically, they repress pharmacologically, using the drug to obliviate the unwelcome. Compulsive activities serve the same purpose.

Regression is retreating to a lower level of development to avoid a more adult task, conflict, or mode of living in the world. Substance abusers and behavioral addicts are often regressed to infantile levels of behavior. It is well for the therapist to note that regression while remembering that much of it may be, and frequently is, a consequence of the addiction rather than an indication of the developmental level of the patient. Nevertheless, the regression serves as a defense against having to operate on a more mature level.

Reaction formation is turning a feeling into its opposite. Sometimes there's more truth than the speaker knows when he says, "I could love you to death." Oversolicitousness often betrays underlying hostility. In a way sobriety and recovery from behavioral addiction is a reaction formation to its opposite, addiction, especially in the beginning. But in this case, therapists support the defense while remaining aware of how fragile it is. Later on sobriety is not a reaction formation against the fear/wish to get high, but a state valued for itself. When the patient pours out love for you before the two of you have a history together, that profession of love is either conscious manipulation or a manifestation of an unconscious defense mechanism—reaction formation.

Denial is the big one in substance abuse and other addictions. It is well to remember that the denial is not only the denial of the substance abuse or compulsive activity, it is also denial of the need for help (Harticollis 1968) and denial of the inner world of feelings (Wurmser 1978).

Externalization goes with denial. It is acting out rather than experiencing feelings and conflicts. It is looking for a solution to an inner problem in the external world.

Splitting is dividing the world and the things in it into two completely sundered categories: all good and all bad. It is the way small children experience others. Splitting oversimplifies a complex world and divides it into gods and devils. Integration of this split, leading to tolerance of ambiguity and complexity, is a sign of growth and maturation. It is helpful, if done in a timely way, to point out to the patient that things aren't so simple or clear-cut. Confronting and interpreting the defense of splitting is usually postponed until the patient is stably sober since this defense, however maladaptive, may help solidify recovery, with sobriety or recovery being the god and substance abuse or addiction the devil. However, it is well for therapists to remember that the early recovery patient is flip-flopping in his or her mind, and sobriety easily becomes the devil and substance abuse the god.

Isolation of affect means separating thought and feeling. The therapist puts them together by naming the feeling that goes with the thought.

Projection is attributing to others aspects of the self. Substance abusers and behavioral addicts project all the time: "It isn't me, it's you." "If my wife didn't nag, I wouldn't drink." "Who's angry, you bastard?" Commenting on (or interpreting projection) is usually extremely helpful and highly desirable in substance abuse counseling and addiction therapy. In any case, therapists should note the projection and what psychological purpose it serves even if they choose not to interpret it at the moment for whatever reason.

Projective identification is an interpersonal process in which an unacceptable feeling is induced in someone else. For example, the patient is filled with rage, which is both unconscious and unacceptable because the patient's self-concept includes being a gentle, loving person. So he has to get rid of his rage. He can't do it directly, so he provokes rage in someone else, say the therapist, by acting in an irritating way. Now the dangerous emotion is in the other, where it can be recognized, acknowledged, and perhaps even identified with. Note how this differs from straight projection, in which the other is experienced as the rageful one, but there is no behavioral induction of rage in the other. Both projection and projective identification are ways of externalizing and getting rid of unacceptable aspects of self, but they do it in different ways.

Substance abusers and behavioral addicts frequently make use of projective identification as well as of projection as defense mechanisms. It is helpful for therapists to be aware that the feelings they are experiencing in the session may be induced by the patient in a process of projective identification. Projective identification is an unconscious defense mechanism, not a conscious manipulation.

Turning against the self is deflection of a feeling, such as anger, away from its original target because of fear of retaliation, and turning it inward against the self. Therapists commonly see turning against the self by substance abusing and addicted patients, and the way to handle it is to put the patient in contact with the fear underlying the defense, and then to help him or her redirect the deflected emotion so it flows outward.

If projection is getting rid of dangerous and unacceptable emotions and aspects of self by experiencing them as parts of the environment, that is, as aspects of others, then *introjection* is the opposite. It is experiencing dangerous aspects of the environment as part of self. For example, the very possibility of having an unloving parent may be so threatening to a child that he comes to experience himself as unloving. He takes something that is awful and puts it inside in fantasy, where it is less dangerous, and perhaps more subject to control—at least that is the unconscious hope. Projection and introjection are ways to deal with "bad" aspects of self and others. When patients are filled with self-hatred, it is helpful for therapists to wonder whether the self-hatred isn't at root hatred of an introjected other.

Identification with the aggressor is closely related to introjection. It is the behavioral part of introjection, which is more about unconscious inner world. The mechanism of identification with the aggressor is "If you can't beat them, join them." In the movie *Gandhi*, we first see Gandhi dressed as an English barrister complete with wing collar and cane. He has identified with the aggressor, the English oppressor of his country. It is only when he is able to liberate himself from this identification, a liberation symbolized by his discarding his business suit and putting on a loincloth that he is able to become a liberator of his people.

Similarly, children raised in homes with substance abusing and/or abusive parents often identify with them. Such patients frequently say, "I can't believe that I'm drinking like my father; I hated it so much when he drank." The patient has identified with the aggressor. It is helpful for the therapist to point this out and to help the patient see that he or she did this as a way of controlling and perhaps winning the love of the violent, alcoholic father.

Rationalization, which means finding weak, even ridiculous reasons, for behavior, and *intellectualization*, which means staying in one's head instead of one's heart, are extremely popular defenses, beloved by substance abusers and other addicts. These patients are superb rationalizers and intellectualizers. Therapists should remember that addicted patients believe what they say; they are using unconscious defense mechanisms, not conscious manipulations, which is not to say that plenty of conscious manipulation may not also be going on. An important part of addiction therapy consists of challenging rationalizations and pointing out their often-transparent absurdity and in trying to pull the patient out of his or her head into his or her gut.

There are many other defense mechanisms, but denial, minimalization (a sort of weaker denial), projection, and rationalization are the ones that keep people stoned or compulsive. The confrontation and interpretation of maladaptive defenses while simultaneously trying to use as much as possible of the patient's defensive style in the service of sobriety is of the essence of substance abuse counseling and addiction psychotherapy. John Wallace (1995) has written a magnificent article on how to help the addicted patient use the characteristic defenses of substance abusers in support of health and sobriety.

The third resistance from the ego is the secondary gain, what the illness (in this case the addiction) does for the patient. Secondary gains range from the tangible, such as remaining eligible for a disability check, to the intangible, such as being the center of family discussion or not having to take part in an aspect of parenting the children that the user wishes to avoid. It is important for the therapist to deal with the resistance flowing from the secondary gain the patient is deriving from his or her substance use. It is good therapeutic technique to wonder, both silently and aloud, "What's the payoff?" "What does the substance abuse do for you?" All of what the substance abuse does for the patient isn't secondary gain. It also serves as a self-medication, companion, lifestyle, and a host of other things. Substance abuse counselors and addiction therapists are sometimes reluctant to inquire into the positive aspects of substance use or compulsive activity. After all, they are advocates of sobriety. Yet it is vital to do so. It completes the picture and it gives the patient a sense of being understood. It also gives the therapist an idea of the needs being met by the substance use or compulsive activity so he or she can better help the patient find healthier means of satisfying them, or better yet, help the patient modify the needs themselves.

Freud said that the resistance from the superego, the patient's feeling that he or she doesn't deserve to recover, and the use of the illness (here the addiction) as a self-punishment were the most difficult resistances to overcome. Freud was right. Guilt is a killer, as is shame. Therefore, helping patients manage guilt; for example, by sharing it at Twelve-Step meetings, or by the therapist pointing out how disproportionate it is (if true), is highly therapeutic. "You drink because you don't think you deserve sobriety," can be an extremely effective intervention.

Resistance isn't something bad that patients do to therapists, even though it may feel that way; it is an inevitable part of the therapeutic process. Freud didn't explicitly mention the strongest resistance we encounter, which is resistance in the service of maintaining the substance abuse or other addiction. But each of the resistances discussed by Freud contributes to it. The real question is how to deal with resistance.

Resistance and Stages of Change

The stages of change research (Prochaska and DiClemente 1984) has demonstrated that recovery is a prolonged, complex process, and the change rarely happens in a sudden moment of illumination, although that may seem to be the case. Rather, substance abusers and behavioral addicts are first in the *precontemplative* stage (that is, not even thinking about quitting); then in a *contemplative* stage (not ready to change but increasingly aware that substance abuse is causing problems); then in the *action* stage (where change actually takes place); and finally in the *maintenance* stage. Prochaska and DiClemente point out that without maintenance, relapse is inevitable, and that the resistance is so strong in the precontemplative stage that the best the therapist can do is to plant some seeds. Even in the contemplative stage ambivalence is strong and the therapist is best advised to not go head to head with the resistance. Rather, both sides of the ambivalence—the reasons for quitting and reasons for continuing—should be elicited, explored, and worked through. Resistance is still present in the action and maintenance stages, but now the therapist confronts the resistance more directly.

Substance abuse counseling is not psychodynamic therapy, but it does borrow the notions of unconscious motivation, defense mechanisms, transference and countertransference, and resistance, and incorporates them into its work with substance abusers and other addicts. And it uses the characteristic techniques of confrontation, exploration, and interpretation of the psychodynamic school where applicable.

Gestalt Therapy

The name associated with the Gestalt school is that of Fritz Perls. Perls's slogan for the Gestalt approach is, "Lose your mind and come to your senses." The emphasis of Gestalt therapy is on moving the patient out of his or her head, out of the squirrel cage of obsession and rumination, into immediate experience. It endeavors to bring the patient into fully experiencing the reality of the here and now. Perls (1969) wrote that the goal of Gestalt counseling was for the patient to become capable of fully and deeply experiencing joy, grief, anger, and orgasm. That's not a bad criterion for mental health.

The word gestalt is the German word for whole, for a completed form. The Gestaltists speak of helping the patient complete the gestalt, of getting closure and moving on, by working on unfinished business. They do that by intense here-and-now interaction between therapist and patient. Confrontation is the most characteristic technique of the Gestalt school. Perls borrowed the term *Gestalt* from the theory of perception, which views perception as an active, rather than a passive, receptive process in which we organize our perceptions to achieve gestalts, or completed forms. In Gestalt therapy the same notion is applied to emotion.

Gestalt therapists carefully observe and comment on the patient's demeanor and body language, pointing out discrepancies between what the patient is saying and what he or she is expressing through body language. Gestalt therapists are very active, engaged, and reactive. It is a lively approach. Gestalt therapists use specialized techniques like the "empty chair": "I want you to pretend that your father is sitting in that chair and tell him how you felt when you were 12 and he came home drunk and pissed on the lawn in front of your friends." They also use a lot of role playing and its elaboration in psychodrama in which conflicts are enacted. Holding a funeral for John Barleycorn, a technique used in substance abuse counseling, is a direct borrowing from the Gestalt tradition.

Gestalt therapy entails opening the patient wide open, so it is important to get closure and to give the patient an opportunity to process what has occurred in the session. If the work has been group work (as it often is), each member of the group has identified with the person on the "hot seat," and they, too, must have an opportunity for closure. Borrowings from the Gestalt tradition are of great value in substance abuse and behavioral addiction work, although the therapist must be careful not to open up feelings prematurely. If the patient can't handle the feelings that are elicited by Gestalt confrontation and role playing, then opening them up is a setup for a slip, as are unprocessed feelings. For that reason, the Gestalt approach is used more in inpatient settings than in outpatient treatment. Ideally, addiction therapists incorporate what they find useful from the Gestalt tradition but use it with discretion, and they try not to let early recovery patients leave while they are still vibrating.

Behavioral Therapy

Behavior therapy targets symptoms and uses the principles of learning theory to help people change. Behaviorists believe that psychopathology (including substance abuse and other addiction) is caused by faulty learning, and they seek to correct that faulty learning. Reinforcement is the most characteristic technique of behavior therapy. Some behavior therapists also use punishment as in *aversion therapy* for alcoholism, in which a painful stimulus is paired with taking a drink in a controlled setting. Behavioral therapists have been ingenious in applying these principles to healing mental and emotional illness. For example, the use of flooding, that is, deliberately intensifying to the max a symptom, such as anxiety induced by not following a compulsive ritual, until it extinguishes is both creative and effective. Here the patient isn't allowed to carry out the compulsive activity, so he or she must experience the anxiety. But lo and behold, nothing terrible happens except discomfort, and after a few trials the anxiety extinguishes and the patient is free not to engage in the ritual. At least that is the theory.

Joseph Wolpe (1969) is the figure most prominently associated with behavior therapy. He developed a technique called *reciprocal inhibition* to treat phobias. He and the patient would construct a hierarchy going from least anxiety-provoking stimulus to most anxiety-provoking stimulus. For example, in the case of fear of flying, Wolpe and the patient might start with a picture of an airplane and work up to actually flying as they imagine progressively more anxiety-provoking situations associated with flying. This is the hierarchy. Then Wolpe teaches the patient relaxation. Next, he exposes the patient to the least fear-inducing stimulus in the hierarchy while in the state of relaxation until the fear (anxiety) is completely extinguished. Only then do the patient and therapist go to the next item on the anxiety hierarchy. They stay there until anxiety is extinguished at that level. This process continues until the goal is reached and the patient is comfortable at the highest rung of the anxiety hierarchy. Wolpe postulated that fear and relaxation can't coexist, hence the term *reciprocal inhibition*. Although substance abuse counselors and addictions therapists are not likely to do reciprocal inhibition therapy, they do borrow Wolpe's reliance on relaxation training and on assertiveness training, which he also used. These, along with the use of reinforcement, are the aspects of the behavioral tradition that have been most strongly incorporated into substance abuse and behavioral addiction work.

Cognitive Therapy

Cognitive therapists believe that irrational beliefs and thoughts cause emotional illness. For example, the belief "I am only a worthwhile person if I get straight A's" confuses a perhaps desirable goal with a condition for having self-esteem. It is an irrational belief or thought, and one that predisposes to depression. An equally irrational belief is, "Drinking helps my depression." Cognitive therapy is about changing ideation, changing the way people think, by challenging irrational thoughts, beliefs, and maladaptive attitudes. It is an active, engaging, anything but neutral approach to therapy. The most prominent names associated with this school are, on the popular side, Albert Ellis (1962), who wrote of "*must*erbation," as in "I *must* have a million dollars to be happy," and, on the academic side, Aaron Beck (1976). Today the majority of the counseling and therapy being done is heavily weighted to the cognitive side. Substance abuse counseling and addictions therapy are essentially forms of cognitive therapy. Substance abuse counselors spend most of their time trying to correct their patients' mistaken beliefs, irrational thoughts, and counterproductive attitudes. The Twelve-Step programs can be understood as being, among other things, a group cognitive therapy. The AA/NA slogans seek to change irrational beliefs and modify attitudes: "Get out of the driver's seat," "Addiction is the disease of more," and "KISS" (Keep it simple, stupid).

The cognitive therapist must sincerely believe that his or her perception of reality makes sense and is more rational than that of the patient. There are obvious dangers here of being doctrinaire and of not examining one's own presuppositions, yet there's no doubt that the substance abuse counselor's commitment to recovery is more rational than the patient's commitment to self-destructive behavior.

The characteristic techniques of the cognitive therapist are confrontation, or what Ellis calls "disputing the patient's irrational beliefs," and education. Cognitive therapists not only work on thoughts in the patient's head, but also are aware that emotion is important, too. For that reason, Ellis called his approach *rational-emotive therapy* (*RET*). Like the character in the Molière play who discovered that he had been speaking prose all his life, if you are a substance abuse counselor you have been a cognitive therapist all along.

Existential Therapy

The existentialist school concentrates on "ultimates," on basic aspects of human existence that none of us can evade. It views mental illness, including substance abuse and behavioral addiction, as an avoidance, an attempt to escape ultimates, the bedrock realities of human life. Of course, they cannot be escaped and the avoider gets paid back in spades. This is obvious in substance abuse. For example, the user endangers his life by his substance abuse, which is driven by his fear of death. The same might be true of sexual addiction if it is driven by avoidance of the fear of death while ironically exposing oneself to a deadly virus. The ultimates the existentialists focus on are mortality, limitation, responsibility for one's life, and the search for meaning, with its concomitant fear of meaninglessness.

The existential school has no particular set of techniques. In fact, it plays down the role of technique. Rather, it is an attitude and perspective. What is important in the therapeutic relationship is genuineness and the therapist's willingness to swim at the deep end of the pool—to struggle with ultimates with the patient. Therapists must be open to their fear of death, their difficulties accepting that some things are not possible, their sense that there can be no escape from responsibility for life's decisions, and their fear that it is all meaningless, "a tale told by an idiot full of sound and fury signifying nothing" (Shakespeare's *Macbeth*). Only then can the patient become open to his or her parallel fears, share them, and begin to come to such terms with them as is possible. There is no one name associated with the existential approach, but in the United States Rollo May (1953) and Eric Fromm (1941), whose best-known work is *Escape from Freedom*, the very title of which tells you its theme, are the most renowned existential therapists. There is no more radical escape from freedom than addiction. The anxiety concomitant with the renewed freedom of recovery and the realization that choice is not only possible but also inevitable can endanger recovery.

Existential themes play a major role in substance abuse counseling and addictions psychotherapy. All addicted patients, in common with their nonaddicted fellows, must come to terms with the ultimates of existence. Their substance use or behavioral addiction has been a prolonged avoidance, but now in recovery that is no longer possible. This is big-time trouble, and it is vital that the therapist swims in that deep end of the pool with the patient.

The Twelve-Step programs know that, and they provide meaning through participation in community and helping others (Twelve-Step work), and they make taking responsibility for oneself tolerable by reducing guilt. This is yet another reason that therapy combined with Twelve-Step participation gives the best odds of recovery.

That brings me to the spiritual. *Spirituality* has become an overused word that has lost meaning, somewhat like *codependency*. These days to say good morning to your spouse is to be codependent. Originally the word had a definite and important meaning: remaining in a self-destructive relationship with an active substance abuser for unconscious emotional reasons. Similarly, these days spirituality refers to everything from going to a séance to wearing love beads, to meditating, to finding meaning. Everything from the most vapid, touchy-feely 1990s charlatanism to the most seriously profound quest to transcend self and connect with the totality of things is spiritual. This is unfortunate, but I am afraid the word won't go away. What it denotes, at its best, is important to patients, and an area of human life therapists must deal with.

Carl Jung, the Swiss psychiatrist and analyst, brought the notion of spirituality into the substance abuse field. The story is told in the AA literature of Roland H., a wealthy American alcoholic businessman, who went to Jung for analysis. He left Zurich, apparently cured, but before long he was back, drunk as ever. Jung told him that he was hopeless and that he would either die or go mad. Roland begged Jung to relent and finally Jung relented and told Mr. H. that there was one hope, namely that he would have a "transvaluation of values," a phrase Jung borrowed from the philosopher Friedrich Nietzsche. A transvaluation of values is a radical change in one's state of being—a deep, strongly emotional realization that the path one is on is wrong and that direction must be reversed. It is what was later called "hitting bottom" and "surrender." Roland had such an experience and joined the Oxford Movement, also known as the Moral Rearmament Movement. It was a sort of upper-class revival movement, led by Frank Buchman, who was something of a con man, albeit an effective organizer. The Oxford Movement had a series of steps of spiritual growth. Roland remained sober and told many people of his spiritual experiences in the Oxford Movement including Ebby Thacker, an alcoholic friend of Bill Wilson's, who was to become the founder of AA. Thacker joined the Oxford Movement and became sober also. He visited his drinking buddy, Bill Wilson, who was drunk as usual and in the last stages of alcoholism. Ebby told Bill his story and Wilson went off for detox. While in Town's Hospital, an expensive drying out tank, Wilson had some sort of "peak" or mystical experience such as Jung had told Roland was the only hope. He never drank again. Leaving the hospital, Wilson joined the Oxford Movement and started working with drunks. Not being one to follow for long, and critical of the Oxford Movement for preachiness and its propensity to talk down to drinkers, Bill Wilson went his own way and founded AA after saving another drunk, Dr. Bob Smith, by "running his story," that is, sharing his experience of drinking and recovery. Ebby Thacker didn't make it; he relapsed and died of alcoholism in a state hospital.

Many years later, Bill Wilson wrote to Carl Jung and told him the story of Roland H. and the founding of AA. Jung wrote back and in his letter punned in Latin that the cure for alcoholism was *Spiritum contra Spiritus* (the spiritual against the spirits). His view is that alcoholism and drug addiction as well as behavioral addiction are mistaken spiritual quests, the quest being admirable but the path deplorable. The only hope for cure is to redirect the spiritual quest. Without a genuine outlet for spiritual needs and aspirations, recovery is not possible. To grossly oversimplify, Freud held that emotional illness (including addiction) was caused by repressed and misdirected sexual and aggressive needs. Jung held that they were caused by repressed and misdirected spiritual needs.

Jung is not my favorite character. He slept with his patients and collaborated with the Nazis, so it is hard to take his emphasis on spirituality seriously. Yet he is indubitably onto something here. Recovery does indeed entail coming to terms with what the existentialists call "ultimates" and the Jungians call the "spiritual." And the therapist must be there for the patient going through that quest without imposing his or her answers or values on the patient. It is also well to remember that not all patients are spiritually inclined and that atheists, agnostics, Sunday Christians, sincere believers, and religious fanatics all suffer substance abuse and other addictions and they all are capable of recovery. There is no particular belief system that is necessary to recovery, and disbelief, and full awareness of the consequences of this disbelief, is as "spiritual" a stand as is religious commitment.

Accepting mortality, taking responsibility for one's life and one's choices, finding meaning or accepting meaninglessness, and connecting with community and the universe or accepting aloneness are more than can be achieved in the course of substance abuse treatment—indeed, more than can be achieved in the entire course of life. Nevertheless, substance abuse counselors and addiction therapists can and should be there for the patient as he or she starts on the new and wondrous yet perilous road, the road to coming to terms with existentialist ultimates—now experienced rather than anesthetized or repressed.

Substance Abuse Specific Counseling and Addiction Therapy

Substance abuse counseling and addiction therapy are unique not only in their integration of schools and techniques. They are also unique in that they have their own knowledge base and their own way of working with patients, focusing sometimes quite narrowly on the substance abuse or addiction itself and on coping strategies for maintaining sobriety or recovery. They most closely resemble cognitive therapy, use the attitudinal components of client-centered counseling, and borrow heavily from the psychodynamic tradition, recognizing the role of transference, countertransference, and resistance in the therapeutic process, and seeking to bring to awareness the existential dilemmas of life so that they don't sneak up and sandbag recovery. When appropriate they also borrow from the Gestalt, behavioral, and directive traditions. They rely most heavily on confrontation, exploration, education, and interpretation, but make use of all techniques when they facilitate the work of bringing people from addiction to recovery—from slavery to freedom.

Addiction as Regression to Pathological Narcissism

This chapter presents a model of the psychodynamic correlative of alcoholism, and of addiction in general, as a regression or fixation to pathological narcissism in a special sense. Drawing on the work of Heinz Kohut (1971, 1977a, b) on the development of the self and its pathological vicissitudes, I define pathological narcissism as regression or fixation to Kohut's stage of the archaic nuclear self. The model may at first seem overly abstract and remote from the concerns of the therapist, but with a little thought, it makes sense to connect the internal psychological and emotional consequences of developmental difficulties with adult vulnerability to addiction. The model is quite practical and I spell out its clinical implications following the case example.

Heinz Kohut was a classical analyst who came to see that classical theory could not account for what went on in his analyses. He realized that certain patients, whom he later identified as having narcissistic personality disorders, did not relate to him as a separate person, but rather related to him as if he were an extension of themselves. Kohut (1971, 1977a) called these ways of relating *narcissistic transferences*. (He later called them *selfobject transferences*.) He built a whole developmental theory from this analysis of the transference. He distinguished between two kinds of such transferences: *mirror transfer-*

ences and *idealizing transferences.* In the mirror transference, the therapist's only function is to reflect back (mirror) the patient's wonderfulness. What the patient seeks is affirmation of archaic infantile grandiosity. In the idealizing transference, the patient puts all of the wonderfulness—omnipotence and omniscience—in the therapist, and then fuses with him or her. I would suggest that the addict's relationship to the substance or compulsive activity can usefully be understood as a combined mirror and idealizing transference.

Kohut spoke of the *transmuting internalization* of psychic structure. By transmuting internalization he meant a gradual taking into the self, a grain at a time, so to speak, of the functions once performed by self-objects, by which Kohut meant not internal representations, but people to whom one relates in a special undifferentiated way. Each nontraumatic failure of the self-object to meet a psychological need results in the acquisition of some capacity to meet the need oneself; for example, tension regulation, once the function of the loving caretaker (self-object) of the infant, becomes an internalized ability to achieve such tension reduction. Kohut's notion was one of optimal frustration: no frustration, no internalization, there is no need for it; too much frustration, no internalization—what is absent can't be taken in. As Winnicott put it, "we succeed by failing." By we Winnicott meant parents and therapists.

Kohut would have been more accurate had he referred to psychic structure as psychic *capacity*, for that is what he meant. He conceptualized most psychopathology, and certainly narcissistic pathology, as a deficit state—something is missing inside. It is missing inside because something went wrong developmentally. Some phase of early object relations went awry. Of course, it makes perfect sense to take something in—alcohol, for instance—to remedy an internal lack. The only trouble is that what is missing can only come from people, from a certain kind of relationship, not from a chemical. So the treatment of addiction must be, in some sense a replacement of rum with relationship. Kohut compared an addiction to a futile attempt to cure a gastric fistula by eating. The food might taste good, but it falls right out the hole without either nourishing or repairing the hole. As Kohut put it, "No psychic structure is built" (1977b, p. viii).

PATHOLOGICAL NARCISSISM

Pathological narcissism is the regression or fixation to the stage of the archaic self. It is characterized by the presence of a cohesive but insecure self that is threatened by regressive fragmentation; grandiosity of less than psychotic proportions, which manifests itself in the form of arrogance, isolation, and unrealistic goals; feelings of entitlement; the need for omnipotent control; poor differentiation of self and object; and deficits in the self-regulating capacities of the ego. Further, affect tolerance is poor. The tenuousness of the cohesion of the self makes the narcissistically regressed individual subject to massive anxiety, which is in reality fear of annihilation (that is, fear of fragmentation of the self). Narcissistic personality disorders are also subject to *empty depression*, which reflects the relative emptiness of the self, or the paucity of psychic structure and good internal objects. In the condition of pathological narcissism, these manifestations of the grandiose self or the idealized self-object or both may be either blatantly apparent or deeply repressed or denied, with a resulting façade of *pseudo–self-sufficiency*, but they are never smoothly integrated into a mature self, as they are in healthy narcissism.

In Kohut's formulation, the overtly grandiose self is the result of merger with (or lack of differentiation from) a mother who used the child to gratify her own narcissistic needs. It is a false self in the terminology of Winnicott (1960). Kohut envisions this false self as insulated by a vertical split in the personality. The reality ego is in turn impoverished as a result of the repression of the unfulfilled archaic narcissistic demands by a horizontal split (repression barrier) in the personality (see Figure 3–1). The salient point to be derived from Kohut's and Winnicott's theories is an understanding of the overt grandiosity of the addict as a manifestation of a "false self," which is isolated, both affectively and cognitively, from the more mature reality ego, which is itself enfeebled by its inability to integrate the archaic self. Hence, some sense can be made of the coexistence of haughty arrogance and near-zero self-esteem so frequently seen in alcoholics.

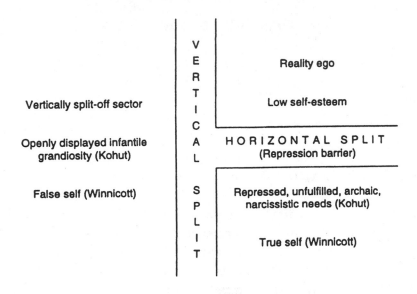

Figure 3–1. Self structure in pathological narcissism.

NARCISSISTIC RAGE

The Kohution notion of narcissistic rage illuminates much addictive behavior. Unlike mature aggression, narcissistic rage is not instrumental in the service of reality-based goals; rather, it is the response of the unmirrored, unnurtured self to narcissistic injury (see Levin 1993). Narcissistic injury is injury to the core self, characterized by deep pain, intense feelings of shame, a precipitous fall in self-esteem, and an unquenchable desire for revenge. It is the response of the offended monarch, "Off with their heads." Kohut (1972) uses as an example Captain Ahab in *Moby-Dick*. Ahab's insane desire for revenge on a "dumb brute," the white whale, destroys him and all but one of his crew.

Narcissistic rage turned against the self can result in suicide. Addictive rage is multidetermined; part of it is pharmacological, the result of the drug's effect on the central nervous system; part of it is in defense of the addiction; part of it is from the accumulation of unexpressed anger (addicts have a lot of bluster but rarely are effectively communicative or assertive); part of it is self-hatred projected outward; part of it is historical (that is, unconscious rage over childhood injury); and part of it is narcissistic rage as a consequence of narcissistic vulnerability. Since most slips are rage responses, helping the patient recognize, contain, and appropriately express, rather than act out, narcissistic rage is of the essence of addiction therapy. I have built upon Kohut's metapsychology to construct a theory of the dynamics of addiction. Kohut inferred a developmental sequence based on his experience of the transference of adult patients. One of the stages in that development is the stage of the archaic, nuclear, bipolar self. I believe that this is the psychodynamic correlative of addiction. This psychodynamic correlative may or may not be etiological. That is, it may be caused by the addiction, rather than be the cause of it. However, in many cases, pathological narcissism as here defined, meaning regression/fixation to the stage of the archaic, nuclear bipolar self, plays a powerful role in the etiology of many addictions.

The Kohutian Self

Kohut defines the self as a unit cohesive in space and enduring in time, the center of initiative and the recipient of impressions. It can be regarded either as a mental structure superordinate to the agencies of the mind—the id, ego, and superego—or as a content of those agencies. Kohut believed that these two conceptualizations were complementary. However, in his later work (Kohut 1984), he emphasized the self as the central or superordinate principle. It is, so to speak, the organized and organizing center of human experience and is itself experienced as cohesive and enduring. According to Kohut, the infant develops a primitive, fragmented sense of self very early. Each body part, each sensation, each mental content is experienced as belonging to a self, to a "me," as mine; however, there is no synthesis of these experiences yet. They are selves, but no unitary self. Nor are there clear boundaries between self and world. Kohut designates this stage as the fragmented self; this is the developmental stage at which psychotic persons are fixated or to which they regress.

The next stage of development, an archaic nuclear bipolar self, arises from the infant's experience of being related to as a self, rather than as a collection of parts and sensations, by empathic caregivers. This self is cohesive and enduring but is not securely established. Therefore, it is prone to regressive fragmentation. It is nuclear in the sense of having a center, or nucleus, and it is archaic in the sense of being primitive, that is, a grandiose and undifferentiated precursor of the mature self. The archaic nuclear self is bipolar in that it comprises two structures: the *grandiose self* and the *idealized parental imago*. The grandiose self is a differentiated self that is experienced as omnipotent, but there are no truly differentiated objects. Objects are experienced as extensions of the self, as selfobjects. The child's grandiose self attempts to exercise omnipotent control of his selfobjects, including the people who care for him. In healthy maturity, all love objects have a selfobject aspect. However, in maturity, the experience of the object as selfobject is a reversible regression in the service of the ego that lacks the rigidity that characterizes experience of objects as selfobjects in pathological narcissism. Pathological narcissism is regression/fixation to this stage of the archaic bipolar nuclear self.

The internalization of psychic structure, that is of the capacity to perform the functions performed by selfobjects, is codeterminous with the formation of the nuclear self. As Kohut (1977a) puts it, "The rudiments of the nuclear self are laid down by simultaneously or consecutively occurring processes of selective inclusion and exclusion of psychological structure" (p. 183). Failure to adequately internalize functions originally performed for the child by selfobjects results in deficits of the self. Addiction is a futile attempt to compensate for this failure in internalization.

It is the inner emptiness, the missing parts of the self experienced as a void, that addicts try to fill with food, with alcohol, with drugs, or with compulsive sexuality. It cannot be done. Whatever is compulsively taken in goes right through, and no psychic structure is built; that can only be done by internalization of relationships. It is their abysmally low self-esteem, their doubts about being real or existing at all, and their terror of regressive fragmentation that addicts try to remediate by their addictions. They always fail.

What the addict suffering from pathological narcissism in the Kohutian sense is lacking is the ability to self-soothe; the ability to modulate anxiety; the ability to maintain a reasonably stable, satisfactory level of self-esteem, a consistent feeling of cohesion and ongoingness, a sense of agency, and the capacity to be alone. It is these self functions that are deficient in the addict that the addict attempts to remediate by substance use.

According to Kohut, the two poles of the archaic nuclear self develop in healthy maturity into realistic ambition derived from the archaic grandiosity, and into values and ideals derived through depersonalization from the idealized parental imago (representation). It is striking, in working with substance abusers, how deficient their ability to be realistically ambitious is. We frequently find one of two extremes. Substance abusers are either grandiose, overreaching, unrealistic, and live in fantasy, indicative of fixation at the level of the grandiose self, or they are at the opposite pole, exhibiting an equally unrealistic underestimation of their capacities, resulting in little attempt at appropriate achievement, indicative of failure to integrate archaic grandiosity into the mature self. Similarly, the pole of idealization in the addictive self has not reached maturity, and substance abusers concomitantly frequently experience radical difficulties in the area of values and ideals. Here, too, we find the two extremes of unrealistic grandiosity and its opposite, the lack of any sort of livable ego ideal. According to Kohut, the experience of idealizing parents is a developmental stage necessary to the achievement of mature ideals. Children need to be able to look up to their parents and to only gradually become nontraumatically disillusioned with them as they go from being ideal to being real objects. In the stormy childhoods of many substance abusers, often in homes rendered chaotic by parental substance abuse, there is little opportunity for idealization, just as there is little phase-appropriate mirroring of the child; the result is massive deficits in the self. The child growing into adolescence then discovers substances that are readily idealized, and just as readily provide mirroring in the form of reassurance and the raising of self-esteem.

Fragmentation is a key notion of Kohut's (1971, 1977a). It refers to the fragmentation of the self; that is, the regressive falling apart of the archaic, bipolar, nuclear self into an earlier stage of self experiences without cohesion. This is an important notion in substance abuse, both because substances can lead to such fragmentation, and because they are commonly used for self-medication in an attempt to abort the panic terror induced by threat of fragmentation. Fragmentation is experienced as psychic death in the sense that it means the loss of the self. So the dynamic import of drugs on fragmentation goes both ways: it causes it, and is often used as an attempt to cure it, an attempt that inevitably fails.

Fragmentation can be understood in many ways, and is clearly a metaphor. Therapists do not literally see the fragments (although they sometimes feel that they do), but they can see evidence of the process of fragmentation. One example Kohut gave was hypochondriasis, in which the patient becomes the various aching body parts and has difficulty experiencing him- or herself as in any way integral or whole.

This brings to mind the story of the man who goes to the doctor and says, "Doctor, I have these terrible headaches, and my bowels bother me, and my legs ache all the time, and to tell you the truth, I myself don't feel so well either." In the state of fragmentation there is no "I myself," there is only the headache and the explosive bowels and the aching feet. Ordinary language also alludes to fragmentation in such phrases as "I'm falling apart" and "I'm going to pieces." The circular attempt to avoid fragmentation by using drugs that fragment is an important dynamic in addiction.

This model of regression/fixation to the stage of the archaic nuclear self accounts for the empirical findings on the clinical addictive personality, which is complex. Its empirically supported traits include elevation on the Psychopathic Deviant (Pd) and Depression (D) scales on the Minnesota Multiphasic Personality Inventory (MMPI), field dependence, confused gender identity, ego weakness, and stimulus augmentation.

The clinical addictive personality, also known as the postaddictive personality, is an empirically determined cluster of traits repeatedly found in populations under treatment for addiction. These findings are robust and consistent across populations. They are statistical averages, and do not necessarily describe any particular addict. Most of this research has been done on white males.

As in much of the psychological literature, personality is operationalized here as scores on objective psychological tests, although sometimes it is operationalized as quantifications of projective test findings, for example the form level on the Rorschach test, reported as % F+.

It is necessary to distinguish the clinical addictive personality from the preaddictive personality, if there be one. Researchers tend to agree that there is a large degree of commonality in people at the end of the addictive cycle. Various psychological measurements on people in detox, rehab, or early recovery show a great deal of commonality. This should not be surprising since addiction is a process of progressive impoverishment at the end of which the addict is left with an empty self, an empty world, and an empty bottle. Recovery is the converse, a process of progressive enrichment. A concomitant of the impoverishment is *dedifferentiation*, a process in which the addict loses his or her uniqueness and becomes similar to everyone else in detox. This is, of course, something of an exaggeration; nevertheless, there is a cluster of findings that is quite consistent across populations and situations, which suggests either that those who become addicted started out much alike or that addiction strips and homogenizes.

Clinically addicted populations manifest pathology on the MMPI, in particular, elevation of what is called the Psychopathic deviant (Pd) scale. This is one of the most consistent and robust findings in addictive populations. Sometimes referred to as the angry scale, it should not be interpreted as evidence that clinical alcoholics and substance abusers are sociopathic or suffer from overt antisocial personality disorder, but rather that they manifest many signs of externalizing defenses, angry acting out, and a devil-take-the-hindmost attitude toward conventions, regulations, and laws. There is some evidence (Loper et al. 1973) that an elevated Pd is antecedent to addiction for at least some addicts, and that it persists, although in an attenuated form, well into sobriety. Alcoholics and other substance abusers also score strikingly high on the Depression (D) scale of the MMPI. However, the depression tends to remit with sobriety. Depression can be primary or secondary, and may be antecedent to the addiction for which the substance use is often a self-medication. Or the depression may be secondary to the substance use on both a pharmacological and lifestyle basis. Awfully depressing things happen to addicts, so they have realistic reasons—connected to declining health, economic loss, and broken relationships—to be depressed. Additionally savage self-hatred that is manifested in the superego's relentless battering of the ego, an unconscious process often coped with by projection, significantly deepens the depression. To add insult to injury, the very substance used to alleviate the depression exacerbates it.

Since cessation of use removes the pharmacological, lifestyle, and one intrapsychic component (self-hatred for the use itself) of the depression, it is not surprising that depression often lifts in sobriety. At least that is what average scores on various measures of depression show.

There are, nevertheless, a percentage of addicts who are primary depressives whose depression does not remit, and this will almost certainly lead to relapse if it is not treated psychologically and/or psychopharmacologically. Combining psychotherapy and psychopharmacology gives the patient optimal odds of remission.

High scores on the neuroticism (Pt) scale of the MMPI characterize high levels of anxiety, low self-esteem, obsessive worry, tension, indecisiveness, and concentration difficulties. These, too, are elevated in clinical addictive populations and tend to improve with sobriety.

MacAndrew (1965) constructed a scale of forty-nine items from the MMPI that accurately identifies 85 percent of male alcoholics. This group is reward-seeking, bold, aggressive, impulsive, and hedonistic, and clearly demonstrates many of the characteristics of those with elevated Pd scale. The 15 percent not identified by those items are identified by other items on the MMPI that are characterized by tension, fear, depression, and fear of punishment. MacAndrew called the first group *primary alcoholics* and the second group *secondary alcoholics*—an unusual use of the primary-secondary terminology.

The second consistent finding in addictive populations is that they are *field dependent* (Witkin et al. 1959). Field dependence refers to a cognitive style in which one does not trust internal cues but rather looks to the environment for guidance in construing a world. It reflects a mistrust of one's own perceptions of the world and a global, cognitive style lacking in differentiation. Field dependence implies some degree of pathological fusion of self and object representations. There is a controversy in the literature as to whether field dependence correlates with pathological interpersonal dependence, either in the direction of defensive isolation or in the direction of symbiosis and loss of identity. Some researchers (Witkin and Oltman 1967) believe that it docs, and that the findings of field dependency in alcoholics and other addicts clearly point to interpersonal difficulties that are present without question; other researchers, while not doubting the existence of the interpersonal difficulties, believe that field dependence refers only to cognitive style. Field dependence is measured in several ways, one of which is the embedded-figure test. Field-independent people readily separate figure from ground, while field-dependent people do not.

The third major trait of the clinical addictive personality is *impoverished self-concept*. This is true whether it is measured by adjective checklist ("Check each item that applies to you"), by projective tests, or by interview. Addicts demonstrate diffuse self-concepts, empty self-concepts, and low self-esteem.

Another trait of the addictive personality is *ego weakness*, manifested by impulsivity; the inability to delay gratification; low affect tolerance; a propensity toward panic level anxiety and prolonged depression; an unclear, confused sense of identity; and lack of clear boundaries. Reality testing, an important ego function, is impaired in ego weakness. So are affect tolerance and the ability to delay gratification. Another aspect of ego weakness is an external locus of control. That is, clinical addicts, on the average, see themselves as controlled by forces outside of themselves, rather than being in control of their own destiny. Of course addicts are not in control of their destiny, their addiction being the tail that wags the dog. Yet another aspect of ego weakness is confused identity. There is much empirical evidence for this in the form of data gleaned from figure drawings, which demonstrate permeable boundaries and lack of differentiation. This may include confusion as to sexual identity manifest in subjects drawing opposite-gender figures on the Draw-a-Person test.

Yet another finding of the clinical addictive personality profile is *stimulus augmentation*, meaning that addicts feel the impact of environmental stimuli more strongly than others. This has nothing to do with malingering but appears to be a largely neurological, though perhaps partly developmental and environmentally determined, personality trait that is quite persistent and enduring. In short, the world impacts addicts hard.

In summary, the clinical addictive personality is characterized by elevated Pd, D, and Pt scales on the MMPI; field dependency; impoverished self-concept; low self-esteem; external locus of central; ego weakness; and stimulus augmentation. Clearly the addiction therapist is treating more than hangnails.

Elevation in the Psychopathic Deviate (Pd) scale of the MMPI, in both active and recovering addicts, can be understood as a manifestation of the overtly grandiose self with its arrogance, isolation, and lack of realistic goals. The elevation on the MMPI Depression (D) scale reflects both the psychopharmacological consequences of active addiction and the impoverishment of the self, riddled with structural deficits and impaired in its capacity for self-esteem regulation, found in pathological narcissism.

Developmentally, the depression reflects the disappointment that results from inadequate phase-appropriate mirroring (approving confirmation) of the child's grandiose self by selfobjects. Additionally, addiction gives one much to be realistically depressed about. Empirical findings, using adjective checklists and self-reports, of impoverishment of the self are to be understood in the same way. The structurally deficient self of pathological narcissism is experienced as an empty depression and is reported as lack of interest, activities, and goals. Even the self is uninteresting to the self. The regression to pathological narcissism concomitant with addiction progressively strips the already enfeebled ego of its investment in objects and activities.

Confused gender identity is another frequent finding in addictive populations. This confusion also can be understood in terms of pathological narcissism. Developmentally, the archaic self arises before the establishment of firm gender identity. Hence, regression or fixation at the stage of the archaic self entails a blurring of gender identity.

Failure to adequately internalize the idealized selfobject of the same sex, which is postulated as etiological in the person's vulnerability to pathological narcissism, renders difficult the establishment of firm gender identity.

Ego weakness is a construct that integrates several empirically confirmed characteristics of the active and early sobriety addict: impulsivity, lack of frustration tolerance, lack of affect tolerance, and lack of differentiation of the self representation. In terms of pathological narcissism, ego weakness in the addict is understood as encompassing the structural deficits in the self. In other words, the failure to internalize by a process of selective and depersonified identification, which Kohut calls transmuting internalization, the functions of affect regulation, self-soothing, boundary maintenance, and maintenance of satisfactory levels of self-esteem, once performed from the outside by the mother and other caregivers, results in ego weakness. In the case of weak or incomplete internalization of the functions of the selfobject, the self is subject to regression to pathological narcissism.

Stimulus augmentation, another characteristic of substance abusers, can also be understood in terms of pathological narcissism as a failure to internalize the mother's function as an auxiliary to the innate stimulus barrier. Although constitutional factors play a role in stimulus augmentation, failures in internalization and structuralization just as certainly play their role.

ALICE: A CASE STUDY

Alice came to me from treatment of a posttraumatic stress reaction. She had been in an automobile accident and was badly shaken. Her face had been scarred and she was deeply depressed. Plastic surgery later restored her face, leaving little evidence of the accident, but when she first came to my office she didn't know that that was going to happen. Alice was young and very appealing. She had been referred by her attorney, who had not mentioned alcohol, so I was surprised when she told me that she was an alcoholic. She said that she had been alcoholic since the age of 12 and had "hit bottom" four years ago. I asked her how old she was. She said, "Twenty-five." My next question was, "How did you get sober?" She replied, "The part about getting sober wouldn't make sense unless I told you about my drinking too. Should I do that?" I said, "Sure."

Well, I don't know where to start. I come from an alcoholic family. Both my parents died of alcoholism. Well, I think my father died of alcoholism; he deserted us when I was 4. I remember the last time I saw him. We were eating dinner and I spilled my food. He screamed at me and said I was disgusting. I always felt that he left because I was so disgusting. I feel like a pig; I'm a compulsive overeater, too. I know in my head that he didn't leave because of the way I ate, but I don't know it in my heart. I still believe it.

Things got worse then. My mother drank more and more and we had very little money. Sometimes there was no toilet paper in the house, but there was always beer. Later we moved to my grandfather's. He was rich, but he grabbed my pussy sometimes and I didn't know what to do. I think he was senile, but he drank too, so maybe that was it. After I grew up, my mother told me she knew what he did to me, but she was afraid to do anything about it because he might have thrown us out. She was drunk when she told me that. Why did she have to tell me? I hate her for letting it happen, and I hate her for telling me that she let it happen. How could a mother do that? I have a daughter. I'd cut off his balls if a man did that to my daughter. How could she? My grandfather got more senile and I don't know exactly what happened after that.

My mother was like two people. When she was sober she was wonderful—beautiful and interested in me. But very snobby and uptight. Then I didn't think she was a snob, I thought that she was a great lady—perfectly dressed and so elegant. I loved her so much. Then there was Mother when she was drunk. Sloppy and falling down, she'd sit with her legs spread with no panties and you could see everything. She'd curse and then try to play the great lady, "Oh, my dear," and all that shit. I hated her then.

I was around 10 when I started having sex play with my cousins and some of the neighborhood kids. Mostly with the boys but sometimes with the girls too. Do you think I'm a lesbian? I loved sex—it felt so good and it made me feel good about myself. Somebody wanted me. Maybe I felt guilty underneath. Later I hated myself and maybe all that sex play had something to do with it. I was raised a strict Catholic, sort of. Once I was naked—I had just gotten out of the tub and I did an imitation of the Virgin Mary—I was about 6—and my mother really whaled my ass with a ruler.

When I was about 10 my mother met my stepfather. Eddy was a complete asshole. He drank all the time, too. Can you imagine marrying a fucking drunk like him? Then Mother really dropped me. She was more interested in drinking with Eddy. I started getting in trouble in school. At 11 I got fucked for the first time. And I mean got fucked, not made love to, by some 20–year-old pervert. Can you imagine an 11–year-old getting fucked? I loved it, or thought that I did. I hung out with all the older boys. They had cars and liquor and pot. I can't tell you how many cocks I had in me. Big ones, small ones, white ones, black ones. And you know I was never sober once. Every one of those guys had something to get high on—beer, pot, hard stuff. I loved pot from the first time I smoked it. It was even better than sex. And I drank a lot. Any boy or man who gave me something to get high on could have me. Sometimes I really liked it, but I liked fooling around with other girls even more. I think I was really turned on by myself when I played with the other girls. My mother and stepfather raised hell when they weren't too drunk to care, and finally my mother had me put away. Can you imagine that? What kind of fucking mother would put a kid in the places she put me? For God's sake, one place had bars and I was locked in. I hate her for doing that. Mental hospitals, homes for delinquent girls, the House of the Good Shepherd, the whole ball of wax. Finally I got out—I wasn't actually in any of those places for very long, it's just the idea: how could you do that to a kid? And then I met Calvin.

What a bastard he was. Oh, I forgot to tell you that when I was 15 I was team banged by a gang who pulled me into an alley and fucked me until my thing was raw and bloody. They beat me real hard too, but not as hard as Calvin did later. Oh yeah, Calvin beat me all the time. I must have been crazy but I loved him. He took me away from my hometown and my mother didn't bother me anymore. He sort of made a prisoner out of me. If I even went to the grocery store without his permission he beat me. He had a big one, the biggest I ever saw and I had seen plenty, so I thought he was a great lover. He always had beer and weed and other stuff and I stayed high most of the time. He's the father of my child. When I went into labor he was stoned. He slapped me and called me a rotten whore. He wouldn't go to the hospital with me. Do you know what it's like for a 16–year-old kid to have a baby alone? Forget it.

I never cheated on Calvin but he never stopped accusing me of being with other men and hitting me. Sometimes he hit me with a wooden plank. I thought I deserved it, that I needed to be punished for all the things I had done. I needed Calvin to beat me. As long as he supplied drugs and alcohol and beat me, I would have stayed. It was the way he acted around the baby that made me leave. One day when he wasn't home and the baby was about 2, I ran away. I couldn't stand his insane jealousy anymore; he was even jealous of the baby. A guy crazy enough to be jealous of his own kid, that's sick. He was real sick; sick in his head. I couldn't stand any more so I ran away and went to a town in the mountains where my older sisters and brother lived. Something in me said *enough*, you've been punished enough. Of course I kept on drinking. There wasn't any more sex, not then, just falling down drunk every day. I went on welfare and sometimes I worked off the books. I was sort of dead—no, not *sort of*, just plain *dead*. That went on for a few years and I hated myself more and more. I tried to be a good mother through it all and I don't think I did too badly, but God, was I depressed!

My stepfather was dead by then and my mother was far gone. I think I saw it in her before I saw it in me. My brother was in the Program— AA, that is. I thought he was a jerk, a real ass, an uptight loser. Who else would join those holy rollers? What I couldn't figure out was how such a raving asshole could be happy, and the damn jerk *was* happy. Even I could see that. He did something really smart; he didn't lecture me. In fact, he never even mentioned my drinking. Damn good thing he didn't, because the way I rebelled against everything and everybody I would never have listened. What he did do was tell me what had happened to him—ran his story, as they say in AA. I didn't want to hear that shit and I told him so, but I did hear it in spite of myself. I was getting worse; I was more and more terrified that Calvin would come back and kill me. I guess I thought that he should because of the way I was living, but I didn't know that then, I was just scared. I was getting sicker and sicker from all the drinking and I never had any money; it got to the point where I couldn't stand any more. If it wasn't for my daughter, I would have killed myself. I don't know why, but one day I asked my brother to take me to a meeting. An AA meeting, that is. I think it was the guilt; once I didn't have Calvin to beat me I couldn't stand the guilt. I *knew*, I mean I really knew what it's like to have alcoholic parents. I loved my daughter—she has such a sick fuck for a father, so I wanted her to have at least one parent with her head screwed on straight. So I went to that fucking meeting. I loved it—I mean, I *loved* it—like I never loved anything. For Christ's sake, I even identified with the coffee cups. When I do something I do it. I went all the way, the whole nine yards. I was sick—sick, sick, sick from my crotch to my toes, not to mention my head. I was so scared; I hadn't had a sober day in years, but I've made it one day at a time. I haven't made it any too swiftly. I still can't stand the guilt and the rage; you wouldn't believe how angry I get, and the crying. I cry all the fucking time, but I don't drink, I don't drug, and I don't care if my ass falls off, I'm not going to. At least not today.

I didn't want to be like my mother. I won't be like her. She's dead now. I couldn't stand it when she died; she died from her drinking. She had an accident while drunk; it was kind of a suicide. I knew she was dead, but I didn't know it. I couldn't let her go—not the awful way it was. If she was sober and I was sober, I could have let her die, but she wasn't, so I knew but I didn't know she was dead. I never accepted it; she couldn't forgive me dead, nor I her. Then one day I went to the cemetery. I looked at her grave for a long time. I couldn't believe she was dead. I started screaming, "Move the fucking grass, move the fucking grass, Mother!" I screamed and screamed but she didn't move the fucking grass and I finally knew she was gone. I went to my home group meeting hysterical. All I said was she couldn't move the fucking grass, and I cried the rest of the meeting. Nobody said a word, they just let me be me; they didn't try to take away my pain, and I didn't want or need anybody to take it away. What I needed was some-body to be with me in that pain, and they were.

I love the fucking program and all the crazy screwed-up people there. They're like me; I'm crazy too, but I'm sober. For God's sake, can you imagine what it would have been like if I was drinking when she died? Thank God I wasn't. I hate her—I love her—I still can't let go of her although I know she's dead. I hate alcohol. I hate drinking; look what it did to her, to my father, to me. How did I get sober? I don't really know. I sort of had two bottoms: a beaten bottom and an alcohol bottom. In that first bottom, I sort of saw myself and saw I couldn't go on exposing my daughter to that stuff; the second was luck or something. No, not exactly luck or not only luck. It had something to do with willingness. I became willing to go to that meeting. Maybe I had just had enough; I didn't want any more pain for me or for the baby; she's not a baby any-more. They say, "Why me?" in the Program. When you're drinking, you have the "poor me's," so you're always asking, "Why me?" If you recover, you say it differently. I don't know why me. The way I lived, I should be dead, but I'm not. I don't know if I deserve it or not, but I'll take it.

Alice is a very clear example of an attempted self-cure of narcis-sistic deficit and narcissistic injury by substance abuse. All such at-tempts at self-cure are futile, eventually leading to further narcissis-tic injury. This was true for Alice. Although alcohol and drugs turned out to be the wrong medicine, Alice had found another way to heal herself or to start to heal herself before she came for therapy, and I largely stayed out of her way and was nonimpinging as she contin-ued. My relative inactivity allowed identification and transmuting internalization to take place. This led to structure building, firmer self-cohesion, and greater ego strength. Most alcoholics and substance abusers do not have Alice's powerful drive for health and they re-quire more active interventions on the part of the therapist.

CLINICAL IMPLICATIONS OF THE MODEL

There are a number of interventions that are extremely effective when working with addicts and that logically follow from the theoretical understanding implicit in my model. In their respective ways, these interventions address what theory understands as narcissistic deficit and narcissistic injury and the attempt at their self-cure through drug use; the attempt to fill the inner emptiness consequent upon failures of internalization and transmuting internalization; the acting out and turning against the self of narcissistic rage; idealizing and mirror transferences to the drug; attempts at omnipotent control through substance use and abuse; attempts to boost abysmally low self-esteem through the use of drugs; and the centrality of shame experiences, both antecedent to and consequent upon, the drug abuse. The following generic ways of translating theory into concrete interventions need to be modified so that each patient can hear them; nevertheless, they are models of great utility when working with addicts.

Most of these interventions are addressed to "actives," those still using, yet their maximum effectiveness is with the "recovering," particularly those in early sobriety. By varying the tense from "you were" to "you are," they can be used with both groups.

1. This intervention addresses the narcissistic wound inflicted by not being able to drink "like other people." In many subcultures, the inability to drug like other people is just as deep a narcissistic wound. The admission that one is powerless over alcohol or drugs, as Twelve-Step programs put it, or that one cannot use without the possibility of losing control, as I would put it, is extremely painful. It is experienced as a defect in the self, which is intolerable to those who are as perfectionistic as addicts usually are. The self *must* not be so damaged and deficient. Additionally, to be able to "drink like a man" or "drink like a lady" may be a central component of the alcoholic's self-concept—his or her identity. This is particularly so for macho men, but is by no means restricted to them. The therapist must recognize and articulate the conflict between the patient's wish to stop using and the patient's feeling that to do so entails admitting that he or she is flawed in a fundamental way. The therapist does this by saying, "You don't so much want to use, as not want not to be able to use." This intervention makes the patient conscious of the conflict in an empathic way and allows him or her to struggle with this issue, and

often opens the way for the patient to achieve a more comfortable, stable recovery.

2. All addictions are one long experience in narcissistic injury. Failure stalks the addict like a shadow. As one of my patients put it, "When I drink, everything turns to shit." It sure does: career setbacks, job losses, rejection by loved ones, humiliations of various sorts, ill health, economic decline, accidental injury, and enduring bad luck are all-too-frequent concomitants of addiction. Each negative experience is a narcissistic wound. Cumulatively, they constitute one massive narcissistic wound. Even if the outward blows have not yet come, the inner blows—self-hatred and low self-regard—are always there. The addict has all too frequently heard, "It's all your fault." The therapist must empathize with the addict's suffering. "Your disease has cost you so much," "You've lost so much," and "Your self-respect is gone" are some ways the therapist can make contact with the substance abuser's pain and facilitate his experiencing this pain instead of denying, acting out, or anesthetizing it.

3. Addicts feel empty. Either they never had much good stuff inside, or they have long ago flushed out the good stuff with alcohol or drugs. "You drink so much because you feel empty" makes the connection, as well as brings into awareness the horrible feelings of an inner void. After sobriety has been achieved, the historical (that is, childhood) determinants of the paucity of psychic structure that is experienced as emptiness can also be interpreted.

4. Addicts lack a firm sense of identity. How can you know who you are if your experience of self is tenuous and its partly unconscious inner representation lacks consistent cohesion? The therapist can comment on this and point out that being an addict or substance abuser is at least something definite, an identity of sorts. When AA members say, "My name is———, and I am an alcoholic," they are affirming that they exist and have at least that one attribute. The manifest purpose of Twelve-Step members so identifying themselves is, of course, to deal with denial. But the latent meaning is existential. Not being sure of their very existence, addicts need to assert it. With sobriety, many more attributes of the self will accrue—the self will enrich and cohere. One way of conveying this to the patient is to

say, "You're confused and not quite sure who you are. That is partly because of your drug use. Acknowledging your addiction will lessen your confusion as to who you are and give you a base on which to build a firm and positive identity."

5. Many people use substances because they cannot stand to be alone. They drink to enjoy someone's companionship (see discussion of Winnicott in Chapters 8 and 10). This should be interpreted. "You use so much because you can't bear to be alone, and getting high gives you the illusion of having company, of being with a friend. After you stop using, it will be important for us to discover why it is so painful for you to be alone."

6. Addicts form selfobject (narcissistic) transferences to drugs and compulsive activities. Relating to drugs as a friend can be regarded as a form of what Kohut called the twinship transference, one form of the mirror transference. Addicts also form idealizing and mirror transferences to their drugs of choice. The image of the archaic, idealized parent is projected onto the drug and it is regarded as an all-powerful, all-good object with which the user merges in order to participate in this omnipotence. "Heroin will deliver the goods and give me love, power, and whatever else I desire" is the user's unconscious fantasy. The therapist should interpret this thus: "Heroin feels like a good, wise, and powerful parent who protects you and makes you feel wonderful, and that is why you loved it so much. In reality, it is a depressant drug, not all the things you thought it was." The therapist can go on to say, "Now that getting high isn't working for you anymore, you are disillusioned, furious, and afraid. Let's talk about those feelings."

7. One of the reasons addicts are so devoted to the consumption of their drug is that it confirms their grandiosity. In other words, they form a mirror transference to the substance. One alcoholic patient told me he was thrilled that a sixth Nobel Prize was to be added to the original five. He read this while drinking in a bar at eight A.M. His not so unconscious fantasy was to win all six. The therapist should make the mirror transference conscious by interpreting it. "When you drink, you feel you can do anything, be anything, achieve anything, and that feels wonderful. No wonder you don't want to give it up."

8. Addicts, without exception, have abysmally low self-esteem no matter how well covered over by bluster and bravado it may be. Self psychology understands this as an impoverishment of the reality ego that is a consequence of failure to integrate archaic grandiosity, which is instead split off by what Kohut calls the "vertical split" and which manifests itself as unrealistic reactive grandiosity. This low self-esteem persists well into recovery. At some point the therapist needs to say, "You feel like shit, and think that you are shit, and all your claims to greatness are ways to avoid knowing that you feel that way. You don't know it, but way down somewhere inside you feel genuinely special. We need to put you in contact with the real stuff, so you don't need drugs or illusions to help you believe that the phony stuff is real." The particular reasons, which are both antecedents to and consequences of the addiction, that the patient values him- or herself so little need to be elucidated and worked through.

9. Sometimes the patient's crazy grandiosity is simultaneously a defense against and an acting out of the narcissistic cathexis of the patient by a parent. In other words, the patient is attempting to fulfill the parent's dreams in fantasy, while making sure not to fulfill them in reality. This is especially likely to be the case if the patient is the adult child of an alcoholic. Heavy drinking or drugging makes such a defense or acting out easy. If the recovering person's grandiosity does seem to be a response to being treated by a parent as an extension of himself, the therapist can say, "One reason you feel so rotten about yourself is that you're always doing it for Mom or Dad, not for yourself. You resent this, and spite them by undermining yourself by getting high."

10. Many addicts have a pathological need for omnipotent control. The drug is simultaneously experienced as an object they believe they can totally control and coerce into doing their will, and an object they believe gives them total control of their subjective states and of the environment. This can be seen as a manifestation of their mirror and idealizing transferences to substances. Addicts frequently treat people, including the therapist, as extensions of themselves. The Twelve-Step slogans, "Get out of the driver's seat" and "Let go and let God," are cognitive-behavioral ways of loosening the need

to control. Therapists should interpret this need to control in the patient's relationship with the drug, with other people, and with the therapist. For example, "You think that when you drink you can feel anyway you wish." "You go into a rage and get high whenever your wife doesn't do as you wish." "You thought of mainlining because you were upset with me when I didn't respond as you thought I would."

11. Substance abusers and their children suffer greatly from shame experiences. Addictive patients are ashamed of having been shamed and often use drugs to obliviate feelings of shame. Therapists need to help substance abusing patients experience, rather than repress, their feelings of shame now that they no longer anesthetize them. One way to do this is to identify feelings of shame that are not recognized as such. For example, "You felt so much shame when you realized you were alcoholic that you kept on drinking so you wouldn't feel the shame."

12. Anxiety is understood and interpreted as panic dread of psychic death in the form of fragmentation of the self. Depression is understood and interpreted as empty depression consequent upon failures of internalization, while rage is understood and interpreted as narcissistic. The management of this narcissistic rage is absolutely critical lest it set up a relapse motivated by vengeance. The therapist must both bring to consciousness and facilitate its appropriate expression while helping the patient contain (rather than repress) the rage. Interpreting the rage as a response to threats to the patient's self-esteem and self-cohesion is the key to doing this.

13. The therapist must sometimes support the defense of splitting in order to preserve the only good object available to the patient until transmuting internalization provides one. Premature attempts at integration of good and bad mother are ill advised, although this is an ultimate treatment goal.

14. The therapist needs to assist the patient in formulating realistic aims and goals that are neither grandiosely inflated nor unrealistically low.

15. The therapist needs to assist the patient in finding and articulating livable ideals and values.

Alice's story amply exemplifies the relationship between narcissistic deficit, narcissistic injury, and the futile attempt to remediate the former and heal the latter through the addictive use of substances (alcohol and food) and compulsive actions (sex and excitement). Alice suffered massive failures of internalization, leaving her with gaping structural deficits. She also felt dead, doubting both her aliveness and her existence, and sought out stimulation of any kind, even beatings, to feel alive. Lacking idealizable parents she found Calvin; having had little phase-appropriate mirroring of her archaic grandiosity, she found alcohol. In addition to mirroring her, alcohol gave her the illusion of cohesiveness. The amazing strength she did display may have been possible because her mother very early on was "good enough." Alice's capacity for splitting also helped her preserve a good mother from whom she could draw some sustenance in face of all the badness of her later, and by then overtly alcoholic, mother. Alice had not integrated the two mothers. Her "bad" mother became Alice's split-off grandiosity and denial. So split off from any kind of reality testing was this side of Alice's vertical split that her unassimilated grandiosity came very close to killing Alice. Alice's mother was not so fortunate; the mother's grandiosity was fatal.

On the other side of the vertical split, Alice's reality ego was impoverished, depressed, empty, fragile, and never far from fragmentation. The phase-appropriate grandiosity of the stage of the archaic nuclear self had never been integrated into her reality ego; it couldn't be because it had never been adequately mirrored. In Winnicott's (1960) terms, her true self was buried for safekeeping from a dangerous, treacherous environment. Whether this is understood in Kohut's or in Winnicott's terms, it is clear that her defensive system made survival possible, *and* that it was now an encumbrance, and that a major aim of treatment had to be its modification.

The child of an alcoholic carries a special kind of narcissistic injury. Humiliation and shame are recurrent and the wounds go deep. Alice's narcissistic injuries were denied, repressed, and acted out, as was the narcissistic rage that is a natural reaction to these injuries. Alice's delinquency was an attempt at self-cure. As Winnicott says, when there is an antisocial tendency, there is hope. Alice found some kind of solace, responsiveness, and, in however distorted a form, mirroring in her acting out. It also allowed her to externalize her rage. However, what saved Alice was her ability to love and to seek love. She never gave up her search for good objects that she could idealize and internalize. Alcohol was one such object—one that traumatically failed her, but she didn't give up. Abandonment depression and abandonment rage were central to Alice's psychopathology, but they could be worked through in the transference, because she did transfer, because she was still searching for relationship. Her love for her baby, probably an identification with the early good mother, got her away from Calvin, and her ability to enter into a twinship relationship with her brother allowed her to identify with him and join AA. The AA program then became an idealized object. She formed the same kind of transference with me, and the working through of her predominantly idealizing transference, which also had mirror aspects, enabled her to build psychic structure. Of course, she was sober by then or this would not have been possible.

The scene in the cemetery was crucial to Alice's recovery. As long as she couldn't let go of the bad mother or of just plain *Mother*, there was no way that she could internalize a good object. Bad Mother was a pathological introject, the content of the vertical split. Only by letting her die and then mourning her could Alice reclaim the energy to love a new object and by transmuting internalization, acquire the psychic structure she lacked. Mourning is not possible during active addiction to alcohol or to other substances. I have found in case after case that facilitating mourning must take priority in the therapy of the stable sober alcoholic. Only then can the work proceed as one hopes it will.

Kohutian analysis is not the treatment of choice for most recovering addicts. Rather, what is indicated is once- or twice-weekly intensive, insight-oriented psychodynamic psychotherapy that is informed by Kohut's insights into the vicissitudes of narcissism. Addicts have an intense need for mirroring as well as a need to idealize their past. They are also particularly narcissistically vulnerable. The treatment should therefore focus on blows to the substance abuser's already low self-esteem, failures of the childhood environment to supply sufficient phase-appropriate mirroring and opportunities for idealization, and the addicts' experience of much of the world as an extension of self. Anxiety is usually understood and interpreted as panic-fear of psychic death, dread of fragmentation of the self, rather than as a manifestation of intrapsychic conflict, and rage is usually understood and interpreted as narcissistic rage, fury at the failure of the self-object to perfectly mirror or protect, rather than as a manifestation of mature aggression.

Much seemingly irrational behavior can be understood in terms of both the addicts' need for omnipotent control and the rage that follows failure to so control. The grandiosity and primitive idealization of the archaic nuclear self also explain the perfectionism of alcoholics and other addicts and the unrealistic standards they set for themselves. Most recovering addicts have not developed realistic ambitions or livable ideals—these are characteristics of the mature self.

The alcoholic's depression can be understood in terms of the paucity of psychic structure, which was never built up through the normal process of transmuting internalization. This empty depression also reflects the repression, rather than the integration, of the archaic nuclear self and the failure to integrate archaic grandiosity. This emptiness does not abate with sobriety. Further, the narcissistic rage to which addicts are so prone can be turned against the self, resulting in intensely angry depression, sometimes of suicidal proportions. Failure to internalize the stimulus barrier and poor resources for self-soothing render the addict especially vulnerable to psychic injury. Therefore, the ordinary events of daily life long continue to threaten the addicts' already tenuous self-esteem.

The insights of self psychology into the dynamics of pathological narcissism are relevant and helpful in working with stably recovering addicts. Further, Kohut's approach can be used in a modified form in which the narcissistic transferences are allowed to unfold, the patient's need to control and to participate in greatness is accepted, and a slow working through of issues is used to help integrate components of the archaic nuclear self into the reality ego.

The empirical psychological and the learning theory literatures both suggest that hyperactivity, learning difficulties, and neurochemical vulnerabilities may characterize the pre-alcoholic and pre-addict but are loath to take seriously psychodynamic conceptualizations of antecedent psychopathology. The "pink cloud" of early sobriety, during which all or most of the negative affect (depression, anxiety, and self-hatred) is lifted, distorts the picture. So does the absence in this literature of a notion of the dynamic unconscious. Most certainly, alcohol and other drugs cause an awful lot of pain, and cessation of self-poisoning radically improves the user's life and inner experience, yet much remains to be done. I treat many substance abusers who return to therapy after extended periods of sobriety. Now the pink cloud is gone and the developmental issues and deficits suggested by Kohut are all too apparent. Of course this is a biased sample and many recovering addicts simply stop and do just fine. Further, I see many adult children of alcoholics (ACOAs) and women, so my picture is necessarily different from the predominantly male clinic and rehabilitation population on which most researchers build their picture of addiction.

As I have said, this model applies both to cases in which it is etiological and to cases in which it is not, so the issue of antecedent psychopathology is not acute. Nevertheless, it is a *deficit model* (as are many of the genetic and biochemical theories); that is, it sees addiction as an attempt to provide something lacking. Whether as cause or as consequence the inner world and style of relating postulated by the Kohut–Levin model is what must be dealt with in the active and early recovery addict.

Treatment of
a Borderline Patient

Sally was first discussed in *Slings and Arrows: Narcissistic Injury and Its Treatment* (Levin 1993). Her case illustrates not only addiction and its vicissitudes, but also the narcissistic injury, the deep wounds to self-esteem and to the core self inflicted by addiction not only upon the addict, but upon all those closely affiliated with the addict, especially his or her children, and not infrequently, albeit in an attenuated way, upon those treating the addict. So this is also a chapter about countertransference, the feelings elicited or arising in the therapist during work with addicts. This countertransferential reaction is illustrated by discussing my feelings in working with Sally. Such self-reference runs the risk of degenerating into narcissistic exhibitionism, but I have decided to take that risk because the countertransference I know best is my own and the therapeutic use of countertransference in the patient–therapist interaction is one of the strongest and most useful tools we have.

Since projective identification is the mechanism by which the patient affectively communicates with the therapist and it is a frequently misunderstood concept, I have interrupted the case narrative to further elaborate this Kleinian notion. I do so in spite of my discussing countertransference and projective identification in other chapters, having decided that a bit of redundancy about a difficult key notion is not a bad price to pay for its clarification.

ACOA means Adult Child of an Alcoholic. Growing up in an alcoholic home does strange things to people. Alcoholism being, on its psychodynamic side, a regression-fixation to pathological narcissism (see Levin 1987, Chapter 3), the alcoholic parent is too self-involved to meet the child's needs. That is the best-case scenario. Frequently, there are parental sins of commission, as well as of omission: active as well as passive injury. Quarrels, fights, family dissension, and angry withdrawal are all common, and far from uncommon are overt sexual and physical abuse by the alcoholic parent. Incest and alcoholism are bedfellows. The same is true of the other addictions. Compounding the various levels of neglect, disregard, inconsistency, and overt abuse is the shame. "Don't tell the neighbors; make excuses for Daddy; take care of Mommy, she has a headache." Cross the street when you see Daddy stumbling home when you are with your girlfriends; blame yourself when Mother slaps you in a drunken rage. I could go on. Subtly or grossly abused, children growing up in a home where one or both parents are alcoholic (or drug addicted or psychotic) suffer repeated narcissistic injury. Being tough, children can absorb an amazing amount of less than optimal care (cf. Winnicott's 1956 concept of the "good enough" parent). Good enough doesn't have to be all that good, but severely alcoholic parents, even if their underlying love for their children is great, simply can't be good enough. The alcoholic family literature describes a variety of roles— the scapegoat, the mascot, the "lost" child, and the hero (also known as the parentified child) that children in such families assume or are cast into. Heroes are particularly prone to become therapy patients. They are classic Alice Miller (1981) narcissists, often outwardly successful, particularly in academic or intellectual pursuits, perfectionistic, inwardly empty, suffering from feelings of meaninglessness and dissatisfaction, and usually having trouble in their interpersonal relations. Heroes, among other things, have a deep need to be in control and often defeat themselves trying to control others who rebel against that control and desert them or retaliate against them. At another level, they are in a desperate struggle to control their underlying rage, which is largely unconscious. Heroes or nonheroes, ACOAs are abysmally narcissistically vulnerable. How that vulnerability manifests itself is individual and highly varied but basically takes either of two forms: the Alice Miller child syndrome described above, or the overtly depressed, poorly functioning, crushed and angry, obviously damaged type of patient.

REPRESSION OF SHAME

Children of alcoholics have to contend with massive amounts of shame, shame that is often denied, walled off, or repressed. That shame comes from two sources: the child's being treated shamefully, and the child blaming himself or herself. As is well known, children blame themselves for all sorts of disasters—parental divorce, parental death, parental desertion, parental abuse, and parental illness, including alcoholism. Children blame themselves because it is less painful to think that they are bad than that their parents are hateful or don't love them. Self-blame is a way of preserving the idealized object and of preventing (denying) the loss of the object or the loss of the love of the object. Freud (1926) postulated a developmental scheme in which anxiety is transformed from fear of annihilation to fear of loss of the object, to fear of loss of the love of the object, to castration anxiety, to fear of the superego, to social anxiety with massive, unmodulated panic dread developing into signal anxiety. Better that I am bad than that Mother or Father doesn't love me. The only problem with this unconscious defense, is that I am ashamed of my badness and develop what John Bradshaw (1988) calls shame-based behavior. It also has the disadvantage of not being true. At the most basic level, the child blames himself or herself because that offers the possibility of control—if I am the cause of these catastrophic events, then if I change (from bad to good), they could cease to be. Of course, this unconscious feeling of having control of a traumatic situation in which one is totally without power is illusory. Self-blame not only makes control possible, it also gives one a way of understanding an irrational situation. It provides explanation and cognitive structure, and that turning of the irrational into the rational reduces anxiety, albeit at the cost of lowering self-esteem. The mechanism of turning a passive experience into an active one is similarly driven. Therapists usually think of turning the passive into the active as doing to others what has been painfully done to us, and indeed this is one meaning of the term. But turning a passive experience into an active one can also mean doing to yourself what has been done to you. In this sense, it is part of the dynamic of the repetition compulsion. The issue once again is control, and avoidance of, or better transcendence of, helplessness. Better to choose than to have done to you, even if the chosen is painful and injurious. We also repeat because we hope the outcome will be different, and because the process of evolution has selected adherence to the familiar because on the average, that behavior has had greater survival value than seeking the novel. We also return to the traumatic in the hope of mastery of the overwhelming feelings engendered by the trauma through repetition, now from an active, that is, self-chosen perspective rather than a passive, that is, inflicted-upon-one perspective.

Be that as it may, ACOAs, like all of us, tend to repeat their early object relations in adulthood so that every object-finding is a refinding, with all too often disastrous consequences. If you are repeating or seeking to repeat early experience with alcoholic parents, you cannot help getting yourself into one mess after another.

Children are resilient and absorb many slings and arrows without suffering serious personality disorder. We all suffered occasional trauma and, for the most part, assimilated it. Not so with what Masud Khan (1974) called "cumulative trauma," the repeated experience of narcissistic injury, and that is precisely what occurs in an alcoholic home. Alcoholism, like any addiction, is the same shit over and over again. Some folks give up active addiction because it becomes so damn boring. Children in alcoholic homes aren't shamed occasionally; they are shamed chronically, and the resultant cumulative trauma asserts its baleful effects over a lifetime. Khan was thinking of the accumulation of relatively minor injuries; here we have the accumulation of not-so-minor ones.

Children of alcoholics have received a great deal of attention in the last decade. There is a plethora of popular books addressed to them. There is a "Twelve Step" self-help group modeled on AA called ACOA, which has been highly successful, certainly in attracting members if not in "curing" them. And there is a glut of "shopping lists" of traits and characteristics of ACOAs in both the pop-psych and the professional literature. Most are so broad that, like the fortune teller's prognostications, they can apply to virtually anyone. I do not wish to add to this literature, and given the fact that literally millions of people are children of alcoholics, they are bound to show considerable variability. The problem is exacerbated by the necessary distinction between those ACOAs who are themselves alcoholic and accordingly manifest the stigmata of alcoholism, and those who are not themselves alcoholic. Having said this—and I abhor the facile oversimplification of the ACOAs' situation—I have to, in a way, add to the ACOA shopping list supply. However, my list is simple, consisting of the belief that it is not possible to grow up in an alcoholic family without suffering profound narcissistic injury with its concomitant shame and rage. This is true for both those ACOAs who are themselves alcoholic and those who are not. The vexed question of whether or not alcoholism is a disease, and the role of genetically transmitted neurochemical vulnerability to (or predisposition to) that "disease," if there is one, need not concern us here. In either case, the children must deal with the effects of the parents' alcoholism on them and their emotional development. Understanding and conceptualizing the parents' behavior as a disease is a double-edged sword; it reduces guilt and shame by giving an alternate explanation of the parents' behavior—"It wasn't because I was bad or unlovable; it was because Father was ill." This understanding of the parents' behavior and the dynamic it induces is complicated by the possibility of the guilt and shame being unconscious or acted out, as it frequently is. It also makes it more difficult to experience and express the repressed rage—"How can I rage against a poor, sick woman, my mother, who couldn't help what she did?"—thereby paradoxically increasing guilt and shame by illegitimatizing the rage the ACOA ineluctably feels. Thus, our interest is in the patient's beliefs about alcoholism being an illness or not being an illness, rather than whether or not it is one. (My own belief is that it is a complex biopsychosocial phenomenon [cf. Levin 1991, 1995].) ACOAs are not cut out with cookie cutters, nor do they conform more than other human beings to the list of characteristics ascribed to them, but they do inevitably suffer serious narcissistic injury, which manifests itself in a wide variety of ways. Many psychotherapists are Alice Miller children, using their highly attuned sensitivity to the nuances of others' emotional states, originally developed adaptively for defensive purposes in an unsafe environment. They are especially vulnerable to countertransferential narcissistic injury. Some of these Alice Miller therapists are ACOAs. Enough of theory and general observation; it's time to turn to case material.

Sally was the most terrified patient I have ever treated. Looking cadaverous, she cringed in the waiting room, flattening herself against a wall as if she wished to be absorbed by it. Hands turned, palms against the wall, this nearly anorexic-appearing woman radiated sheer terror. My office is a flight above the waiting room. When I would call her in, she would go up the stairs half-twisted to keep her back against the wall, not relaxing—if moving from terror to tension and anxiety can be called relaxing—until she entered the office and I closed the door. In her mid-thirties, she was potentially attractive, given a 20–decibel reduction in her tension level and a 20–pound gain in weight, but her distress made her no more appealing than a frightened animal. Not only her movements and her body language, but her eyes radiated her fear. Although I wouldn't have described her as fragile, her tension was so great that I feared she might break, even shatter. I mean this not metaphorically, but concretely—bodily. It took some time before the basis of her fear, guilty secrets and terror of her alcoholic and abusive father, became apparent. As she sat rigidly on the couch, the tension in the room was palpable. It made me anxious. I figured that I wasn't going to be able to be very helpful to her unless I could reduce my anxiety level, but this proved elusive— I couldn't do it. It was as if the terror were contagious. Perhaps I too believed that her father would kill me. I think I also sensed the infinite rage behind her fear, and that too frightened me. Some sort of projective identification was occurring. A concept originating with Melanie Klein (1955), projective identification is the notion that infants project unacceptable aspects of themselves onto the environment in order to protect their inner goodness from their inner badness. Essentially it is projection of the death instinct and its derivatives. Once the projection is in the environment, it takes on an object characterization and becomes a persecutory object. The persecutory object is then reintrojected because it is too dangerous in the environment, and a whole sequence of introjection and projection ensues. More contemporary understandings (Ogden 1982, 1990) view projective identification as a process in which a child or an adult patient gets rid of an unacceptable feeling by engaging in behaviors that will induce the very same feeling in someone else, in this case the therapist, where ideally it is processed; that is, the projected affect or state of being is contained and tamed. Projected, not now by Klein's mysterious phantasizing process but rather through a behavioral inducement, the affect state is now present in the therapist, who has more mature resources to handle the feeling, and in that sense, processes it in such a way that it is tamed. The projector, in this case the patient, is now able to identify with what he or she has projected, which is now in a more benign state, so it's his stuff, but his stuff in a more manageable form, and now through identification, is able to take it back in, where it will now be more easily handled by the person who originally projected it. In this version, there is nothing mysterious about projective identification. It's about behavior-induced affective states in both the projector and the recipient of the projection; the recipient of the projection doing something with it, which the projector was unable to do, which now induces a behavioral state in the one who originally projected it, so he or she can easily identify with it.

Something like that seemed to be going on with Sally and me. Like most people, I get anxious about being anxious, and a vicious cycle sets in. Being in that state lowers my self-esteem; I like myself less—although I also know (at least cognitively) that there is nothing wrong with my being anxious; I am entitled—and that liking myself less constitutes a narcissistic wound, albeit a shallow one. Of course, I didn't want to appear anxious, and my social fear of being perceived in a way I didn't want to be perceived added to my discomfort. Since I was functioning in a professional role, my concern there was not purely psychopathological; it had a real social referent, and there were reasons not to appear anxious, which would only make things worse for Sally. I started to dislike my new patient for "making" me so uncomfortable. I dealt with this by mulling it over and trying to understand it, as well as by turning my attention away from myself to Sally. That sounds contradictory, even paradoxical, but it isn't. My bit of self-analysis included her and her projections, and the objectification calmed me and turned me away from my subjective discomfort so I could more easily focus on her, which in turn further reduced my anxiety by making my self-perception closer to my ego-ideal of the dispassionate understanding of others, at least in my professional role. Other ways of understanding my countertransference: Was it induced by projective identification, as speculated about above? Was it truly transferential, echoing and arousing similar affect states in me by putting me in contact, albeit unconsciously, with terrifying experiences of my own? Or was it an unconscious attempt at understanding through identifying with, and empathizing with, Sally?

PROJECTIVE IDENTIFICATION REVISITED

Projective identification is a vexed, complex, multiple-meaning concept that has been understood in a bewildering variety of ways. Some redundancy may be helpful here. For our purpose, I am going to take the term in its implicit and most concrete meaning, one that doesn't require belief in the projection of internal objects or object states from one mind to another. It involves three steps: first, behavior of some sort, usually highly emotive, by the projector, which is driven by an unconscious wish to induce a usually but not necessarily disruptive and painful affective state in the recipient (the affect as well as the wish may be unconscious). Second, the induction of that state in the recipient, who is usually puzzled by the subjective experience he or she is undergoing. The recipient does something with the induced change in his/her state of being to broaden it from a relatively clear-cut feeling; this is usually referred to as containing and processing the feeling. Third, the projector now becomes cognizant of the processed state of being and identified with it, such identification leading to a reintrojection or internalization of the state of being, which is now manageable. Step three takes place with various degrees of awareness (consciousness), but usually what the original projector experiences is a change in state of being which is mostly a change in affective state. This too need not be entirely conscious.

David Scharff, whose work is also discussed in Chapters 8 and 12, has an interesting pictorial representation of identification, projective and introjective, based on Ronald Fairbairn's object relational model of the mind. It is reproduced in Figure 4–1.

There are several problems here: although we speak of "stuffing feelings," or repressed affect, it is not at all clear how or where repressed affect could be stored. Affect always has a somatic component that is either present or not present and doesn't lend itself to storage in the unconscious. It makes more sense to conceive of the process of repression of affect as a repression of ideation that would release the affect, so with derepression a thought, image, concept, or memory triggers the feeling. But thought doesn't travel through or between minds without being verbalized; hence, projective identification seems impossible. But not so; the affect state induced in the recipient becomes associated with the recipient's ideation, which may be more or less similar to the projector's, and this is what is processed, to varying degrees, beneath awareness. Freud wrote that identification precedes object relating, and is a kind of psychic cannibalism, an almost literal oral incorporation. The boundaries and sense of separation needed for object relations are lacking. Hence, projective identification is a primitive process, and its very archaicness induces anxiety in the recipient. That is, Freud says that identification is more archaic than object relating in that there is no separation. He speaks of an object relation regressing to an identification.

Part of my anxiety with Sally came from this primitiveness. As Ogden (1990) points out, there can also be projective countertransference, which is particularly likely to occur when the therapist is

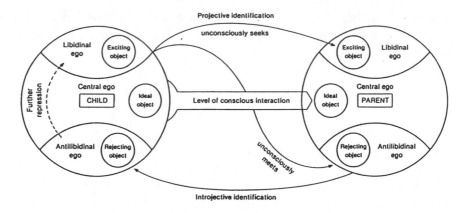

Figure 4–1. The action of projective and introjective identification, by David E. Scharff, from *Refinding the Object and Reclaiming the Self.* The mechanism here is the interaction of the child's projective and introjective identifications with the parent as the child meets frustration, unrequited yearning, or trauma. The diagram depicts the child longing to have his needs met and identifying with the similar trends in the parents via projective identification. The child meeting with rejection identifies with the frustration of the parent's own antilibidinal system via introjective identification. In an internal reaction to the frustration, the libidinal system is further repressed by the renewed force of the child's antilibidinal system. (Reprinted courtesy of David E. Scharff.)

working with highly regressed patients. If a projective identification/ counterprojective identification is proceeding without awareness, that is, unanalyzed, the result is confusion and frequently pain for both parties. This confusion and pain can be narcissistically injurious to both patient and therapist and can easily lead to premature termination of therapy.

To return to Sally, certainly part of the anxiety I felt in her presence was the result of projective identification. Accordingly, how I dealt with the portion of my anxiety so induced would be highly determinative of how well the patient would do. She needed me to contain and process the anxiety that was overwhelming her in some way that soothed it without denying it, so that she could in turn internalize that at least somewhat tamed anxiety. I also had to look at whatever countertransference this woman was inducing in me. I could not immediately identify any. She simply didn't resonate any important figure in my life. That didn't mean that I wasn't having any countertransference in the narrow sense, but for the moment, it wasn't in evidence. Not so countertransference in the broad sense. Being around anxious people sometimes makes me anxious, and Sally sure did. How about the third possibility, that I was simply feeling what she felt so I could better understand her? (To be more accurate, I certainly wasn't feeling what she was feeling, only a highly attenuated version of it.) Perhaps, but that didn't seem particularly salient. Projective identification can simply be a communication, an attempt to make another feel what we are feeling, so they can better understand us. Some such mechanism is the basis of all empathy. No doubt Sally wished to be empathized with; otherwise she wouldn't have been there, and her unconscious doubtless did what it could to obtain that empathy, but that wasn't mostly what was happening to her and between us. On the contrary, she was simply terrified, and her terror was so extreme for an outpatient office setting that I was shaken and discomfited.

The question of diagnosis arose. Of course, I knew nothing about her, but her appearance, demeanor, and behavior suggested that she was crazy. As I get older, I have a harder and harder time seeing psychopathology. What I see are human beings struggling to deal with their lives in ways that make some sort of sense when viewed from their vantage point. I find it harder and harder to judge them as pathological. I see shades of gray rather than black and white. People get by with all sorts of patched-together arrangements, making do, compromises, and who am I to judge them? Nevertheless, diagnose I must. Some conditions are correlative with neurochemical anomalies and require referral for their remediation; some conditions, such as active addiction, require direct confrontation; while other diagnoses also have implications for technique. So I diagnose but do so tentatively, aware that I may be missing something or just plain wrong. I didn't yet have a working diagnosis for Sally, but she seemed pretty disturbed. Diagnoses objectify, and that objectification, necessary as it may be, is often the source of a deep narcissistic wound for the patient, who feels like an insect impaled on a dissecting stage. One patient said to me, "I feel like the postage stamp mounted in someone's stamp book. The only thing about me that matters is that I be placed in the correct position on the correct page." Much of the work we do is helping people with problems in living, hardly diseases, but we don't like to admit it; it gets in the way of third-party reimbursement—insurance companies don't pay for personal growth—and far more significantly, it makes us feel less important, less scientific, less professional. To relinquish diagnosis is to lower our self-esteem, to narcissistically injure us. Somewhere in the course of our work together, I flirted with many diagnoses for Sally. Why don't you diagnose along with me as Sally's story and treatment unfold?

Sally's anxiety level was so high that it was almost impossible for her to speak. She sat rigidly, not quite trembling although threatening to, and said little. Her initial communications made little sense. She told me a garbled account of triangles, squares, and circles, which evidently had special (magical?) meaning for her. Try as I did to understand their significance, I could not. Did they have some sort of sexual symbolism? Triangles could represent both the male (penis plus two testicles) and the female (pattern of pubic hair, two breasts and vagina) genitals. The circle—the breast? And the square? This sort of analysis was a dead end; it went nowhere. Eventually it became clear that the geometric shapes represented modes of confinement, of being imprisoned within them, but for the moment, they seemed to be representative of the magic world of the schizophrenic. Was my patient schizophrenic? I began to think so. She was unemployed, terribly worried about finances, and struggling to find work. She was able to talk about this with difficulty. I also learned that she was married, but not much else.

I usually do an "intake"—another potential source of narcissistic injury in treatment. Badly conducted intakes can really batter: they make the patient feel not just interrogated (which of course is happening) but interrogated the way a detective might interrogate a suspect (which need not happen). What should be the beginning of a rich interpersonal experience is turned into another instance of being processed, categorized, pigeonholed, quantified, just as if the patient were a loan applicant at a finance company. The patient feels objectified, turned into an object, scrutinized for weakness and flaws, and perhaps rejected, the loan turned down. One of the Victorian poets wrote, "We murder in order to dissect." A badly done intake is a dissection that turns into a "soul murder." I figure that I can always obtain a systematic history later, and although I prefer to conduct a structured intake, I do not insist on it. If an intake is done, it must be done sensitively; aspects of the patient's life relevant to the treatment must be elicited in such a way that the patient feels the inquiry is part of the treatment, as indeed it should be, not the filling out of forms antecedent to it. Perhaps the key is empathy—discovering with, rather than voyeuristically finding out about, the patient. In Sally's case, conducting a standard intake would probably have driven her out of treatment, so I deferred it. In retrospect, that was the correct decision, but it put me at a disadvantage, and I resented her for it.

We did manage to reach a contract, in which time and fee were set. She agreed to twice-weekly sessions, and to say what came to mind, while the fee would be paid by her husband's insurance (her circumstances made treatment impossible without that third-party payment). The fee is always a narcissistic injury. Nobody expects to pay for Mother's milk. Too often we forget this, and do not sufficiently uncover the patient's feelings about the fee. Even with the patient who feels important because he pays a high fee, the flip side is, I shouldn't have to pay this—this guy is an emotional whore—he only cares about me because I pay him. This inflicts a narcissistic injury on us, the therapists. It's true, sort of, or too true for comfort.

Terror and hesitant speech were our mode of being together for some time, until Sally asked, "May I sit on the floor?" adding, "I'll feel more comfortable there." Without really thinking, I nodded, and she did so. In retrospect, I wonder where I was coming from. With almost any other patient, I would have "analyzed" her request. "Tell me more about wanting to sit on the floor." "What does sitting on the floor bring to mind?" "I wonder why you are asking me that now?" I think I nodded unreflectively because I wanted a tension reduction at almost any cost. I wanted the impasse broken. Sally needed to control something, and where she sat was one thing she could, perhaps, control. Though I was proceeding on unconscious intuition, it is true that to have analyzed her request would have increased the distance between us, further reducing her self-esteem and increasing her fear. The longer I practice, the less I say. If I don't get in the way, most patients cure themselves (cf. Anna O.'s "talking cure" and "chimney sweeping" [Freud and Breuer 1895]). Sally immediately moved to the floor. Once there, she looked up at me imploringly, yet with the first manifestation of warmth I had seen in her, and asked, "Will you join me here?" Sensing nothing seductive in her request, I did. We sat silently for a long time—she was no longer terrified—then she said, "I used to sit like this with my mother, eating the cookies we baked together or just playing." After that, the therapy, hitherto frozen, exploded.

A TRAUMATIC DEREPRESSION

What followed was the most rapid derepression I have ever witnessed. A series of hitherto inaccessible memories flooded the patient. The earliest concerned physical abuse by her mother: throwing her against a wall, hitting her with a rolling pin, and throwing her out of the way. This abuse was apparently episodic and rare. The way it came to consciousness was interesting. Sally had been to a chiropractor who had discovered that she had a cracked coccyx. He had treated her kindly, and she had had a strong attachment to him. His kindness had reminded her of the warm side of her mother, and when I sat on the floor with her, the transference to her chiropractor, which was a good-mother transference, transferred to me. Feeling safely and firmly held by the "good mother," she was able to tolerate memories of the "bad mother." The recovered memories of being between her parents, her father throwing her aside (was she getting in the way of his sexual advance, or of a physical assault on the mother?), and of her mother throwing her against the wall disorganized her. In terror, she became hysterical. Her father's hostility was not news, but her mother's was. Devastating news. Here we have two narcissistic injuries: the original was inflicted by the mother, and the second inflicted, in a sense, by me, who had facilitated the discovery that the parent who seemed to love her had not always been loving. A child needs a good object, and lacking one, uses the best material available to create one. In a sense, Sally's good mother was more of a transitional object than one-half of a split, although she was also that.

The transitional object is a concept of Winnicott's (1951) in which he postulates that the child's infusing of a blanket or stuffed animal with symbolic meaning as a substitute for the mother is the basis of all human culture. The most familiar example of the transitional object is Linus's blanket in the comic strip *Peanuts*. It is not the animal or blanket but the meaning the child gives it that makes it a transitional object. Patients often make therapists their transitional objects, assigning them meanings as substitutes for parents, much as a child does with a blanket or toy.

It was as if a "good mother" transference established by our "eating cookies on the floor" provided the security and safety needed to experience the bad mother. This transference and the derepression it enabled were facilitated by Sally's positive experiences with her chiropractor; her rapport with him (or, if you prefer, positive transference to him) accrued to me before she even walked in my door. Without it she would have been too afraid to enter psychological treatment. Transference often works that way; rather than being a re-creation of an early object relation, it is a carryover from a previous adult experience with a teacher, physician, previous therapist, or another authority figure. All therapists know this, yet there is little note of it in the literature. Of course, the previous relationship was also a transference, but the intervening relationship modified the transference in crucial ways that powerfully influence the patient's relationship with us. Transference as usually understood is a "reenactment instead of remembering," (Freud 1914b, p. 150) but that does not adequately account for what happened between Sally and me. Freud said that in the transference the patient acted instead of remembering. That is, instead of remembering the traumatic events of childhood, he or she enacts them in the relationship with the therapist.

Here the reenactment of the good mother transference enabled Sally to get in contact with the traumatically bad mother, without the split; historically and developmentally in the patient's life, as well as contemporaneously in the transference, neither the degree of health the patient had achieved nor the facilitation of further growth through treatment would have been possible. Not only is splitting developmentally normative, its defensive elaboration, although usually viewed as pathological, is often highly adaptive. ACOAs grow up in chaotic environments, where Jekyll-and-Hyde—sober and drunk—parental behavior is the norm, so alternation of good and bad mothers and fathers is reality. This reality is reflected in and reinforces developmentally normal and defensive splitting, and may be the only way the child can experience love and goodness. The problem lies in the deeper reality that the two parents are in fact one person, and far more fundamentally that, as Melanie Klein (1946) pointed out, you can't split the object without splitting the self, so ultimately integration must occur for the self to be experienced as a centered whole. But that integration lies in the future, after the therapeutic work that can only be accomplished while the split is operative has been done. Although many disagree with me, I don't believe that therapy is possible unless the positive transference dominates. In ACOAs and many others whose early experience was horrendous—cumulatively traumatic—the reenactment of those horrors in the transference, if that be possible, only further lowers self-esteem and reinforces narcissistic injury. Patients who were abused as children need to feel loved by their therapists, and good-mother or good-father transference makes that possible. Syrupy as that may sound, there is nothing sentimental about it; it is simply true. The difficulty is that these patients feel neither love nor lovable, and that makes the establishment of a therapeutic alliance and/or a positive transference extremely difficult. A good deal of the skill in their therapy lies in facilitating its development. None of this prevents the patient from reliving and working through painful experiences in the transference, but this comes later, after the splitting has given the patient some sense of safety. In Sally's case, the central trauma of her life was reexperienced transferentially, fortunately only after a powerful bond had been built. As my first analytic supervisor, Claude Miller, used to say, "You have to build the trampoline before you can jump up and down on it."

The chiropractor had a nontransferential impact on Sally's recovery of the traumatic repressed. He told her that her X-rays showed an old fracture of the coccyx. Had she been injured? This information—the existence of a fracture—became operative within the safety of her transference to me. We were sitting quietly on the floor when Sally's face turned wooden; contact seemed broken as she retreated inward; then she started screaming. The screaming was brief, followed by prolonged, broken, haunting sobbing. I said nothing. Her convulsive sobbing continued. Gradually quieting, she cried herself to exhaustion. Tears became whimpering, and then ceased. After an interlude, Sally said, "She broke my back." Over the next week, Sally recalled how her mother, in an uncontrolled fury, had picked her up and smashed her against a wall. She was about 5 when that occurred. The remembrance was devastating. Mother had been the stable, caring parent, while Father, nightly drunk, had been cold, uncaring, hostile, withdrawn, and sometimes violent. The threatened loss of Mother as a good object was almost unbearable. Was the broken coccyx a screen memory for many such happenings? A screen memory is a memory that acts as a screen and conceals as much as it reveals. Freud suggested that they be analyzed much in the same way as a dream, with the patient free-associating to each element of the screen memory. Sally's memory didn't appear to be a screen for multiple abuses. The mother of Sally's infancy, toddlerhood, and latency had been remarkably caring in a home of persistent hostility and violent arguments. That love had been interrupted by a small number of brutalities (additional widely separated similar episodes were uncovered.)

Having little history, I knew nothing at that time of her parents' drinking. After about three weeks of alternating disbelief and all too convincing belief that her beloved mother had so mistreated her, Sally stopped talking about her mother's abuse, risking cutting off her feelings (we seemed at an impasse), and began talking about her parents' drinking. She had perfect recall of most of this, and she proceeded to relate how her father, who always worked and who used his status as a "good provider" to justify doing anything he damn well pleased, drank every single night. He "held it well," meaning that he rarely slurred or staggered. What he did do was scream and argue, virtually continuously. Utterly self-centered, Father could not tolerate not having his way. When he could not dominate, he ranted. Sally's memory of the "baseline" status of her childhood home was of parental fighting: loud, vulgar, occasionally physical, and always terrifying. The terror she had exhibited in the waiting room, trying to disappear into the wall, was the terror she had lived with night after night as a small child. The attempt to disappear was a re-creation of her earlier attempts to disappear, which was her way of coping. She literally hid in the closet, under the bed, and when older, in the woods in back of the house. Constant fighting meant constant terror. Sometimes Sally's mother interposed her, literally frequently and metaphorically constantly, between herself (the mother) and the father. Sally was Monkey in the Middle with a vengeance. Her mother's use of her as a shield was totally repressed until these episodes flooded back during the period of traumatic derepression in therapy. They, too, were traumatically disillusioning. Sally was tossed around— pushed aside by her father, and sometimes flung across the room. Although not quite explicit, it was clear that what the mother was using Sally to protect herself from was, at least sometimes, sex. Sally was almost literally fucked by her father as he thrust toward her mother. "How could she? I thought she adored me," sobbed Sally in a thousand variations. Children need to idealize their parents. Clearly her father was not idealizable, which left Mother. Disillusionment, nontraumatic, gradual disillusionment, is inevitable and normal. This was not possible for Sally. Being thrown against a wall so hard that her coccyx was broken, and being put between Mother and her enraged father, could not be integrated with Mother, the loving baker, so instead of phase-appropriate, gradual deidealization through nontraumatic disillusionment, Sally maintained a pathological, albeit adaptive, conscious, primitive idealization and repressed unconscious reservoirs of traumatically disillusioning memories. Early in treatment, this defensive structure, stable for thirty years, disintegrated with startling rapidity, leaving Sally nakedly vulnerable.

When Sally was thrust in front of Mother, Father was not usually physically violent toward her. Rather, his attitude was one of scorn, rejection, hostility, and barely repressed rage. He had contempt for "girls." Her older brother, although hardly well-treated, was more accepted and later sent to college. Sally, in what was one of the most damaging of the many injuries inflicted on her, was not. Father didn't believe in education for girls. It was a waste, since they soon married anyway. Needless to say, this highly intelligent woman's being deprived of higher education had reality consequences in terms of her earning power and inability to find meaningful and satisfying work that went far beyond the already indelible psychological damage that her father's dismissal of her as insignificant had inflicted.

There was an exception to the father's not hitting her outside the sexualized fighting between the parents. When Sally was trying to disappear, she sometimes had temper tantrums. Her rage had to have some outlet. When she was 4, she had a particularly intense and prolonged one. Her father came, pulled down her pants, put her across his knee, and spanked her with a strap. Her conscious memory was of the experience being humiliating and enraging. Yet, as an adult, she sometimes found being spanked in exactly the manner her father had spanked her highly sexually exciting. This was one of her most guilty secrets. In addition to what was a secret to herself (the repressed), Sally had a number of guilty secrets that she had confided to nobody. Her pleasure in "erotic" spankings was one of them. She blushed scarlet when she finally told me about them (they didn't play a major role in her sexual life, being an occasional behavior). Sally was ashamed of the pleasure she gleaned from being spanked. That shame was threefold: it seemed perverse; it had first occurred in an affair she was deeply ashamed of; and most saliently, the idea that the original spanking by her hated father had been sexually stimulating was repugnant, violently unacceptable. Yet it almost certainly had been, the pleasurable (or, better, the stimulating) effects having been repressed. Sally tried to detach her pleasure in erotic spanking from her father, saying that a reddening of the skin of her buttocks was physically stimulating and had no psychological meaning (my wording). I didn't believe that was the case, but I didn't interpret the genetic source of her pleasure for years. Children who are severely beaten do not find spanking erotic, although they may otherwise seek to repeat their experiences. (Freud interpreted shame as a reaction-formation to sexual pleasure. Sally's shame over pleasure in spanking was partly exactly that.) To have told her this would have been premature and would have inflicted needless narcissistic injury. Sally would have hated herself for "enjoying" anything "sexual" with her father. She had more than enough self-hatred. This was knowledge she didn't need yet. Eventually, we did discuss it, and I pointed out that her temper tantrums were states of high arousal from which the spanking, which had not been so painful for the pain to override the pleasurable cutaneous stimulation of the spanks, had brought a resolution, a sort of "climax." Sally's temper tantrum had put her in a high state of arousal; the spanking, with its affective discharge, was in effect a detumescence. That episode was also one of the few times in which Sally's father had paid much attention to her, so for a few moments he was intensely engaged with her, rather than ignoring her contemptuously. At a more unconscious level, sex-play spankings were an eroticization of terrifying, traumatic experience in order to gain mastery. The pulling down of her pants, the father's attention, the father's sexual excitement, her own state of arousal, all fixated this experience in her mind so it was one she returned to in adulthood with intense, highly guilty pleasure. Further, the pain that did exist was a trade-off for the forbidden pleasure and sufficiently reduced guilt for her to experience it. Sally then said, "My father got an erection when he spanked me. I think I can remember feeling it. That's why he stopped." I said, "He stopped because he came." I went on to suggest that it was no accident that she first experienced this form of eroticism in a relationship with a man who was in many ways like her father.

I return to Sally's parents' drinking. As the years went on, the parents' fighting intensified. The father's alcoholism was stable in the sense that he continued to drink in the same way, with the same effects of sullenness, barely contained rage, and contempt. He often said that he had never wanted children, and that they were a burden he couldn't wait to get rid of. When Sally was in her early teens, her mother started to drink heavily. She did not drink well. Unlike the father, she staggered, vomited, slurred, and was a public humiliation. Her drinking hastened her premature death from a series of strokes.

Sally's parents finally separated and divorced when she was in her late teens. At the time Sally came to treatment, her father was dying of cirrhosis of the liver and other somatic complications of his alcoholism. Surely, you say, what went on in Sally's home was psychopathological, the result of her father's extremely narcissistic, virtually sociopathic personality disorder, and of her mother's inability to cope with his pathology. Sure, but don't underrate the impact of alcoholism alone. Narcissistic regression, if narcissistic fixation doesn't already exist, is the ineluctable psychodynamic concomitant of alcoholism (see Chapter 3, this volume, and Levin 1987), and narcissistically regressed/fixated parents cannot help inflicting narcissistic injury on their children. Sally's mother would have been "good enough" if it wasn't for her alcoholism, and Sally's father, although unlikely to have been "good enough," would not have engaged in constant fighting if he had not been drinking. Further, parents' drunkenness is always a source of shame, self-blame, self-hatred, humiliation, and injury to the self, all of which always engender rage, which is frequently turned against the self, inflicting further narcissistic injury. Alternately, it is acted out in self-destructive ways that also eventuate in self-harm.

Even as a best-case scenario, being an ACOA is no bed of roses. Another patient recalled walking down the street in a small southern city with her high school girlfriends and seeing her father, now separated from the family and in the last stages of alcoholism, stumbling along, looking every bit the Skid Row bum he had become. Indelible shame permeated her body and soul. Cringing, she hid herself between the other girls and got by her father without being recognized or greeted. The thought that her friends would have known that that was her father was more than she could bear. Twenty years later, her shame overwhelmed her as she recounted what didn't but only threatened to occur. She felt as worthless as she felt her father was. Yet another patient remembered running, at about the age of 6, with his brother to greet his father getting off the bus upon his returning from work. Thrilled that Daddy was home, Tom ran eagerly to greet him. Daddy, although not staggeringly drunk, had drunk enough to react irrationally and cruelly. He shouted, "You're mocking me—running up to jump on me with your shoes untied," and slapped Tom across his face. Daddy had a thing (a pathological thing) about neatness, and in his paranoid alcoholic rage, thought his children were deliberately making fun of him. Again the patient never forgot and never fully or unselfconsciously loved again. The narcissistic injury from growing up in an alcoholic home need not be so blatant. Kelly's father never cursed, ranted, fought, or abused. He simply got drunk every night and discussed deep philosophical issues with his drinking companions. Although her physical needs were all met and her father treated her in a superficially affectionate and kindly manner, Kelly might just as well not have been there. Her injuries were not as debilitating as Sally's or Tom's, but neither were they slight. I could go on, having treated scores of ACOAs, but won't. You have the idea.

Sally's account of her mother's alcoholism gave me an opportunity to offer her a reconstruction—a reconstruction that allowed her to regain some self-esteem and proved vital in her rehabilitation. I told her, "Your mother must have been drinking, even drunk, when she threw you against a wall, and when she interposed you between her and your furious father. You remember her alcoholism as developing in your teens, but it is highly unlikely that she started drinking then. She went downhill too fast. It is far more likely that she had drunk episodically for years and was ashamed of it because she could hardly drink and object to your father's drinking in the way she did. She must have drunk secretly, and it was when she was drunk that she involved you in their fighting and broke your coccyx."

"Do you really think that's so?" she asked pathetically, pleadingly, so strong was her need to make sense of her mother's behavior and to feel loved by her. "Yes," I said. "I can't be sure, but it fits, makes sense. Why else would your loving mother, who usually protected you from your father, act in that way?" Sally's relief was enormous. It was her mother's alcoholism, not her hatred, that injured.

This brings us to a need to understand alcoholism. I believe that it is a disease—a biopsychosocial disorder with complex determinants (Levin 1987, 1991, 1995) and I tell my patients so. I do that in a rather didactic way, not very differently than I would deliver a classroom lecture. I explain the constitutional, neurochemical, genetically transmitted predisposition to alcoholism, the evidence for such a factor, the sociocultural determinants of alcoholism, and how emotional factors (psychodynamics) enter into pathological drinking. I do so succinctly and try not to get into a position where my presentation of the disease model seems to judge the patient's negative feelings toward the drinking parent(s). As the great slogan of pre-Hitlerian Austrian Liberalism had it, "*Wissen macht frei*," "knowledge liberates." Didactic interventions can be woven into psychodynamic work very nicely. In Sally's case, I wanted to give her a rationale for her mother's behavior without blocking the emergence of her rage toward her father by "dismissing"—explaining away—his brutal rejection of her. Later, much later, after fully experiencing and expressing her rage at him, she would be able to see that he too was ill, and to quote Erikson, "accept the inevitability of the one and only life that was possible." Having to do so prematurely would have been catastrophic, preventing her from externalizing the rage now turned inward.

During this period of derepression, Sally's behavior and demeanor would alter abruptly and totally. One minute she would be engaged, in the room on the floor with me; the next minute she would "leave," either freezing in terror, or going into a cold, withdrawn, immobile rage (not experienced as rage) reminiscent of the catatonics I encountered in my psychiatric hospital days. Her utterly frigid rages were unnerving. I tensed when she went into them, sometimes for reasons that I could not discern and sometimes in response to some slight disturbance in our relationship—the phone ringing, or my being two minutes late, a failure of empathy on my part. These withdrawals, with their psychotic quality, were frightening. I worried that she might not come out of them; they were too close to psychosis, and regression is sometimes irreversible. They also angered me; I don't like to be cut off, and I felt punished. To the best of my self-scrutiny, nobody significant in my past or present life had treated me that way, so I figured that my reaction to Sally's withdrawals was here-and-now stuff and that her interpersonal impact on other people was being gauged pretty accurately by my response. When she spoke again, sometimes not until several sessions later, she often talked of not wanting to live or, more actively suicidal, of wanting to die. I did not

doubt that she did and that her rage was quite capable of being enacted in a suicide. I felt threatened and controlled, both of which
enraged me. I calmed myself by telling myself that none of this was
personal—it wasn't—and that helped; nevertheless, the situation remained intrinsically scary. As a result of my interventions, a highly
disturbed patient was undergoing overwhelmingly intense emotional
experiences, and discovering intolerable things that might well make
her feel so hopeless that that hopelessness, if not her rage, might very
well kill her. It was a high-risk situation and I knew it.

I had had patients suicide before. I suspect most therapists, if they
work with the seriously pathogenic at all, have lost patients. Losing
a patient to suicide is one of the worst narcissistic injuries that a therapist can suffer. Of course, one's reaction to an event such as the suicide of a patient is not fixed, and the therapist could respond to it
without experiencing it as a narcissistic injury, but I would question
whether that reaction was not a defense against the awareness of injury. Therapists, one hopes, are highly invested in their work and seek
to enhance their patients' lives rather than see them end—patients
suffering from chronic, painful, terminal illness excepted. To have a
therapy patient suicide is to fail, fail oneself and fail one's patient.
Feelings of failure are accompanied by feelings of shame, lowered self-
esteem, and self-hatred. We feel angry at those who contribute to
our failures. So here are rage, shame, and feelings of humiliation—
the triad of emotions associated with narcissistic injury.

There is a phenomenon called postschizophrenic depression. In it,
the patient recovering from a schizophrenic episode goes into a profound depression and, all too frequently, suicides. Such depressions
are usually understood as manifestations of the depletion of available
catecholamines, norepinephrine and serotonin, following the neuro-
leptic treatment of a schizophrenic episode, and as the patient's reaction to the realization that he or she has a chronic relapsing and
highly disabling disease. All of that is true. Yet, there is another way
of looking at it. In Kleinian and object relational theory in general
(see Chapter 8), there is a developmental sequence in which the infant goes from the *paranoid-schizoid* position, which is a stage of
preintegration of good and bad, into the integration of the *depressive*

position, in which the child realizes that the good object and bad object are one, and that his or her aggression in part created the bad object. This is the stage in which guilt is developed, or in Winnicott's (1963) terms, there is a development of the "capacity for concern." It is extremely important developmentally, and makes possible human empathy. However, the guilt experienced in the depressive position is a primitive guilt, and the superego that drives it is an archaic, savage superego. I would suggest that part of the etiology of postschizophrenic depression, with its suicidal potential, results from the rapid integration of preambivalent, good and bad split self- and object representations into more complex, unsplit representations enabled by pharmacological treatment through neuroleptics, and that the patient is overwhelmed by the primitive guilt of this chemically induced progression into the depressive position before he or she has the resources to cope with the new experiential world of the postambivalent depressive stage.

The first patient I lost was a severely borderline woman who had just been released from her second hospitalization. I had arranged for her to attend a day treatment program, and when I met with her the day she suicided, she was future-oriented, talking about her expectations of that program. Only hours later, she swallowed pills and died, after having jumped out of the car as her parents rushed her to the hospital. Looking back on it, I see that she clearly wanted to die, seeing herself with a career as a mental patient to look forward to. She just didn't want it. I don't want to sound like the existential psychoanalyst, Ludwig Binswanger (1944), justifying the death of his patient Ellen West as the only possible fulfillment of her destiny, but I doubt if any intervention would have kept my patient alive. But I didn't know that then, and I suffered greatly, questioning my judgment and ability as a therapist. My professional self was profoundly shaken. Some of that was healthy; I wouldn't want to be the kind of therapist who wasn't upset by a patient's suicide. The consulting psychiatrist who had discharged the patient felt even worse. What is needed in such a situation is peer support and consultation. I sought both, and they helped. I learned that my powers are limited, that my illusion of omnipotence was just that, an illusion that needed to be relinquished, and that hospitals can't always do the job either. Relinquishing some of my omnipotence freed me up to be a better therapist, not to mention making me less vulnerable to narcissistic injury. Recovering from the narcissistic injury of this patient's suicide didn't lessen my feelings of sorrow at the waste that her life had been. The lessening of grandiosity always lowers the risk of narcissistic injury.

Another patient I treated who suicided videotaped his suicide for the benefit of his wife. I was so enraged at this sadism inflicted by the patient, who had refused psychiatric referral and dropped out of treatment, that I felt only anger. My last experience was with a Donald Manes-type situation (Donald Manes was the Queens borough president who succeeded in killing himself on his third try after he was caught in a political scandal), of a man who had been hospitalized thrice after three attempts and clearly preferred death to indictment. I had scant relationship with him and felt no guilt.

Three were more than enough for me; I didn't want Sally to suicide. Neither did I want her to limp through life terrified and half-alive. Therapy is a serious and sometimes dangerous business. All therapists take risks and expose themselves to emotional injury. If they are never on the edge, they aren't doing their job. On the other hand, failure to protect patients as fully as we can is inexcusable. What to do with Sally? Hospitalize her? Not if I could help it. The narcissistic injury of hospitalization is profound, and in her case, would have been experienced as a violation of the tenuous trust we had established. Naturally, I would rather lose the case than lose the patient, but damn it, I didn't want to lose the case. Things were happening, and Sally just might go far if she could live through the violence of the emotional storm of traumatic derepression. So I decided not to recommend, let alone insist on, hospitalization at that time. It was a decision that cost me no little sleep.

The question of the diagnosis that I preferred not to make reoccurred. Was Sally psychotic? Were her catatonic-like states more than transferential repeats of her rage at and flight from the traumatic disruptions of the self-object relationships (see Chapter 3, this volume and Kohut 1977a) of her childhood? I decided probably not, and that the intensity of her reactions to "minor" disturbances in our relationships were reflections of her intense need for all of me and all of my attention and understanding for her to feel safe enough to do the work that she was doing. As it turned out, she reacted as she did largely because any lapse in my self-object ties to her, that is, my being there to meet her needs, meant that I could no longer protect her from her father's vengeance, which would be to murder her. But I didn't know that then. If not psychotic, what then? For quite a while I thought I was working with a multiple-personality disorder. So rapid and so total were the shifts in her state of being that I considered consultation with a multiple-personality specialist. Her third-party payment diagnosis was dysthymic disorder, which was true enough. In retrospect, Sally came very near to fragmenting, regressing to the stage that precedes integration of the self which Kohut thought of as the intraphysic correlative of psychosis, in this stage of therapy, but fortunately that fragmentation was not so total as to preclude communication between alternate states of being.

Just as things seemed to settle down, Sally was hit by—and that was what it seemed—another wave of derepression, this time of sexual abuse by her father. This was possible only after my interpretation of her mother's violent behavior toward her as being an early manifestation of her mother's chronic alcoholism, which helped Sally feel loved and protected by her mother once again. After that interpretation, an interlude of relative serenity was certainly welcomed by me and must have been by her. However, that interlude was brief, and Sally's extreme terror returned. She spent several sessions rigid and far away. There was little communication, and I could not seem to make contact with her. In the fourth such session, I was sitting and worrying that she might be slipping into psychosis, when Sally erupted in convulsive, prolonged sobs. When she sobbed in that way, which I had seen before, her face reflected all the pain of a heartbroken child. As her tears poured forth, the triangle formed by her eyes and nose seemed to regress inward, so that her face split into two planes, much like a crushed cardboard box. At first I though my visual impression was hallucinatory, and to some extent it was, but I now believe that her musculature actually changed her physiognomy. After about fifteen minutes, Sally started speaking through her sobs and her face regained its normal contours.

"He tore me; he's going to kill me for telling you. When I was 3 and 4 and 5, Mother worked nights as a waitress, and he would baby-sit me. He hated it. Taking care of kids was woman's work. When he put me to bed, he would lie beside me and hold me very tight. At first I liked being held; it made me feel secure, but then he would hold me too tight, very tight. It hurt, and I was scared. He would rub up against me and I would feel something hard. I guess he would come; maybe I partly liked it. I don't know." (More convulsive sobbing, during which Sally again retreated far inside herself.) "One time—one time—one time." (Silence.) "One time," I prompted her. "Oh, it hurt, it hurt. He tore me. There was blood. Then he took my panties and threw them out, telling my mother I had wet them. I think that happened. I know the rubbing did; I'm not sure about the rest—oh, it hurt."

During the ensuing month, Sally's terror reached an apogee. Her petrification against—into—the walls of my waiting room became continuous unless she was sitting on my floor. She moved only her head, searching for danger.

I told her I thought that the events she remembered were real, that they had actually occurred. Could I be sure? No. But here is a problem that has vexed psychoanalysis from the beginning. Were the confessions of Freud's hysterics about childhood seduction true? (Seduction is an odd word for what is sometimes rape and always involves an extreme power differential, which already says something about the need of adult theorists [of childhood sexuality] to exculpate adults.) Or were they fantasies? Historical truth or narrative truth? Although Freud himself abandoned his seduction theory, he never denied that adults sexually abused children and that such abuse is traumatic and etiologically powerful in the formation of neurosis. On the other hand, there is currently an atmosphere of near hysteria in which any physical affection expressed by an adult toward a little girl is suspect. I do not wish to contribute to that hysteria and make no general statement judging the veracity of accusations by children, or by adults remembering childhood, of sexual abuse. However, I am inclined to believe my patients, at least without evidence to the contrary. In Sally's case, her father drank heavily every night and was certainly near drunk when he "baby-sat" her, and we know that sexual abuse is highly correlated with alcoholism. Sally's father was in a constant rage because his wife was "cold," and Sally was involved in their violent quarrels over his sexual demands. Further, the way Sally remembered this "seduction," and the emotionality accompanying that remembering only made sense if her memory was a memory of a real event. The only possible alternate explanation is that she is crazy, and/or that her remembered father is a projection of her own pathological rage. Do I believe that? No way. I was there, Sally's struggle to *not* remember was at least as powerful as the affects that accompanied that remembering.

Sexual abuse of children by drunken adults isn't confined to girls. Mark's story has many parallels to Sally's: a father who had been alcoholic and indifferent throughout Mark's life. There was constant fighting between the parents. His mother, who had initially been loving and warm in early childhood, eventually joined her husband in heavy drinking, becoming alcoholic herself. After that, the parents would go to the tavern together, come home blind drunk, and violently quarrel. From the age of 11, Mark and his two-years-younger brother would get between the parents, who were too drunk to resist, and lead them to separate beds, the younger brother remaining with the father while Mark slept with the mother. One such night, he awoke to his mother playing with his genitals, trying to induce an erection. Mark's sexuality was permanently inhibited by that incident (which was probably a screen memory for many such instances), and he "chose," if that's the right word, a celibate life. When I treated him for panic attacks forty years later, he had cognitive memory, but no affective memory, of that "seduction." Only when he experienced and expressed the rage he had been afraid to feel for forty years did his panic attacks subside.

I concluded that Sally wasn't crazy, but I was concerned that she was becoming so. Maybe she just couldn't handle knowing that both parents had loved her so little that they had each violently attacked her. Even more ominous, she remained convinced that her father, now old, seriously ill, and 2,000 miles away, was going to kill her in my waiting room. That did seem near psychotic. I asked her if he had threatened to kill her if she "told." I was convinced that he had, but Sally couldn't remember such a threat, only that she had always been terrified of him. I tried reassurance and supplementation of her reality testing, to no avail. I wondered if a need for punishment was fueling her delusional fear, if it was delusional—her father sounded pretty crazy. Was he capable of coming north and killing her, if he knew of her "betrayal" of him? Did she need to be killed because she had enjoyed the pre-tear rubbing? Did she have other (conscious or unconscious) guilty secrets? I was soon to find out. Sally was poorly differentiated. During the first years of treatment, she would relate events that I interpreted as incidents in which she lost her identity in merger with casual acquaintances, in which she would be overwhelmed by their misfortunes. It was as if she became them, especially when they shared great pain with her. As Freud would have said, her object relations all too easily regressed to identifications. Was her lack of firm boundaries contributing to her terror? I asked her if she thought her father could read her thoughts. She replied, "I don't know." My telling her that he couldn't did not help. Confessing her "guilty secret" did.

For Freud (1917), an identification is a regression to a pre-object relations state of being, that is, to a state before the separation of subject and object. It is both a regression and a defense. If you can't have the object or the object's love, then you can become the object. Alternately, Freud describes this process as an internalization of the object. We have already looked at the mechanism of projective identification and the mechanism of introjective identification, in which there is no projection but simply the taking in of the object. So in identification we become the object, and in introjective identification we somehow put the object inside us and identify with it. Identification is also used in a less technical way in ordinary speech, and in the ideology of the Twelve Step programs. Here, identification is seen not as a regressive state, but as a powerful mechanism through which guilt is deliquesced, and denial and resistance broken down though identification with those who are further along the process of recovery. In the Twelve Step setting, identification is all of the things Freud said it was, but it is something else as well, whatever the underlying mechanisms. Perhaps the best way to put it is that identification can be not only a regressive defense but also a highly adaptive mode of intrapsychic functioning, which is the ultimate basis of empathy.

Like so many ACOAs, Sally had married an alcoholic. In the early years of their marriage, he was daily drunk, frequently unemployed, and totally irresponsible. In a sense, she had traded down; at least her father had consistently worked. (She had also traded up, as we shall see. Hank wasn't only an alcoholic, and Sally's "object finding being a refinding" was complex, being simultaneously a refinding of her father and refinding of her "good" mother.) Sally and Hank recapitulated her parents' arguments. Finally she emotionally detached, threatening divorce if he didn't stop drinking.

At that time, Sally was working for Steven, a physician, as a sort of all-around assistant office manager and untrained nurse. Outwardly, he looked as different from her father as possible, a nondrinking educated professional. Needless to say, she became his mistress. He too was unhappily married. (As someone once said, clichés are clichés because they are true.) Sally became friendly with the wife, and was soon monkey in the middle, just as she had been as a child. Further, Steven turned out to be a dominating tyrant who used the power differential (employer-employee, upper middle class-working class) between them to exploit her sexually and otherwise, sweating long hours out of her and demanding total devotion. Steven did give her something in return: he taught her a great deal about medicine. For Sally, grievously hurt by her lack of education, this affiliation was, among other things, an attempt at remediation. It raised her self-esteem and gave her vicarious if not real status. Steven, whatever his character defects, was masterly at his profession, and Sally adored that. At first their sex had been mutual and highly gratifying. Then Hank stopped drinking to save their marriage, and Sally grew close to him. The sober Hank was remarkably different from the drinking Hank: loving, considerate, responsible. Sally no longer wanted sex with her employer. He pressed her relentlessly, demeaning her and belittling her—"Who else would employ you?"—and she usually gave in. When she didn't, he would grab her in an empty examining room and push her head down on his penis; when she swallowed his ejaculate, which she enjoyed doing and then was sexually aroused in spite of herself, he ranted, "That was disgusting," and that only whores swallow cum. She came to hate him, yet couldn't break with him. Now that she was in love with her husband, Sally's guilt knew no bounds. Finally, she quit her job, but her guilt never left her. It was exacerbated by her naïveté and lack of caution in agreeing to go for a ride with her podiatrist, who raped her. He threatened to kill her if she told, and fear of him added to and was displaced onto her already great fear of her father. Sally continued to have lunch with her physician ex-employer, hating it but not knowing why she did so.

Confessing to her affair and discussing the rape somewhat lessened her terror, one source of which was her fear that she would confess to her husband. Telling me obviated that need and removed that component of her terror. Sally didn't connect Steven with her father. I made the connection for her, going on to give her one of my passive-active interpretations (I see so much pathology driven by that mechanism, which can be understood as a futile attempt to remediate [heal] a narcissistic injury by enacting power rather than experiencing powerlessness, that I frequently use it; patients readily understand turning passive into active—it resonates), saying "When your father forced himself on you and tore your vulva, you had no choice. You were powerless. When you found Steven, who as your employer was a father of sorts and shared your father's domineeringness, self-centeredness, and ruthlessness, you unconsciously repeated your relationship with your father, but you were now choosing it instead of having it inflicted on you. Your relationship with Steven was an attempt to master a trauma by repetition." That was the most I had said for months. My interpretation was instantly understood, and the response to it was profoundly emotional. Neither Sally's terror nor her guilt left her, but the intensity of both abated.

In the next session, Sally arrived with a large paper bag, blushing beet red. "Can I show you something?" I nodded. Whether or not she was a multiple personality, psychotic or whatever, I had by now come to trust Sally's drive for health, and let it direct the treatment. After all, she had opened things up with her move to the floor, had bonded with me to enable her to experience and integrate her childhood traumas, and had told me what she feared she would destructively blurt out to her husband. Out came Charlie—a large and obviously well-loved teddy bear. Sally, looking about 2 years old, cuddled Charlie. At last she felt safe. One didn't need to have read Winnicott and his theory of transitional objects to understand Charlie and Sally's relationship to him. In one creative act, an illusion if you prefer but a transmuting illusion, Sally had provided herself with a reliable object, one who cared and loved and could be cared for and loved. She was doing as an adult in treatment what she hadn't been able to do for herself in childhood. Few of my patients have had Sally's gift for creative, restitutional, healing regression. We spent many sessions talking about Sally's relationship with Charlie. I offered no interpretations. It was during this relatively serene period of our work together that Sally revealed other sources of her strength—her love for nature and her reading of Norman Vincent Peale.

We stopped "doing therapy" and talked about hiking, woods trails, and mountains, and how the power of positive thinking had prevented her from suiciding during her giving in to Steven's sexual demands. Should I have told her that both nature and Peale were transitional objects? Analyzed instead of shared? No way. You don't take away before replacing. Triangular relationships in psychoanalysis don't usually refer to patient, therapist, and teddy bear, but this particular triangle bore fruit. Did I enjoy regressing with Sally? You're damn right I did. Is such regression on the therapist's part dangerous? Sure, but therapy is a dangerous business. The trick is to have binocular vision—to regress and not regress simultaneously. I decided to risk being too tolerant of my and my patient's therapeutic regression rather than to risk distancing myself and inflicting a narcissistic wound by making her feel foolish. So to speak, I chanced turning (on my side) an object relation into an identification.

Charlie enabled Sally's next, and vital, "confession." Out of the blue, Sally said, "I don't know how to tell you this, but I'm addicted to amphetamines. I get them from Dr. X., my diet doctor. If I get fat, I'll kill myself. I can't stand being fat. I went off them once, but I got so depressed I nearly suicided. I've never wanted to live, and I'm afraid if I go off, I'll kill myself." Sally's fears of suicide were all too real. I was taken aback. I shouldn't have been. So many ACOAs themselves become addicted to alcohol, perhaps partly on a genetic susceptibility basis, or marry alcoholics, that such behavior is expectable. Addiction to other drugs or to compulsive activities is also extremely common among ACOAs, yet I had totally missed Sally's addiction. Looking back, I could see that her extreme tension, body rigidity, fear, near anorexia, runaway anxiety and near psychotic ideation, whatever their psychodynamic determinants, were pathognomic of amphetamine addiction. I'm an addiction specialist, and should have (Horney's right about the "tyranny of the shoulds") spotted it. Here was a place where diagnosis was important. I felt stupid— my professional self-concept was being threatened, and I was narcissistically wounded—I felt shame, lowered self-esteem, and rage at myself. If—if I had taken a standard intake as I almost always do, I would have inquired into Sally's alcohol and drug usage. If I had done my job more thoroughly, in all likelihood she would have lied and felt so guilty that she would have had to quit, so maybe my error wasn't such an error. Rationalization? Perhaps, but in any case, no harm was done, and the facts were now on the table. Sally's diagnosis was becoming clearer. She was an ACOA and amphetamine-dependent.

ACOAs who aren't addicted to some substance are usually addicted to perfectionism and "people-pleasing"; nevertheless, their treatment is importantly different from the treatment of chemically addicted (or alcohol-addicted) ACOAs whose addiction must be confronted and arrested before their narcissistic injuries and deficits can be worked with. In Sally's case, we were working in reverse order. Sally had told me that she had smoked pot a lot in the past, and sometimes drank too much, but had minimized this, putting it all well back in time. She felt ashamed not only of her addiction, but of having "lied" to me through minimalization and omission. Addiction, to anything, is *always* searingly narcissistically injurious. Something else has power over the self; feelings of shame, humiliation, and guilt are ineluctable. That's saying too little. The self-hatred of the addict is the essence of his problem. Feeling powerless, he or she can only recover through a paradoxical admission of powerlessness—powerlessness over the addictive substance or activity. I borrow that from AA and the Twelve-Step movement because it's true. Some form of "surrender" (Levin 1987, Tiebout 1949), which is simultaneously narcissistically injurious and narcissistically sustaining is required. The paradox lies in the relinquishing of the reactive and compensatory grandiosity that the self-object (simultaneously idealizing and mirroring) transference to the substance of abuse confers in return for a slight but real gain in self-esteem. Sally wasn't ready to surrender; she was too scared. Amphetamine, a "good mother" psychodynamically and an antidepressant pharmacologically, seemed to be something she couldn't live without. She also couldn't live with it—not anymore—the guilt and shame and self-hatred were too great. That is why she "confessed" her addiction.

Here was the missing piece of Sally's terror. Her need for punishment for her addiction was handily projected onto her all too terrifying father. Of course, he would kill her; she deserved to be killed. Her use of pills and, as it turned out, more than a little pot, also contributed to her poor reality testing and her tendency to confused mergers. "Can't live with and can't live without it," is the terminal point of all addictions. It is a dangerous point always. Suicide is an ideal way out for any addict at this point, and Sally had long been suicidal. I again considered hospitalization, deciding against it. Instead, I kept her talking about her shame, her need to lie and evade, her constant fear that her husband would find out, her need to play money games for her supplies, her fear that Dr. Feelgood might cut her off. She repeatedly tried to cut back, always failing. The more we talked about drugs, the more she wanted to be off them, but she could not do it—her fear was too great. Now I discussed going into rehab, but she would have none of it. Hank would find out she had been deceiving him about her drug use if she went into it. Unlike an alcoholic at a parallel stage of the "disease," her physical health was not immediately threatened, nor was she pharmacologically regressing in such a way that therapeutic gains were swept away and meaningful relationship was impossible. Her consumption was stable. For several months, we were at an (apparent) impasse.

A CREATIVELY CURATIVE REQUEST

Then Sally made another one of her creatively curative moves. She came to session more frightened than I had seen her for a long time. With trembling lips and shaking voice, she asked, "May I pray?"—a request no patient had ever made. I was taken aback, although I don't think I showed it. I nodded. Speaking now in a low but increasingly firm voice, she prayed, starting: "When two are gathered together in My Name" (which made me, being neither a Christian nor a believer, vaguely uncomfortable), and went on to ask God "to help Dr. Levin help me get off amphetamines." At her final "Amen," I almost cried. That prayer was what Leston Havens (1986), borrowing from the English philosopher John Langshaw Austin, calls a "performative utterance," a use of language not to denote, connote, or emote, but rather to act. Such speech is an action. Sally's petition was clearly self-fulfilling. The act of asking God to help me help her released her, even if not entirely, from her paralyzing fear. It was also a commitment at a deep emotional and psychic level to getting off drugs. I knew at that moment that Sally would soon be drug-free. It was her "surrender," her admission that the two of us were powerless over her addiction. For her performative utterance to be efficacious, I too had to surrender—admit my powerlessness, thereby becoming a participant in her sanctifying and enabling ritual. It was humbling, and that was good. If, in her surrender, she relinquished a grandiose illusion of control in order to transfer that control to an idealized object—God—then I, too, relinquished a part of my grandiosity and transferred my illusion of control to an idealized object—the anabolic forces of the universe manifest in the therapeutic process. It was a healing moment for us both.

We were not yet home free. I tried to send her to a psychiatric consultant to determine how much amphetamine she was on and propose a safe withdrawal schedule. Sally resisted this referral, not wanting to tell anyone else of her addiction. Finally, I sent her pills to the consultant, who identified them and worked out a detoxification schedule without actually seeing her. I was angry about this, but she was adamant. Psychiatric referrals by non-medical therapists are frequently experienced as narcissistically injurious by patients, and not all that infrequently by therapists. Both halves of this must be addressed. Generally, if you talk through the patient's feelings about being sent to a "shrink"—that usually means that they must really be crazy—and deal with your feelings about the patient's feelings that someone has more magic than you do, such referrals go well. No so in this case.

Fortunately, we got by that and Sally started cutting down. All went well until we approached ground zero. At that point, Sally panicked and upped her dosage. We went around that merry-go-round several times. I was by then doing a lot of analyzing and interpreting. I pointed out as many meanings of her addiction as I was aware of, starting with the unconscious identification with her mother's and father's addictions, and ending with amphetamine's role as an idealized, magical object that would soothe, satisfy, thin, and mood-elevate. I told her that contrary to her expectations, she would feel better off the drugs, her self-esteem would get a huge boost, and her self-hatred would diminish. I was very active, very didactic, and very firm in my assertion that things could only get better for her if she were drug-free. It finally worked, and there she was feeling bereft, naked, more vulnerable than ever, after I reassured her that she would feel better without the drugs. She was as angry as she dared to be with me. I repeatedly urged her to go to NA (Narcotics Anonymous) meetings, and/or to an ACOA meeting. She resisted but finally went. Sally never became a deeply committed member of the Twelve-Step movement (so-called for AA's Twelve Steps of Recovery), but her intermittent, rather tepid involvement significantly helped. It reduced her shame and lessened her social isolation.

Sally dealt with her fear of people by superciliousness and contempt, which kept her socially isolated. Of course, her fear that people would "know" that she was an addict and adulteress made matters worse. Fortunately, neither was now nearly as salient, and NA provided her with a first socialization experience in an alcohol- and drug-free environment. She was still too troubled and struggling too hard to ward off depression to become socially involved outside of NA, but a seed had been planted, and she became less defensively contemptuous of others. A year later, she would start to have lunch with fellow workers and develop some friendships with women, but that was yet to come. For the present, she had only Hank and me.

Psychotherapeutically, "curing" an addiction always involves a transfer from dependence on a substance (seemingly much safer) to dependence on people. Relationship cures. Therein lie both the opportunity and the problem. Sally's transference to me was so overwhelming (for both of us) that the slightest deviance on my part (e.g., being a few minutes late), threw her into a panic, and she responded to a perceived narcissistic injury with narcissistic rage, punishing me with catatonic-like withdrawals (which were also self-protections), suicidal threats (not experienced as threats), and frantic calls at all hours of the day and night. I understood her desperation, yet felt enraged and controlled. I did not for a long time point out the aggression (narcissistic rage) behind much of this behavior; she would not have understood such an interpretation. Instead, I set such limits as I needed to function and otherwise remained tolerant of and empathic toward her need to cling, control, and position. That behavior diminished only slowly. Even more troublesome, Sally lived in dread of my going away, which inevitably would occur.

At this point, her fear of her father returned. Now I pressed for and encouraged her to express her rage toward him. Fearing fatal retaliation, she found this very difficult. However, our bond was now so strong (confining and infuriating as I sometimes experienced it to be) that she was able to do this work.

Her most characteristic defense was turning against the self. I actively intervened when she would tear into herself. During a particularly virulent orgy of self-deprecation in which she insisted on her worthlessness, I said, "It isn't you but your father who is worthless." That opened things up. Once begun, her rage at him was poured out volcanically, yet her fear didn't abate. She oscillated wildly between wanting to kill him and wanting to kill herself. I pointed out this confusion. She asked me if she should call him and express her feelings. Technical neutrality would have been disastrous. Sally needed to actively experience and express anger to her father and not be killed. I actively and strongly encouraged her.

Technical neutrality refers not only to the analyst's noninvolvement in the patient's life but also to the analyst's neutrality toward conflicting aspects of the mind, equidistancing him- or herself between id, ego, and super-ego. It is a technique of extraordinary power and efficacy when used appropriately. This simply was not such a situation.

After several weeks of "I will," and "I can't," (confront Father), Sally came in and said, "I called him and told him I hoped that his prick would fall off, and hung up." I shook her hand. Sally fully expected to be murdered, but the longer nothing happened, the less fearful she became. Several months later, her father died. His death was a liberation for her. Probably for the first time in her life, Sally wasn't terrified. What she feared may have been a memory, but the death of the objective correlative of that memory dislodged it and, so to speak, it was expelled. Sally felt no guilt, or at least none I could detect—and I probed for it. Her only regret was not seeing him buried, so that she would be absolutely sure he was gone. I wondered if she would have driven a stake through his heart if she had been at the funeral.

The momentous events following Sally's ceasing to take amphetamines were largely adaptive. However, she certainly experienced a "postwithdrawal crash depression." Amphetamine withdrawal is dangerous because of the rebound depression. Such depressions can and often do lead to suicide, hence my making myself available as much as possible during that period. Whatever nonpharmacological psychodynamic determinants her behavior had at that time, it was powerfully psychopharmacologically driven, and her clinging behavior was the clinging of a drowning person to a life raft. In other words—it was necessary and restitutional.

THE LIBERATING POWER OF HATRED

If love and forgiveness can liberate and cure, so can hate. We don't give hate its proper place in the restoration of the self. Sally's hatred of her father, a well-earned hatred, derepressed, experienced, and expressed, was the single most potent force driving and enabling her recovery. I deliberately say "hate" and not "rage," for it was truly hatred. Therapists, generally identifying themselves with the angels, are usually uncomfortable with hatred, especially hatred of parents. It goes against the grain of our professional self-images as healers and restorers of harmony. Some things can't and shouldn't be fixed, and some families and some parents are toxic. We need to help our patients hate them, and use that hatred in the service of separation and individuation. Sally's boundaries firmed up once her internalized father ceased tormenting her. Of course, being off amphetamines also helped her differentiate. The pills, which she literally internalized, were, along with being an all-powerful, loving mother, also her hateful and hating father—safer within her than without—yet, like him, tormenting and persecuting her. Part of her fear of giving up the pills was a fear that he, no longer symbolically within, would be even more dangerous without. I told her all of this while she was still struggling for abstinence, and warned her that she would suffer a rebound depression—a rebound crash—which would be neurochemical, intensely painful, but self-limiting and without emotional (psychodynamic) or symbolic meaning.

After a prolonged working through, all went well until my vacation grew closer. Sally regressed to near psychosis. Her phone calls became more frequent and increasingly unmanageable. I now found them invasive and intolerable. Sally's voice assumed the same remoteness that her face expressed during her quasi-catatonic withdrawals. Glacial, dead, astral, were some of the adjectives that came to mind listening to her calls. She seemed to be a different person. Was she indeed a multiple who split, perhaps to prevent complete and total fragmentation when her anxiety reached panic proportions, when faced with disruption of a life-sustaining self-object transference, by abandonment by the self-object—me? Sally constantly threatened (she didn't experience it as a threat) to return to her old friend, her previous self-object, amphetamine.

In *Inhibitions, Symptoms and Anxiety* (1926), Freud described a developmental sequence of anxiety, starting with fear of annihilation, followed by fear of loss of the object (separation anxiety), fear of loss of love of the object, castration anxiety, and social anxiety. In his revision of his anxiety theory, Freud moved from his earlier view that we are anxious because we repress—that anxiety is a somatic product caused by a toxin, the degeneration product of bottled-up libido—to the opposite view, that we repress because we are anxious, in which anxiety is more psychological and communicative than somatic, although Freud never entirely abandoned the belief that anxiety had some sort of somatic basis. In the revised theory, anxiety is a signal of an external or internal danger that calls forth defenses. However, the move from fear of annihilation to *signal anxiety* is a developmental achievement, subject to regressive loss. Sally had reached the level in which anxiety is a signal, but her development was tenuous and insecure. Kohut (1971) offers an alternate explanation of the same phenomenon when he speaks of "regressive fragmentation" to panic terror of the loss of the (archaic nuclear) self, in response to loss or disruption of a self-object transference. They (Kohut and Freud) offer alternate and complementary ways of conceptualizing Sally's anxiety.

My impending abandonment threatened the ultimate narcissistic injury, destruction of the self. That threat was being defended against by going away, by not being there, and by the cold, murderous fury of narcissistic rage. That narcissistic rage could easily prove fatal. This time, I was fully convinced that Sally was capable of killing herself as the ultimate way of not being there—of avoiding annihilation and of punishing me for my abandonment. An eye for an eye, a tooth for a tooth. I was abandoning her—she would abandon me. We were in deep shit. This time I decided to make hospitalization a condition of treatment if things didn't change before I left. Now I interpreted the aggression—narcissistic rage—behind her frantic calls and suicidal ideation. She couldn't hear it, although much later she did and was able to use it. I went back to empathizing with her terror, saying in more emotive and personal terms what I said earlier about Freud's and Kohut's understanding of anxiety. I emphasized that it felt *as if* she would shatter, but that it wouldn't happen. It worked. Sally now asked, in a less enraged, albeit still desperate way, "How can I survive your vacation?" She then had another one of her creatively curative breakthroughs. She asked, "Can I come and sit in your waiting room (which was shared and accessible) during the times we would be having our appointments?" I was relieved that the hospital, which would have been shattering for her, wouldn't be needed. I spontaneously went her one better and said, "I'll give you the key to my office, and you can go in and sit in the usual place, at our regularly scheduled times." She now had her self-object back, and panic terror of annihilation turned into more ordinary forms of separation anxiety. It's just as well that I don't need the approbation of the "classical school." Eissler (1958) spoke about *parameters*—deviations from analytic technique as a temporary expedient in the course of the analysis. "Parameters all right, but isn't this ridiculous?" The classicist would say, "This isn't analysis; this is unvarnished gratification. Allowing Sally to use your office has to arouse memories of the primal scene, anal invasion, and oral incorporative fantasies that will remain uninterpreted." Not so, say I. First things first, as they say in the Twelve-Step programs, and the first thing was to get this patient through my vacation without her either suiciding or having to be hospitalized. Of course being in my office did have all of the above meanings; it had to, but they were secondary. The salient meaning of being able to sit on the floor in my office while I was away was that Sally would spend my vacation baking cookies with her mother. Another way of conceptualizing Sally's problem is to say that she had failed to develop *evocative memory*, a prerequisite to *object constancy*. Evocative memory is the ability to get in touch with object representations when we need them. Lacking this ability and regressing in the face of great anxiety, Sally needed the concrete sensory stimuli of my office to conjure me (and what I represented). Safe in the womb, if you want to see it that way, she could feel connected with me even though I wasn't there, even though she lacked object constancy—the ability to libidinally cathect (to revert to the language of drive theory) an object (representation), even in a state of need and deprivation. Of course, I did encourage Sally to explore all of her feelings about being in my office and interpreted some of them after the vacation (or to be more accurate, after many vacations).

The security of knowing that she would be able to stay in my office stabilized Sally. And she had a dream, the associations to which led her to one of the most traumatic events of her life. This wasn't really, strictly speaking, repressed, but it had never come up, and Sally didn't connect it to her present panic. When she was 12, her mother, by then far advanced in her alcoholism, stated, screaming, "I can't stand you fucking kids anymore. I'm leaving." And she did. She got in her wreck of a car and drove away, not returning for weeks, and only then because she couldn't make it on her own. Sally was devastated. She was abandoned, on the verge of adolescence, to the mercies of her drunken, sexually obsessed father. The weeks her mother was gone were sheer hell for her. All security and safety, however meager, vanished. Nothing dramatic happened during her mother's absence, and the incident was never talked about. Life, such as it was, slowly returned to the status quo ante, but things were never the same for Sally again. It was Mother's second traumatic failure: a broken coccyx and a broken heart—strange legacies from a good mother. (Of course, there was a good mother, not entirely of Sally's creating, but the degree to which she had defensively and adaptively idealized what was idealizable about Mother was now clear.) The primary meaning of my leaving was now apparent. I, like Mother, was abandoning her to Father, who would kill her horribly, sexually, mutilatingly, if she didn't kill herself first.

A wall had been breached. Sally's frozen, furious withdrawal was no more. Now sorrow and fear, rage and fury, poured forth. I pounded away at the transferential link. Time and time again, I took her back to Mother, also pointing out that I wasn't Mother (which in her near psychotic transference was not always clear to her), and that Father was dead. Much was accomplished before I left. As the date of my departure neared, Sally's fear, as was to be expected, escalated again. I insisted that she see a covering therapist, as well as sit in my office. With surprisingly little resistance, she agreed. Ensuing vacations were almost equally traumatic for her, but each was a little less traumatic than the last, and as the years went on, Sally steadily improved. It took her several years to be completely comfortable without amphetamines or pot. She knew few people who weren't into drinking or drugs, but as her defensive devaluation of people subsided, her social anxiety (really fear of rejection and fear of a consuming and annihilating merger) abated and she made new connections. Her self-esteem rose and her anxiety level fell as she progressively individuated.

An enduring current narcissistic injury was lack of meaningful or fulfilling work, a constant source of pain that I could do little, beyond empathizing, to alleviate. She came to terms with her father: "I don't forgive him, yet I understand him more now. He never wanted children and resented us. If there is an afterlife, perhaps his punishment could be helping me now. He owes it to me, and I deserve it," and experienced more and more rage toward her mother. She did a lot of mourning work (her mother had died of complications of her alcoholism), and it paid off. Sally's rage seemed to separate her from her mother, her bond to me giving her the security to do so. She was becoming more and more her own person.

My next vacation approached. As usual, Sally was upset, but this time she was more nervous than terrified. Just before I left she said, "I'll miss you." That wasn't transference. That was here-and-now real relationship stuff. Leston Havens says, "If there is one moment without transference, the patient is cured." I don't know that there is any moment completely without transference, and I doubt that any of us is "cured," yet something was profoundly different. I said, "You are going to miss me because you are you, and I am I, and you like being with me, but I will be away. You used to think that you would cease to exist if I went away because you could not be, except as a part of me. Now you are secure in your own identity, as evidenced by your growing interest in intellectual activities, hiking, and bicycle riding. And you don't need me in the same way. Your missing me isn't about your mother, it's about us. You used to get confused with your mother. You weren't sure what was you and what was her, but the more we talked about her dying and your feelings about her dying, and of her earlier leaving, the less confused you became [here I cited the evidence in several dreams of her progressive separation-individuation] about who you are and who she was. You knew perfectly well that Mother wasn't you in the sense that you had separate bodies and were separate people, but in your mind, you had images of you and your mother that were blurred, confused, and merged. Now those images are clearly demarcated. When you get very upset, they may temporarily blur again, and when that happens, I will point it out to you; however, you have moved on to a different space, a different way of being, and that achievement is indelibly yours. It was only after you separated, in your mind and heart, from your mother, finally felt her loss, experienced her as a whole person, good and bad, loving and hating, there for you and not there for you, that you yourself could become a full person, loving and hating, joining and separating, joyful and sorrowful, fearful and secure, and it was only after your mourning allowed you to experience your mother as separate and whole, forever gone and forever a part of you, but not to be confused with you, that you could experience yourself as separate and whole with all the feelings you have about that separation and wholeness; that you became able to experience me as separate and whole, as there and not there, as focused on you and as having my own needs, as magnificently capable of helping you and as frequently flawed and sometimes inadequate. It is you, the separate, individuated, and whole Sally who will miss me as a separate, individuated, and tired therapist. I will miss you too, but not so much that I won't have a hell of a good time."

Sally wept a little, but she was not fearful. "I hate your going away, but I hope you have a good time, if you know what I mean." I did and said so.

Underlying Emotional Issues

I had met Sarah in her capacity as a real estate agent. In the course of our business together, she had noticed my books on alcoholism. She volunteered that her husband, a rabbi, had an interest in addiction. Assuming that he did pastoral counseling and that he might be a referral source, I gave her my card. My impression of Sarah was that of a rather anxious, moderately overweight, reasonably pleasant, and rather friendly salesperson who did not put much pressure on me to buy the lot I was considering as an investment. She seemed to know her business. Not very important to me, I soon forgot her. Months later, I got a call from her husband, Rabbi Simon. Assuming he wanted to refer a congregant, I returned his call. "Doctor, it's for me," blurted out the rabbi. We made an appointment. The second he entered the office it was apparent that the rabbi, a short, muscular man in his late forties, was angry.

"I don't fucking want to be here. God should be enough; I shouldn't need you. I'm angry at God. If he did his job, I wouldn't be here. But I had no choice. I goddamn have to be here. I am in recovery, and I want to drink. It happens every time I get two years together. I get involved with a woman and I can't handle it, so I start drinking again. It's my wife's fault. Before we were married, she gave me oral sex; now she won't. Nine years she hasn't gone down on me. It was FALSE ADVERTISING," boomed the rabbi. "False advertising! I didn't even want to marry her! She misled me. I know I shouldn't blame it on her. I should 'take my own inventory.'" As he fell back on an AA slogan, the rabbi, who had been deep red as he protested his wife's "false advertising," visibly calmed. But not for long. Although he was obviously comforted by his reconnection with AA, I had doubts about his commitment to the program. He "talked the talk" but did he "walk the walk"?

As he related the precipitating event that brought him to therapy, his speech became more and more pressured. "I was conducting a *Shabbos* service. I was about to give my sermon. I had written a winner. It had some really good stories in it, and I couldn't wait to get some laughs. I have a terrific sense of humor—maybe I'm too funny and nobody respects me, maybe not . . . Doctor, what's your fee? I don't have much money. Do you give professional courtesy—clerical reductions or anything? . . . Well, I started my sermon and my eye caught Rachel. What a piece! Her kids are in the Hebrew school and we talk sometimes. I could tell from the way she looked at me that she wouldn't mind some action. While in the middle of the sermon, I started thinking, 'I bet she gives great head,' and I couldn't get the thought out of my head. Then I heard a voice saying, 'Hershel, you're going to get drunk tonight,' and I wanted a drink so bad my tongue was hanging out. I have no idea what I said to the congregation, but I recovered and continued the service. Then as I was putting the Torah back in the Ark, I started thinking, 'What's the *bracha* [blessing] for a blow job?' and I couldn't get that thought out of my mind." (Some sort of projective identification must have been going on because I had exactly the same thought.) "I felt tremendously guilty. I couldn't stand the guilt, and all I could think of was drinking. What do I need you for? I can do the same thing with my sponsor. What did you say you charge, again? It's not just Sarah. I'm having trouble with my congregation. We're in contract negotiations and they're offering me *bubkes* [beans]. They expect me to take next to nothing and they don't fix a thing in my house!"

I thought, this sounds like the "Catholic crazies" with the sacrilege and the guilt over drinking or the thought of it. His drinking simultaneously stops the obsessive sacrilege and punishes him for it. Not exactly a Jewish scenario. In this age of multiculturalism it is perhaps useful to note cultural determinants of neurosis and other psychopathology. They are there, yet underneath its all the same stuff.

Alcoholism being endemic in the Catholic clergy and the Church willing to pay for treatment, I have treated many "religious" over the years. I found myself remembering Sister Beth Ann, who had obsessive scatological thoughts concerning the Virgin Mary during Mass, and Sister Judith, who burned with erotic desire for Jesus. Both of them got totally blotto as often as they could, which was nightly, and both became so ill that their superiors insisted that they seek treatment for their alcoholism. I also thought of Brother Thomas, less tormented by sacrilegious thoughts than by guilt over homosexual fantasies, who wound up with panic attacks, disastrously self-medicated by alcohol.

I also thought of Alice, nun, social worker, and nurse, who was clinical director of the dual-diagnosis unit of a famous psychiatric hospital and in her seventh year of recovery when she picked up a drink. When she came to see me after going AWOL from an inpatient rehabilitation facility, she spent her session spewing obsessive hatred of the Pope. Daughter of a tyrannical career officer father, she had been pushed into the cloister although she did believe that she had a vocation. During her thirties, she had fallen madly in love with a brilliant priest, who was president of the college in which she taught. They planned to leave their respective orders and marry. He did—someone else. Her alcoholism followed. In her recovery, she had once again fallen in love, this time with the medical director of her unit. It was a classic doctor–nurse relationship. She wrote his professional papers for him, ran the unit to his professional benefit, and attended his kids' birthday parties. She waited for the promised leaving of his wife. He too abandoned her. It was a short distance from there to the bar. Once she picked up a drink, it took less than a week for her to escalate into around-the-clock drunkenness, a progression that eventuated in her entry into the rehabilitation unit and subsequent treatment with me. We had barely connected when my vacation loomed. I feared that she would get drunk shortly after I left, and struggled mightily through interpretation and probing of her feelings to help her experience rather than act out her feelings of abandonment. I failed. Alice had a spectacular and almost fatal fall—a literal one, down a flight of stairs while drunk, and entered a long-term treatment facility. I never heard from her, but years later learned that she was running her own rehabilitation program in a distant state.

Her obsessive hatred of the Pope, no doubt displaced hatred of her father, priest-lover, and doctor-paramour, had brought her to mind. But why was I thinking of my Catholic patients instead of listening to my rabbinical patient? I was doing the same thing he had done during his sermon—going into a reverie instead of staying with my professional task. Given that I was a deeply resented substitute for a lazy God and an expensive, useless, double of a sponsor, perhaps it was less than amazing that I should have stopped listening to him. With a conscious effort, I tuned back in on what he was saying.

"Nobody in my congregation knows I'm in the Program. I live in terror that I'll meet a member of the congregation at a meeting. Then I think, 'Well, it's something I overcame.' They'll respect me even more—who cares about those *shleppers*, a bunch of schoolteachers. Not a single doctor in the whole congregation.

"My father's crazy. I was born in Jerusalem. Doctor, you don't understand. I'm afraid I'll leave here and go to a bar. I've done it three times—put together a few sober years and gone out again. What did you say your fee is? I'm a poor man, Oh yes, Jerusalem. That reminds me. I was officiating at the interfaith banquet—community relations is one of my strong points. I was invited to lead the interfaith Memorial Day service, too—that and kids. I'm really good with kids, too. It's my sense of humor." I couldn't help thinking that his sense of humor was singularly not in evidence in this session. "Oh yes, my father, he's crazy. He can't hold a job. Sometimes he works as a *shammes* (sextant) in a synagogue or as a building super. He can't get along with people, so either people won't hire him in the first place or they fire him. Thirty years in this country and he can't speak English. And his cheapness—it's an illness. When I was a kid, one of my chores was to vacuum the carpet. I'd be vacuuming and he would start shouting, 'Stop walking on the carpet! It's expensive! You'll wear it out! Can't you vacuum without walking on it?' The same with the radio: 'Don't play it so much, it will burn out!' Lots of stuff like that. He's crazy. But I've forgiven him. I had lots of therapy, and I've worked all that childhood stuff through. Not my wife! She never dealt with her issues. She needs therapy! Oh yes, the interfaith banquet. Let me finish with my family. My mother, she's a dishrag. He walks all over her. All she does is whine. But it's okay. I've learned to deal with them. Besides they are over 80. My brother, he was a great athlete. You wouldn't expect it in such a religious family, but he was, a quarterback and a basketball star, and what a ladies' man; had them by the dozen. Now he's depressed; he finally married and his wife cheated on him. 'What goes around . . . ' Oh yes, the banquet. My brother hates religion. When he was a kid in Jerusalem, my parents sent him to an ultra-Orthodox school where they beat the kids with whips. My crazy parents said, 'It's good for him.' Oh yes, the banquet. It was a great success. Everyone was laughing and applauding when I started thinking, 'Theodor Herzl was a faggot.' I couldn't get the thought out of my mind. I've thought that before, but not like that night. It just wouldn't get out of my mind. Then all I could think of was getting out of there and having a double bourbon. Actually I started to think about Herzl when I was getting a hard-on looking at the Presbyterian minister. Boy, is she beautiful! I guess I started thinking about Herzl to get her out of my mind. The idea of fucking a minister really excites me! Then I thought, Hershel, this is a sin. What's wrong with you?' And then I remembered Herzl was a faggot, and I hadn't thought about that in years, but when it gets in my head I can't get it out. What am I doing here? God should be enough. I shouldn't need you. I hate you—nothing personal, Doctor. It doesn't cost anything to talk to my sponsor. Then it came time to say the benediction, and suddenly I was afraid that I would say, 'Either way with LBJ at the YMCA.' I wanted to shout that. It was then I decided to have an affair with Rachel. I knew I could, and that for a while I would feel better. But then would come the guilt and I would drink. I know. I've done it before. Doctor, what are you going to do to prevent me from slipping? I know you can't do it; I have to, yet I want you to. My parents never took care of us. They were too crazy. What's your fee? Whatever it is, it's too much!"

I was getting bewildered. Was the rabbi "crazy" like his father? His pent-up conflicts and anxieties poured out of him like pus from a lanced boil, jumbled and desperate, and defended against by devaluation and contempt of me, therapy, his congregation, his wife. Feeling overwhelmed, I let my mind wander to Theodor Herzl. Was the founder of Zionism indeed homosexual? Not so implausible, given Herzl's obsessive love for Heinrich Kana and his deep, deep grief after his friend's death by suicide, and his distant, estranged marriage. Again I was leaving the rabbi, no doubt because he made me anxious, and as angry as he himself was, in a classic projective identification. I recovered, dropping my speculation about Herzl's alleged homosexuality and brought my attention back to Rabbi Simon. Surely his identification with Herzl said as much about grandiosity as it did about sexuality. All in all, Herzl was a fascinating identification figure. Rich, handsome, powerful, deeply sexually conflicted, feeling repugnance for sensuality except for his attraction to young girls, having an intense male friendship with sexual overtones, and being the embodiment of charismatic leadership. The Hershel/Herzl echo must have facilitated this unconscious identification. The rabbi was starting to sound more like Freud's Rat Man than a case of the Catholic crazies. This tormented man, born in Jerusalem, linked himself through obsessive repudiation with a handsome, charismatic leader who had made his birth in Jerusalem possible. Herzl had something Hershel didn't—power. It also occurred to me that Herzl had died at about the rabbi's age, and wondered if there was a death wish behind his self-destructiveness. I also associated to the 1964 presidential campaign when Walter Jenkins, a Johnson aide, was caught performing fellatio in the men's room of the YMCA and the jingle the rabbi wanted to use as the benediction at the interfaith banquet made the rounds. I later bitterly regretted voting for Johnson.

"I should tell you about my negotiations with my congregation. I'm an educator, the religious school principal, as well as the rabbi, and I do both jobs. I want—I demand—*double salary*! Two jobs, two salaries! And I refuse to prepare the little *momzers* [bastards] for their bar mitzvahs. The religious school teachers should do that. The rabbi should be a scholar. I should be able to spend my time studying the Talmud. I know I won't get exactly double, but it better be close!"

"What do you get paid, Rabbi?" I asked him.

"Eighty-five thousand dollars plus my home and a travel allowance."

I decided he really was crazy. He was at the top of the scale for a rabbi of a southern Jersey small-town synagogue with a not-too-populous middle-class membership.

Preparing their kids for their *bar mitzvahs* was exactly what they were paying him for. I wondered if being alone with pubescent boys was too threatening to him. Trying to inject a little reality, I said, "You describe your congregation as a bunch of *shleppers*—could they afford . . . ?" He cut me off ragefully, fulminating about what a gang of cheap bastards they were and how badly they treated him. I said, "You're in a rage because your wife won't suck you off and neither will your congregation." He took that as an empathic statement and calmed down. I suggested that his rage at his congregation was partly driven by his experience of them as withholding, indifferent, and unnourishing, being all too reminiscent of his experience with his parents.

He replied, "It's their irrationality—that's what's like my parents! The board says they don't have the money, but they do! I can tell them how to save enough on other things to pay me what I *deserve*! It's my right!" He fell silent, looking hurt. After a few minutes, he resumed his tirade.

"My wife, my board of directors—don't think that I don't have friends in the congregation, some of them love me—won't give me my due. I'm a terrific speaker. I was a child prodigy, good at everything I did. I started working young, and that got me away from my crazy parents. That and sports. I was real good at sports. Not as good as my brother. He could have been a pro. And I got along real good with all the kids—Jewish, Gentile. It was the streets that saved me. At 14, I had my first piece of pizza—not kosher, you understand. And my first piece of ass, then my first joint. I didn't drink 'til much later. But I loved pot. Then I got sick. I developed bone cancer and almost died. I think it was my parents, they made me sick. I hated them so!

Not now, I've worked all that through. Anyway, when I was 19, I had an amputation, I have an artificial leg. They gave me Demerol, and when I got out of the hospital, I started using heroin. Nobody knew. I went to college and got a degree in business. My habit got out of control and I wound up living in the street. I did a little dealing, too. Do you think I'd make a good businessman? I think about leaving the clergy and going into business. Clergy is a business, too. Go to a rabbis' convention. You don't hear about God; you hear about contract negotiations and how they hate their congregations. I wasn't the most successful dealer, so I was in withdrawal half the time. It was terrible. Finally I went into a TC [treatment center] and stayed 18 months. I was the favorite. The director treated me like a son. I was afraid of women because of the amputation. The director gamed me, 'You think your stump is more important than your dick? When are you going to get laid, Hershel?' Finally, I did. Now I tell myself that makes me more attractive; it shows how strong I am and how much I've overcome. The same with my addiction, as long as I don't see a congregant at a meeting. The director really helped me. In those days, you got drinking privileges at a certain stage of your recovery, so I never thought alcohol was a problem. I left the TC, went back to school, and got a degree in religious education and married the rabbi's daughter. In my days as religious school principal, I fucked quite a few while their fathers were conducting services. I have a grown daughter. We have an okay relationship, but she still resents I wasn't there for her when she was growing up. I started losing jobs because of my drinking. After the first few times I went back to heroin. My wife left me. We divorced, and I really went wild. Finally I met Sarah. She was secular but she loved me. I was the only one who ever gave her an orgasm. She has an odd problem. When she was born, she had a missing clitoris. I talk to her about a reconstruction, but she won't get one. That's okay. I understand, she's ashamed. I can give her a vaginal orgasm, no one else ever did. (Shouting) I get her off and she doesn't give me what I want! That's why I have to have another woman. My slips have serious consequences. I wound up in rehab four times, and each time Sarah stayed with me. The last time she said it's over if I drink again.

I thought, "It's no accident that these two people, each missing a vital body part, have found each other." I felt more empathy for the rabbi now. He had indeed overcome much—crazy parents, near-fatal illness, disabling and shaming surgery, and drug addiction. And he had reached out for help as much as he resented and hated it when he feared enacting his repetition compulsion.

The rabbi continued, "Doctor, I don't want to drink again. This is the longest period of sobriety I've had—over two years. When I got out of my last rehab, I decided enough of being a religious educator. Principals are always under some rabbi's thumb and most of them are tyrants. I play all sides of the street—Reform, Conservative, and Orthodox. It's all the same to me. Like I said, it's a business." (It occurred to me that "spirituality" wasn't the rabbi's strong suit.) "If you can fuck their daughters, it isn't too bad, but usually you can't, and most of the time, you wouldn't want to. So I went to rabbinical school. This is my first job as a rabbi." (I thought his behavior more irrational than ever.) "Another problem, doctor, I have four children with Sarah. I didn't want them. But of course I love them and take good care of them, but I resent them. I did it for her, and she doesn't keep her part of the bargain." (The rabbi became furious again.) "She's a terrible mother; the kids don't get the attention they need because Sarah's always depressed, and she won't give me oral sex. Even intercourse is infrequent, I want to kill her! I'm going to go out and get a woman—Rachel, probably, if something doesn't happen, and then I'll slip for sure! Doctor, you have to help me. The only hope is marriage counseling. I want you to see us together and resolve this."

I almost fell off my chair. Couple therapy? That was the last thing in the world that I thought he would ask for, or that I was willing to give him. My fantasy, in all probability close to the reality, was that he wanted to bring the *rebbitzin* to me to coerce her into going down on him, and if I failed his response would be rage. All in all, not a task I was anxious to engage in. It also occurred to me that the women and the homosexual thoughts were smoke screens, and that he was setting himself up to drink, the real motivation being his desire to get blasted. I am sure that this was true, but equally sure that the causal vector went both ways. In any case, I was dubious that couple therapy was the answer. I tried to dissuade him.

"Rabbi, you have so many problems. You're in such emotional pain, you need individual therapy."

"No, no. I've had that—TC, six rehabs, counselors—no! I want marriage therapy! I told Sarah I would come to see you and arrange it."

I equivocated, "Couple therapy can be very helpful, but I think you need individual attention. What if I see you individually and refer the two of you for couple therapy?"

"No! No! Sarah wouldn't go. She only wants *you*!"

I let my surprise get away from me. "What?"

"Sarah's not a therapy person. She had a shrink but she never went. That infuriates me. Her depression brings the whole house down. She won't see any other therapist, but she really liked you even though you didn't buy the lot from her. She's agreed to come here."

I wondered if God shouldn't provide the couple therapy, and felt resentful at being manipulated into doing something I really didn't want to do. So I was feeling exactly what my patient felt about being in therapy, and I, like him, agreed to do something I resented. I said, "The way you present it, there is no other treatment possibility other than you and Sarah seeing me."

He snapped back, "That's right. If you don't see us as a couple, I'll surely slip."

Going against the grain and burning with resentment at the manipulation I replied, "Rabbi, you know that's outrageous bullshit and if you slip it's your own doing, but let's try it. Would you be willing to see another therapist individually? You're in so much pain . . . "

He interrupted with an icy "No!"

My attempt to get the rabbi into therapy with someone else having failed, we held couples sessions, which went on for three months. They were nothing like I anticipated. In these sessions, the rabbi showed a different side of himself—the negotiator—and something of the businessman he sometimes yearned to be. He became increasingly reasonable as the sessions went on, and I came to see that however much he resented and felt tricked and cheated by his wife, he wanted the marriage. Sarah was certainly depressed, clearly sitting on infinite rage and much in her husband's shadow. As the sessions progressed, she slowly bloomed. The rabbi's first negotiating point was that she go on antidepressants. After some hassle, she did. Emulating her sales approach with what I hoped would be more success, I took a soft-sell antidepressant stand: "You're certainly depressed, and medication seems worth a try. What are your objections?" This opened the way for her to say, "It's not the medicine; it's my husband's insistence. It's another way he controls me." With that she started taking the pills and they helped. As time went on, Hershel's rage subsided, especially after she gave him his "birthday blow job," her refusal of oral sex having more to do with her depression and her resentment of Hershel's using his insistence as a form of control and dominance than on objection to the physical act—and her rage surfaced. I helped her articulate her feelings through here-and-now interpretation. We never went "deep," sticking to facilitating communication and expressing feelings. I avoided genetic interpretations sensing that this couple was not available for such work. Similarly I offered few transference interpretations, although I tried to be as fully aware of their transferences and my countertransferences as possible. Sarah's rage was primarily over being controlled. This was her perception, first denied, then grudgingly admitted by Hershel. I did make a connection with her domineering father's control, but didn't push it when she didn't run with that ball.

Another part of her rage was over his "slips." If she knew about the women, which I thought she did, she never said so. The slips had a devastating effect on their economic and family life. At first defensive, Hershel shared increasing empathy, eventually weepingly apologizing for the pain he had inflicted on her. She in turn allowed herself to be "negotiated" into spending more time with the kids, started being a better marital partner insofar as she ceased being sullen, and became more available emotionally as well as sexually. The rabbi didn't drink. He directed his rage away from his wife and family and at his congregation, particularly at the board of directors. Sarah completely supported him, thinking even his most outrageous demands reasonable and his feelings of injury justifiable. Having a common enemy brought them together. Needless to say, his contract was not renewed, and he left town unemployed. They both blamed me for this. Even though the rabbi's narcissistic and sexual problems were never really addressed in the therapy, it must be considered a success. He came to avoid slipping, and he did. My goals for him would have been more ambitious, but that is irrelevant. The freedom he wanted was freedom from clinical dependency, and he achieved that. And his wife gained, too, emerging from her apathetic, depressed state. The marriage, troubled as it was, endured, and I think both parties wanted it to. Sobriety doesn't guarantee an end to obsession, and I doubt that his obsessions were much different at the end of therapy than they were at the interfaith banquet.

Several years later he sent me a note thanking me for helping him sustain his recovery and save his marriage. He went on to say that the two of them had opened their own real estate office and were doing "fabulously." He also wrote that he was to be the speaker at the next Chamber of Commerce meeting. I won't share my fantasy of his fantasies at that meeting.

❖ C H A P T E R   6 ❖

Sexual Addiction
and the President*

When the Monica Lewinsky scandal broke, I said to an old friend, "Clinton sure looks like a sex addict. All the prerequisites are there: biological predisposition, early trauma, and a history." She said, "You're right. You ought to write a book." So I did, *The Clinton Syndrome: The President and the Self-Destructive Nature of Sexual Addiction* (Levin 1998a). It is a book not only about the president, but about sexual addiction in general. This chapter is an updated adaptation from that book.

Later in this chapter, I adapt the *DSM-IV* criteria for substance abuse and dependence to sexual addiction. I think there is compelling evidence that Bill Clinton fits the rubric. What characterizes sexual addiction is its compulsiveness; its use of sex to meet unconscious needs of a nonsexual nature, especially to reassure and to quell painful, often unconscious, feelings of shame, guilt, and rage; and its ignoring of reality and of consequences for self and others. Clinton's behavior meets these criteria. As long ago as Yale Law School, he

---

* This chapter, in modified form, is reprinted from *The Clinton Syndrome: The President and the Self-Destructive Nature of Sexual Addiction* by permission of Prima Press, Rocklin, CA.

and Hillary were publicly fighting over his infidelities; his sexual behavior more than raised eyebrows in a very permissive Little Rock, and Betsey Wright, his chief of staff, begged him not to run for the presidency after putting together the "doomsday list," a compilation of not only his "conquests" but also of how dangerous his often less than sterling choices might be.

Bill Clinton is hardly the first political leader to be caught up in a sexual scandal. From Cleopatra and Mark Antony to Kitty O'Shea and Charles Stewart Parnell, the fates of empires have turned on the private passions of their leaders. Antony's lust for Cleopatra cost him the Roman Empire, while Parnell's passion for Mrs. O'Shea cost the Irish their strongest leader and probably delayed for a generation their liberation from English rule. There have been legions of autocratic, decadent, licentious rulers. Clement VII, the Renaissance pope, had a relationship with a woman such that she was his daughter, daughter-in-law (by marriage to his son), and the mother of his child. Franklin Roosevelt had a thirty-year affair with Lucy Mercer Rutherford and John Kennedy had one with Marilyn Monroe. Therefore, the intrusion of private sexual conduct into the realm of the public and political is hardly news. However, there is something different about President Clinton's sexuality and the political ramifications of that sexuality. It appears that it is neither the grand passion of a Mark Antony or a Parnell, nor the overripe decadence of a Renaissance pope, nor the longtime love of an essentially lonely man. Rather, it is something quite different: the irrational behavior of a basically decent middle-class democratic leader, behavior that has had tragicomic consequences for both the man and the nation.

When the country learned that tapes existed of former White House intern Monica Lewinsky discussing her sexual relationship with President Clinton after he had denied having had sex with her, there was a sense of shock. First Lady Hillary Rodham Clinton, true to form, quickly came to her husband's defense, asserting his innocence and the existence of a vast right-wing conspiracy aimed at her husband and herself. However, the tapes that might contradict the president's story had already fallen into the hands of Special Prosecutor Kenneth Starr, and talk of impeachment arose. It appeared that Clinton, in testifying in the Paula Jones suit that he had not had sex with Lewinsky and in allegedly urging Lewinsky to lie about their relationship, was guilty of at least perjury and most likely obstruction of justice as well. Although most Americans thought that the president's sex life, like their own, should be a private matter, they felt *betrayed*. During the 1992 presidential election, Clinton first denied having had an affair with Gennifer Flowers yet more or less admitted it on national television when he gave an interview to "*60 Minutes*." During that interview, Clinton stated that he and Hillary had had marital difficulties but that they had overcome them and that their marriage was stronger than ever. Essentially, Clinton had promised to straighten up in the White House. Now, suddenly, that did not appear to be the case.

After the initial sense of shock, public reaction ranged from rage to hurt to amusement to indifference to joy (on the part of Clinton's enemies). Despite the multitude of emotions felt, the public shared one common thought: Why would Bill Clinton do something so stupid? Why would he put his historical role in jeopardy?

My initial reaction was one of anger. I remember asking, "Why did he play into the hands of the most destructive elements in American politics?" My reaction began to temper, however, as I realized that Bill Clinton was exhibiting the symptoms of someone in the grip of an untreated addiction. Had the Monica Lewinsky affair been an isolated event, I never would have entertained the thought of Clinton as a sex addict. However, the Lewinsky affair was *not* an isolated event, and the more I thought about it, the more I realized that Clinton had about as much chance of leaving her alone as a cocaine addict has of passing up a line.

If it were merely a matter of having an orgasm, Clinton assuredly could have found a less risky, more suitable partner, but sexual addictions are not about sex. They are about insecurity, low self-esteem, and the need for affirmation and reassurance. The sex addict feels unloved and unlovable and therefore looks obsessively for proof that this is not so. The sex addict disguises his feelings of worthlessness from himself and from the world and uses sex to deaden and avoid psychological pain and conflict, to reassure and bolster fragile self-esteem, and to bury deeply embedded feelings of self-hatred.

Monica Lewinsky was only 21 when Bill Clinton's sexual relationship with her began, and the contrast in power between them was striking. Not only did the age difference contribute to this power differential, but the vast disparity between their respective ranges of experience and their status as intern and president, respectively, made this little better than "robbing the cradle." It was a tawdry business at best, one of secret sex with a young student, perhaps literally behind a stack of state papers.

Clinton knew that both the special prosecutor and Paula Jones's attorneys were scrutinizing his behavior in microscopic detail. Given this, and in the absence of an addiction, his relationship with Lewinsky would make no sense whatsoever, unless he is regarded as self-destructive to the point of madness. However, I do not believe that Clinton is that self-destructive. People who will their own downfall may not be aware of the destructive nature of their actions; however, to an outside observer, the destructiveness may be readily apparent. Nothing in Clinton's background, history, or life up to the Lewinsky incident indicates that he is a man who is his own worst enemy in any motivated sense. In other words, Clinton's behavior is indeed self-destructive, but that destruction is not the primary motive for his actions. Richard Nixon, another extraordinarily complex public figure, provides a ready contrast. You could feel the man sharpening the knife with which his enemies would slit his throat. Nixon's self-destructiveness was manifest in his self-pity ("You won't have Nixon to kick around anymore"), in his clumsy attempts to cover up, and most spectacularly in recording evidence of his own guilt and not destroying the incriminating tapes when he still could do so with impunity. It was as if Nixon clung to the tapes in order to destroy himself. Little evidence exists for anything of this sort in Clinton's life. Clinton is a man driven to succeed, to climb the ladder, to go from triumph to triumph.

The Lewinsky affair resulted from a mix of many factors. The first and most important factor that drove Clinton toward Monica Lewinsky was his history of having been raised in a violently alcoholic, dysfunctional home. With a mother and grandmother who showed many signs of compulsive gambling, a father who was apparently a sexual compulsive and perhaps an alcoholic, and a half-brother who is a recovering cocaine addict, Clinton grew up completely enveloped by addiction. Studies have shown that predisposition to addictive behavior is partly biological and partly environmental. Exactly what goes into the mix is debated by scientists, but no one in the field of addiction—researcher or clinician—doubts that addiction in the family powerfully predisposes children to addiction, as does violence in the family, and Clinton was witness to such violence from an early age. The consequences of such an upbringing are indelible. Only with extensive treatment do people overcome the legacy of such childhoods. Although Clinton has, by the world's standards, done extremely well, the external achievement does not heal the inner devastation. Clinton was left with powerful, repressed, un–worked-through feelings of shame, guilt, and rage, feelings later anesthetized and deflected by sexual compulsion. He also learned to cover up and to lie. To conceal the horror at home was a noble act. It protected the family. Clinton was further traumatized by his mother's leaving him when he was a year old to return to school and by the sexualized competition between mother and grandmother for his attention. One of Clinton's earliest memories is of his mother's weeping as he looked back on her dormitory as his grandparents pulled him away. Such traumatic separation from a woman could very well predispose to uniting with as many women as possible, being the one in control who first possesses and controls and then leaves. It is a perfect turning of a passive experience into an active one. He was to repeat the pattern of having two women vie for his love throughout his life. He was also left with repressed hostility toward women and a need to control and dominate them.

The second factor was Clinton's previous record of infidelity. His affair with Lewinsky has many antecedents. As far back as his first campaign for public office in 1974, when he ran for the U.S. Congress shortly after receiving his law degree, his reputation for philandering was such that Hillary, at that point engaged to Bill, sent her father and brother ostensibly to work in his campaign. It was common knowledge, however, that they were there to spy on Bill, who already had two girlfriends on the side. Clinton lost that election, but went on to become attorney general of Arkansas in 1976. Bill and Hillary had married in 1975, and by this time (according to all of Clinton's biographers) the allegations of sexual misconduct on Bill's part became routine and expected. By the time Clinton met Lewinsky, he had developed a lifetime habit of taking sexual pleasures wherever they could be found. Old habits are hard to break, and Bill Clinton is no exception to the rule.

The third factor was the two-year period during which Clinton suffered three major losses. His mother, Virginia Kelley, died on January 6, 1994; Israeli Prime Minister Yitzhak Rabin, an important father figure to Clinton, was assassinated on November 4, 1995; and U.S. Commerce Secretary and friend Ron Brown was killed in a plane crash on April 3, 1996. Clinton was muted in his public sorrow for his mother, but not for the two men.

Clinton's loss of his mother, although perhaps both privately and deep within his psyche the most wounding of his losses, is the one that elicited the least public expression of emotion. This is puzzling, for Clinton is, by nature, an emotionally expressive man. This unexpected lack of emotion suggests deep and strongly conflicted feelings about his mother. Whatever the nature of that conflict, Clinton's attachment to her is manifest and documented by all his biographers, both friendly and unfriendly. Clinton's mother was a strong, flamboyant, extroverted gambler and lady-about-town, and she had a reputation as a flirt. This certainly suggests that Clinton's sexual proclivities may stem, at least in part, from his identification with his mother. This identification may be a conscious modeling of his mother or, as is far more likely, an unconscious reenactment of her traits and behaviors. For all his attachment, Clinton had mixed feelings about his high-flying, wide-ranging mother. Such ambivalence impedes mourning and therefore makes moving on with one's life more difficult.

Clinton's experiences with father figures have been filled with tragedy. His biological father, William Jefferson Blythe, was killed in a car accident before Clinton was born; his stepfather, Roger Clinton, was a violent drunk; and there have been a long series of surrogate fathers who either failed him, died, or became unavailable to him.

Clinton's ongoing search for a father likely has been one of the strongest motivators in his life.

The assassination of Rabin, which might have derailed the Middle East peace process, rendered Clinton helpless, and it was as though fate had derailed his plans to go down in history as a peacemaker. The president was appalled by both the fanaticism of the assassin and the assassin's cause. It is not surprising that Clinton would be extraordinarily distraught by both the loss of an admired ally and by his natural identification with the assassination of a political leader. Nevertheless, Clinton's reaction was so overtly emotional (he almost lost his composure at Rabin's funeral) and so deeply felt that some additional factor must have been at work. Clearly, his relationship with Rabin had some further deep and personal meaning to him.

As numerous commentators wrote at the time of Rabin's death, when the intensity of Clinton's reaction was being widely commented on, Rabin had been not only an important father figure to Clinton but also a famous warrior who had manifested the kind of courage in battle that Clinton's draft evasion had prevented him from claiming for himself. Rabin accepted Clinton and did not criticize his behavior during the Vietnam War. Rabin, though not an alcoholic, was known to be a heavy drinker, so Clinton had found a father who could drink yet function—and function magnificently—the exact opposite of Clinton's pathetically alcoholic stepfather. Rabin was a man's man who had not only physical but moral courage, a trait to which Clinton aspired and was frequently condemned for lacking. Rabin and Clinton had become allies in a supremely important quest: to bring peace to the Middle East. All these factors made Rabin an almost perfect father surrogate for President Clinton. Anyone watching the video of Clinton at Rabin's funeral would be unable to deny his devastation. This was a loss that really stunned him. Rabin was the last in a long series of father surrogates in Clinton's life, and his passing left Clinton vulnerable. A hole needed to be filled, one that could not be filled by another surrogate father. This was one loss too many, and it became unlikely that Clinton would risk—on any level, conscious or unconscious—becoming that emotionally tied to a "father" again.

Having lost his mother and the last of his fathers, both real and surrogate, Clinton truly was an orphan. Then came another devastating blow, the loss of an older-brother figure, friend, and political ally, Ron Brown. Clinton was once again extremely emotional in his public reaction to Brown's death. Dying in a plane crash is both sudden and unexpected and, in this manner, not much different from dying in a car crash. Therefore, Brown's tragic death had to have brought to mind Clinton's biological father's equally tragic death. Although Clinton expressed deep emotion over the losses of Rabin and Brown, the pace of public life left him no time to work through these losses and complete the mourning process. Clinton was reeling under the impact of three profound losses, each imperfectly and incompletely mourned.

The fourth factor was Bill Clinton's beleaguered presidency during the Republican sweep of Congress in 1994 and the country's subsequent turn to the right. These actions marginalized him and robbed him of much of his leadership role—again another major loss. And it appeared that he was going to lose the presidency. However, the 1996 presidential campaign was made easier by the Republicans under Newt Gingrich closing down the government, the nomination of a weak Republican candidate, Bob Dole, and the presence of a third-party candidate lacking credibility, Ross Perot. Clinton displayed political genius and turned the tide on his opponents.

Things were beginning to look better for Clinton, but with his political resurrection came a different kind of emotional danger. Having pulled the chestnuts from the fire in an extraordinary way, he was suddenly in a strong leadership position, despite the opposition party's control of Congress. He now had ample proof that the American people supported him, however tempered that approval was by a lack of confidence in Dole and Perot. Clinton was insecurely, yet strongly, in the driver's seat again. The danger now lay in whether this renewed position of power would feed his grandiosity and lead him to behave recklessly. Would newfound arrogance, overconfidence, and overweening pride covering deep insecurity lead him into reckless actions because he believed that he was invulnerable? Here is a fifth factor, feeding yet another stream into the river that would sweep him into Monica Lewinsky's arms. It has been said, and wisely so, that "those whom the gods would destroy, they first make proud." Clinton's political comeback may have done exactly that by increasing his vulnerability to reckless sexual behavior.

A predisposition to addiction, a lifetime behavioral pattern of infidelity, three deep and devastating losses, and a political comeback engendering arrogance all pulled Bill Clinton in the direction of Monica Lewinsky. What happened after that was circumstance.

There is an interesting photograph of Virginia Kelley (Clinton's mother) and William Jefferson Blythe (Clinton's biological father) in the archives of the *Washington Post* (reproduced as photograph 2 in David Maraniss's (1996) biography of Clinton, *First in His Class*). Kelley looks extraordinarily like Lewinsky. Kelley's hairstyle, heavy makeup, and overall impression are strikingly similar to Lewinsky's. Bill Clinton, the man who had lost his mother, had found a replacement for her. Whatever oedipal longings Clinton may have had toward his overtly seductive mother may have been fulfilled with a woman who somewhat resembles his mother. Of course, I cannot know what was in Clinton's mind, consciously or unconsciously, or whether he ever made such a connection, but the resemblance is noteworthy nonetheless.

Now there is no mystery as to why Bill Clinton would have gotten into a virtually suicidal relationship with Monica Lewinsky. His legacy as an adult child of an alcoholic (ACOA) compelled him to fill the emptiness of his childhood and to repeat the addictive pattern of both his biological and adoptive parents. His relationship with Lewinsky revived a long-standing behavioral pattern; she fulfilled a complex nexus of unconscious needs—needs that were exacerbated by the loss of three important figures in his life. He derived reassurance when his political fortunes were in doubt and then continued to pursue that reassurance with a grandiose recklessness once the pendulum had swung. Last, but not least, she was there, and she was available. Absent any insight into what he was doing, he had no choice but to fall into a really stupid trap.

Clinton had bared his throat to a hoard of savage enemies led by the special prosecutor for the sake of an apparently meaningless relationship with Lewinsky. A man of acute political awareness, Clinton surely heard the baying hounds at his heels, yet he stumbled toward their jaws. In making himself vulnerable to devastating disclosure, public scrutiny, and persecutory zeal, he endangered not only his presidency and place in history but also the political agenda of moderation, tolerance, and the pursuit of peace to which he appears sincerely committed. To do this for the sake of having oral sex bespeaks of either recklessness bordering on madness—recklessness beyond that associated with grandiosity—which simply is not Clinton, or the irrationally compulsive behavior of an addict seeking affirmation and reassurance.

Assuming that President Clinton did half the sexual things he is alleged to have done over a lifetime, not to mention in the immediate past, he undoubtedly lost control. He became powerless over sexual impulses and his reputation is indelibly stained.

SEXUAL ADDICTION

The very concept of sexual addiction is fraught with controversy and no small degree of skepticism on the part of many. However, it is not a new idea, and the vast amount of sexual addiction literature strongly attests to the fact that the problem has become widely recognized.

The American Psychiatric Association's (APA) (1994) *Diagnostic and Statistical Manual of Mental Disorders* (*DSM-IV*), now in its fourth edition, has no category of sexual addiction, but I predict there will be in the fifth.

Psychiatric diagnosis is a fallible business, not because diseases come into (and go out of) being but because our perceptions and therefore our evaluations of psychiatric disease change. The APA's definition of and criteria for the various psychiatric illnesses have changed and continue to change as new editions of the *DSM* are published. The *DSM-IV* does not have a category for addiction as a diagnosis at all; rather, it speaks of substance abuse and substance dependence.

Although criteria somewhat overlap, the two are distinguished by their degree of severity. Substance abuse is less severe than substance dependence, because abuse is the natural and necessary precursor to dependence—one cannot become *dependent* on a substance without having first *abused* the substance. Therefore, addicts both abuse and depend on their substance of choice.

Although these categories apply to substances, such as alcohol or drugs, many mental health professionals have expanded these categories to apply to behaviors as well.

The following list is my adaptation of the *DSM* diagnostic criteria for substance dependence to compulsive sexing:

1. Repeated sexual activity resulting in a failure to fulfill major role obligations at work, school, or home.
2. Sexual activity in potentially dangerous situations.
3. Repeated sex-related legal problems.
4. Continued problematic sexual activity despite persistent or recurrent social or interpersonal problems.
5. Tolerance.
6. Withdrawal.
7. Larger amounts of sexual activity over longer periods of time than originally intended.
8. An enduring desire to control sexual activity and simultaneous failed attempts to do so.
9. Increased time spent in activities necessary to obtain sexual activity and/or to recover from its effects.
10. Decreased social, occupational, or recreational activities directly related to sexual activity.
11. Continued sexual activity despite knowledge of persistent or recurrent physical or psychological problems that are caused or exacerbated by the activity.

Repeated sexual activity resulting in a failure to fulfill major role obligations at work, school, or home.

For sex addicts, the addictive behavior can certainly affect work- or school-related obligations, but it most commonly affects one's obligations at home.

John was the manager of a support service department at a research facility. He was known to be tyrannical and to engage in bizarre acts such as putting lighted matches to papers on his subordinates' desks. He also habitually hit on lower-level employees, especially the secretaries. Because he "produced," his behavior was ignored by his superiors until his suggestive verbal advances progressed to groping. The subsequent demoralization within his department resulted in faltering productivity, and as a result he was dismissed. In John's case, the failure to fulfill a major role obligation was most manifest in the workplace.

Clinton certainly meets this criterion; difficulties at both home and work consequent upon his sexual activities have long plagued him and reached new heights in the Lewinsky affair.

Sexual activity in potentially dangerous situations.

The sex addicts with whom I have worked have, without exception, engaged in sex despite dangerous risks. Their compulsion commonly resulted in having unprotected sex, during which they repeatedly risked contracting sexually transmitted diseases including HIV.

Additionally, because most sex addicts engage in sex with complete strangers, many risk ending up in unsafe places where, should danger arise, no help is available. I have treated many addicts who have been roughed up.

Larry, a gay sex addict, came close to being killed by two "gay bashers" he had picked up. He is now permanently physically disabled and walks only with difficulty and with the aid of mechanical appliances, yet even this event failed to keep him from engaging in more addictive behavior. The risk of getting caught in the act also constitutes a danger. For example, I've treated addicts who have had sex in crowded public parks in broad daylight. Despite such dangers, sex addicts' desires for new conquests are so strong that such outrageous risks are repeatedly taken.

For some, perhaps including Clinton, the risk is intrinsic to the pleasure.

Repeated sex-related legal problems.

Many sex addicts expose themselves to blackmail, put themselves in positions to be financially castrated by vengeful spouses, and risk civil (and sometimes even criminal) proceedings as a result of their sexual behavior. Despite these consequences, they continue to behave in the same way.

Nancy's husband was hell-bent on proving her an unfit mother and gaining custody of their children. Yet, despite knowing that her husband had her apartment under surveillance, she brought home a seemingly endless stream of men. So addicted was she to sex that she lost custody of her children.

Clinton's legal problems hardly need comment.

Continued problematic sexual activity despite persistent or recurrent social or interpersonal problems.

If the addiction is marked and advanced, nearly every sex addict suffers social or interpersonal problems. This is because addictions invade every aspect of life. Despite these problems, however, addicts continue to engage in the addictive behavior.

Harry sincerely loved his wife and repeatedly told her so, yet he always had to have some action on the side. Because Harry was not a skillful liar, eventually his wife learned of the affairs. This led to violent fights at home and the suffering and depression of the wife he loved. As a result, Harry suffered intensely from guilt. Even so, he could not alter his behavior.

Clinton, too, persisted in his problematic sexual behavior in spite of negative consequences.

Tolerance, as evidenced by either of the following:

(a) Needing increased amounts of sexual activity to achieve the high or the desired effect.

(b) A markedly diminished response to the same amount of sexual activity.

Some sex addicts become compelled to engage in increasingly frequent encounters to achieve the same effect. That effect, on a conscious level, is sexual pleasure; however, and more important, on an unconscious level, the effect is an emotional one, such as warding off depression, feelings of inadequacy, or loneliness. Just as the drinker must drink increasingly more to get the effects of alcohol, the sex addict needs to increase the amount of sexual activity to achieve the same desired effect of meeting the unconscious emotional need.

In Eugene O'Neill's 1946 play, *The Iceman Cometh*, a group of skid row bums are hanging around Harry Hope's dead-end saloon when Hickey, a traveling salesman, arrives for his annual visit. The rummies are in a state of great excitement because Hickey always pays for drinks while he is staying at Harry Hope's. However, this year Hickey has been transformed—he is on the wagon and preaching temperance. The denizens of Harry Hope's are appalled. Despite all Hickey's preaching, he continues to pay for the men's drinks; however, the alcohol no longer has an effect on the men. The booze just doesn't work anymore. Throughout the play is a haunting refrain, "Harry, what have you done with the booze, it doesn't have the old magic anymore." The same thing happens to sex addicts when the same amount of sexual activity no longer has the power to even temporarily fill the emotional void and a tolerance has indeed been built.

John, the manager who set fire to his employees' desks and hit on department secretaries, well illustrates the notion of escalation. When verbal harassment no longer satisfied him, he moved on to groping and was subsequently fired.

Another patient, Joey, was once satisfied with his nightly practice of "turning a trick." Soon, however, he was no longer satisfied with just one, and after finishing with his first trick, he had to return to the bar for one more conquest. Eventually, he experienced such a lack of satisfaction that no matter how many times he scored, he returned home depressed.

Clinton's turning to an immature, neurotic, blabbermouth intern may very well represent such an escalation. Certainly the risk and excitement associated with it escalated dramatically.

Withdrawal, as evidenced by either of the following:

(a) Withdrawal symptoms characteristic for (addictive) sexual activity.

(b) Use of sexual activity, or similar compulsive behavior, to alleviate or avoid withdrawal symptoms.

Sex addicts may experience all the psychological symptoms of substance withdrawal: anxiety, irritability, anger, depression, restlessness, insomnia, and mood swings. However, unlike addiction to substances, the psychological symptoms of withdrawal from sexual addiction are not physically dangerous. Therefore, although no one will die from the withdrawal symptoms associated with sexual addiction, individuals may *feel* so miserable that they wish they would die.

The use of sexual activity to alleviate or avoid the withdrawal symptoms has been reported in studies conducted by Dr. Wayne Myers (1994), professor of psychiatry at Columbia University Medical School. Dr. Myers believes that many (if not most) sex addicts use sex as an antidepressant. In this way, they ward off the withdrawal symptoms of depression, anxiety, irritability, anger, and mood swings. This sets up a vicious cycle in which they return even more compulsively to sex to escape these withdrawal symptoms that are then exacerbated if and when the addict again stops the addictive behavior. Sex addicts commonly turn to other compulsive activities (such as gambling) or to substances to hold their potential withdrawal symptoms at bay.

Larger amounts of sexual activity over longer periods than originally intended.

Carrie's addictive pursuit of sex partners prevented her from working on the novel she was writing. Her addiction invaded more and more of her life until she literally had no time for anything else. She needed to be engaged in sex—looking for it, having it, or recovering from it—to the exclusion of all else.

Although it was not clear that Clinton had withdrawal symptoms, his apparent period of recovery (if it was one) ended as soon as he once again needed his "antidepressant."

An enduring desire to control sexual activity and simultaneous failed attempts to do so.

I regularly hear statements like the following from sex addicts: "I was going to work yesterday and I swore I wasn't going into the park to cruise, yet I somehow ended up there. I don't even remember walking into the park, but the next thing I knew I was behind some bushes engaged in oral sex. I enjoyed it, but I was furious at myself. I was not only late for work again, but it just wasn't what I had wanted to do."

Susan, one of my patients, liked to go out dancing. Her husband rationalized that even though she went out three, four, and sometimes even more nights per week, it was okay because he was not much of a dancer. She swore on each occasion that she would not be unfaithful to her husband, and she was perfectly serious and focused on her intent to dance and do nothing else. Inevitably, however, she wound up having intercourse, often unprotected, with someone she met in a bar. Afterward, she would feel frightened, depressed, and guilty.

For addicts, the repeated resolution to stop or control their behavior and the failure to do so is not only common but also extremely painful. This failure to control leaves addicts feeling powerless, as indeed they are, and their sense of being out of control is terrifying. All addicts seek to avoid this terror by engaging in more of whatever their soothing activity is, in this case, sex. Again we see the makings of a vicious cycle. The addict becomes depressed and anxious, partly because of his or her sexual activity, and then needs even more sex to quell the anxiety or deaden the depression.

Clinton himself has testified as to his attempts to control his sexual impulsiveness and his failure to do so in his taped conversations with Lewinsky.

Increased time spent in activities necessary to obtain sexual activity and/or to recover from its effects.

Ken, like Carrie, the woman whose whole life became sex, spent hours preening himself before going to the singles bars. Because he was compelled to stay until he scored, he was often exhausted the next day when he would obsessively wash his genitals in an attempt to magically escape disease.

Since Clinton was apparently on the phone with a congressman, who later voted for his impeachment, discussing an important appropriations bill while Monica was going down on him, he would appear to meet this criterion.

Decreased social, occupational, or recreational activities directly related to sexual activity.

I have written elsewhere (Levin 1987) that at the end of the alcoholic process the drinker is left with an "empty bottle, empty world, and empty self." This is because addictions invade every aspect of life, including mind, body, and spirit, and in this way, lead to progressive impoverishment.

The first manifestations of such impoverishment are emotional and mental. The addict experiences a narrower range of feelings than before, and those feelings that are experienced are often distorted and incredibly intense. The sex addict's emotional life becomes more and more twisted, constricted, and distorted. The addict regresses to using primitive defense mechanisms, the most common of which is denial. Just as the emotional feelings decrease in scope, the addict's mental processes become increasingly narrow and limited. Huge amounts of mental energy go into defending the addiction and finding supplies—into lying, scheming, rationalizing, and defending—so that little mental energy remains for anything else.

The second manifestation of such impoverishment is physical— the body is progressively damaged. This effect is glaring in chemical addicts, although sex addicts may also suffer bodily damage from exposure to diseases—both fatal and nonfatal. Death from medical complications of sexually transmitted diseases affects not only homosexuals but heterosexuals as well.

Finally, there is spiritual impoverishment. One does not have to be religious to be spiritual. Spirituality includes ideals and values that are necessary to mental health. These ideals and values can be quite secular in nature, yet they must in some way provide for transcendence of self. When these ideals and values are lost, spirituality is lost, and life becomes empty. The growing self-hate and self-loathing, the loss of all hope except for the hope to grope, and a numbing bitterness and cynicism combine to form a bleak and negative perspective on life. The sexual addict winds up spiritually impoverished, self-hating, and hopeless.

The sexual addiction progresses, more and more of the addict's life is taken away until nothing remains except the pursuit of sexual activity. Not only was more and more of Tim's time spent preparing for, seeking, and recovering from sexual experiences, but his inner world contracted until, unless compelled by economic necessity, he barely thought about anything else. One by one, his friends dropped out of his life, his interest in books and sports died, and his emotional range became restricted to briefer moments of euphoria after he scored and longer periods of anxiety and depression when he didn't.

Although this criterion doesn't seem to fit Clinton too well since he is emotionally involved in politics, he himself has spoken of his spiritual impoverishment and his need for spiritual nourishment. Accordingly, he has acquired spiritual advisors in what is almost certainly in part a public relations ploy, yet may also be, who knows to what extent, sincere.

Continued sexual activity despite knowledge of persistent or recurrent physical or psychological problems that are caused or exacerbated by the activity.

As previously stated, some sex addicts knowingly engage in their addictive behavior in spite of clear danger of physical illnesses such as venereal disease or even HIV. Sexual exposure to HIV is sometimes motivated by a self-destructiveness of suicidal proportions. Sometimes it's motivated by such a strong compulsion to have sex that nothing else matters, and in such cases denial ("It can't happen to me") also plays a role. Sex addicts also continue their behavior despite knowing that their activities are causing them psychological distress, including deep shame, guilt, and anxiety.

Sammy came from an Orthodox Jewish family. He was homosexual, a condition his pious grandfather considered worse then death. Sammy was tormented by conscious guilt about his homosexuality and by unconscious rage he felt toward his family. He had two obsessive thoughts. His first thought was "Maimonides [a medieval Jewish sage] taught that homosexuals should be stoned to death." His second thought was, "Grandfather should shove the Torah up his ass." The only thing that relieved Sammy's guilt and obsessive thoughts was sex. Yet the more sex he engaged in, the more guilt he felt and the more tormenting were his obsessive thoughts, which in turn required more sex to temporarily relieve them—ad infinitum. Sammy was caught in a vicious cycle, and he soon became a sex addict.

The applicability of this criterion to the president, at least on its psychological side, hardly needs elaboration.

It is important to note that one need not meet all eleven diagnostic criteria to qualify as a sexual addict. Only three of the eleven symptomatic behaviors need be present for the diagnosis to be made. Diagnostic criteria should not be applied mechanically; rather, the entire context of behavior(s) and the person's life circumstances should be taken into account. Indeed, there is much danger in taking any of these behaviors in isolation from one another, or even in concert, and labeling them "addiction." Nevertheless, I can't help but note that Bill Clinton comes up with a score of nine positives and two maybes on the eleven criteria for sexual compulsion.

Moving away from the *DSM-IV* adaptation I would like to offer some conclusions drawn from clinical practice as to the salient definers of sexual compulsion. I have observed certain characteristics in those whose sexuality is driven by unconscious demons:

1. It is compulsive in the sense that the sex addict has little choice but to engage in the sex act or be consumed by the sexual preoccupation regardless of consequences to self or others.
2. It has a driven quality because it is an attempt to fulfill unconscious needs and resolve unconscious conflicts, which, by its very nature, it cannot do. The attempt is futile, and this futility results in meaningless repetition.
3. It is out of control at the behavioral level and engenders conscious or unconscious anxiety at the emotional level because the sex addict "knows" at some level that he or she is out of control.
4. It persists over time.
5. It continues despite damage to health, career, relationships, reputation, or self-esteem.
6. It is at variance with community standards, meaning that it exceeds and goes beyond culturally accepted standards and is damaging to the individual.

7. It progresses in the sense that its negative consequences accelerate and become more serious.

The sexual addict seeks reassurance, a guarantee of cohesion and continuity of the self; a feeling of being loved, needed, and wanted; and a rise in self-esteem. The problem with using an addiction to fill these voids is that it actually works in the short term. Each time a sexual compulsive scores, he or she feels a little more powerful, a little more in control, a little more together, a little more lovable, and a little more worthwhile. If that were the end of the story, it would be a wonderful fix to certain kinds of emotional distress. Unfortunately, that is not the end of the story. In the long run, the fix backfires. The temporary power, control, and feelings of worth give way to an emotional hangover in which guilt, shame, and feelings of powerlessness cause sex addicts to feel even worse about themselves than they did before.

There are three requisites for recovery from any addiction, including sexual addiction:

1. Relinquishing denial.
2. Learning coping mechanisms to establish behavioral control.
3. Working through underlying conflicts, mourning losses and traumatization, and coming to terms with repressed shame, guilt, and rage.

This suggests that the therapy should proceed in three stages: confrontation, cognitive behavioral teaching of alternate behaviors and strategies for avoiding relapse, and finally psychodynamic work to surface and deal with unconscious conflict and pain. Although Bill Clinton had some brief family counseling after his brother was busted for cocaine dealing, he has never had this kind of in-depth treatment. This is regrettable since he seems to be a brilliant man, fully capable of insight if only his denial had been penetrated. (Note how difficult it is to avoid sexual overtones in writing about Clinton.) As one who voted for Clinton twice and would do so again, and who considers his enemies, led by Kenneth Starr, a threat to the republic, I am particularly regretful that the president never sought treatment.

The line between philandering and sexual addiction, like the line between problem drinking and alcoholism, is often hard to draw, and an argument can and has been made that Clinton simply acts the way alpha males act. Nevertheless, his involvement with Lewinsky was so reckless, so oblivious of consequences, and so irrational that it can only be explained in one of three ways: the president is stupid, which he is not; the president is crazy, which he is not; or the president is addicted. Given his possession of all the predisposing factors, his history, and his recent behavior including his denial-driven failure to settle with Paula Jones, I vote for the last possibility, sexual addiction. One can only hope that he is in stable recovery.

Telephone Therapy of Addiction

I hate telephones. They intrude on my life and greedily gobble up any interlude in my schedule. They deprive me of museum breaks when I'm working in my city office and of swimming breaks when I'm working in my country office. They make a mockery of my desires for contemplative time and ridicule my plans to steal an hour for writing. I look at my list of calls to return and cringe. Beware of the telephone; it is a tyrant. After a day of talking and listening, some days I can't help wistfully envying the analyst in the old story of the two friends who meet after many years; "Abie, it's been so long, what's happened to you? What are you doing?" "Hymie, I've become a psychoanalyst." "*Oy vay iz mir*! How do you stand listening to *tsouris* all day long?" "Who listens?"—the last thing I want to do is to talk and listen. At one time the message on my answering machine was, "Remembering that brevity is the soul of wit, leave a message." I reluctantly changed that message when I discovered that it didn't in the least discourage those I wanted to discourage and offended those I didn't want to offend, prospective patients, for example. My acerbic answering machine message hadn't reduced the number of calls I had to return.

When we became too social, too committed to activities involving other people, my wife likes to say "schizoids should remain schizoid," a sentiment I heartily endorse. I sometimes fantasize a practice devoted exclusively to the treatment of schizoids who would neither speak nor expect to be spoken to. After ten therapy sessions I would enjoy hearing the roaring of lions or the howling of wolves, but the last thing in the world I want to hear is the human voice. Just about then the telephone rings.

Telephones exacerbate my distractibility. If I were on Ritalin I would up my dose before a telephone session. It's difficult to maintain my focus and I find myself thinking of Lacan, my least favorite psychoanalytic thinker, no doubt because of his advocacy of the short session. I'm sure that part of my feelings about the telephone derive from my gender disability, otherwise known as maleness. I'm not sure what it's about, but it is women who, on the average, enjoy the phone in a way few men do. Most of the successful telephone sessions I have had have been with women.

An additional reason I hate the telephone is that often I can't think of one meaningful thing to say to a patient in crisis or pseudocrisis on the other side of the line. Silence over a phone line is a very different thing than silence in a room. The latter is often productive, the former usually tense, awkward, and unproductive. When I am holding the phone in an absolute blank as the distraught mother is imploring me to tell her what to do now that her son has come home stoned for the thousandth time, I think of a colleague's story of the time his daughter woke him, saying, "Daddy, the car broke down. It's freezing out and there's no one around for miles." Her half-conscious psychiatrist father muttered into the phone, "Can you tell me more about it?" That's a reply I would like to make to the distraught mother until I remember my friend's daughter's response, "Daddy, stop that shit and come get me." One of the worst things about the phone is it doesn't give you much of a place to hide. Like it or not, you have to go get them.

Having expressed my negative transference to Bell's child and by implication to his grandchildren, the fax, the beeper (I don't do beepers) and e-mail, I feel duly bound to express the other half of my ambivalence. However reluctantly, I have to concede that the telephone has its uses in therapy and that much of my hatred of it relates more to my administrative than to my clinical duties. In fact the telephone can be a lifesaver, especially for patients struggling through the early days of sobriety. I've even had some experience with successful ongoing phone therapies, but not much. Rather, I find that brief phone sessions can get people through crises and that they can help substance-abusing patients avoid slips and maintain stable sobriety. Even more important than actual phone contact—the phone session in itself—is therapeutic *availability*, the fact that the patient knows the therapist can be reached, and reached *any time*. It's the telephone that makes that possible.

You may be surprised to learn that I am a very available therapist. You can't work with substance abusers or other high-risk patients without being willing to make yourself available. This imposes a real burden on the therapist. You must be willing to check the answering machine—and you need one that you can retrieve from no matter where you are several times a day—and to return urgent calls immediately. That sometimes means talking from less than ideal public phones (the mere thought of a cell phone sends cold chills down my spine) and always requires the ability to think on your feet. All of this is a real intrusion in my life and, as you can tell from my opening paragraphs, it engenders real resentment. Yet, you can't do substance abuse work solo unless you can tolerate that intrusion. And one thing that facilitates tolerating it is experiencing and acknowledging your resentment. Otherwise you will act it out by not returning calls, by retaliating, or by finding other employment. The other thing you can do to make the intrusion tolerable is to limit it; to establish boundaries, however permeable; and to communicate where those boundaries lie.

I tell patients early on that I am available and I *want* them to call me if they really need to, and I *mean it*. I strongly urge you not to say that or anything like it if you don't mean it. Patients will pick up on your insincerity and either call you relentlessly to test you or not call you when they really do need to call. Either result is a disaster. Some patients need to learn to restrict their use of your availability while others need to learn to utilize it.

Although I tell patients to call me if they are afraid they will "pick up" (a drink or drug), or if they are experiencing intolerable anxiety or despair, I also convey both verbally *and* less directly, by manner and intonation, that I don't wish to be called for trivial reasons. Surprisingly few patients call frequently (or at all) and the frequency of those who do tapers off rather quickly. The idea is to convey that you truly care and that you want to be there for your patients, especially in the torment and terror of learning to live drug-free *and* that you have your own needs and your own life. More disturbed borderline patients are like small children who have difficulty accepting that their parents have their own needs. They literally don't know this. They need to be told. Less disturbed patients regress at times of great stress and become so needy that they too "forget" that their therapist has a life.

There are patients in the substance abusing population who literally have not achieved object constancy in the psychodynamic sense of being able to believe that the object is there and capable of love or caring during times of tension in the relationship or even in the Piagetian sense of securely believing that the object exists when out of sight. This may be a projection. When the patient is angry or upset with the therapist he or she may be incapable of caring for the therapist; all that good history together is wiped out and only a call can reestablish the existence of the good object. Or the patient may fear that his or her hostility, envy, and hatred have destroyed the therapist (the good object) and may need to call for reassurance that this is not so. Substance abuse induces regression, and patients who were once functioning on higher developmental levels and had securely established object constancy may have regressed to a point where this is no longer so. Any and all of this can be interpreted, but such interpretation should not be delivered reflexively. Therapeutic tact and a good sense of where the patient is at should help the therapist to distinguish between situations where it is best just to be there and situations in which it is best to interpret. Remember, you can always interpret later; the premature interpretation can be off-putting and can shut the patient down. There is nothing wrong with telling the patient that you have your own needs and your own life; in fact, it is therapeutic. Many therapists are hesitant to express their own needs and that hesitancy should be explored in supervision and/or personal therapy.

I find my approach works. I get few calls, and the vast majority of those who do call should have called. Using fairly directive, didactic interventions, combined with some interpretation of, for example, the hostility behind harassing, demanding calls, I help those patients who are so impulse-ridden that they cannot accept boundaries to tolerate them. If they don't have boundaries, I do, and my willingness to talk about my boundaries helps them to establish some of their own. I find this happens rather rapidly. As firm as I am, I am equally insistent that the boundary-transgressing patient call when genuinely needy. This is a difficult discrimination for some and the therapist should give concrete examples, drawn from the patient's life and circumstances, of what is and what is not an appropriate call. This less than dynamic sort of schoolmarmish work is nevertheless highly therapeutic.

The patient who is unable or unwilling to call when such a call would prevent a slip or other high-risk behavior (including suicide) is handled with a similar combination of directive, didactic, and psychodynamic interventions: "I want you to call the next time you are seriously contemplating taking a drink." "The reason you didn't call before you copped is because you were afraid the call would be effective and that talking to me would stop you from going out for heroin." "The reason you didn't call was that you feared rejection. Your parents were rarely available when you were in trouble and needed them so it was perfectly natural for you to expect I wouldn't be there for you either. It was too dangerous to find out. Better to believe I would have been there for you if you had called than to call and find out I wasn't. Such a disappointment would have been awful. Next time take a chance and call me." Exploration rather than direction or interpretation is also highly therapeutic with both types of patients, but is more effective with the telephone-shy or phobic patient: "Do you have any thoughts on why it was so hard to call me last night?"

I will try to make all this real with some case material. But first I would like to explain why substance abusers need as much access to the therapist via telephone as they do. Like most things psychical the substance abusers' need for close contact is overdetermined. The following dynamics may or may not apply in a given case, but it is not unusual to find that they all apply to the emotional condition of a particular substance abuser.

First and perhaps foremost, active substance abusers and those in early recovery tend to be developmentally regressed. That is to say their inner worlds and interpersonal relations are marked by lack of differentiation and weak integration, poor impulse control, low affect tolerance, ego weakness, poorly defined boundaries, diffuse identity, and a reliance on primitive defense mechanisms, especially splitting, denial, and projection. Insecurely established object constancy and a paucity of inner resources are part of the syndrome. This dynamic-emotional status may be the result of the substance abuse itself, in which case it is best understood as a regression, or it may have been antecedent to the substance abuse, in which case it is best understood as deficit or fixation, which is etiological of the substance abuse. Often the impoverished inner world is the outcome of a complex interaction of antecedent and consequent factors. Be that as it may, it is clear that a patient with such limited emotional resources is going to need a good deal of support and structuring from the outside and that that support must be available when it is needed.

A great many substance abusers use isolation—literally avoiding human contact to the maximum extent possible—in defense of their addiction as a result of the paranoia often secondary to substance abuse, and as an interpersonal and intrapsychic defense, particularly against feelings of rage, guilt, and shame. Paradoxically, these isolators, who hide out of fear, may have failed to develop what Winnicott (1958) calls the "capacity to be alone," so that they are caught in the dreadful trap of not being able to be part of community while not being able to be comfortably or creatively alone. For these people, the use of the telephone may be a perfect halfway house toward full participation in the human community—a connection that is not too threatening. Here the telephone and the conversation on it becomes something like a transitional object (Winnicott 1951). For the isolater, learning to use the phone to reach out for help is highly therapeutic in and of itself, quite apart from content. The Twelve-Step (AA type) self-help programs know this and put great emphasis on their members availing themselves of what they call "telephone therapy," contacting their fellow members for support. The telephone speaks to both sides of the defense: it allows the isolators to come out of hiding relatively easily since it engenders less fear than face-to-face contact and it replaces the substance as companion (which is what it is in one of its meanings) for those who have not developed the capacity of being alone.

Yet another aspect of the substance abusers' relationship to the substance is that of a *selfobject*. That is to say the substance abuser has developed a selfobject transference (Kohut 1977b) with both mirroring and idealizing components to the substance abuse. This is a hypothesis that I have elaborated elsewhere (Levin 1987, 1991, 1995, 1999 and in Chapter 3, this volume). The disruption of a selfobject transference or relationship that a move toward abstinence entails may induce profound anxiety and deep despair. The patient in early recovery, however exhilarated by his or her escape from a life-threatening addiction, is also utterly bereft of selfobject, companion, script, defense, and a deeply ingrained way of life. Any one of these may be so threatening as to set off a slip, (i.e., relapse), but the loss of the selfobject relationship is particularly difficult to negotiate. The ensuing anxiety and despair may make sobriety intolerable, so it is vital that another selfobject relationship—that to the therapist—replace the one lost to the substance. The telephone facilitates this relationship. In the idealizing transference the ideal object is experienced as omniscient, omnipotent, and omnipresent. Telephone accessibility provides a simulacrum to omnipresence and the contact made assuages anxiety and provides hope as an antidote to despair. The key to treating substance abusers is to replace rum with relationship and the telephone assists this process.

Yet another reason telephone access is necessary is that the substance-abusing patient is playing with half a deck. He or she has a poisoned brain, and, not infrequently, other somatic complications. There is a Twelve-Step neologism that refers to the mental confusion and emotional turmoil of early sobriety. That word is *mokus*. When AA or NA members say that Dave or Sally is mokus they are making an onomatopoetic statement. The very sound of the word *mokus* conveys the confusion induced by a poisoned mind, of suffering from an organic brain syndrome. The fact that the Twelve-Step movement, which has vast experience in this matter, has a word for and recognizes the state of mind with which the early recovering patient must struggle says a lot about what the therapist must deal with and about the necessity of being available to the patient in that state: an availability best provided by open access to telephone therapy.

While the nonmedical therapist should never attempt to practice medicine, those in the field do acquire a good deal of knowledge about the somatic complications—enough to recognize symptoms that may be quite dangerous and to use that recognition to appropriately warn and refer. Better to have the substance abuser with a serious somatic symptom, whether from the direct toxic effect of the drug, from withdrawal, or from malnutrition (surprisingly common even in comfortably middle-class substance abusers) call you at 3:00 a.m. (since he or she probably wouldn't call anyone else) as you sleepily say, "Call 911 immediately," then to find out in the morning that your caseload has been reduced by one.

Related to the somatic complications and poisoned brain is what is known as the prolonged (or attenuated) withdrawal symptom, which is characterized by emotional lability; cognitive difficulties; and impairments in short-term memory, in sleep disturbances, and in the ability to abstract. This is the neurological correlative of the psycho-dynamic-interpersonal regression I spoke of above. The patient is doubly damned, so to speak, by emotional regression/fixation to a primitive level of development and by neurological deficit concomitant with the substance abuse itself. As they say in AA, "Nobody is here for hangnails." Patients struggling with so much require tremendous support, including open feeding (or feeding on demand), which is what telephone access is. So characterizing active addiction and early recovery in the way I have, I do not mean to imply that substance abusers lack strength or that many do not do splendidly in recovery—they do. But it takes time, sometimes a very long time. The prolonged withdrawal symptom commonly lasts upward of a year. The Twelve-Step slogan "It takes five years to get your marbles back and the rest of your life to use them" has it right. Here both clinical experience with substance abusers and empirical research support the folk wisdom of the Twelve-Step movement. The more we study recovery the longer it seems to take and by implication the longer telephone sessions, however short, are needed on a demand basis. I should note that the prolonged withdrawal syndrome is not the acute withdrawal syndrome that can be life threatening and should *always* be monitored under medical supervision.

Yet another reason telephone therapy is needed in early recovery is the fact that once the patient has been released from the utter slavery and compulsion of addiction that dictates his or her every move, the newfound freedom to make decisions engenders tremendous anxiety. All of a sudden many things become possible and the patient is in no shape to make decisions that may profoundly alter his or her life, whether in the area of work, personal relationships, or relationship to self. The patient is also incapacitated in making more subtle decisions requiring access to internal states. Søren Kierkegaard (1849) called the anxiety that goes with choice the "dizziness of freedom." This dizziness of freedom not only implies that decisions about basic personal and existential matters should be postponed. It also argues that the patient's anxiety about the suddenly bewildering range of options and choices is sobriety threatening and requires open contact with the therapist to help quell moments of panic, which are indeed sobriety threatening, and which arise in premature confrontation with unmanageable freedom. My clinical experience here is congruent with the Twelve-Step programs' advice to their members that they postpone decisions on these matters during the first year of recovery. The therapist's very simple intervention, "You don't have to decide that right now," during a telephone contact is often sobriety saving.

Another reason telephone access is necessary in substance abuse treatment is the simple, obvious, but often forgotten fact that drugs are dangerous. They are not only dangerous pharmacologically. Their use gets people into dangerous situations, their use is often associated with violence of many kinds, their use may lead to difficulties with the law, withdrawal can itself be dangerous, and suicide is highly correlated with substance abuse. Relapses are common and we treat active users and patients for whom abstinence is not a goal, so that imminent danger is intrinsic to substance abuse and its treatment. We cannot completely protect our patients from these dangers, nor can or should we try to live their lives for them, but we can be reachable when the patient is in danger and we can intervene appropriately, whether the intervention is advice, calling the police, talking the patient down, or interpreting the underlying dynamic of the current craziness in the patient's behavior and crisis in the patient's life. Once again, the telephone is the indispensable tool.

Substance abuse has been understood as a mistaken attempt at self-medication, a hypothesis elaborated with great subtlety and specificity by Edward Khantzian (1999). Substance abusers may be self-medicating anxiety, depression, attention deficit disorder, various personality disorders or, more rarely, psychosis, particularly paranoia. Although this self-medication may work for a while, over time it ineluctably exacerbates the very condition it is being used to treat and a vicious cycle is set up of medication of a condition caused by the medication. Nevertheless, when the self-medication is stopped, the underlying conditions is now neither medicated, anesthetized by the drug, nor masked by its use, and it may be a very serious condition. That leaves the newly and sometimes not so newly recovering patient struggling both to maintain sobriety and to live with what are sometimes major emotional disorders. To do that successfully requires all the help one can get, and the therapist's telephone accessibility, especially to help modulate anxiety, is absolutely necessary. Once again, the telephone session need not be long, but it must be timely.

There is a phenomenon known as *state dependent learning*, which also argues for the necessity of metaphorical, symbolic demand feeding via free access to the therapist on the phone. If you train a mouse to run a maze while it is high on some drug and then ask the mouse to run the same maze sober, the mouse can't do it. Give it cocaine or opium or alcohol or whatever drug it was on while learning the maze and lo and behold, Mickey or Minnie sails right through the maze. The learning is *state dependent*. I have argued elsewhere (Levin 1995, 1999) that something very similar happens to people, so that the recovering person has a great deal of re-learning to do. He or she literally doesn't know how to do it, whether "it" be having sex, giving a speech, or handling a feeling, while sober. The newly sober person is reborn not only in the spiritual sense, but in the sense of being a child, indeed an infant, relearning to negotiate the world within and the environment without. Although I exaggerate to make a point and state dependent learning is a partial rather than total phenomenon, it is clear that anxiety induced by the relearning process and the anxiety of not knowing how to handle the self and the world sober threaten that sobriety. Therefore, the therapist must be available to give the "infant" guidance. Of course, the therapist should not infantilize or do for the patient what the patient can do for him- or herself, but neither should the therapist underestimate or criticize the patient's real incapacity and need for concrete guidance in early sobriety.

Martin Seligman's (1989) well-known studies of learned helplessness also argue for the therapist's accessibility on the telephone when treating substance abusers. Seligman trained dogs to escape a noxious stimulus (a shock delivered by electrifying the floor on which they stood) by jumping over a barrier. Then he pulled a really dirty trick; he electrified the floor in the escape area. The dogs jumped back over the barrier where they were shocked yet again. After a few such trials the dogs gave up and just lay there whimpering. Seligman now turned off the current, and when he turned it on again, the dogs could escape. There was now no current on the other side of the barrier. All they had to do was jump. But they didn't. They just lay there and whimpered. Seligman called this *learned helplessness* and argued that it was a paradigm for at least one form of human depression. He then instructed his students to drag the dogs across the barrier to the safe unelectrified area of the floor. The learned helplessness turned out to be highly resistant to extinction and it took an average of ten trials of dragging the dogs over the barrier before they returned to spontaneous active escape behavior. Substance abusers have learned and overlearned that action is futile, whether that action be relinquishing the substances themselves, or trying to achieve while handicapped by their substance abuse. They have been shocking themselves on both sides of the barrier, so-to-speak, and they have learned passivity. This suggests that the substance abuse therapist needs to be highly active and directive, at least in the beginning. Many dogs have been dragged across the barrier on the telephone. The very act of calling the therapist breaks the learned helplessness quite independently of what the therapist says or does. Of course the content of the therapist's interventions (here a symbolic pulling over the barrier) has significance also. The phenomenon of the substance abusers' learned helplessness and need for the therapist's activity to counter it argues from yet another perspective that the therapist should be available on the phone in active and early recovery substance abuse treatment.

There is a strong correlation between substance abuse and suicide. In his seminal work *Suicide*, the great sociologist Emile Durkheim (1897) argued from an empirical-statistical as well as from a theoretical standpoint that suicide was strongly correlated with anomie and alienation. There are few populations that suffer more anomie and alienation than that of substance abusers. Additionally, substance abuse depresses pharmacologically and psychologically. Further, the lifestyle of substance abusers is itself highly depressing. These are people who are often already depressed and attempting to self-medicate that depression. This, too, reinforces the connection between suicide and substance abuse, and a considerable number of empirical studies in the century since Durkheim's work confirm the intimate association of suicide and substance abuse. The mental confusion induced by the drugs themselves increases the suicidal risk even more. Needless to say, the telephone is an important tool in reducing this risk.

There is another risk associated with the endgame of substance abuse that therapists have not often recognized. I speak here of the point where the patient comes to believe that he or she can no longer live drunk or stoned but cannot envision a life without drugs: "I can't live with it and I can't live without it." The danger here is very great and is not only inherent in the last stage of substance abuse, but is intrinsic to early sobriety, to recovery itself. It is very real, and here the telephone can literally be lifesaving. Don't forget that the user has been fleeing intolerable feelings in the only way he or she knows, namely by substance use, and that door has now been closed, so suicide readily becomes the only viable alternative. Why, you may ask, if the danger is so great, aren't these patients hospitalized? The unfortunate answer is that with the relentless pressure of managed care it is harder and harder to get patients who are in potential danger admitted. Therefore telephone therapy in early recovery is more salient, necessary and central to treatment than ever.

Finally, substance abuse is in itself traumatizing. It is traumatic to be out of control, it is traumatic to have the things happen to you that usually happen to substance abusers, it is traumatic to do the sort of violence to the self that substance abuse does, and there are at least a dozen other ways in which substance abuse traumatizes. The victims of trauma suffer anxiety, impulsive thinking, compulsive thinking, fixation on the trauma, rage, shame, guilt, and depression. Those traumatized by substance abuse suffer every one of these symptoms—this is in addition to the antecedent childhood and adult trauma the majority of substance abusers have experienced. The consequences of traumatization dovetail and resonate with the psychodynamic and neurological conflicts, deficits, regressions, and fixations already discussed to exacerbate the active and early recovery patient's susceptibility to intolerable pain and to relapse. This, too, argues for the maximal possible strength of the holding environment the therapist seeks to build for the patient and the telephone is an intrinsic and necessary part of that holding environment.

Having made a case for telephone therapy being a necessary evil (evil for the therapist and necessary for the patient) the form of such therapy becomes the issue. As I have said, I am temperamentally averse to ongoing full telephone sessions in spite of having conducted a few such therapies successfully, but I know that others are not. Nevertheless, I cannot recommend ongoing regular telephone therapy with substance abusers as the sole modality. I've never seen it work.

The telephone too readily lends itself to deception, game-playing, minimalization, and concealment in the service of denial of the substance abuse. My experience with patients, even those with some sobriety behind them, who have moved away and wish to continue their therapy on the phone is that it doesn't work. They need the reality and intensity of face-to-face sessions. Without the intimacy of being in the same room with the therapist, these patients all too readily return to acting out of one sort or another. Part of the problem may be the failure of evocative memory so even with the reinforcement of the disembodied voice the therapist soon fades and loses potency for the patient.

On the other hand, short (meaning five- to fifteen-minute) sessions on an as-needed basis or prearranged during periods of stress are not only highly therapeutic, indeed they can be and often are lifesaving. I don't charge for these short telephone sessions; most are less than five minutes, frequently consisting of a brief exchange of a few sentences each. That does not mean that full telephone sessions should not be scheduled when for whatever reason the patient and therapist cannot meet face to face and the need is there. The "extra session" on the telephone strengthens the therapeutic alliance and facilitates recovery. Of course in these instances, the patient should be charged for a full session. Now to those examples.

Henry was sober for several years when he came to see me. His problems seemed to have little to do with his alcoholism, which had been severe but was in stable remission. Rather, he was concerned with being intensely uncomfortable with his homosexuality. Growing up in a depressed alcoholic home that was treated as a shrine for his dead older brother by his parents, Henry had all sorts of difficulties with relationships, whether at work, or in the gay world, or in therapy. We had been working on his relationship problem both within the transference and outside of it for about six months, dealing, but little other than historically, with his alcoholism, which was nicely contained by his consistent albeit somewhat timid and tepid participation in AA, when he was sent to China on an extensive business trip. An important part of his business activities was to be social. As a museum curator trying to put together a traveling exhibit he would be expected to attend banquets in which drinking was de rigueur. Suddenly, his sobriety was threatened. How could he handle the banquets? We rehearsed and strategized together and made conscious the part of him that wished to drink and welcomed the banquets far from anyone he knew as situations in which "sipping a bit" could be easily rationalized. It soon became clear that valuable as this work was, it probably wasn't going to be enough to keep Henry sober on his trip. Being alone in China was too much an emotional recapitulation of being alone with his depressed parents and dead brother—the dominant "spirit" in his home—and drinking to quell the fury, sadness, shame, and guilt that had welled up in the adolescent boy struggling with an unwelcome sexuality and all the rest of the feelings he could neither repress nor accept. I suggested phone sessions.

Henry was reluctant. He didn't want to admit how much he needed me. I interpreted, trying to preserve his fragile self-esteem and less fragile, but nevertheless jeopardized, sobriety, that being alone for so long in such difficult circumstances was simply too much. I went on to comment that it was not a pejorative commentary on his capacity for self-regulation to reinforce it with phone sessions with me. After much resistance, Henry agreed to prescheduled and as-needed telephone sessions. In the two months he was in China we had six prearranged half-hour sessions and several short ad hoc ones. As it turned out, we talked but little about drinking. Henry's having decided in his own mind that he would return rather than drink made a real difference. What we spoke of was separation, aloneness, and the emotional abandonment by his parents after the brother's death by drowning. I asked, "Was it an accident that you almost drowned yourself in drink?" Henry's hitherto unconscious yearning for a connection to a father, and the ways in which alcohol was a pseudo-meeting of this need became another theme of our phone sessions. For the shy, rather withdrawn young man it proved easier to talk about these things over 5,000 miles than face to face, but once the ice was broken the therapy heated up and became more emotionally intense when we returned to our face-to-face sessions. The telephone had facilitated the strengthening of the fragile therapeutic alliance and made possible more in-depth work. It also kindled feelings of gratitude in Henry, since I had gone out of my way to insist on the protective structure of the telephone work. Henry felt loved without feeling so threatened by the sexualization of his yearning for a father that he needed to flee into an emotionally shallow relationship with me, or more direly into drinking. Although Henry felt that his sobriety was never threatened in China, I am convinced that the telephone accessibility contributed importantly to his relative ease in not drinking and that it indeed may have made his maintenance of sobriety possible. Whatever my feelings about the telephone, this work proved gratifying.

The Smiths, on the other hand, were the kind of couple whose telephone calls I dreaded. Theirs was a necessary evil, open access, unscheduled phone relationship. Larry was an alcoholic, marijuana-using manic-depressive with severe personality pathology. Drinking or high on pot he was impossible, whether as a husband or a patient. Before he achieved stable sobriety he was frequently in and out of the V.A. hospital. I was seeing him on contract for the V.A. in those days. For whatever reason, I was able to talk him down from incipient manic episodes if he hadn't gone too far and was not high on alcohol or grass. Not infrequently, that talking down was on the phone.

After his last decompensation his wife managed to get him admitted to a private psychiatric hospital with a substance abuse rehabilitation unit. After he was stabilized on the "flight deck" (AA slang for the closed ward), he was transferred for a month's stay in the substance abuse rehabilitation unit. Having had many seeds planted during his years of therapy with me, Larry got the message. He never drank or smoked pot again. However, he was always on the verge of doing so and sometimes used to threaten a relapse when he and Sally, his third wife, would fight. And fight they did. Sally was fragile, suffering extraordinarily low self-esteem and vulnerability to depression. She was prone to see offense where there was none and Larry provided too much reality-based offense. Sally was hard to diagnose, but if I had to I would come up with a dysthymia, not infrequently associated with exacerbation into major depression, in a borderline personality with paranoid tendencies. All in all, not a marriage made in heaven. Yet these two gravely damaged people loved each other and when they weren't attacking each other they could be mutually helpful. Neither could have survived without the other. All in all a symbiosis that worked—sort of.

With Larry sober, things weren't too bad until Sally had a baby. Larry had a grown son from his first marriage and a stormy relationship with his stepdaughter from his second marriage. Although they both sincerely wanted to be good parents their resources were just too limited and the stress of having the baby set off wild screaming matches usually ending with Sally sobbing and threatening suicide and with Larry threatening to leave or to get drunk, usually followed by his being crushed by remorse. Then would come the telephone call. First Sally would pour out her despair, begging me to stop Larry from controlling and demeaning her; then Larry would chime in with less than helpful complaints about Sally's inadequacies, which were not entirely of his imagining, forcing him to "take over." Meanwhile the baby could be heard screaming as Sally taking the phone again would sob, "I just can't stand it—I can't stand the baby crying and Larry screaming." I never had the slightest idea of what to say so I would sit there, holding the receiver, feeling stupid, inadequate, frustrated, and annoyed. After ten to fifteen minutes of this seeming futility they would calm down, and I would say something to this effect, "I'm glad you called out for help. You seem to be feeling calmer now so I'll see you next week as scheduled," as I hung up with relief. Not entirely honest, but the best I could come up with. The Smiths were always grateful. Just being there to listen, to pacify, and to defuse helped. Nobody drank or drugged, nobody attempted suicide, nobody decompensated, and there was no violence. No matter how much I dreaded their calls there is no question that the calls helped them. I can't tell you that the Smiths improved much even with the more interpretive work I did in what were now couple sessions, but the combination of face-to-face and telephone therapy got them through—and through sober. That would not have been possible without the phone sessions.

Martin exemplifies another kind of telephone intervention. He was a multiple drug user, but his drug of choice was alcohol. A rather schizoid, strongly narcissistic middle-aged man whose family of origin had nicknamed him the "Baron," he used a façade of arrogance, condescension, devaluation, and contempt for others to barely paper over an extremely fragile sense of self and an even more fragile self-esteem. An artist whose successes were intermittent and far apart, he was rageful, perpetually hurting, and chronically frustrated. In spite of these many personality problems, his developmental arrest, and primitive defenses, he managed to become stably sober as an AA member about a year before he came for therapy. He had also managed to marry a wealthy businesswoman, whom he simultaneously admired, envied, loved and hated. She saw him as the archetypal romantic hero-artist whom she had saved from a life in the garret—or the gutter. I had no idea of how good his work might have been. He didn't really work at it during the period I knew him, but she believed in it, expecting Martin to be discovered "any day now." His wife's belief in him no doubt raised unfulfillable expectations in him, which, however gratifying his wife's support of his at best intermittent artistic efforts might have been, also set him up for crushing feelings of failure and inadequacy.

Seemingly fixated at the anal stage, Martin used language that was obsessively anal "Blow it out your ass," "My brother (a successful corporate type Martin envied and hated) doesn't know which hand to wipe himself with," and pretty much everyone in his AA group was an "asshole." Although he went to meetings on a regular basis, Martin's contempt for AA and its members knew no bounds. Those who weren't assholes were "shits" and the whole thing smelled like a sewer. I wouldn't have bet much on his continuing sobriety.

I did what I could to shore up Martin's fragile self-esteem without encouraging unrealistic expectations, in the hope that feeling better about himself he might grow less contemptuous of others. Although there was no real therapeutic alliance, he found my encouraging his artistic activities and expressing admiration (which was sincere) for his accomplishment and courage in achieving and sustaining sobriety in spite of painful feelings gratifying, so he kept coming for treatment. I figured that as long as Martin stayed in treatment there was hope. I began to gingerly confront and interpret, suggesting that much pain and massive depression must underlie his contempt and devaluation. I kept it in the here and now, staying away from the genetic sources of his "baroncy." Even so, he couldn't tolerate much of this and I dosed my confrontations very carefully. I believed that maintaining Martin's sobriety was quite ambitious enough a goal for the moment and Martin did stay sober.

Martin (or more accurately his wife) had a country home, which they visited weekends. Martin complained incessantly about the trip, the bugs, the landscaper who didn't show up, and his wife's wealthy, sometimes distinguished friends. Thanksgiving weekend they planned a big party and Martin, who took inordinate pride in his gourmet cooking, was preparing a feast. Of course there would be wine and cocktails before dinner. I sensed danger and tried to alert him, but to no avail. He was on one of his highly emotionally invested quests for admiration of his cooking skills.

Not readily able to ask for help, Martin had never availed himself of access to me on the telephone, so phone therapy had played no role in our relationship. Late the Saturday night of Thanksgiving weekend my phone rang. It was Martin crying out and screaming in acute physical pain. As was almost predictable, he had dismissed my suggestion that the party was a danger to his sobriety and had, as he later put it, "found" himself sipping the wine he was using to cook with, the very first night he was in the country. He rationalized, "Oh, it's only cooking wine it doesn't matter." He continued to drink and things went precipitously downhill. At the party Friday night he was roaring, falling-down drunk. The party was a disaster. His wife left him there drinking and went back to the city in the morning. Martin had been drinking ever since.

As he described the excruciating abdominal pain, projectile vomiting, and the inability to straighten up he was experiencing, I guessed that Martin was having an attack of alcoholic pancreatitis, a potentially fatal complication of alcoholism. As it turned out my surmise was correct. But the relevant thing here was that he called me. Even if I was a therapist without knowledge of the medical complications of alcoholism, I would have known that this was a medical emergency and could have acted accordingly. My previously scorned invitation to call me if he needed help saved Martin's life. Because he was too drunk and too sick to help himself, I arranged for suitable medical intervention. Martin never forgave me for his having needed me and for my having "seen" him in such a condition, so therapy was at an end, an end I wasn't altogether sorry to see. But Martin was alive and had another chance to recover, a chance perhaps enhanced by his brush with death from his alcoholism. It is interesting that Martin had no previous history of somatic complications and that it had taken only a few days of drinking to bring him to death's door. His body had apparently lost its tolerance for alcohol and his drinking days would be few. For him it was probably recovery or death. This sudden decompensation—somatic, psychological, or psychotic—is not uncommon in substance abuse and is yet another reason for keeping the phone line open.

Sandy was the borderline substance abuser from hell. Twenty-three and going on two she wasn't the sort of case you hear about in analytic school: crisis-ridden, unreliable, dishonest in therapy and in life, manipulative, desperate and very, very sad. It was hard to know what to do with and for Sandy. Mostly I didn't know, and stumbled from crisis to crisis keeping her afloat, more or less. The two best interventions I made in the year we worked together were: "If you treat other people the way you treat me, it's no wonder people drop you," which she managed to hear and take in although it had only a brief effect on her behavior, and "You're convinced that your problem is the pain other people inflict on you, but you don't have a chance of feeling better unless you stop inflicting the sort of pain you do on other people." Sandy heard the second of these interventions and was successful in curbing her aggressive acting out for a period. My interventions sound angry, even retaliatory, but they weren't; they were actually empathic. Sandy did better with confrontation than with more overtly supportive interventions. When her substance abuse, which was multiple, but mostly prescription drugs—Valium and other benzodiazepines—and alcohol weren't out of control, she was manageable. She had literary ambitions and had written some pretty decent poetry. Although it would be less than truthful to say I enjoyed her, I did like her. The telephone played a major role in our relationship from the beginning. Most of our telephone sessions were in the nature of crisis intervention, but occasionally there were calmer, longer, more interpretive ones that anchored Sandy and perhaps even produced some insight.

Sandy was madly, and I use the word advisedly, in love with a middle-aged alcoholic who was more or less continuously trying to end the relationship, except when he was lonely or horny. Although he sent mixed messages, my sense was that he genuinely wanted to end it. Sandy was just too crazy. Several times, when he had insisted she leave his home, she had become violent and more than once the police were involved. On one occasion, Sandy deliberately ran her car into a tree, cutting her head and face so that there would be a reason he would have to keep her around. She had told him another driver had forced her off the road. Who knows what the truth was, but her head and face were some mess. She was a case of what Karen Horney (1945) called "morbid dependency."

Sandy insisted that she simply couldn't live without Daryl. I interpreted the hostile, controlling aspect of her behavior, the temper tantrums over not getting her own way, and the regressive symbiotic need behind her actions phrased as, "You hope to get from Daryl what you never got from your mother," and conveyed a dozen other confrontational, genetic, and transferential observations to her. All to no avail except for short periods of remission of her acting out which coincided with her relative abstinence from substances. Unfortunately, Sandy's "love addiction" didn't improve. Finally, with the assistance of the police, Daryl forcefully removed her and made it clear that she was not to return. He was finally unequivocally finished with her.

That was when I got the call about the gun. Sandy called to tell me she had a gun and she was going to kill herself. I didn't know where she was, so I wasn't able to call the police. I believed her, although I knew she must have had some ambivalence about dying or she wouldn't have called. I had always used black humor with Sandy, it was a language she understood. So I said, "Sandy, my office is rather drab. It needs a splash of color, so would you mind shooting yourself in my office so I can get some red on my gray carpet?" Amazingly, she agreed. I paced during the half hour she took to get to the office, but then she was there, gun and all. I told her she wasn't in her right mind and it was her depression, her disease that was telling her to kill herself. I insisted she go to the hospital. By then she had put the gun away, but she adamantly refused to go to the hospital. I told her that I would call 911 if she didn't go voluntarily. Sandy countered with, "Call Daryl. If he goes with me, I'll go to the hospital." The telephone again! I called Daryl ,who knew who I was, and explained why we needed him. I played on his guilt, hoping that he was not too strongly psychopathic. It worked, and within an hour Sandy was happily ensconced in Daryl's car with me following on the way to the hospital to meet my psychiatrist colleague-friend who had privileges there. The telephone again was the means of making arrangements. After some struggling with the threat of involuntary commitment Sandy signed herself in. She didn't want to die. She wanted what she wanted—Daryl—but she might very well have died if she hadn't called and reached me. Yes, the telephone is a necessary evil in substance abuse treatment.

Psychodynamic Treatment of Addiction

Psychoanalysis and addiction have been intertwined since the beginning. Freud was seriously involved with cocaine and addicted to nicotine. The *Ur*-patient of psychoanalysis, Anna O., was addicted to choral hydrate and other drugs; Freud's disciple and biographer, Ernest Jones's common-law wife, Leo Kahn, was addicted to morphine; the Wolfman's second analyst, Ruth Mack Brunswick died of complications of her alcoholism, and so it goes. Much like the rest of the world psychoanalysis, in common with psychiatry and medicine in general, has dealt with alcoholism and drug addiction within its ranks by denial, minimalization, rationalization, and not uncommonly by enabling.

In spite of this blindness, which rendered whole herds of elephants in the consulting room invisible, psychoanalysis and psychodynamic psychotherapy have made magnificent contributions to our understanding of addiction. Addiction is too much of a core human dilemma and too central to much psychopathology for it to have been ignored by dynamic thinkers. And it has not been. Every major theorist, from Freud on down, has dealt with addiction in one way or another. Their writings are not only theoretical; they have clinical implications and utility, in some cases made explicit by the theorists, and sometimes implicit in their work. It is important to note that psychodynamic theories of addiction are not necessarily etiological, although some are. Rather, they are dynamic, meaning that they give an account of the addict's inner world—his or her conflicts and deficits. They are descriptive of the intrapsychic and the interpersonal, of the conscious and the unconscious, aspects of the addict's subjective experience. As such, they facilitate therapists' making contact and empathetically connecting with patients whose behavior, affect, and cognition often seem bizarre. It is this enabling of insight into the other's, the patient's, inner world that makes these theories so practical, so therapeutically useful, quite apart from their particular contents. No one dynamic perfectly accounts for the addiction of a given patient, and every patient partakes to some extent of every dynamic elucidated by our theorists.

There are many dynamic theories of addiction, some of which derive from drive theory, some from ego psychology, some from object relations theory, and some from self psychology. One of the earliest formulators of a dynamic theory of addiction is Thomas Trotter. In his early nineteenth century work, Trotter (Jellinek 1943) stated that addiction, in this case to alcohol, is the result of premature weaning and heredity. It was not a bad guess he made, that the causes of addiction lie in early trauma and in constitutional predisposition. Other theorists who have written importantly about the dynamics of addiction include Freud, Karl Abraham, Edward Glover, Karl Menninger, Thomas Szasz, Sandor Rado, Henry Tiebout, Henry Krystal and Herbert Raskin, Leon Wurmser, Peter Hartocollis, Edward Khantzian, Robert Knight, Ernst Simmel, Otto Fenichel, and Heinz Kohut.

SIGMUND FREUD

In *Civilization and its Discontents*, Freud (1930) stated:

> The service rendered by intoxicating media in the struggle for happiness and in keeping misery at a distance is so highly prized as a benefit that individuals and peoples alike have given it an established place in the economics of their libido. We owe to such media not merely the

immediate yield to pleasure, but also a greatly desired degree of independence from the external world. For one knows that, with the help of this "drowner of cares" one can at any time withdraw from the pressure of reality and find refuge in a world of one's own with better conditions of sensibility. [p. 78]

Freud, the cocaine devotee and nicotine addict, was most certainly not oblivious to the pleasures of substance use.

In a letter to Wilhelm Fliess, Freud (1897) states that all later addictions are displacements of and reenactments of the original addiction to masturbation. This may seem far afield from everyday work with substance abusers; however, it is a dynamic that highlights the dead-end nature of addiction, its compulsive repetition, the guilt and shame that accompany the failure to follow through on the resolve, originally not to masturbate, later not to use, a failure that is driven by withdrawal into a world of fantasy and narcissistic pleasure. Just as one's love object in masturbation is one's self, or one's fantasy of another, but not an actual other, one's love object in addiction is the substance experienced as an extension of self. In his essay on the great Russian writer, *Dostoyevsky and Parricide*, Freud (1928) analyzes Dostoyevsky's compulsive gambling and plays upon the word *play*, saying Dostoyevsky's gambling addiction is a displacement and reenactment of his addiction to and inward conflict about masturbation. But Freud complicates the picture by condensing masturbatory guilt with oedipal guilt and with guilt for the addictive activity itself. He points out that Dostoyevsky's violent alcoholic father was murdered by his peasants, enacting Dostoyevsky's unconscious wish to kill that father, and that the enactment in reality of the fantasy, inculcated guilt—overwhelming guilt—in Dostoyevsky. This analysis allows Freud to focus on the payoff in Dostoyevsky's compulsive gambling, namely losing. The pleasure is in the pain. Addictions offer one a rare opportunity to express aggression and be punished for it simultaneously. This is an extraordinarily powerful hook.

In *Beyond the Pleasure Principle*, Freud (1920) speaks of the repetition compulsion as a manifestation of the death instinct. He uses addiction as one of his examples of the repetition compulsion. The centrality of guilt and the use of substance abuse for self-punishment is highly salient, and its interpretation is often mutative in treating substance abusers. Additionally, many addicts describe themselves as "doing nothing but jerking off." The masturbatory nature of addiction is often recognized by patients and can sometimes be usefully interpreted. Of course, if one were dealing with a 250–lb. truck driver who is an angry man, it is probably unwise to interpret, "When you drank, all you did was whack off," even though it may be dynamically true.

Whenever I ponder whether or not to interpret an addiction to a substance as a displacement of an addiction to masturbation, I think of the probably apocryphal story of Ms. Henderson who sat in the front row of Bruno Bettelheim's lecture hall at the University of Chicago, ostentatiously knitting as the august professor held the rest of the auditorium spellbound. Week after week the universally feared Dr. Bettelheim would glower at Ms. Henderson, but to no avail. Finally, he could take it no more and halted his presentation to address the offender. Speaking in his coldest and most contemptuous manner, the professor said, "Ms. Henderson, do you know that knitting is symbolic masturbation?" The hall was enveloped in a silence you could cut with a knife until Ms. Henderson, totally unruffled, replied, "Professor Bettelheim, when I knit, I knit; and when I masturbate, I masturbate." Some addicts use when they use and masturbate when they masturbate, but then some don't.

KARL ABRAHAM

Abraham (1908) wrote one of his first psychoanalytic papers on addiction, his topic being the relationship between sexuality and alcoholism. Abraham teaches us two very useful things. First, he amalgamated and bridged the sociological and the psychological. His analysis of alcoholism is in terms of male drinking in the beer *stubba*, the taverns of Berlin, around the beginning of the twentieth century. His awareness of the social dimensions of that behavior very much informs his paper, just as we need to inform our understanding of our addictive and substance abusing patients by understanding their cultural setting. Second, Abraham emphasized the use of alcohol, and by extension, any drug, to express forbidden wishes—explicitly, forbidden homosexual wishes. He pointed to a more or less open expression of homoeroticism in the bleary-eyed camaraderie of the beer *stubba*, and this in a highly homophobic society. Only with the consumption of alcohol were these men capable of putting their arms around each other, sometimes kissing each other, and expressing love toward each other. Abraham points out the psychosexual regression that accompanies drunkenness, as the component instincts (see Freud 1905a) come to be expressed directly. Abraham here is thinking primarily of sadistic enactments, but also of masochistic ones, as well as of the expression of ego-dystonic homosexuality. He also highlights delusions of jealousy in the alcoholic. As the alcoholic's potency diminishes as a consequence of his drinking, he now accuses his wife of being with other men. This too is a defense against homosexual wishes—"It is she, a woman, and not I, a man, who desires another man."

The first decade of the new millennium is another time and place. Nevertheless, we encounter many patients who drink in order to express forbidden sexual desires—sadistic, masochistic, homosexual, what have you. They then discount them. I have treated many men who have had homosexual experiences while drunk who disclaim that experience totally. It had nothing to do with them, it was just the booze. The same is true for other drugs. Cocaine, in particular, enables or induces sadomasochistic fantasy and enactments. The therapist needs to interpret the unconscious wish that finds expression in the state of being high and help the patient own the wish, or fantasy, or drive.

EDWARD GLOVER

Glover, an English analyst chiefly known for his notion of ego nuclei, self precursors that coalesce into an ego, also highlighted a central dynamic in substance abuse, namely, drinking or drugging in order to express rage at someone. Glover (1928) speaks of oral and anal sadism as the central dynamic in addiction. I prefer to talk of the "fuck you martini." Most slips, that is, relapses, are driven by unconscious and sometimes conscious rage. They are angry acts, eating or drinking or smoking or drugging or sexing against somebody. That somebody may be an external object or an internal object and the therapist needs to be alert for the possibility that the rage directed at the external object is transferential and really belongs to one or more internal objects. The patient's rage, usually over some narcissistic injury, must be interpreted. That rage often comes from narcissistic vulnerability, from feelings of worthlessness, from low self-esteem, or from an inability to deal with the slings and arrows of outrageous fortune. In that state of narcissistic vulnerability, the injury, real or imagined, is often, by any reasonable objective standard, slight indeed. But in the addict's mind, it is an overwhelming offense to "His or Her Majesty, the Baby" (Freud 1914a), and elicits narcissistic rage. "Off with their heads" is the sentiment behind the "fuck you martini."

KARL MENNINGER

Menninger (1938), one of the few American analysts to subscribe to Freud's (1920) notion of the death instinct, wrote a book, *Man Against Himself*, depicting many forms of self-destruction. Both alcoholism and drug addiction receive prominent treatment in that text. More than almost any other dynamic thinker, Menninger emphasizes the self-punitive and self-destructive dynamic of addictive behavior. He calls addiction "chronic suicide." This is also known as suicide on the installment plan. Drug addiction is highly correlated with suicide, as is alcoholism, and such suicide may indeed be acute rather than chronic. There is a debate in the literature about the meaning of addictive self-destructive behavior. Some thinkers, such as Edward Khantzian (1981), believe that the self-destructive behavior is a by-product of the addict's use of the substance for adaptive purposes. The behaviorally oriented researchers believe that addiction is biphasic in the sense that it initially provides pleasure, and only much later in the addictive process does it have serious negative consequences. Therefore, it is perfectly rational for users to continue doing something (drugging or drinking) that provides them with positive reinforcement. If users are addictively inclined, they continue to seek that positive reinforcement (euphoria and/or anxiety reduction) until they are hooked, that is, addicted. Only later do the negative consequences come, and by then they cannot escape them because they are now addicted. So, from both an ego psychological and a behavioral point of view, the self-destruction of the addict, which is certainly real enough, is not dynamically motivated.

Menninger believes the opposite. I believe the two positions are not incompatible. As we know, contrarieties do not trouble primary process thinking. Thus, one may be using a drug in an adaptive fashion to meet some ego need one cannot meet on one's own, and one may be destroying one's self, in terms of health, financial well-being, relationships, and relationship with self simply because one is hooked and doesn't know how to escape, *and* one may be motivated by the dynamic unconscious to destroy one's self—all at the same time. It is vital that the therapist be alert to each of these possibilities and to discuss and interpret them all.

> Randy "slipped" repeatedly, and I suggested that her slips were motivated, or at least rationalized, by claims to special privilege—"a princess has the right to go on a bender"—a hypothesis for which there was much evidence, although she denied it. When I went on to suggest that her slips were acts of aggression ("fuck you martinis") against me and sundry others, she also denied it, offering the countersuggestion that she drank when she simply couldn't find another way to cope (drinking to remediate or self-medicate self and ego deficits). I agreed with her and told her so (although I continued to believe that her slips were "overdetermined" and that the dynamics I had suggested were also operative). After acknowledging the adaptive function of the slips, I suggested that they had yet another purpose—self-punishment and self-destruction. She ran with that ball as my interpretation resonated. Our mutually constructed understanding of the complex dynamics of Randy's slips proved highly mutative and those slips became progressively less frequent.

SANDOR RADO

In a prescient paper of 1933, Rado captured in a highly poetic way the tragic trap of addiction—the viciousness of the addictive cycle. He spoke of a state of tense depression, a sort of agitated depression that is felt to be intolerable, and its concomitant feelings of worthlessness or, at best, of very low self-esteem. The drug is then taken for its euphoric properties. It is an elatant. The user rises from tense depression to manic joy. In that manic joy, the constraints of reality are obliterated. So far, so good. Who would not want to be in such a state of elation? Unfortunately, it cannot be sustained and there is the crash, returning the developing addict to an even tenser and deeper depression. The claims of reality come back in spades, necessitating another round of drug use. But the drug is less effective this time, and the manic or euphoric state is more tenuous, briefer, and less effective, necessitating yet more use of the drug, ad infinitum, until there is almost no euphoria and almost continuous bleak and black depression. In his elucidation of this cycle, Rado noted the close similarity between drug addiction and manic-depression. And, indeed, there is a far greater than random correlation between manic-depression and addiction, particularly alcoholism. But even if the patient is not technically manic-depressive, his addiction is a manic-depressive process.

Further, Rado underlines the centrality of self-esteem in the entire process. What the drug does is to raise self-esteem. That is the single most salient quality it has, and is the primary reason the user uses. The therapist will never go wrong in centering on self-esteem; there is almost nothing I would say without qualification about drug addiction with this exception. There are no addicts who do not have absolutely abysmal self-esteem, however defended against by bluster and bravado. It is vital that the therapist interpret this: "You think so little of yourself that you have to have, or at least believe you have to have, cocaine in order to feel better about yourself." "When you drink you feel you are on top of the world." "The only time you really like yourself is when you're smoking pot." Correlative to pointing out or interpreting the function of the drug in raising self-esteem, the therapist also needs to help the patient experience his or her abysmally low self-esteem, indeed, self-loathing. Karl Menninger, concentrating more on aggression, particularly aggression against the father and self-punishment for it, stated that the first step in recovery was for the alcoholic to realize he was "a real bastard." Interesting choice of words by Menninger, but that's not very relevant here. Somewhat similarly, focusing now not on the angry acted-out aggression but on the self-loathing, patients need to be able to feel how really bad they feel about themselves in order to begin to move toward a more realistically based self-esteem. Therefore, the therapist needs to say things like, "You really feel like shit, and therefore you have to make all sorts of claims of greatness so you won't know that you are shit."

ROBERT KNIGHT

Knight was one of the first analytically trained psychiatrists to work with alcoholics. He was also one of the first to describe the borderline syndrome. It is no accident that Knight's interests were in both borderline and addictive problems. There is, indeed, a substantial overlap between borderline and addictive populations. However, it is important to note the nature of that correlation, namely that it is not the case that all substance abusers are borderlines, but it is the case that the vast majority of borderlines develop substance abuse, if not dependence. Working in a closed setting at the Menninger clinic in the 1930s, Knight treated many male alcoholics. Knight (1937, 1938) commented on their dynamics, and realized that they were roughly distinguishable into two different types. The dynamic that Knight saw was self-punishment for forbidden aggression against the father. That aggression took place on both the level of fantasy and the level of reality. In the latter it was acted out in terms of living a lifestyle that embarrassed the father, necessitated rescue, and generally made the father's life miserable. This aggression against the father added a layer of guilt to the son's already guilt-ridden psyche, although there was also satisfaction in that aggressivity. This new level of guilt echoed earlier oedipal guilt, building layer upon layer of guilt until the burden was intolerable. The answer, of course, was to continue to drink. Guilt can be anesthetized with alcohol. And this drinking to deaden the guilt of previous aggression is only yet another aggression, but it is not only that—it also leads to failure, humiliation, shame, and often poverty. The male drinker hurts not only the father but himself. Knight is not too far from his boss Karl Menninger's notion that alcoholism and other addictions are forms of chronic suicide as punishment for forbidden death wishes toward the father.

Life doesn't offer many deals this good. Where else but in addiction can you express your forbidden murderous wishes and be simultaneously punished for that expression? This dynamic is an extraordinarily powerful hook that keeps some people drinking/drugging to death. This dynamic is interpretable and that interpretation is often heard and acted on, that action being movement toward sobriety.

In his study of his patients' families, Knight noticed that the fathers were very erratic, as well as erratically punitive, and that the mothers tended to be passive, subordinate, and ineffectual. Although we work in a different time and place, this is a family constellation we still see very commonly in the families of male addicts.

Knight also noticed that in spite of the fact that all of his patients had very serious alcohol problems necessitating hospitalization, they were not the same. In fact, his population seemed to be bimodal. Elucidating this bimodality, Knight distinguished between what he called *essential alcoholics* and *reactive alcoholics*. Essential alcoholics were those who had been in trouble with booze from their first drink, who had very spotty educational and vocational histories, and whose interpersonal relationships were stormy, distant, symbiotic, or otherwise highly disturbed. In short, they never really matured into anything approximating healthy adulthood. The reactives, on the other hand, often had substantial, even spectacular, academic and career success. They had, for the most part, succeeded in marrying and establishing families, and, at least until their addictions had progressed, had behaved in more or less caring and responsible ways; that is, they appeared to have been capable of love, even if they were no longer so. They were simply a different population than the essentials. Knight called this syndrome reactive because he believed that this type of alcoholism was a reaction to some major narcissistic wound. Although this was probably true in some cases, it is more likely that Knight was describing patients who had been functional alcoholics until their disease progressed and they had deteriorated to the point where admission to the Menninger Clinic was necessary.

Almost all workers in the field have made similar distinctions, both for alcoholics and for other substance abusers. The way this is sometimes put is that some patients require habilitation and others rehabilitation. Clinically, the two groups feel very different. The essentials require a very long period of time to make even minimal gains, while the reactives, if they stop drinking, often turn their lives around rather spectacularly and rapidly, which is not to say that many emotional and psychological problems do not remain.

Another way of looking at Knight's differential is that the essential alcoholics are probably borderline, while the reactive alcoholics are probably narcissistic. Borderlines and narcissists do indeed make up much of the addicted population. In general, borderlines have a terrible problem functioning in any area of life, while narcissists often do quite well in school and work, but run into trouble in their interpersonal lives. Knight really doesn't present us with much data about the marital and parental relationships of his reactive alcoholics, but one suspects that even though they seem like upright, responsible citizens, when compared to the essentials, they probably had highly troubled relationships with both their families of origin and families of procreation.

Knight's treatment recommendations are also of interest. For the essentials, he believed that abstinence was the only possible cure, and that the best psychological treatment was an expressive, supportive therapy with many didactic and educational components, more or less what a modern substance abuse counselor does.

Knight's essentials may have been people who had a constitutional predisposition to alcoholism, and it may be the case that part of their difficulties around drinking resulted from biological vulnerability. This would support Knight's intuitive feeling that abstinence was their only hope.

The reactives, according to Knight, had once drunk normally, and he thought that if it was important to them perhaps they could drink normally again. His treatment for reactives was psychoanalysis. Believing that their core problem was intrapsychic conflict between id and superego, analysis made perfect sense as a treatment modality. But Knight was hardly a fool, and he had these patients under lock and key for a long period of time, often up to, or in excess of, a year, during which the analysis was going on. They did not have an opportunity to drink during that time. From our perspective, the practicality of a return to controlled drinking by this population is questionable. There are, of course, some reactives who, with insight, can drink without getting into difficulties, but the therapist must be cautious in negotiating treatment goals and not give the patient unrealistic hope that he or she can become a social drinker with impunity. For most, this is not possible, although for a few it is.

OTTO FENICHEL

Fenichel (1945) is credited with the observation, "The superego is that part of the mind which is soluble in alcohol" (p. 379). In the sections on alcoholism and drug addiction in his classic text, *The Psychoanalytic Theory of Neurosis*, Fenichel points to the use of drugs to resolve irreconcilable id-ego conflicts. He also discusses at length and was the first to highlight the narcissistic regression in alcoholism and drug addiction. By narcissistic regression, Fenichel means the relinquishing of the object world (reality) for an inner world of fantasy. Drugs enable this living in fantasy. Typically these fantasies are about omnipotence and grandiosity. In exchange for the world, the addict becomes the ruler—His or Her Majesty—of an empty world, empty self, and empty bottle. Fenichel also recognized that narcissistic fixation, a developmental arrest which would now be called pathological narcissism, powerfully predisposes to addiction.

THOMAS SZASZ

Szasz (1958) wrote a fascinating paper on the counterphobic mechanism in addiction in which he postulates that a great deal of addiction is driven by a desire to master overwhelming fears. The addict is essentially making the statement "I am indestructible. I can engage in the most dangerous self-destructive acts and emerge unscathed." This feeds into and strengthens denial. There is a kind of grandiosity in that position that can be very resistant to therapeutic intervention. It is perhaps heroic to defy the gods once, but to do it on a daily basis is madness, and that is exactly what the addict does. I would elaborate on Szasz's notion of a counterphobic mechanism and postulate that many addictions are enactments of a drama of death and resurrection. The substance abuser, at least in his more advanced state, ingests the drug until he or she collapses and goes into a state of oblivion. This is certainly an enactment of death, a kind of little suicide. In a way, the addict's little suicide is similar to Dostoyevsky's epileptic fits, which were also a little death, as interpreted by Freud (1928), as a punishment for his murderous wishes toward his father.

The most powerful part of this drama lies in the fact that the addict, at least most of the time, comes out of the stupor and is resurrected, proving that he or she is immortal. It is an extremely powerful dynamic. The addict who is tormented by fear of death enacts death counterphobically, and miraculously is resurrected from the underworld. This drama not only reinforces the addiction but affirms the addict's grandiosity. After all, one who can die and be reborn is indeed a powerful and wonderful being. The therapist can interpret this drama and say to the addict, "Like all of us, but perhaps more so, you are absolutely terrified of death. Yet, when you drink yourself into unconsciousness, you in effect kill yourself, choose death, enact death, render yourself unconscious and insensate. So, in drinking, you go into the very fear that is most powerfully in you. Yet, you wake up in the morning, however hung over, and you've survived, and that's enormously reassuring to you. It also affirms how powerful you are. But you don't really feel powerful; on the contrary, you feel profoundly powerless and need this reassurance. Ironically, your very

attempt to master your fear of death is killing you. Given your cir-
rhotic liver, you know and I know that you can't live much longer if
you continue to drink the way you do."

HARRY TIEBOUT

Tiebout was the psychiatrist of the founder of AA, Bill Wilson. Wilson was a lifelong depressive, perhaps what we would now call a dual-
diagnosis patient who went to Tiebout for treatment of his depression long after he was a world-famous figure. The two men taught
each other a great deal. From Tiebout, Wilson heard the phrase, "His
or Her Majesty, the Baby," from Freud's 1914 essay, "On Narcissism."
He incorporated it into the AA literature, which sees pathological
narcissism as the central dynamic of addiction. Tiebout, in turn,
learned a great deal from Bill Wilson about the "surrender" experience, the experience in which the addict throws in the towel and
admits he or she is powerless to control that addiction and reaches
out for help. This is also known as hitting bottom.

Tiebout (1949, 1957), in his papers on surrender, emphasized the
grandiosity in addiction, the saliency of "His or Her Majesty, the
Baby." Tiebout called for "ego deflation in depth." He was using ego
not in the sense of the executive part of the mind, as it is used in
Freud's structural model, but in the everyday sense in which one says,
"He has a big ego." Tiebout's emphasis on ego deflation has an un-
pleasant, moralistic, even sadistic, tone to it, a kind of crush-'em-and-
rub-their-noses-in-it flavor, which I find offensive; nevertheless, he
has something important to say. Reactive grandiosity, as a defense
against underlying feelings of worthlessness, is an extremely potent
dynamic in addiction, and must be dealt with in one way or another.
In deflating this grandiose ego, one can simply inflict more narcissistic wounds and do more harm than good. Yet, the therapist must
confront that grandiosity, at least during the phase of active addiction, because that grandiosity will keep the substance use going forever, making it impossible to work through the grandiosity in a more
accepting and neutral way. So, something like Tiebout's ego defla-

tion is often a vital part of substance abuse treatment. Fortunately, that deflation often comes about spontaneously and is a by-product of both treatment and the addictive process, rather than through the therapist self-consciously pin-pricking the balloon of ego inflation.

HENRY KRYSTAL AND HERBERT RASKIN

Krystal and Raskin (1970) made one of the most clinically useful contributions to the literature on the dynamics of addiction when they spoke of affect regression as a central dynamic. What they were alluding to cannot be understood unless we look at their developmental theory. It is the theory about the development of affect in which it is postulated that affect is originally a massive, undifferentiated, vague, and overwhelming experience that they call an *Ur*-affect, a primitive precursor of more finely discriminated feelings and emotions. This *Ur*-affect is preverbal, experienced as somatic, and undifferentiated. In the normal course of development, affect is differentiated so that, for example, Rado's tense depression becomes anxiety and depression, now experienced as qualitatively different. Further, the differentiated affects can be verbalized. By giving feelings labels, they can be spoken of, instead of being experienced as bodily states, and they become available for psychic elaboration and working through, obviating the need for somatization and/or acting out.

The process of affect development not only involves the unfolding of an innate biological potential, but, importantly, is an interpersonal or object relational process. We learn what we are feeling by being given labels for our feelings, words for them, by empathic caregivers. When a mother says, "You're crying because you're feeling blue, and you're feeling blue because your doll broke," or "You're crying because you're angry," she is giving her child the means by which to verbalize feelings.

For many substance abusers, this process went poorly. The loving caregivers were not there to help them sort out and verbalize their feelings, so the feelings remained massive and undifferentiated, somaticized and unverbalized, or they became differentiated and verbalized, but weakly and insecurely so. In other words, substance abusers commonly suffer either fixation at a stage of primitive affect, or have a vulnerability to affect regression consequent upon early trauma and deprivation. In traumatization of all sorts, there is affect regression. Addiction is a form of chronic traumatization. This is true even though it may not seem so, and it may appear that the trauma is mostly inflicted on others; nevertheless, it is traumatic to the self, which experiences one narcissistic wound after another as the addiction progresses. This in addition to historical trauma—either acute or chronic, or both.

Thus, there are many reasons for substance abusers to be vulnerable to affect regression, including the addiction itself and its pharmacological effects. By the time they seek treatment, we find that they have *alexithymia*, that is, they cannot put their feelings into words or can do so only in a confused and imprecise way. Further, resomatization is the rule, rather than the exception, and anxiety, in particular, is experienced not as a signal but as overwhelming. Such anxiety is commonly experienced as a bodily catastrophe such as an imminent heart attack or stroke. Leon Wurmser (1978) believes that sexualization is also an aspect of affect regression. It is necessarily the case that the addict coming for treatment at the end of the addictive process, or deep into it, is suffering from affect regression characterized by dedifferentiation, resomatization, deverbalization, and sexualization. The therapist's job is to help the patient reverse this process and move up the scale of affect development into differentiation, verbalization, desomatization, and desexualization. That sounds complicated but in practice is fairly simple. One simply helps the recovering substance abuser find labels for feelings. One interprets the patient's affects: "You're sad," or "You're angry," or "You're confused." These are interpretations and the therapist may misperceive the active or recovering addict's emotional state, but with experience this happens infrequently. Generally speaking, the therapist is on target and has a better sense of what the patient is feeling than the patient does. Even more importantly the therapist has words for those feelings. In the reverbalization, discriminations are made and differentiation takes place. Also in the verbalization, a means of symbolization and working through comes into being, and somatization is no longer necessary. Similarly, the sexualization of affect diminishes with its differentiation and verbalization.

There is a famous experiment by the social psychologist Stanley Schachter (Schachter and Singer 1962), in which he assigned research subjects to one of four conditions. Two groups received adrenaline, two groups received sterile water, and every group had a confederate who was placed among them as they were told they were waiting for the experiment to take place. One confederate was happy and jolly, and when those that received the adrenaline were asked what they were feeling, they said they were happily excited. The other confederate was angry and complaining and cursing out the stupid scientists, and when those who received adrenaline were asked what they were feeling, they said they were feeling angry and unhappy. Those who received sterile water were not very influenced by either confederate. This would seem to argue that affect is a result of an interaction between physiological arousal and cognitive labeling, and very much supports the theory of Krystal and Raskin.

FRANZ ALEXANDER

Franz Alexander, the long-time head of the Chicago Psychoanalytic Institute, was the father of psychosomatic medicine. He is probably best known for his insistence that therapy is a "corrective emotional experience," a view of therapy that minimizes the role of insight in enabling change. In addiction therapy we often provide more of a corrective emotional experience than anything else.

Alexander taught that a psychosomatic illness required three etiological factors: constitutional predisposition, infantile trauma, and a current stress. Although with the exception of a paper on alcoholism Alexander didn't write explicitly about addiction, his theory is highly relevant to addiction therapy. Addiction can be understood as a psychosomatic illness and it is useful for the therapist to look at the role of these three factors in any particular case. Constitutional predisposition is there more often than not, infantile or childhood trauma is virtually ubiquitous in this population, and current stress plays a role not only in relapse but in development of the disorder in the first place. The current stress is often the *Sturm und Drang* of adolescence, particularly conflict around separating and individuating. All of this is usefully discussed with the patient.

JOHN HUGHLINGS JACKSON

John Hughlings Jackson was one of the greatest neurologists of the nineteenth century, as well as a feature of Victorian London life. His historical influence is vast, ranging from his impact on Sigmund Freud to his influence on the gestalt psychologists. There are several aspects of his work that are relevant to substance abuse treatment. Perhaps the most important is his notion of *dissolution*. That is the idea that pathology is a regression to a lower stage of evolution and of development. Pathology of the nervous system is the stepping back to a less highly developed mode of functioning. This has obvious relevance in work with substance abusers. As we have seen from several angles, both outward function and inner world become less highly elaborated, suffer dedifferentiation, and become more global and more primitive. Jackson's theory gives a neurological basis to a wide set of clinical observations. Freud, who knew Jackson's work well, the two men having a common interest in and both publishing seminal works on aphasia, the loss of the capacity to speak, transmuted Jackson's notion of neurological dissolution into the psychological notion of *regression*. It is important to note that the dissolution or regression is across the board, that it affects all areas of functioning since there is less highly articulated integration and a general falling off of highly discriminated thinking, feeling, and acting.

Another Jacksonian notion of great importance in substance abuse treatment is his criticism of the notion of "localization of function." Jackson thought that both function and dysfunction could only be understood globally. He believed that what was observed as loss of function in one area was not the result merely of damage to some particular tract in the brain, as held by his opponents in the localization controversy such as Broca, the equally eminent neurologist for whom Broca's aphasia is named, but that the damage was far more diffuse and involved a failure of integration of an almost infinite concatenation of circuits and feedback loops. This is almost certainly correct. What that means for us is that we need to realize that although our substance abusing patient's functioning is uneven, and certainly better in some areas than others, there is going to be some degree of impairment across the board because the higher levels of synthesis and integration have regressed, have de-evolved, have suffered "dissolution," in Jackson's terminology, under the impact of both pharmacological poisoning of the nervous system by drug use and by the psychological regression ineluctably concomitant with that substance abuse.

The particulars of Jackson's work, including his work on epilepsy, has relevance to substance abuse that will not be elaborated here. The important lesson we must learn from Jackson is that we must look at symptoms both in terms of their specificity, at a neurological level, the localization of function, and in terms of their global consequences as a far-more generalized impediment to and regression to a lower level of all mental and emotional development.

KURT GOLDSTEIN

Kurt Goldstein learned a great deal from Hughlings Jackson and developed Jackson's ideas even further. He is the foremost proponent of the global versus localization understanding of psychic functioning in the twentieth century. Goldstein's understanding of the nervous system and of human behavior grew directly out of his work with brain-injured soldiers in World War I when he was a physician in the German army. What he saw was that brain injury had consequences not only in terms of loss of a particular function—say a paralysis, or loss of a sensory mode—but had far more global consequences in terms of a reorganization at a lower level of complexity, and regression to a lower level of development of mental functioning in general. This was a striking clinical affirmation of the theories of

Hughlings Jackson. Not surprisingly, what is generally considered to be Goldstein's masterpiece is entitled *The Organism*. According to Goldstein (1939), psychopathology always involves the entire organism. The influence of this point of view, which he argues primarily in neurological rather than psychological terms, on the Gestalt psychologists is quite direct and easy to understand. The Gestalt psychologists simply confirmed in the area of perception what Goldstein had found in his broader clinical work with brain-injured soldiers.

What this means for the therapist treating the substance abuser is that he or she must always be alert for a more generalized regression to a lower level of functioning, to a less complex integration of experience, and in particular to a loss of what Goldstein and Scheer (1941) called the "abstract attitude" resulting in functioning on the concrete level. Goldstein and Scheer called this the assumption of the "concrete attitude." This loss of the abstract attitude and regression to the concrete attitude has direct implications for substance abuse counseling technique. It confirms a point made in Chapter 2 that the counselor/therapist's interventions must be simple, clear, redundant and particular, that is, concrete. The more vivid and emotive the language of the therapist, the better. It is easy for the therapist to underestimate the degree of impairment in the ability to abstract, caused by the assault to the brain by the various drugs used, in highly educated patients who are verbally glib. Nevertheless, they are not tracking nearly as well as they sound and it is always wise for the therapist to assume that there is at least a transient impairment in the ability to understand and process abstract language.

Another crucial conceptual contribution of Kurt Goldstein is the contrast he drew between *catastrophic anxiety* and *neurotic anxiety*. Catastrophic anxiety elicits defenses, especially compulsive ones, which serve to protect the organism from awarenesses that would be so devastating as to be destructive. Goldstein had in mind the way in which some of his brain-damaged soldiers lined up their clothing in their bedside cabinets with great rigidity and compulsiveness, arranging and re-arranging until every T-shirt and pair of underpants lined up precisely with every other one. Traditionally this would have been seen as evidence of obsessive compulsive neurosis and the defense analyzed. Goldstein saw that when there was an attempt to prevent these brain-injured soldiers from using their compulsive defenses they went into castastrophic anxiety, that is, they were panicked and overwhelmed. He realized that they needed to simplify their world and to structure it in a highly rigid way in order to process what information they could. They needed simplicity, clarity, rigid lines, routine, repetition, order, to a degree an organism not so damaged does not require. The correct therapeutic stance to catastrophic anxiety is to support the defense. Neurotic anxiety, on the other hand, is Freudian anxiety, the anxiety coming from unconscious inner conflict. The correct therapeutic response to that is to analyze the defenses and to make conscious the underlying conflict. They are two quite distinct things and require two quite distinct approaches if the therapist is to be helpful rather than destructive.

We frequently see in early sobriety patients a move from impulsivity to compulsivity. The compulsiveness and rigidity are often apparent to the therapist who in his or her countertransferential zeal feels compelled to confront, analyze, and soften the defense. This is a mistake. Goldstein is right. In early sobriety, such compulsivity is a necessary defense against catastrophic anxiety that would arise from trying to process information at a more complex level than the organism, the patient, is able to handle. As recovery proceeds, the nervous system evolves, rather than devolves, and once again complexity and abstractness can be better handled and higher levels of integration, subtlety, and complexity are to be encouraged. It is important to note that it may also be necessary to support defenses against neurotic anxiety in early sobriety in order to give the patient a chance to secure his or her recovery before attempting to deal with maladaptive defenses and the intense anxiety that may lead to a slip if they are prematurely encountered by the counselor or therapist. This is not to say that more traditional insight work is not appropriate with substance abusers—it most certainly is. Rather, it is a question of timing and of therapeutic tact. Such work should not be attempted unless the conflict is sobriety-threatening too early in recovery. Defenses, particularly compulsive ones, against catastrophic anxiety must be respected and supported. One reason Twelve-Step programs are so successful is that they are highly ritualized and encourage considerable compulsivity in their members who are, after all, using a higher-level defense in being compulsive and are operating at a higher developmental level than they did in being impulsive. Kurt Goldstein's contribution is truly illuminating and gives a theoretical basis upon which to build an efficacious therapeutic technique with substance abusers.

LEON WURMSER

Wurmser (1978) addresses the degree to which the addict externalizes internal conflict and looks for external solutions, and how our society so often reinforces such an externalizing defense in its denial of the saliency of the inner world, particularly of the unconscious inner world. Further, Wurmser describes a complex process depicting and elaborating the addictive cycle, a cycle that begins with a narcissistic crisis (stage one), a state in which self-esteem plummets and the integrity of the self is threatened. This is intolerable, and leads to instant defense. This narcissistic crisis leads to a breakdown of affect defense (stage two), so that affects become overwhelming and the addict undergoes affect regression. Then affect is experienced as massive, archaic, somatic, sexualized, deverbalized, and dedifferentiated. At that point, the patient feels uncontrollable intense rage, or shame, or despair, but cannot put those feelings into words. In the third stage, the affect disappears and is replaced by a vague, unbearable tension, as the addict begins a frantic search for excitement and relief and experiences craving. At this point, there is massive denial of inner reality and a frantic search for an external solution. This leads into the fourth stage, the wild drivenness for action, for an external concrete solution to the internal conflict.

There is a great deal of magical thinking in the fourth stage. The addict swings into action, which is characterized by both self-destructiveness and by aggression. It is a breaking out in which boundaries are transgressed, social limits are violated, others are attacked, the self is destroyed, and the addict is consumed with hurting and being hurt, humiliating others, and being shamed. Then despair takes over, and there is a splitting of the superego to allow for whatever action must be taken to end this intolerable state of affairs. This eventuates in feelings of entitlement. Finally, the drug is found, consumed, and the narcissistic crisis is ended, self-esteem is restored, and manic-euphoria results in pleasure. In summary, the cycle consists of acute narcissistic crisis, affect regression, search for affect defense and the use of denial and splitting, the use of externalization as a defense in a search for magic power, the mobilization of aggression, the split of the superego, and finally the pleasure of being high. At that point, the substance abuser is in the state of even greater narcissistic vulnerability, consumed with shame and guilt, albeit unconsciously. The pleasure soon ends, and the next acute narcissistic crisis occurs, now even more easily set off because of greater narcissistic vulnerability. It is truly a horrible situation in which to be trapped.

Wurmser is reminiscent of Rado in his sensitive and, underneath the technical language, moving depiction of the addictive cycle and the entrapment in which addicts find themselves. His recommendations are twofold: multimodal treatment (because addiction is a very hard condition to combat and requires heavy artillery for its successful resolution), which might include self-help, group therapy, family therapy, psychopharmacology, psychoanalysis or modified analytic therapy; and psychodynamic treatment. Wurmser feels that analysis, or at least psychodynamic treatment, is essential in order to help the addict move from externalization to contact with the inner world of affect, cognition, aspiration, and fantasy.

Wurmser makes other points that are highly salient in the treatment of substance abuse. He believes that much contemporary analytic and psychodynamic theory focuses too much on deficit and not enough on conflict. His belief is that much that appears to be deficit, that is, to be holes and gaps within the patient, often turns out to be defenses against conflicts, or unconscious potentials that need to be realized. Wurmser is not unaware of deficit, as in his citation of affect regression based on vulnerability derived from early trauma, which he borrows from Krystal and Raskin. Nevertheless, his emphasis is on the uncovering of unconscious conflict. He takes this position partly because he views it as more hopeful. Conflict can be surfaced and worked with, while deficit is much harder to ameliorate.

Wurmser also emphasizes a dynamic he calls "flight from conscience" as driving not only substance abuse, but severe neurosis in general. The problem is not that patients lack a superego, but that the superego is so harsh, primitive, and unforgiving that there is a flight from that superego into sometimes gross and outrageous antisocial behavior. Patients act out to escape their conscience. Wurmser's notion of flight from conscience is perfectly consistent with his emphasis on working with conflict and with his view that many contemporary analysts and psychodynamic therapists miss conflict in their all-too-ready acquiescence in the patient's self-estimation. To focus on deficit can be a way of devaluing the patient—"He can't do this, that, and the other thing; he's missing parts; he's a mess."

Wurmser also coined a term, *psychophobia*, which refers to our culture's repudiation of the inner world of fantasy, drive, unconscious conflict, and unconscious aspiration. Substance abusers are highly psychophobic. They externalize and act out in every possible way to avoid contact with their inner worlds, particularly with the stringencies of the superego. The psychophobia of a culture that emphasizes manipulation through technique and behavioral change (as desirable as that may sometimes be) reinforces the patient's unwillingness to look inside and experience the inner world.

PETER HARTOCOLLIS

Hartocollis (1968) was one of the first to point out the high prevalence of borderline and narcissistic personality disorders in addiction. It is counterfactual to say that all addicts are borderline. It simply is not true, but the contrary tends to be true. Most borderlines become substance abusers, usually polysubstance abusers. It is also contrary to fact to say that all substance abusers are narcissistic personality disorders in *DSM-IV* terms. Nevertheless, narcissistic difficulties seem to be at the core of addiction, and there is a reactive narcissism that goes with the addiction that may or may not be ameliorated by recovery in and of itself. In Chapter 3 I argue that regression/fixation to pathological narcissism, in Kohut's sense, is the psychodynamic correlative of addiction. Hartocollis emphasizes that the borderline and narcissistic character elements of the addict must be dealt with psychodynamically if any sort of satisfactory stable sobriety is to become possible. Hartocollis also noted that alcoholic denial is a denial not only of the drinker's alcoholism but of the drinker's need for help; that is, it is a form of counterdependence and pseudo–self-sufficiency, both of these states being characteristic of borderline and even more of narcissistic pathology. This can be usefully interpreted.

EDWARD KHANTZIAN

Khantzian (1981, 1999) is the author of the *self-medication hypothesis*, the notion that people use drugs to remediate ego deficits and developmental arrest. In his view, the taking of the substance is an initially adaptive attempt to cope with a deficit state. He sees these deficits as involving both ego and self. Although these deficits encompass many areas of functioning and of self-regulation, they are primarily deficits in the areas of self-care, affect regulation, self-esteem, and a subjective sense of well-being. The self-medication hypothesis has also been called the prosthetic theory of drug use and abuse. In this formulation, the drug is seen as a prosthesis that supplies the missing part or the missing function. Khantzian is very clear that the motivation, conscious or unconscious, driving substance abuse is the attempt to relieve suffering.

Khantzian's view is of the utmost clinical saliency. If the therapist does not recognize, as one of the most central dynamics of addiction, the adaptive nature of drug use and the attempt at self-cure through that use, there is no way in which the alcoholic or drug addict will feel understood. However mistaken the belief, however many years have passed since the drug ameliorated, rather than exacerbated, deficit and conflict, the taking of the drug was at one point a rational attempt to cope, despite developmental disability. The therapist must acknowledge this and, indeed, reflect it back to, or even interpret it to, the patient, who may have no conscious awareness that that was what he or she was trying to do. This in no way negates the importance of confrontation of denial, or of the need to repeatedly point to all of the negative consequences of the addiction. Nor is it incompatible, though Khantzian would probably think that it was, with interpretations around self-hatred and psychodynamically motivated self-destruction. One may indeed have begun using drugs in an attempt to cope, and either simultaneously or sequentially have come to use the drug as a self-punisher.

Khantzian's emphasis on the suffering driving substance abuse, on addicts trying, however futilely, to alleviate their pain, powerfully alters the therapist's countertransference. Frustration and rage at the seemingly irrational behavior of the substance abusing patient evanesce, and the therapist's ensuing calm and acceptance is communicated to the patient.

Khantzian highlights the specificity of the attempt at self-medication: for example, the use of amphetamine, crack, or cocaine as an unconscious attempt to treat attention deficit disorder (ADD) and hyperactivity. For Khantzian, the drug of choice says a lot about the substance abusing patient that the therapist needs to attend to, both to understand and to treat the ADD or depression or anxiety psychopharmacologically and/or psychotherapeutically. Khantzian makes an interesting and clinically useful distinction in the use of cocaine as self-medication. One group of users is self-medicating depression while another group is sensation-seeking and on the manic side. They are looking to get even higher. The therapist needs to be alert to which of these dynamics pertains as well as to be on the lookout for self-medication of ADD.

Khantzian's colleague John Mack (1981, Khantzian and Mack 1989) has developed with him an elaboration of the notion of deficits in the areas of the capacity of self-care and self-governance driving addiction. Part of being sane is knowing how to be sane, and the basic idea here is that the alcoholic or drug addict simply does not know how to be sane. There is, in behavioral language, an enormous learning deficit, or, speaking more psychodynamically, there are massive failures of internalization of parental functions, so that self-care and self-governance have never been internalized. It is not possible to internalize that which never existed externally, and in the case of many substance abusers who grew up in chaotic, even violent, homes in which there was little consistent care, there was scant opportunity to internalize the ability to care for oneself.

In Kohut's terms, there has been a failure to transmutably internalize the functions of the selfobject (see Chapter 3). Mack and Khantzian elaborate the notion of self-care, and amalgamate it, to some degree, with other ego and superego functions to arrive at the notion of self-regulation as an ego function, with perhaps some superego aspects to it. In their view, self-regulation, which includes limits on behavior, is, even in the best of circumstances, not completely internalized and always depends on external reinforcement. That is to say that some ego functions and some superego functions constantly require reinforcement from the environment. To take a trivial example, few of us are so self-regulated or superego restrained as to always observe the speed limit; only the possibility of getting a ticket slows us down. Khantzian and Mack are saying that something like this pertains to many areas of life. If we are not part of a social system that gives us feedback, we are not going to be able to regulate ourselves effectively. And that will be the case no matter how fortunate our early circumstances, or how well we have internalized regulatory ego and superego functions. Human beings always need a social context and corrective feedback from that context.

In Khantzian and Mack's view, it is precisely the people who have the weakest internal structures who are most likely to be alienated and in a state of anomic isolation. Those who need it most lack social support for their precariously internalized ego and superego functions, rendering them highly vulnerable to turning to substances to make up for both internal and current environmental deficits.

In Khantzian and Mack's analysis, it is precisely the power of the Twelve-Step programs to provide an auxiliary ego and, to some degree, auxiliary superego, that makes them so highly effective for recovering persons. Khantzian and Mack's term for this amalgamation of ego and superego functions seen to be both internal and external is *self-governance*. Addicts are radically disabled by their deficits in their ability to self-govern, and it is precisely the genius of the Twelve-Step programs to provide the external component of that self-governance, which in the course of time becomes internalized, but never completely. As is the case for all of us, the recovering addict continues to need the external support, feedback, and constraint that the program provides. This seems to me to be very realistic. Whatever other ways there may be in which we are necessarily interdependent, it is most certainly the case that ego and superego functions are not completely internalized, as a classic psychoanalytic model would maintain, and indeed they require continuous environmental reinforcement. This reinforcement permits them not only to maintain their existence, but to evolve into more mature forms.

STEPHANIE BROWN

Brown (1985) emphasizes the developmental arrest in addiction both of the addict and of the children raised by the addict. She considers it absolutely vital that the therapist figure out when growth stopped and the arrest began. Only then can the therapy successfully put the addict back on the pathway to emotional maturity. She understands the Twelve Steps as facilitating ego growth in a way parallel to that of a psychodynamic therapy informed by psychoanalytic developmental theory. In the case of patients raised in alcoholic or addicted homes, the therapist should determine what age the patient was when the family became overtly dysfunctional. The arrest occurs at that point.

Brown also emphasizes the traumatization ineluctably consequent on being out of control—and every addict is out of control. The therapist should make the patient aware of this. Brown regards every case of addiction as a case of posttraumatic stress disorder—the trauma being the experience of being out of control—and treats the addicted patient accordingly.

ERNST SIMMEL

Simmel created the first inpatient drug rehabilitation center, Schloss Tegel, outside Berlin in the 1920s. He didn't think of Schloss Tegel as a rehab. Rather, he considered it a psychoanalytic sanatorium. In both his understanding of the dynamics of drug addiction and in his treatment, he emphasized the symbolic meaning of the drug. Simmel noted that many of his patients could taper down to such a low dosage of their drug, usually alcohol, that its pharmacological effect was minimal, yet they clung to it and refused to give up the "last drop." This suggested that the drug served a psychodynamic function quite apart from its pharmacological action. It had some symbolic meaning—mother, magic potency, elixir of life, elixir of love, selfobject, semen, blood, milk, magic, or preserver of the integrity of the self. Central to Simmel's treatment was interpretation of the symbolic meaning of the drug. This is no less useful now than it was seventy-five years ago. Interpretations around the symbolic function of the drug are often mutative. It takes a good deal of listening before the clinician has the knowledge necessary to make an accurate interpretation. Treating people in the sanatorium, Simmel was in perfect position to wait them out as he worked with them analytically. This is much less feasible in an outpatient setting where the patient's ongoing use may make such interpretation irrelevant.

It is of some interest to note that Freud, coming to Berlin for an adjustment of his prosthesis for his ablated jaw, which had been removed to treat a carcinoma secondary to his addictive smoking, stayed in Simmel's sanatorium while he was having his mouth worked on. Ironically, Freud had no insight that he too, was an addict and his resting in his friend's sanatorium for addiction was entirely appropriate. Then again, perhaps Freud did know at some level.

Simmel created a milieu therapy in which every member of the staff was part of the treatment team, from the cook to the gardener. He built in feedback loops so that his patients learned about themselves in all of their activities. Similarly, in modern recreational therapy or occupational therapy, how patients play the game or make the vase reveals an enormous amount about them, and this is very usefully commented on or interpreted.

In creating his milieu, Simmel did something unique. He split his staff into a highly supportive nursing team that indulged the patients, self-consciously infantilized them, and tried to meet all their needs, in an attempt to belatedly remediate early environmental deficit and trauma, and a medical team. The first component of the staff provided a corrective emotional experience. It was, indeed, a *nursing* staff. The second component, the physician (in that time and place almost certainly a male), was, on the other hand, the representative of reality, the setter of limits. So, part of the staff represented the pleasure principle and part the reality principle. Simmel's notion was that addictive patients, at least the ones in his sanatorium, were too regressed to deal with reality, including the reality of their own addiction, unless they were embedded in a highly supportive environment. That notion still has utility, perhaps not in such a direct form as Simmel prescribed it at Schloss Tegel. But most certainly something like this happens in most inpatient rehabilitation units, and the Twelve-Step programs very much provide support and reality checks simultaneously. As Claude Miller, a wise analyst, was fond of remarking in his seminars at the American Institute for Psychotherapy and Psychoanalysis, "All of our lives, we need mother's milk and corrective feedback, preferably from the same person." Simmel intentionally did not provide it from the same person, yet all of his staff were part of the same institution, and in the patient's transferential fantasies were surely amalgamated in some way.

Simmel came to the United States when the Nazis came to power in Germany, and continued his interest in the treatment of alcoholism in New York City. Here, too, he anticipated and indeed made possible some of our current understanding of addiction. Shortly after World War II, he wrote a paper, part sociology, part psychology, continuing in the analytic tradition of bridging these realms of discourse, a tradition going back to Karl Abraham (1908), in which he forecasted a huge increase in addiction and severe psychopathology following the end of the war. He hypothesized that the kind of dislocation the war had brought, and the unleashing of primitive aggression concomitant with it, combined with the difficulties that the veterans would have reintegrating into civilian society, would lead to an increase in all kinds of acting-out behaviors, including addiction. He proved to be entirely right. Something similar to that happened after the Vietnam War, when the veterans who used pot and heroin in Vietnam returned to the United States and, for the most part, put aside the narcotics, but showed up in Veterans Administration hospitals a few years later as alcoholics. These veterans, like Simmel's World War II veterans, often suffered undiagnosed post-traumatic stress disorder, which they sought to self-medicate with alcohol and other drugs.

Simmel did not live to finish his 1948 paper, but in it he reached out to the self-help community, then barely known, and attempted to interpret the twelve steps of Alcoholics Anonymous in terms of ego development. In our own time, Stephanie Brown (1985) has continued this work and has elaborated such a developmental hypothesis (see above). Simmel, in his advocacy of collaboration between mental health professionals and self-helpers, has much to teach us about how to deal with our countertransference to the Twelve-Step programs. If we are to successfully work with addicts, it is necessary that we come to terms with that countertransference. Simmel's attitude toward the Twelve-Step programs is one worth identifying with. He neither abdicates his professional stance nor condescends to the self-help movement; on the contrary, he is entirely open to learning from it, while feeling that he, as a professional and analyst, has much to teach self-help movement members.

ERICH FROMM

Fromm's (1941) best-known book is entitled *Escape from Freedom*. As I have suggested in Chapter 1, Fromm's social-political-psychological analysis is the subtext, in one way or another, of most of this book. There are few more total escapes from freedom than addiction. Fromm's central notion, written in the shadow of the totalitarian movements of the mid–twentieth century, elaborates a social-political dynamic in which the anxiety of being free, having to make choices, and being responsible is more than people are sometimes able to bear. In that state, they all too readily abdicate freedom, and enter into an orgy of submission to authoritarian figures or movements. This is a pattern that we have seen over and over again in the twentieth century with enthrallment to figures as diverse as Hitler and David Koresh, who led his followers to mass suicide. Fromm was right. Human beings do have a difficult time bearing the responsibility of being free. Whatever the ultimate truth of the free-will determinism debate, experientially we have feelings of agency, and those feelings often frighten us. Addiction is very usefully understood and interpreted as a flight from freedom. Fromm was elaborating not only a social dynamic, but a psychological one.

Dostoevsky had a similar insight into the dread of freedom. In the Myth of the Grand Inquisitor in his novel *The Brothers Karamazov* (1880), Christ returns to Earth in the midst of the Spanish Inquisition and offers men freedom and responsibility in exchange for relinquishing mythological hope. Christ is sent away. Dostoyevsky's Grand Inquisitor tells him that what he offers human beings is too difficult, they cannot manage it; only the elite, the Inquisitor and his peers, can know the truth of the human condition. The rest of us must be protected, infantilized, and reassured. Something similar goes on in the 1990s in the United States, just as surely as it did in Dostoyevsky's vision of fifteenth-century Seville. People find all sorts of ways to relinquish their freedom—addiction preeminent among them. What the Danish philosopher Søren Kierkegaard (1849) called the "dizziness of freedom" has led to many a slip. Addiction is total enslavement. All of the addict's actions are predetermined by his or her need to obtain the drug, to use the drug, to recover from using the drug. The same is true of the "process addictions" such as compulsive gambling. Choices there are not. The addict's world becomes progressively narrower and more constricted. In recovery the process is reversed and the recovering person becomes more and more aware that a range of choices is open in every area of life. This can, and frequently does, cause enormous anxiety. The drive to escape from this anxiety commonly leads to a return to drug use. The Twelve-Step programs tell people not to make major decisions in the first year of sobriety. The manifest reason for this is that people change a lot during the first year of sobriety and it is therefore unwise to make avoidable major decisions during this state of transition. But the latent reason is even more powerful: the anxiety of making choices is so overwhelming for people in early recovery whose egos are still too weak to withstand it, that choosing makes them vulnerable to relapse. Therapists should interpret the danger of the dizziness of freedom in early sobriety and support delaying making major decisions until the recovering addict has his feet on the ground.

HOWARD BLANE

The dependency conflict theory elaborated by Blane and others states that people who cannot find healthy interdependent interpersonal ways of meeting their dependency needs are prone to turn to substances. Rather than turning to people, they turn to drugs, doing so from a stance of pseudo–self-sufficiency. Denying their need for human support, they consider themselves self-sufficient, meeting all their needs for support and security through the use of substances or by engaging in compulsive activities. Such counterdependents are blind to their dependency on chemicals.

As the addiction plays itself out, the counterdependent user slowly, or sometimes rapidly, collapses, and winds up overtly dependent on other people for care. At the end of a spree, the user often has to be nursed. The whole cycle is played out right back to the infant nursing at the breast.

In *The Personality of the Alcoholic: Guises of Dependency* (1968), Blane describes three types of dependency in alcoholics: (1) *Open dependents* are characterized by an attitude of "take care of me." "Here I am at my therapy session so I can collect my welfare check." Blane's open dependents are much like Robert Knight's essential alcoholics. He considered their prognosis poor. (2) *Counterdependents*, whom therapists frequently encounter in their clinical practices, are characterized by an attitude of "Fuck you, I don't need anyone." However pathetically and transparently untrue, it is a powerful defense that is extremely difficult to penetrate. The best the therapist can do is try to address the fear behind the counterdependency, interpreting how deeply afraid the addict is of any form of closeness, intimacy, or indeed of any relationship. The reasons for that fear need to be uncovered and explored. The Twelve-Step programs are extremely good at addressing counterdependency with such slogans as "We need each other," "Keep coming back," and "Nobody graduates." The Twelve-Step programs continually try to make interpersonal dependency acceptable to a counterdependent population and to undercut the pseudo–self-sufficiency. Therapists need to work with patients on this issue also. Blane considers counterdependents to have a poor prognosis. Although the more extreme counterdependents are fairly antisocial, and more or less unworkable in most therapy, not all counterdependents are unreachable. Addressing the underlying fear is the key. (3) *Dependent/counterdependents* are those addicts who are in great conflict about how to meet their dependency needs. Blane considers them by far the most treatable because their conflict is the most active and unresolved, and they can be engaged in psychotherapy because they are in pain.

The cowboy with his horse and bottle who rides off into the sunset needing nobody is the classic counterdependent. But the same scenario gets played out in New York City in the year 2000 just as it once got played out in Silver City in the 1880s. Those cowboys who look back, however furtively, to town, are the ones who are most likely to succeed in treatment.

MELANIE KLEIN

Klein's (1921–1945, 1946–1963) developmental theory is a useful adjunct and necessary background for understanding the developmental theories of Mahler, Kernberg, Masterson, and Kohut. Klein believes that that death instinct must be projected out onto the environment, lest it destroy the neonate. The projected death instinct then becomes the persecutory object (otherwise known as the bad breast), and the persecutory object is hated, feared, and envied.

The death instinct is also projected in order to protect the good within from destruction. But the good aspects of the self can also be projected outward, creating ideal objects and the good breast. So the child is now living in a world of split part-objects (all good and all bad). According to Klein this is a biologically programmed developmental sequence that is reinforced by the inevitable frustration of the world, in this case the frustration of mother not always being there. The good and bad breast are now identified with and introjected by the infant so that they now become internal objects. Kleinian developmental theory starts out as an instinct theory, but it does not remain one. It becomes an object relations theory. Instinct essentially drops out, leaving internal objects and external objects.

The abused substance is experienced as the good breast until it turns on and fails the user. It then becomes the bad breast.

Once the inner badness is projected, the infant lives in a split (or schizoid) and persecutory (or paranoid) world. This state of being Klein calls the *paranoid-schizoid position*. It is both a developmental stage and a state of being that stays with us throughout life.

Klein originally called this development stage and existential stance the paranoid position until Ronald Fairbairn (1940) suggested that the aloneness of the infant greatly added to anxieties of psychotic proportion, and that schizoid defenses were instituted to protect the infant from persecution by the bad breast. Accordingly, he suggested that Klein change the name of the position to paranoid-schizoid, which she did.

In Klein's developmental scheme the next stage involves a recognition that the good breast is the bad breast and that there is only one breast, which entails an integration of self and object representations. The characteristic defenses of the paranoid-schizoid position are splitting, denial, and devaluation, and the affective states accompanying it are terror, hatred, and envy. In the depressive position, which Winnicott (1963) called the acquisition of the capacity for concern, not only are good and bad integrated and splitting healed, but there is a realization that I have created the bad breast by spoiling the good breast through my hatred and envy. This results in primitive guilt, which leads to savagery against the self by the primitive superego.

According to Klein, who based her theory on clinical evidence from her analysis of children, in my realization that I have transgressed against and spoiled the good breast—feelings derived from my desire to bite, piss on, and shit on the good breast—I develop a wish to make reparation for that spoiling. Thus an important part of arriving at and living in the depressive position is the making of reparation for my aggression.

But my envy of the good breast prevents me from making that reparation. Melanie Klein is to the breast what Freud was to the penis—both theorists putting great emphasis on envy of those body parts by those who do not have them, either by reason of their gender or their infantile state. (The Spanish existential philosopher Unamuno wrote of male womb envy.) But Klein goes a step further and says that that reparation becomes possible because I am able to overcome my envy and hatred through feeling gratitude for the goodness of the good breast—and later, gratitude for whole objects.

This sounds like it has an awful lot to do with the dynamics of substance abusers. Substance abusers are often filled with primitive rage, hatred, and envy, and they aggress in all kinds of ways against the good things of their lives and this world. They also live in a split world of part-objects—split not only into good and bad, but into less than whole units, this being seen particularly clearly in sexual addictions in which the person is irrelevant and the genitals are the only area of interest. But substances, too, are part-objects in the minds of those who abuse them, most often good breasts or good penises, but not infrequently bad breasts and bad penises. Perhaps even more to the point is the degree to which substance abusers live in the Kleinian paranoid-schizoid position, that is, in a state of terror in a persecutory world.

In the Kleinian vision, that persecution is entirely the product of the projection of the death instinct and of aggressive and murderous wishes, and certainly substance abusers struggle with murderous wishes. As their addiction progresses, they regress to living almost exclusively in the paranoid-schizoid position. Users often become overtly paranoid, refusing to answer the door, being afraid to open their mail, and hiding from the world and from themselves.

All of us live throughout our lives, except for the very earliest months, in dynamic equilibrium between the depressive and the paranoid-schizoid positions. Creativity and spontaneity, discontinuity and novelty, are more a product of paranoid-schizoid functioning, something we would not wish to live without, while steadiness, reliability, responsibility, and rationality are all concomitant with existence in the depressive position. There is, so to speak, more sanity in the depressive position, and substance abusers are not any too sane, so they are definitely not spending most of their time in the depressive position. The difficulty in substance abuse in terms of the Kleinian developmental scheme is the predominance of paranoid-schizoid functioning rather than its presence, which is universal. Some substance abusers never reach the depressive position, or do so only insecurely. They are the patients described as essential alcoholics, as primary addicts, as habilitation cases. But most substance abusers have regressed to predominantly paranoid-schizoid functioning.

Thomas Ogden (1990) has added a position even more primitive than the paranoid-schizoid to the Kleinian developmental scheme, which he calls the *autistic-contiguous position*, a coming-into-being phenomenon. But this is not terribly relevant to the treatment of substance abuse except to explain the utter lostness of those substance abusers who have regressed all the way. They have literally lost themselves and must come back into being.

Klein's important notion of projective identification is discussed in Chapters 2 and 4.

DONALD WINNICOTT

Although there are many aspects of Winnicott's theoretical and clinical writings that have application to the understanding of treatment of substance abusers, by far the most salient is his short essay, "The Capacity to Be Alone" (1958). In it, Winnicott postulates that the capacity to be alone is a paradox. It comes from the experience of being alone in the presence of another person. If we are fortunate enough to have been with a loving, non-impinging parent who allowed us to be alone as we explored the world, even as he or she was there with us, we slowly internalize that parent so that we can now be alone without really being alone, because mother or father is inside of us. This process can go awry in either of two ways. The parent may be, to use Winnicott's term, too impinging, too controlling, too unable to let the child be, or the parent may not have been available. In either case, there will be pathological deficit in the capacity to be alone. Counterintuitive as it may be, the capacity to be alone is not a given, is not innate, but is a human achievement. It is important to note that Winnicott's capacity to be alone is not defensive isolation; it is quite the opposite. It is the kind of being alone that is necessary for creativity, for inner peacefulness, for serenity, for contemplation. Defensive isolation occurs out of fear and is what the Twelve-Step programs call isolating, which they quite rightfully see as a danger to sustaining sobriety.

One of the most frequent reasons people use drugs is to be companioned. One of the capacities that must be internalized during development, namely, the capacity to be companioned by the self and its internal objects, never occurs so that aloneness becomes terrifying abandonment. It cannot be tolerated and must be immediately alleviated by providing one's self with the companionship of reefer, line, or sexual partner. The therapist should interpret this.

ERIK ERIKSON

There are many aspects of Erikson's (1950, 1968) developmental scheme that are highly relevant to substance abuse treatment, but I will highlight only two. The first is the development of basic trust at the very beginning of life, or the failure to do so. As Erikson tells us, his is an epigenetic scheme in which each succeeding stage enfolds even as it builds on earlier stages. It follows that if we miss out on, or fail to successfully master, an earlier developmental task, it will make mastery of all the later ones more difficult. Many substance abusers have severe problems with trust. That is one reason they use substances instead of relationships to meet their needs, an insight that gives us another perspective from which to view the counterdependency so often concomitant with substance abuse. The substance abuse therapist needs to be aware that many, if not most, of these patients have never developed basic trust, and that makes for extraordinarily fragile therapeutic relationships (which are fragile enough on many other counts, including defense of the addiction). And that failure to successfully master this first developmental task means that all of the subsequent developmental tasks will be fraught with difficulty and achieved tenuously if at all.

The other Eriksonian developmental task particularly relevant to work with substance abusers is the achievement of identity, or the failure to do so, which Erikson variously calls *identity defusion* and *identity confusion*. Whether as fixation or regression, identity disturbances are ubiquitous among substance abusers. When an AA member says, "My name is John, and I am an alcoholic," he is performing what the ordinary language philosopher John Austin (1961) called a "performative utterance." A performative utterance is a use of language that actually does something, and does not merely denote something. When the judge says, "Ten years," he's not merely pointing to something in the statute book; he is speaking a performative utterance. When John says, "I am," he is not only denoting his existence, he is creating, or at the very least, affirming it. Further, he is specifying his existential assertion by naming one characteristic of that existence—being alcoholic. This is the beginning of having an identity.

Substance abusers are very confused about their identity, partly because of the confused state that the substance induces by its cognitive damage and partly because of developmental deficit. To be something—an alcoholic or an addict—is better than to be nothing, and this affirmation of existence as an addict is the beginning of accruing a more complex identity. We have empirical evidence (Conners 1962) for this. If patients in a drug rehabilitation unit are asked to fill out an adjective checklist of self-descriptive terms, they check very few items on the list, indicating a vacuity in their self-concepts. If the same people are tested five years later (if they remain sober), they now have a very rich self-concept, and check many adjectives.

Problems around identity, even existence, are absolutely crucial in the treatment of patients early in recovery from substance abuse. Over and over again, the therapist needs to return to issues of identity, changing identity, and the confusion of having been one person drunk and one person straight, and to emphasize to patients that once they have a core identity as an alcoholic or an addict, then they can, and will, add all sorts of attributes to their identity as they slowly accrete and accrue an enriched self-concept.

Erikson's epigenetic developmental scheme has more implications for substance abuse treatment than those derived from difficulties around the establishment of basic trust and identity, transcendentally vital as they may be. Failure to successfully negotiate any of Erikson's psychosocial stages, which is more the rule than the exception for substance abusers, renders the work of negotiating each of the succeeding stages all the more difficult. This is especially apparent in working with adolescent substance abusers struggling with the vicissitudes of the identity crisis without having mastered the previous stage of industry vs. inferiority, the stage in which Erikson tells us that the "tools" necessary to function in a given culture are acquired. The failure manifests as massive educational deficits that must be remediated if the youngster is to have any shot at a stable and satisfying sobriety. This task seems so daunting that many youngsters give up and relapse. The therapist needs to be empathic to the seeming impossibility of playing catch-up, as well as to be able to offer the teenager a realistic plan of remediation that kindles hope.

At the other end of life, imagine the virtual impossibility of arriving at final integrity, which Erikson counterposed to senile despair or disgust and which he tells us entails "the acceptance of one's one and only life cycle and of the people who have become significant to it as something that had to be and that, by necessity, permitted no substitutions" (1968, p. 138), without having reasonably satisfactorily mastered the stages of intimacy and generativity because of substance abuse. For the older patient in early recovery, the sense of its being too late can be crushing. The best the therapist can do is to engage the patient in major mourning for lost opportunity, while paradoxically focusing on the now, and perhaps suggest that the patient read *King Lear*.

JAMES MASTERSON

Masterson's (1976) theory of the dynamics of borderline personality syndrome is highly relevant to work with many substance abusers. Masterson postulates that the borderline has been raised in a situation in which separateness and autonomy are punished and symbiosis is rewarded, and that the borderline patient has internal representations reflecting these experiences that are activated in current interpersonal relations. The internal representations are both enacted and projected in these relationships, including the relationship with the therapist in which they can be usefully interpreted. People with such internal worlds have great difficulty with their interpersonal relations and are quite prone to turn to substances. Substance use gratifies and rewards the drive toward symbiosis, yet simultaneously gives the illusion of autonomy and separateness. Drug use thus provides (at least in the beginning) a way out of the dilemma of the Masterson borderline who is trapped between fear of abandonment and fear of engulfment. If the therapist detects such a pattern in the patient, interpretation of the drug as yet another rewarder of fusion and being a substitute for and reincarnation of the parent who would not let go will be mutative. For borderlines with the kind of internal world Masterson describes, drug use is perfectly ego-syntonic behavior. The fact that the substance use provides a pseudo–self-sufficiency, a kind of artificial and illusionary sense of separation without the accompanying punishment by abandonment by the love object—now the drug—is an extraordinarily powerful hook that makes it extremely difficult for the user to relinquish the use. Naturally, not all substance abusers fit this rubric, but surprisingly many do, and the addictions therapist needs to be alert for this pattern of internal object relations that Masterson characterized as a split between a maternal part-object that is attacking in the face of efforts at separation-individuation and a maternal part-object that offers approval and supplies for regressive and clinging behavior. The borderline's part-self representations are also split between the bad, helpless, guilty, and empty, and the good, passive, compliant child. We see this all the time in work with substance abusers.

OTTO KERNBERG

Kernberg (1975) sees substance abuse as a correlative of borderline personality disorder, although he realizes that this correlation is imperfect. A great deal of Kernberg's work has been on the treatment of borderlines. And as we have seen, most borderlines are substance abusers, although the converse is not the case—most substance abusers are not borderline—so that it is natural for Kernberg to concentrate on the internal world and dynamics of the borderline in his discussions of substance abuse. He has definite treatment recommendations, the most important of which is that the patient may not use while he or she is in treatment. He greatly encourages his patients to take part in Twelve-Step programs and does strict limit setting. His way of handling substance abuse is strikingly like his way of handling attempted suicide. He tells his patients that if they attempt suicide, he will do everything possible to save their lives, but the treatment will be at an end. He is not quite so strict on terminating if the patient breaks the contract by drinking or drugging, but he holds a fairly tight line, and being a therapist with a great deal of charisma and one who projects a great deal of power he may be able to get away with things that other therapists cannot. Nevertheless, the recommendation that the patient must be abstinent in order to participate in the treatment is quite prevalent in the substance abuse treatment field, and often makes sense. But I do not believe it always makes sense. There are times when one must work with the user while he or she continues to use, even if the ultimate goal is abstinence. This is a controversial treatment recommendation with which Kernberg would not agree.

In viewing the borderline personality aspect of substance abuse, it is useful to look through the lens of Kernberg's theory of the dynamics and development of the borderline personality structure. According to Kernberg, an object relations theorist who speaks of internal object representations, we start out with an undifferentiated, amalgamated selfobject representation, which essentially is without boundaries and without demarcations. Those fixated or regressed to this developmental stage are, by definition, psychotic, since reality testing is not possible without separation of self and object representations. Kernberg calls this stage one of object relations development.

In Kernberg's second stage of development, there is division of the undifferentiated stage one representation along affective lines, resulting in a separation into a good selfobject and a bad selfobject representation. This is to say that differentiation has not yet occurred in terms of separation of self and object, but that affective differentiation has taken place in a kind of global way. The infant experiences a good mother who feeds and soothes, and a bad mother who frustrates. These experiences are internalized as selfobject representations in which both the good and bad mother become part of me and of my internal representation of myself. Fixation/regression to this stage of object relations development also results in psychosis, because there is still no separation of self and object.

In Kernberg's third stage, there are four internal representations, namely of the good object, the bad object, the good self, and the bad self. Now there is separation, but not yet integration of the positive and negative aspects of our experience of the world and ourselves. A drive theorist in spite of his object relations orientation, Kernberg depicts the goodness or badness of these representations as resulting from the cathexis by libido or by aggression of self and object representations. This is the internal world of the borderline patient, and, in Kernberg's view, it is responsible for the chaotic interpersonal experience and the wild fluctuations in self-evaluation borderlines experience. There is no integration of good and bad self representations, or of good and bad object representations. The patient is not psychotic, reality testing being possible, but his or her affective life is chaos. When the Twelve-Step slogan speaks of there being only two people who can get a person in trouble, the great "I am" and "poor me," it is speaking of Kernberg's good self representation (here grandiose), and bad self representation.

Kernberg's treatment is aimed at the integration of these representations so the patient can move into a mature internal world. This stage four internal world consists of complex self representations in which the positive predominates over the negative, but that are, nevertheless, amalgamations of the good and the bad. People who reach stage four of object relations development are capable of ambivalence. Similarly, the representations of others become complex as good and bad object representations are integrated.

Melanie Klein, whose work has been one of the major influences on Kernberg, would conceive of the developmental move from stage three to stage four as a move from the schizoid position to the depressive position. In Klein's depressive position, ambivalence and mourning become possible.

Kernberg's way of working and facilitating motivation is to interpret the transference in here-and-now terms. He makes few genetic interpretations; that is, he rarely comments on the historical source of what is happening now in the treatment. Rather, he interprets extensively, and often at length, what is going on between the patient and the analyst or therapist. These interpretations serve to make maladaptive defenses conscious. Manifestations of splitting into all good and all bad, the most characteristic borderline defense, are confronted. Kernberg talks about the borderline defenses of devaluation, primitive idealization, and denial, as well as of splitting, considering these pathognomonic of borderline personality disorders when they are the predominant defensive mechanisms.

These are precisely the defenses we see in substance abusers: the primitive idealization of the substance; the primitive idealization of the grandiose self; devaluation of others (including the therapist) as a defense (a manifestation of negative transference, which Kernberg is particularly prompt and vigorous in interpreting); and denial. All are highly characteristic of substance abusers, as is projection. Denial is the defense most characteristic of substance abusers.

Kernberg also addressed narcissistic personality disorder. In his view, the narcissist's internal world is dominated by a pathological representation that is an amalgamation of ideal self, real self, and ideal object. The real and ideal are confused, boundaries are blurred, and the grandiosity characteristic of the great "I am" is a natural consequence of having such a selfobject representation.

Kernberg sees substance abuse as common among and very characteristic of many narcissistic personality disorders, as he defines them.

Peter Hartocollis (1968), whose work I have already cited, sees the internal world of substance abusers similarly to Kernberg. However, his presentation is more ego psychological than object relational. He sees the characteristic difficulty of the borderline as historical, as rising from disturbances in parent–child relations. The borderline adult interpersonal difficulties are derivatives of difficulties in the rapprochement subphase of separation-individuation. Hartocollis is here drawing on Margaret Mahler's (Mahler et al. 1975) well-known developmental schema, of the autistic stage, the symbiotic stage, and the stage of separation-individuation with its four substages—differentiation, practicing, rapprochement, and separation-individuation proper. In Hartocollis's view, the borderline has suffered either traumatic rejection and abandonment or a refusal to let go in the rapprochement subphase, and this makes for the very stormy interpersonal relations driven by fears of abandonment and engulfment. The borderline turns to substances because he finds his relationship to them more manageable. This is strikingly similar to Masterson's presentation of what he calls the "partial object relations unit" in which separation is punished and symbiosis rewarded (see above).

So these four thinkers—Kernberg, Masterson, Hartocollis, and Mahler (by implication, as I don't know anywhere she writes explicitly about substance abuse)—all see the difficulties of the borderline substance abuser as arising quite early in development, and being more determined by developmental arrest and deficit in object or ego development than by intrapsychic conflict. That is not to say that borderlines do not experience intrapsychic conflict. Like all human beings they do, but these conflicts are not central to their dilemma.

The treatment implications of all of this is to be aware of these various ways of thinking about what happens, internally and interpersonally, to people with borderline and narcissistic characteristics. That is where substance abusers tend to be, and even if their level of object relations and ego development is a regression consequent upon the drug use, it is what therapists have to deal with. This knowledge lessens the therapist's anxiety in face of the patient's irrationality. The therapist looks for the unfolding of the patient's internal world in terms of relationships to self, to others, to therapist, and to the substance. All of these relationships and their interconnections can be usefully commented on.

HEINZ KOHUT

Heinz Kohut, the founder of self psychology, has particularly important things to say about addiction which I have incorporated in my dynamic/treatment model of addiction exposited in Chapter 3 so I won't say more about Kohut here. However, I would like to note that interpretations related to narcissistic issues such as reactive grandiosity, narcissistic injury, and self-esteem resonate with addictive patients. They hear them and understand them and they are mutative. Addiction therapy is indebted to Kohut for pointing us in this direction.

DANIEL STERN

Daniel Stern's theory of the development of the self has direct implications for addiction treatment. For Stern, the self is experiential. He defines it as the sense of agency, the sense of physical cohesion, the sense of continuity, the sense of affectivity, the sense of a subjective self that can achieve intersubjectivity with another, the sense of creating organization, and the sense of transmitting meaning. Definitions are prescriptive as well as descriptive, and Stern opts for a self or series of selves that are sensate, vaguely inchoate, or sharply experienced sensations and organizations of sensations. These selves are essentially preconscious most of the time, although for the most part they can emerge into consciousness without difficulty. It is not clear how or how much the Sternian selves are dynamically unconscious. Perhaps figure and ground is a better metaphor than conscious and unconscious; Stern's selves most commonly serve as ground, albeit an active and organizing ground, but they become figure in some situations.

Stern's selves correspond to discontinuities—quantum leaps in development. The sense of the emergent self comes into being during the first two months of life. It is a "sense of organization in the process of formation" (Stern 1985, p. 38). Stern emphasizes the experience of the process more than he does the product. This process is an ongoing organization of bodily concerns resulting in experiential cohesion of the body, its actions, and inner feeling states. These will form the core self that is now emerging. The emergent self is both the process and the product of forming relations between isolated events. It is the giving of cohesion. In adult life, the emergent self is the basis of creativity and potential for ongoing development.

In the next stage, that of the core self, there is a consolidation of that which has emerged from the emerging self. The core self is characterized by experiences of self-agency ("I can do things"), self-cohesion ("I have boundaries; I am a physical whole"), self-affectivity ("I have patterned inner qualities of feeling that are the same across experiences"), and self-history ("I endure, go-on-being, because there are regularities in the flow of my experience, in the stream of my consciousness"). These four self-experiences of the core self are preconceptual. They are "senses of," not concepts, not cognitive knowledge or self-awareness. They are not reflexive or reflective. The core self is a self without self-consciousness. In normal development, it is consolidated at about 8 months.

Stern's inclusion of affectivity as one of the most salient aspects of self-experience has important implications for the experience of the continuity of the self. Stern maintains that affect is the most constant experience we have, in the sense that affects remain more the same across time than any other experience. That is, our experiences of anger, sadness, joy, and pain are essentially the same in infancy, in childhood, in adolescence, in young adulthood, in maturity, and in old age. Therefore, our experience of affect very importantly determines and is constitutive of our experience of going-on-being. There is clinical implication in this as well, in that putting patients in contact with their feelings, their affects, in addition to whatever else it may do, should increase their sense of self-cohesion and self-continuity.

The subjective self develops from 8 to 15 months. Essentially, infants discover that there are inner subjective experiences—thoughts and feelings—that are theirs alone. Simultaneously, or slightly later, infants "discover" that others also have minds (i.e., inward, private thoughts and feelings that are potentially the same as theirs). This opens up the possibility of intersubjectivity. They can share (or not share) or connect (or not connect) with other creatures who are subjects like them, who have an inner world of sensations, feelings, and thoughts. For Stern, self and objects are co-emergent, not from a symbiosis, but from genetically and temporally prior, less organized, inward experiences of self and others. There is a prior primitiveness of self and others (primitive in the sense of less organized and less self-aware), but no prior confusion or merger. In the state of the subjective self, the subjectivity of the other is also established, and multitudinous possibilities for relatedness come into being. It is only now that merger or symbiosis becomes possible, but only as a union of that which was initially experienced as distinct.

During the second year of life, the verbal self comes into being. Now the self can be represented as a narrative: the story one tells to oneself about who and what one is. The narrative self is reminiscent of Freud's notion of the secondary revision of dreams, the process by which the dreamer gives the dream more cohesion and a better narrative line than it actually has. In a sense, the verbal self is a secondary revision of the dream that is one's life. The verbal self cannot adequately represent the other selves. It creates a world of concepts and abstractions that carry with them the danger of alienation from the vividness, uniqueness, and vitality of the preverbal experience characteristic of the emergent, core, and subjective selves. Thus, the four selves are equally necessary. The temporally later does not supplant the temporally earlier; rather, they provide different self-experiences. The four selves endure and mutually enrich each other across the life span. In the full flower of the Sternian self, it is simultaneously the experience of coming into being, the experience of being, the experience of interiority of self and others, and the experience of having or creating a history verbally, a narrative.

Stern's theory of the four selves helps the therapist make sense of some aspects of the addictive experience and the addict's behavior. Most substance abusers seem to have mastered the stage of the emergent self. It has been noted by many authors that creativity and substance abuse have not infrequently been linked. The reason for this may be that substance abusers live a great deal in the world of the emergent self. And, indeed, the very experience of getting high—changing one's state of consciousness and then returning to the sober state—is a whole process of emergence and reemergence. Therefore, it is possible that the dynamic behind some substance abuse is the drive for mastery of Stern's very first developmental stage—the coming into being—by its constant rehearsal and reenactment; on the other hand, it may be the case that substance abusers are relatively fixated at this stage, and that explains both the ease at which they reenact it in their substance use, and the above-noted linkage between creativity and substance abuse.

The core self seems much more problematic for substance abusers. They seem to have very real confusion about boundaries, about ongoingness, about centeredness, and about solidity of self. The substance use is both an attempt to self-medicate this tendency of the core self to collapse into the emergent self and a cause of the fragility of the core self, which is disorganized by the substance use itself. This is well worth talking about in the therapy. Without using technical language, the therapist can talk about the shakiness of the patient's sense of self, his or her insecurity as to boundaries, going on being, centeredness, and solidity, and suggest that the substance use is an attempt to firm up the patient's sense of self, which tragically does the exact opposite, setting up a vicious circle. This interpretation, properly timed with the right patient, can be highly mutative.

Stern's subjective self is also a problem area for many substance abusers. They have great difficulty experiencing their own interiority, including their affects. If Stern is right, that affect is the experience that most makes for a sense of continuity, then it is not surprising that many substance abusers experience themselves as so discontinuous and fragmented.

Wurmser's notion of psychophobia also dovetails with the notion that substance abusers suffer deficiencies in their experience of Stern's subjective self. They externalize compulsively to compensate for the inner emptiness and inadequacy, or the relative paucity of content and arrested development of the subjective self. Once again, the treatment worsens the disease, and the self-medication with the usual concomitant acting out and externalization impoverishes the subjective self even more.

The notion of affect regression discussed above in the section on Krystal and Raskin also comes into play here, although Krystal and Raskin's notion of affect development is at odds with Stern's notion of affect constancy. With a relatively weak sense of subjective self, affect differentiation is bound to be fragile. Similarly, the addict's sense of the inner subjectivity, of the interiority, of others may also be impoverished. Having little contact with his or her inner world, the chances of bridging—through empathy—to someone else's inner world are not great. These deficiencies, difficulties, conflicts, and attempts at remediation through substance use can also profitably be discussed in therapy.

Therapy is essentially about revising the narrative self, helping patients tell a different story to themselves to account for their life. There are few more radical revisions in the narrative self than the change that comes about in the story that addicts tell themselves about the self before and after achieving sobriety. It almost seems to be the story about a different life. And this change in the narrative self is crucial if a sustained recovery is to become possible.

ALEXITHYMIA, SYMBOLIZATION, AND THE INEFFABLE

David had recently lost his wife. The death had been unexpected and David was having a very rough time. A psychiatrist who often used intellectualization as a defense, he was also capable of using technical language insightfully and productively. Earlier in his life he had had a severe drinking problem. He had spent a decade in AA, stably sober, but had decided to leave the Program, as it is called, when he started resenting being there. As he put it, "I didn't want to be angry at something that had been so wonderful." David has been sober for more than a quarter of a century; alcohol is not an issue in his life or in our therapy. He had also suffered from panic-level anxiety and moderately severe depression. This, too, was long in the past, at least in its more severe manifestations, but David was definitely one who was acquainted with the night. He had had a successful—successful in the sense of being extremely helpful—analysis, and had been relatively unplagued by anxiety and depression for the past twenty years. Yet—yet, he had had his moments of doubt—doubt that his work was meaningful or that it helped anyone, doubt about his skills, doubt about his courage and integrity—necessary qualities in a psychotherapist. For the past few years, he had begun to wonder if he believed in anything, if he had any ideals, let alone upheld them. Guilt for sins of omission and sins of commission—real and imagined—in the present and in the past, intermittently tormented him. Flawed he certainly was, yet he was capable of joy, intermittently loving, and at times strongly productive. These doubts, guilt, and occasional moments of self-hatred had brought him back into therapy. I like him and readily identified with much of what he reported. There was too much vitality in him, too strong a capacity for relishing life for me to give him a diagnosis of dysthymia, let alone major depression. Once when we were kicking around his diagnosis, I spontaneously said to him, "Your problem is your species." He looked at me oddly, then said, "You mean being human?" I nodded. His existential crisis had many ingredients, but his relative isolation from community and from extended family certainly had something to do with it. His circle was too narrow; he was too reliant on his wife, both for love and to love. He was aware of this and we were working, I think successfully, on these issues when totally out of the blue tragedy struck. Ann, seemingly healthy, vigorous and asymptomatic, awoke one morning in pain and two hours later she was dead. Two weeks after his wife's death, he reported the following experience. The experience was his, the understanding of it and the generalizations drawn from it were a joint effort; but here I put both the experience and the understanding of it in his mouth.

I was walking on the beach, feeling relatively good, although there was an underlying sort of subliminal anxiety. It was warm for November and very beautiful. Part of me felt peaceful, but something else was happening. I didn't know what, but I had a lot of physical symptoms—the right side of my head felt odd, blocked and tingling, weird and frightening, and my right arm felt peculiar and almost numb. It went all the way down to my hand. I had had these symptoms all week, but I wasn't as frightened by them as I had been since my internist had said that they were caused by tension. But I wasn't altogether convinced. At times the fear came back. Was it an ischemic episode? Was my carotid artery blocking? I tried to forget about my body and be one with the sea and the sky but I couldn't sustain it. I kept going back to the strange feelings in my head and my numb hand. I walked a very long time, never able to completely get away from my physical symptoms. At times I felt tears running down my cheeks, yet I wasn't thinking about Ann or losing her or really of anything else except what was happening in my body. There were moments when I was one with the sea but they didn't last long. I felt confused, out of contact, unfocused. Then—and I'll never know why—I started thinking of Mozart's *The Magic Flute*. All sorts of emotions I had no name for suffused me. I thought, Mozart understood, Mozart understood everything, as I saw Tamino about to enter into the mysteries, into his trial by fire. Then I saw Pamina approach him with the magic flute as she took his hand, and, fused together by love and music, they entered into their trial. I remembered a character in a Bergman film saying, "There's hope, Pamina lives." Then I could feel Ann's hand in mine and I knew that Ann too lived in me, so there was hope. I don't know what happened after that, execpt for the deep, convulsive sobbing that went on, I don't know for how long. It wasn't a temporal experience, nor did I seem located in space when it went on. It-I was utterly unreflective; it-I just was—pure experience outside of time and space. I have no words for my state of being. When I reemerged and once more saw the beach and sea and sky I was overwhelmed by their beauty. I fell to my knees in a paroxysm of gratitude. Gratitude for all that beauty, gratitude for Ann and our years together, gratitude for all I'd learned in AA and my analysis, knowledge that allowed me to experience rather than act out, repress, or anesthetize my grief, gratitude for art and culture, and, to my surprise, gratitude for religion, for Judaism with its tradition and symbol system I could draw on, gratitude for the love of so many people and such exceptional people. I thought of the 23rd psalm, which had been incorporated into Ann's memorial service. I realized that goodness and mercy had indeed followed me all of my life in the form of the wonderful people in it—parents, friends, sponsor, analyst, mentor, and, of course, Ann. I was grateful for every bit of it—all that love in spite of my often best efforts to be unlovable. I stayed on my knees for a long time, weeping hard but no longer in an altered state of consciousness. When I got to my feet I was once again overwhelmed with love for Ann and this world with its manifold beauties. I went back on my knees and again I thanked I know not what. When I got up the second time I felt lighter. Although there were people around, I took off my clothes and went into the sea. There was nothing exhibitionistic about it and I was utterly without self-consciousness. After I dressed I started walking again, weeping intermittently, and I began to reflect on what had happened to me. As I walked I knew, with the knowledge deep within my bones, that I could face whatever demons, pass through whatever fire, because Ann was a part of me—alive within me—just as Tamino had been able to pass through his trials because Pamina was with him. As I continued to walk, thoughts arose within me that carried deep conviction. It felt like insight, however delusional it may in reality be. My physical symptoms were gone. These were my thoughts.

It seemed to me that I had been in a state of alexithymia. My feelings were inchoate, unnameable and unnamed, hence incapable of vocalization or communication. My inner world was a seething cauldron of chaos. The inchoate unnameable was somatized in my head and my hand, in strange feelings and numbness. Insofar as I was capable of giving a name to a feeling it was terror. Then a miracle happened. I was able to leave the desolation of isolation that is an ineluctable concomitant of alexithymia, since what cannot be represented cannot be symbolized, cannot be verbalized, cannot be communicated, so community is not possible—and I found both community and representation in my accessing *The Magic Flute*. I was no longer alone. Mozart and Bergman, Tamino and Pamina, were with me. Tamino's terror before the mysteries, before life without the love of Pamina, gave representation to my inchoate feelings of dread and terror, just as his alliance with Pamina and Bergman's echoing of Mozart's "There is hope—Pamina lives," allowed me to hope and give representation to a truth that I had

had no way of knowing—that Ann lived within me. Now symbolized and verbalized, my feelings could be elaborated, expressed, shared, and worked through. I no longer had to turn them into bodily states—the only course open to me since I rejected acting out or anesthetizing.

I then had a new and different understanding of art, of culture, of religion, of therapy, and, I think, of life itself. They all served the same purpose. They gave voice to the previously unexpressed and inexpressible, allowing the supplicant-patient, through an act of projective identification with the cultural product, religious ritual, or therapeutic interpretation, to verbalize, express, communicate, give form to, and work through what had been chaos. I knew then that the function of all these human institutions was to move people from the inarticulate isolation of alexithymia into the realm of the representational that makes community possible. I had a new and different understanding of the function of interpretation in psychotherapy: interpretation doesn't so much explain, although it sometimes does that. Far more primordially, it gives voice to. And in giving voice to, it moves the patient, in an act of projective identification (projection onto the therapist of what he or she can't express, which the therapist then processes and gives expression to, which in turn allows the patient to identify with his own projection and to re-internalize it, once again making it his own but now verbalized, vocalized, and shared) into community, communication, and potential for working through. Hegel was talking about exactly the same thing from an ontological perspective when he spoke of cultural products as "concrete universals" in his dynamic of history. Further, the work of art, the cultural product, the religious tradition or ritual, and the interpretation serve as a self-object function, but more of this later.

I did not remain in the realm of symbolization, verbalization, and articulation when I felt Ann's hand in mine. I passed another nonverbal state characterized by convulsive sobbing without reflection or self-awareness. It is a state that can have no representation. Experientially it is neither temporal nor spatial. Yet this nonverbal state of being is the antithesis of the alexithymia. I call it the ineffable or pure experience. It is simultaneously the apotheosis of individuation and the culmination of relatedness—relatedness both immanent and transcendent. One then returns from the ineffable—the state of pure experiencing—to the realm of the represented in which verbalization, communication, and embeddedness in community are again possible. The ineffable is to whatever extent possible incorporated into and worked through in the realm of the mundane symbolic. It seemed to me, walking on the beach, overwhelmed and ravished by love and beauty, that all of life is a dialectic of alexithymia to verbalization to—if we are very lucky—the ineffable of pure experience and the return to verbalization. That is what development is about. And what all institutions, traditions, and procedures that human beings have evolved to enable that development are about.

I further realized that all these activities required sanctification for them to be maximally efficacious. They all partake of the sacred and require a sacred space; that is, they necessarily require ritualization. The ritual serves to demarcate the boundary of the sacred space. The idea of the therapy session needing ritualization in order to demarcate it as occurring in a sacred space that provides sanctification to the activities performed there has something in common with Winnicott's notion of therapy occurring in a "transitional space." What occurs in the transitional-sacred space is projective identification.

The cultural-therapeutic projective identification does three things: (1) It gives voice to and articulates the inchoate, gives structure and meaning to chaos; (2) It provides the security that enables movement out of the alexithymia. The articulation and the projection onto it, along with its subsequent reintroduction, constitutes a holding (Winnicott), contextual (Scharff), selfobject (Kohut) transference. There is a dialectical relationship between (1) and (2) as the contextual transference enables the articulation even as the articulation enables the transference. (3) The embeddedness in the articulated transference eventuates in the discharge of what Freud and Breuer magnificently called the "strangulated affect" and this derepression experience ends the somatization, acting out, and/or anesthetizing with drugs and alcohol of the affect now expressed, experienced, and potentially worked through.

As a result of both the derepression and the symbolization and verbalization of the emotional, both communication and work become possible and community is established with therapist, with the creator of the cultural product, and with each and all of the human beings who have struggled on this earth, expressed the same feelings, fled from them, drowned them, worked with them, acted on them, and sometimes transcended them into the realm of pure experience. The patient-participant is no longer alone, and in that transcendental community, his pain, although no less intense, is transmuted and given meaning.

Seen from this perspective, therapy becomes the most vital of activities and the practice of this impossible profession, which deals with elusive intangibles, becomes of supreme importance. In the movement from the alexithymic to the articulated and the expressible to pure experience lies the hope of "cure"—cure of depression, anxiety, and addiction. Facilitating this dialectic is of the essence of their treatment. The relationship between the inner and the outer, between the inchoate within and the representation without, is truly a projective identification. Of all the millions of cultural artifacts that might have come to mind, it was *The Magic Flute* that precisely expressed what I could not express, which allowed me to objectify an inner state with which I then identified and was able to then make my own in a way that was articulated, communicable, and expressible. Similarly, of all the interpretations the attuned therapist might make, it is the one that is being induced by the inchoate unexpressed and inexpressible within the patient that gives rise to a feeling state within the therapist which is then objectified and identified with by the patient, who can then work with it.

Just as insight into this dynamic gives meaning and salience to therapy, it changes one's understanding of art and of culture (at least it does for me), which are no longer seen as decoration and entertainment, however valuable these may be in themselves, but as yet another manifestation of the dialectic of alexithymia to articulation to experience and back to articulation.

And so I learned from David that the dynamic of life is the dynamic of culture is the dynamic of psychotherapy, and that it is this dynamic that makes love and work possible.

Countertransference Ensnarlments

One of the subtlest, yet most ensnarling forms of enslavement is countertransferential. Here it is the therapist, not the patient who loses his or her freedom either through overidentification, sometimes to the point of blurring of boundaries, even of merger, or through bonds of powerful passion either of love or of hate. If the therapist is substance involved, or turns to drugs or alcohol in a mistaken attempt to master his or her countertransferential feelings, the situation is even more dire. Perhaps the most famous case of countertransferential self-destruction is fictional, that of F. Scott Fitzgerald's Dick Diver, the psychiatrist in his novel *Tender Is the Night (1933)*, who falls in love with a patient, marries her, and destroys himself with alcohol.

Dr. Sonnenshein also had his problems. His analytic career had gone swimmingly until he met Karen, an "abductee," that is, someone who has been kidnapped by aliens and has now returned. Abductees are also known as "experiencers." At first Dr. Sonnenshein was, to say the least, skeptical, particularly when Karen replied to his objections to her descriptions of the aliens and their spacecraft, not to mention their sexual experiments on her, as being right out of "The X-Files" and other science-fiction stories and films, by saying, "That's another manifestation of the alien's superior intelligence. They implanted those descriptions and narratives in the script writers' minds by tele-communication so that any story experiencers like me told would be discredited and their presence remain unknown." But as time went on, Sonnenshein came to believe her. For the first time he lost his boundaries and became pathologically overidentified with a patient, probing deeper and deeper into the alien world that had come to fascinate and obsess him. He lived for Karen's sessions until, in a denouncement reminiscent of Robert Lindner's (1954) tale of the "Jet Propelled Couch" in his autobiographical classic *The Fifty-Minute Hour*, Karen came to a session infuriated, screaming, "Damn you! I finally found a competent psychiatrist who correctly diagnosed me and put me on antipsychotic medication! I'm suing you for malprac-tice!" His malpractice insurance and a brief reanalysis took care of this episode, but Sonnenshein's troubles were just beginning.

THE PROSTHETIC AMYGDALA

"Mrs. Hyman Dreck called for an appointment." "Mrs. Dreck? You must be kidding, unless she's crazy." "I'm not kidding. She was very insistent. She wants to see you immediately. She wants you to fit her husband with a prosthetic amygdala." Dr. Sonnenshein stared at his secretary as if she had gone out of her mind. "Prosthetic amygdala?" Nancy nodded affirmatively. "What is this routine. Isn't it enough I have to listen to *mishegas* all day without your going around the bend?" "All I know is that Mrs. Dreck, wants a prosthetic amygdala for her husband. I gave her an appointment for three this afternoon. Mr. Highboy canceled." "Nancy! Why do you do things like this to me? Highboy pays whether he shows up or not! What do I need this lu-natic for?" "You're a psychiatrist aren't you?" "All right, I'll see her, but if I hit the button, call 911 immediately." Sonnenshein had been trying to fire Nancy for years. Only his certainty that she was unem-ployable elsewhere restrained him. Mumbling loud enough for Nancy to hear, he ruminated, "If this turns out to be trouble, I really will fire her this time." Half amused, half curious, and fully furious, Sonnenshein entered the inner sanctum of his consulting room, flipped through the *Playboys* he found wedged between analytic journals, and waited impatiently for his first patient.

Sonnenshein's concentration wasn't what it once had been and by his fourth analytic hour of the day he regularly had trouble keeping his mind on what his patient was saying sometimes even interpreting the previous patient's dream. Fortunately, patients took his totally off-the-wall interpretations as evidence of his brilliance and worked hard at understanding their analyst's cryptic comments, but this degree of inattention was rare. Most of the time Sonnenshein quickly pulled himself back from his reveries and attended to the weeping or raging body on the couch. But not today. Sonnenshein just couldn't get his mind off Mrs. Hyman Dreck and the prosthetic amygdala. He pictured her in many guises, finally settling on an image of a sexless, 200-pound, disheveled, near psychotic, coprophagic who didn't have a husband. Perhaps she will turn out to be analyzable with the aid of a suitable dose of neuroleptics.

As the day wore on, Dr. Sonnenshein thought less and less about Mrs. Hyman Dreck and more and more about the prosthetic amygdala. Could there be such a device? Could it be programmed to give the patient a simulacrum of a normal emotional life? Sonnenshein was fantasizing a Nobel when Mr. Hyperbland's session came to an end. Sitting through Hyperbland's hour was always torture; staying awake took prodigious effort. But not today. He hadn't heard a word of Hyperbland's continuing lament thanks to his obsessive fantasizing about the prosthetic amygdala. Sonnenshein's fantasy was cruelly interrupted by Nancy's nervous announcement, "Mrs. Dreck is here to see you." Sonnenshein thought, "Damn her, she's always buzzing at the worst possible time." Mrs. Dreck entered. She was nothing like the doctor's fantasy, but rather young, pert, self-assured, and sexy in a classy way; she was almost beautiful. Losing his analytically neutral equanimity that normally made it impossible to discern his state of mind, Sonnenshein's amazement was all over the room. What had this enticing creature to do with the tormented nut Sonnenshein had anticipated?

Recovering, Sonnenshein moved into professional high gear. Objectively assessing the situation he drew on his long experience to reflect that lunacy can be well packaged. Still thinking about the meaning of the call and of the woman standing before him, he greeted her cordially, but not too warmly, as he did all patients. Although well-packaged lunacy was possible, it seemed more likely that this was a put-on of some kind. But why such a put-on? Wasn't such behavior symptomatic? But symptomatic of what? Fully engaged, Sonnenshein reached for a provisional diagnosis. Such a hypothetical formulation allowed him to integrate the often bewildering complexity of the data gleaned from an initial interview. Sonnenshein was as good as he was because unlike some of his colleagues he knew that such diagnostic formulations were hypothetical scaffoldings to be disassembled when their usefulness was superseded by the edifice of relationship. What happened in the room between the patient and the analyst was real, not hypothetical. But for now, an organizing probe was useful. But which probe to use? Assumption of madness or assumption of strange eccentricity—or some capacity for bizarre humor serving some unconscious emotional purpose or merely some unconscious emotional need? Sonnenshein concluded that it was impossible to know. Did he need to? Better to simply listen for now? Mrs. Dreck, anything but self-possessed by now, was pouring out a litany of complaint about her unfeeling husband. It rambled and made little sense. No, active listening wouldn't do. She was unraveling before his eyes. How to center her, help her organize? Aha, thought Sonnenshein. The name! Get her off her husband—who knows if he even exists—and off the prosthetic amygdala. That psychotic stuff we can go into later. Pull her into the room and into relationship by commenting on her name!

Sonnenshein prided himself on making contact, and his ability to bring his patient into emotional reality, into the here and now of relationship with him. He had to wait several minutes for Mrs. Dreck to pause long enough to get her breath to interject, "Mrs. Dreck, I'd like to learn a little more about you before we discuss your husband. Your name is a bit unusual; it isn't perhaps a stage name? Or one you gave yourself?" Mrs. Dreck laughed. "Oh, no. It's my married name. Hymie comes from a long line of Drecks. I was very young when I married; still a student at Vassar. Everyone I knew told me not to marry him, that he was a *grubber yung*." The Yiddishism sounded strange in the mouth of this histrionic Seven Sisters sophisticate. "A *grubber yung*, crude as they come. God knows what attracted me to him." Sonnenshein's mind wandered to the story of Mollie meeting Rachel. "Mazel tov, Mollie. I heard your daughter was married." "Mazel tov? Some mazel tov! You should see the groom. So crude, such a *grubber yung*, such a *balagoola*. You know my Rosie, so gentle, so educated, so refined, so delicate, so pure. And she had to marry such a *grubber yung*. So crude is he that when he stepped on the glass to smash it, it was with such violence, such force, that my delicate, *edel*, refined, educated, pure Rosie almost miscarried." Sonnenshein trusted his unconscious; it hadn't gone to the joke for no reason. Had Mrs. Dreck married Hymie because she was pregnant? Returning from his reverie, Sonnenshein came in in the middle as Mrs. Dreck was discussing her fatal attraction to Hymie. "Yeah, I thought *grubber yungness* was toughness and crudeness strength; I mistook Hymie's crudeness for masculinity. I was raised in Westchester in a town where no one knew how to fart. Hymie had no trouble farting. I fell head over heels in love with him. He was the antithesis of the kind of faggy preppie my family wanted me to marry. To me he was an exotic. Hymie turned out to be as manly as a stone, as exotic as a pile of shit. The only thing he turned out to be good at was making money. I'm not sure how. I'm pretty sure his business is some kind of racket. He's probably linked in some way to the mob. I didn't need the money anyway. My father made a fortune as a silent partner of his Wharton roommate. They manufactured votive candles. You can't have a mass without candles from Finkelstein and Stasilone. Of course, my father's name couldn't be on the candles and I couldn't really say what he did. No wonder my parents wanted me to marry some straight-arrow proctologist. My father went to temple on Rosh Hashanah to pray for the well-being of the Pope yet—to get more Catholics back in church to light more votive candles. My dad's a worm. Hymie is a *starke*."

Sonnenshein was reeling. Was this husband, if he really existed, a strongman for the Mafia? Was Sonnenshein in danger if he treated the wife? Her story was less and less probable. Perhaps she was delusional after all. Sonnenshein could feel waves of anxiety passing through his body: a gangster and a crazy, who needs this? I'll refer them to some marriage counselor I can't stand. Once again Sonnenshein pulled himself back into the room by centering on Mrs. Dreck's anality. Forcefully concentrating his mind to focus his thoughts on her material felt like tightening his anal sphincter. Was this a projective identification? Was Mrs. Dreck's preoccupation with things anal inducing his comparison of focusing his thoughts to tightening his asshole? Was her anal fixation the key to understanding her behavior? Sonnenshein filed his thoughts on Mrs. Dreck's anality away for future use and tuned in on her increasingly frantic verbalization.

"My maiden name was Sadie Finkelstein. I couldn't go back to Vassar for my senior year as Sadie Dreck so I changed my name to Samantha. Now I'm Samantha Dreck." Sonnenshein thought, "Oh, God—from the frying pan to the fire, or should I say from the toilet to the cesspool?" He tried to imagine what it must have been like to have been Samantha Dreck that senior year at Vassar. Such a feat of imaginative empathy was beyond him.

"I tried for years to get him to change his name to Derk or Perk or anything rather than Dreck, but Hymie is stubborn as an ox—he won't. He says he's proud to be a Dreck and he thinks it's funny and it's part of his borderline sadism, his exhibitionism, and his narcissism." Sonnenshein noted the strange combination of attractively lucid casualness, vulgarity, and psychoanalytic terminology characteristic of her speech. He was surprised to note that he was enchanted by it. It never descended to psychobabble, but this was no psychoanalytic virgin. Samantha had been on more than one couch. She became more and more engaged as she related her failed attempts to get Hymie Dreck to change his name. Her indignation rose to a climax as she screamed, "Fuck him, fuck him," for a full five minutes, before collapsing. Screaming was followed by weeping as she related humiliation after humiliation consequent on being Mrs. Dreck. Her sobs racked her body until the whole room seemed to shake. They stopped as abruptly as they started.

"Enough of that. Being Mrs. Dreck isn't so bad—I'm used to it. That's not what I came here to discuss. It's my husband's lack of feeling. He's dead. He never expresses anything. He's like a piece of wood. I can't stand his woodenness. It's like being with a corpse. I'm still in love with him. I'm crazy about him. God knows why; he's terrible, just horrible." She wiped away a tear or two, this time delicately. Sonnenshein wondered if there wasn't more feeling in those two tears than in the oceans wept over her appellation. He wasn't sure. She was so protean. Perhaps she was acting now.

"The other day we were making love; that is, he was fucking me. It was after that I decided he needed a prosthetic amygdala. I know about them, the amygdalas, I read *Scientific American*." There was something about the little-girl way she said she read *Scientific American* that touched Sonnenshein. It was the first human, as opposed to professional or self-probing, feeling he had had during the session.

"Anyway, we were in bed and then the whole thing started to shake. I screamed, 'Bad dog!' He was flattered; he thought I meant him, but I didn't. I meant 'Bad dog.' Tiny, our dog, was climbing into the bed. I pushed Hymie off and rolled over onto my stomach to push Tiny down. And then . . ." She started screaming. Sonnenshein said, "And then?" The screaming followed by wild weeping continued. "And then?" "I was trying to push Tiny down—he's a mastiff for God's sake—he weighs 180 pounds! So there I was on my tummy, wrestling with Tiny who was turned on and hot to go when Hymie got on top and started butt-fucking me." No sound-proofing could contain Samantha's piercing shrieks. "Butt-fucking me—the fucking bastard—while a 180-pound dog was trying to fuck us both. How could he do it? Only one way—he can't feel a thing—at least not outside his dick! Didn't he know I was terrified? No feelings!" Samantha settled into quiet crying. Wiping her eyes, she said, "That's when I thought of the prosthetic amygdala. Hymie objectifies me. I was just a hole to come in. He didn't even care what hole. Nothing about me or how I felt—not even acknowledgment that I felt—that I had feelings at all. How could he think about my feelings when he has none except genital ones? Oh, he makes me come if he can, that he understands; otherwise he's an affective mute. Tiny has so much more feeling, although sometimes he's caninistic, like that night in bed when he got turned on by the smells. But he's a very loving beast, not like my husband. I thought if only Hymie could be more like Tiny."

Dr. Sonnenshein thought of the patient who had had a heart attack in his office and died in his waiting room. His next patient more or less stepped over the body the EMS personnel were working on and insisted on having her session as usual, reflecting, "Why couldn't that be my husband?" The autopsy was positive for cocaine. Samantha repeated, "Why can't my husband be more like that wonderful, expressive mastiff? As I lay there crushed, I reached down to give Tiny a paw job. I did it partly out of love, I knew Tiny was really fired up, frustrated and hurting. I wanted to give him release and pleasure. And partly out of fear—what would he do if he didn't get relief? Hymie paid no attention as he went on butt-fucking me. They came at the same time. Tiny licked my face and went to sleep. Hymie didn't even notice I was getting Tiny off. He pulled out and fell asleep too. I was so hurt, so hurt. How could he treat me like that?"

Samantha desolved once again into tears; this time the paroxysm was explosive. It seemed that her sobbing would never cease, but it did—abruptly and dramatically. She wiped her eyes on her Brooks' sweater sleeve, smiled her most engaging little-girl smile, and continued her story. "I was crushed. I just couldn't stand feeling that hurt. And then it occurred to me that it wasn't his fault. He didn't have an amygdala—at least he didn't have one that worked the way it was supposed to work. There is a circuit board, or a connection, or a ganglia, or something missing. Then I felt enormous compassion for him. The poor thing doesn't have an amygdala. He can't help it; it's not his fault that he hurts me so horribly. At first I thought about a transplant. Maybe Tiny's amygdala could be transplanted to Hymie—I thought, he really is only a dog, so why not? And then I thought Hymie should only be a dog, as lovable and loving as Tiny, and I knew I could never sacrifice Tiny's affective life to give Hymie one even if it were possible. I started to despair again, and then just as I was sticking some Vaseline up my butt-hole with my finger—it was so sore—I thought of you. I had read an article in *Scientific American* that referred to your work in trying to build a bridge between psychoanalysis and neuroscience. Then I felt a peace like the peace that passes understanding that the mystics talk about and I knew that you would build a prosthetic amygdala for Hymie and all would be well. Even the soreness disappeared and I don't think it was the Vaseline. Just thinking about you soothed my soul and my body. I felt completely relaxed and warm as if I were floating in a warm, wonderful bath. Hymie was out, and sharing my peacefulness with him seemed impossible in any case since being close to him felt abhorrent. So I climbed down to the floor and curled up with Tiny and slept the most wonderful sleep I had ever had. In the morning I called for an appointment."

Sonnenshein's mind was reeling. This wasn't a person, this was a bundle of fragments. Nothing held them together. Too many styles, too many ways of expressing herself, too many emotions, and none of them was convincing. Or, at least he was less than convinced. But who knows, maybe the husband and dog and the bizarre name were real. Sonnenshein started feeling as fragmented as his patient. His head spun. Was she a *dreikopf*? Was she a multiple? Was she an hysteric? A psychopath? An actress? A con-woman? A deluded, terribly ill woman? All were possible. Sonnenshein needed to know which was the case, just as he really needed to know what made the patient tick. He realized that he was in danger of being enchanted by her. Without being seductive, she seduced. He wasn't Sonnenshein anymore. He was the *dreikopf*, the multiple, the hysteric, the sociopath, the actress, the con-woman, the psychotic. He was falling apart. Consciously pulling himself together, Sonnenshein shook off his enthrallment and regained his professional identity. He dismissed his confusion, his state induced by his patient's fragmentation, and turned toward examining his countertransference, seeking a clue to his patient's true state. Few shrinks have Sonnenshein's capacity to understand patients by experiencing and understanding how he is reacting to the patient's behavior. Training, inborn talent, and experience had given Sonnenshein an almost preternatural capacity for gaining empathic understanding by reaching into self. Sonnenshein didn't feel bewildered now. He was fully in possession of himself, but he was puzzled. His inward journey had come up with nothing except his moment of being touched by her little-girl voice. In a flood of insight he realized why. There had been no emotion in the room, it was all hysterical, not playacting, but shallow—an attempt to feel by someone who could not feel except through exaggeration and hysterics.

Using his renowned capacity for masterly confrontation, Sonnenshein translated his insight into an intervention that he hoped she would be able to hear. Abruptly pulling himself out of his reverie, he raised his hand to check her babbling about how wonderful Dr. Sonnenshein will build a prosthetic amygdala for her husband, a babbling he tuned out and said, "Samantha, I couldn't feel your pain, and I don't think you felt it either. I felt hardly anything during our session. Your hyperemoting is a desperate attempt to feel. It isn't your husband that needs a prosthetic amygdala; it's you. You came here to feel and asked me to magically help you by building an amygdala for Hymie." Samantha turned white. This time there was no doubt about the depth and reality of her emotion. Biting her lip hard she stammered, "You're right."

Sonnenshein was certain that something important had been achieved, that a therapeutic breakthrough had occurred. Samantha eagerly accepted his suggestion that she enter analysis. During the ensuing months Samantha was no longer hysterical or histrionic; she no longer spun fantastic stories that might or might not be true; her anal preoccupation was no longer in evidence. Her obsessive preoccupation with her husband ceased. She took responsibility for her actions, her state of being, and such feelings as surfaced. It was a cure of sorts, but the patient was dead. There was little in the way of genuine emotion replacing the hyperemotionality of her first session. Sonnenshein used every therapeutic device in his extensive armamentarium—the truth being known, including many nonanalytic ones—but it was to no avail. Session after session Samantha turned up cute as a button in a sweater and pleated skirt looking like Betty Co-ed in a 1940s movie. She talked easily and fluently, but about nothing of consequence. Sonnenshein wasn't sure if he had cured her or killed her. He would have been hard-put to give her a diagnosis—affable, related, functioning adequately. It was hard to justify continuing the analysis, now in its seventh month. Bored to distraction, Sonnenshein had decided to suggest a termination date, when out of the blue, just as she was talking about picking out a new rug for her living room,

Samantha asked, "Dr. Sonnenshein, will you build me a prosthetic amygdala? It's true, I'm not unhappy and life isn't so bad, but I'm not here, there's no me—I'm a robot. I know feeling would help me, and I know that I can't experience joy without experiencing suffering. I'm willing to chance it, so build me an amygdala." She paused and then said, "I do not want to get to the end without having been." Two barely perceptible tears slowly rolled down her cheeks.

Sonnenshein thought of Freud's mordant comment at the end of his life when a visitor said of his reconstructed study in his London exile, "Oh, Professor Freud, it's all here." Freud replied, *"Ya, aber Ich bin nicht Heir."* Samantha was *nicht Heir.* Sonnenshein was being himself—on familiar territory—in relating his patient's experience to some bit of analytic lore. It was the way his mind worked. Then the wholly unexpected occurred—Freud was banished far beyond London and from Sonnenshein's mind as if he had never lived. A conviction emanated from Sonnenshein's groin and radiated upward until it pierced his entire body, that he was helplessly in love with Samantha Dreck. Loving in a way he had never been in love. In love with an intensity that dwarfed the love that he thought he had had for his wife. This was a love that possessed, tormented, consumed, encompassed, shattered. There was no precedent, no precursor, no intimation that such a love could be, let alone be his in Sonnenshein's experience. He had known lust; he had known caring; he had known wanting to be with; but he had never known this ineffable state of being.

Sonnenshein reached deep within to regain possession of himself. The effort was futile. The best he could do was to fall back on his professional identity and analyze his falling in love. It was the tears, something about the two tears and the little girl pleading and the courage. How often he had tried to convince patients that there was something to be gained from revisiting trauma and working through pain, that it was worth it to give up defenses against experiencing it. How often did he try and persuade the reluctant that their feelings, no matter what they were, are good for them. More often than not, it was to no avail. Sonnenshein wasn't sure he believed it himself and here was this lovely young woman solemnly asking to be taken on a journey to pain for the sake of living more abundantly. How could he not love?

Analysis might explain, but it changed nothing. Sonnenshein sat and stared as if beholding a beatific vision as he self-consciously became capable of once again perceiving what she said.

"Doctor, it shouldn't be so hard. I've read that they're now implanting pacemakers to stimulate the vagus nerve as a treatment for depression. That must have something to do with the amygdala. You can do it. Give me a life, Dr. Sonnenshein, I beg you to give me a life!"

Sonnenshein rallied for the last time. Pulling himself away from his enthrallment to regain an analytic posture he said, "Samantha, in the very act of asking for a prosthetic amygdala you become the feeling person you want to be, so you no longer need a prosthetic amygdala."

"Doctor, to feel that I don't feel isn't enough. Even feeling sad that I don't feel isn't enough. It's insight with a bit of emotion attached, not a full affective life. I want more. I want a prosthetic amygdala."

"You spoke of feeling like—that is, being—a robot. Won't having a mechanical device to enable you to feel leave you as robotic as ever?"

"No, doctor. My new amygdala wouldn't feel for me; it would enable me to feel, just like my glasses enable me to see, yet they do not themselves see."

Sonnenshein was washed in such a wave of love that he feared that he would literally dissolve. Trying a last time, he said, "Surely we could build on the sadness you feel at not feeling until you have a full range of emotional experience and expression."

"I know in my gut that I can't do it, my amygdala isn't capable of doing it. My sadness and yearning exhaust its capacity. Listen to me. I know my only chance is a prosthetic amygdala. Please!" Sonnenshein remained silent.

"Doctor, there is something else I should tell you. I've been taking cocaine. I get it from my husband who's been taking it for years. My amygdala can't even let me feel I'm not feeling without cocaine. I need to feel *something,* so I can't stop using coke without a replacement. I beg you! Build me a prosthetic amygdala."

Sonnenshein knew he was being blackmailed. But it didn't matter. He had seen too many destroy themselves with drugs. He thought,

I can't let this wonderful, wondrous creature destroy herself. Incredibly, he heard himself saying, "Oh, my darling, I'll build you Xanadu. I'll build you a prosthetic amygdala." Sonnenshein hadn't actually verbalized these thoughts although he believed he had. What he actually said was, "I'll try."

In the ensuing months, Sonnenshein mastered all there was to know about the limbic system and the amygdala. He saw fewer and fewer patients, ceased attending professional meetings, seldom saw his family, slept little, and worried much—all to no avail. There was no way that knowledge of the microscopic anatomy of the amygdaloid body, as it is sometimes called, could be used to make a prosthesis. Sonnenshein lost weight; his hair whitened; he sank into a depression. Samantha, on the other hand, who was by now addicted to cocaine, seemed to flourish. Her sessions revolved around her attempts to reassure him. The more faith she expressed in his genius, the more responsible he felt. As has been often noted, in responsibility begins guilt. As failure after failure piled up, as one extravagant scheme after another for building the prosthetic amygdala proved illusory, guilt turned to self-loathing. Thoughts of suicide seldom left Sonnenshein's mind. Only the remote possibility that he could help Samantha sustained his life.

By now Sonnenshein's office was more of a laboratory than a consulting room. His few patients had to wind their way through a maze of wires, apparatus, and chemical retorts. On the day he had decided that Samantha was better off without him, his one patient related how he had dreamt that Dr. Sonnenshein was an alchemist. Commenting that children attribute magical power to their parents that gets transferred onto the analyst, Sonnenshein dismissed the bewildered patient, who tripped on the emotionizer, one of Sonnenshein's failed attempts, and almost killed himself on the way out. Sonnenshein mumbled something about the insurance company as he slammed the door. Just as he was reaching for the poison, an idea occurred to him. My God, of course, every first year medical student knows that the limbic system is called the reptilian brain! Reptiles have the finest amygdalas! Dummkopf! You don't have to build an amygdala, you can transplant one! All you have to do is find a way to attach a reptilian amygdala to the putamen and the tail of the claudate nucleus as well as to the neocortex of the frontal and temporal lobes. Of course, I'll have to connect it to the hippocampus and hypothalamus. Six wires and some immune suppressants to prevent rejection and it's done. Sonnenshein grabbed the yellow pages and looked under "C" for crocodile. There was no listing.

A year later Sonnenshein's office was awash in vessels containing reptilian amygdalas. His savings had gone to exotic animal suppliers, but he had done it! There was a lizard with a rattlesnake amygdala who was just fine, and a rabbit with a Gila monster amygdala who was acting rather strangely, yet remained a rabbit. It was time.

Sonnenshein had noticed that the closer he got to his goal, the less he felt. Instead of feeling exhilaration he felt blah. Even his love for Samantha was more a memory than a reality. The only thing that mattered was his obsession—transplanting the reptilian amygdala into a human who was affectively challenged, as he started to phrase it. Sonnenshein began to wish that someone would give him a prosthetic amygdala. It was true that he had never been a feeling guy. He had always lived in his head, not his heart. His analysis had helped, but not much. His love for Samantha had been an exception, but that had faded. It was almost gone. Yes, that's why he agreed to construct the prosthetic amygdala. It was not only identification with her and her unfeelingness; it was an unconscious wish and hope that he would cure himself. His identification with her had been wonderful; it allowed him not only to understand her but to experience love. Yet what was that love? Was it not narcissistic at root? She was but a mirror in which he saw himself. No, he needed a prosthetic amygdala in the form of a reptilian transplant. Besides, how could he operate on her without a trial? So it was decided. He would operate on himself and install an alligator's amygdala.

The work with the engineers and machinists had been more arduous than the work on the neurochemistry of the limbic system. Still, in only six months the apparatus had been constructed. The helmet with the drills, and the mechanical arms that would be programmed to install the amygdala so carefully dissected out of the baby alligators that lived in the bathtub and that could be programmed to make the six connections, were a technological wonder. Sonnenshein allowed himself a modicum of pride.

With the alligator amygdala floating in sterile saline, Sonnenshein placed himself in the operating chair, injected himself with anesthetic, and pressed the start button just before he lost consciousness. Two hours later, his wife, who fortunately had come to his office to serve divorce papers on the grounds of insanity, found him lying in a pool of blood with the baby alligators who had escaped from the tub gnawing at his extremities. Just as Sonnenshein regained consciousness in the intensive care unit, Samantha rushed in. Embracing him, she cried out, "Thank God, you're still alive! Thank God, you're going to be all right! And there's been even better news! I no longer need a prosthetic amygdala. Hymie and I stopped using cocaine and I'm all right, but he has post–cocaine abuse anxiety disorder so he's expressive as hell and constantly trying to please me. He's even willing to change his name. My life is unbelievably wonderful now! It was him after all; now that he's emotionally alive, I am too. We were on the wrong track. But that doesn't matter, you cared for me when no one else did and that got me through. Thank you for trying to help me. I'll always remember our work together. I hope your brain heals all right and the animal rights people aren't too tough on you."

Sonnenshein, suddenly overwhelmed with sadness, wept inconsolably at the follies and illusions of humankind. He, too, no longer needed the prosthetic amygdala, or looked at from a different perspective, perhaps the prosthetic amygdala worked after all.

TRANSFERENCE

The analyst had been deaf for years. He learned to coordinate his "Umhums" with variations in his patients' breathing. Somehow he sensed when to say, "You are thinking how much I am like your mother." If the patient writhed on the couch, he knew he had scored. If the patient's body language gave no clue and his breathing pattern remained constant, the analyst would wait until the stillness of the patient's head signaled an interruption in the flow of associations and say, "You reject, not even reject—simply act as if I didn't exist—my interpretations. You are doing to me what your mother did to you—turning a passive experience, having it happen to you, into an active one, doing it to me, as a way to master the trauma of being treated like you weren't there. And you want me to feel what you felt—shame, humiliation, hurt—deeper than you can imagine—and rage—the rage you express by treating me as if I didn't exist."

The analyst had learned long ago that all of his patients were so narcissistic they inevitably felt that they had not received their just due, that both family and world hadn't recognized their greatness. So the "You reject my interpretation" interpretation rarely failed. More often than not, it brought tears. In his more sadistic moods, the analyst would add, "You felt so impotent, so small, so like a piece of shit—a tiny insignificant turd—and that's the way you want me to feel." That inevitably brought tears.

If a patient remained silent for any length of time, the analyst would say, "You are thinking of sucking my cock." If the patient seemed unmoved, the analyst would continue, "Or, perhaps of my fucking you up the ass. Sucking or fucking—either way you take in my strength, the strength you wanted from your father, a wish you could never admit." The analyst prided himself on the directness of his communications. This, too, almost inevitably worked—none of the analyst's patients felt that they had connected with their fathers.

Just to make sure the patient didn't think he was fixated on the homosexual transference, the analyst handled the patient's next protracted silence by interpreting, "You were thinking of killing me, but you were afraid to say so because you fear that I will castrate you." Sometimes he added, "Just like you feared your father would do when you wanted to kill him when you were six." However, over the years the analyst had noticed that patients became more anguished if he did not make the connection with the father, so now he only did so out of boredom.

The analyst wasn't quite so deft with female patients. Yet, with the aid of the biographies he asked them to write as part of the treatment and some lip reading in the initial face-to-face sessions, he had enough information to say "Um-hum" appropriately. All in all deafness wasn't so much of a barrier to doing analysis. Besides, what difference did it make? As Freud had said, "They all—the most hidebound conservatives as well as the most fire-eating revolutionaries—want consolation—and I have none to give them." Life sucks and analysis can't change that. The analyst also often thought that the best that analysis can do is to change neurotic misery into ordinary human unhappiness, as the father of his profession had said. And most of the time he believed he couldn't even do that. So deafness didn't much matter. They all say the same thing anyway.

The analyst often mused that being deaf wasn't so bad—perhaps it was even an advantage. After all, there were so many things that he didn't want to hear. It was true that gender was a bit of a problem. It was harder to fake it, although the analyst didn't really think of what he was doing as "faking it" with a woman. Fortunately, most of his patients suffered gender confusion, so it didn't really much matter if he gave a male response to a female. In any case, androgyny was in, and it wasn't too hard to turn lack of therapeutic tact—as disastrous misstatements on the part of the therapist are euphemistically called—into therapeutic triumphs—a challenge that the analyst really got off on.

The analyst missed Mozart, but otherwise found that not hearing what people said was no great disadvantage. When he needed to he could lip-read, which he did quite well. The analyst's sometimes frantic need of reassuring himself that his deafness was inconsequential was expressed in a sort of rehearsal—a rehearsal of what had become an almost obsessive thought—"I can smell a fart readily enough, who needs to hear it, too?" Anal themes had played a central role in his training analysis and he usually gave his seminar students an assignment to "contemplate the asshole." No, it wasn't being unable to hear with his two outer ears that troubled the analyst; rather, it was the deafness he had developed with his third ear—the one lengthily and painstaking trained to listen to and for the manifestations of the unconscious, to hear the dynamic process inherent in the self-absorbed narratives patients had spewed on his couch for thirty years. The analyst's gaze frequently wandered from his analysand's almost convulsively heavy breathing to the worn crumbling paperback volume of Theodore Reik's classic, *Listening with a Third Ear*, and he cringed. This third ear had grown ever deafer years before he had lost his hearing in the other two. He had first become aware that it was dwindling away years ago when he became anxious over his growing inability to make sense of dreams. It was something like a deepening tone deafness. He just couldn't catch the resonances. The analyst's interpretations became progressively more mechanical, banal, stereo-typical—and he knew it. In the old days he had been able to virtually dream along with the dreamer, and had been able to see behind the manifest content to the underlying meaning. Now dreams were opaque. It was as if he had lost not only his third ear, but his third eye—blind and deaf in the realm of the unconscious. Should he become a behaviorist? He was hardly an analyst anymore and he knew it. But dreams—however much they might be the "royal road to the unconscious"—weren't the only road. There was the transference. But that too grew opaque. The dynamics of interpersonal relations now befuddled him. Half the time the analyst had no idea what was going on between him and his analysand. What was projection? What was realistic perception? Who knew? All was a mystery. It was only after his third ear failed that the analyst's hearing in his other two ears dimmed and within a few years failed altogether.

Ironically, it was his deafness that prevented the analyst's suicide. Now that he couldn't hear, he was protected from crushing feelings of failure and loss. Deafness spared him catastrophic anxiety and the blackness of despair. He was no longer capable of knowing what he did not know. Besides, his stereotypic interpretations and well-timed "Um-hums" worked magnificently. Not troubled by the nuances of true analysis, or the discomfort of penetrating interpretations, patients flocked to him. The analyst might almost have been said to start a new school of psychoanalysis—the collusion school. It worked beyond anyone's wildest dreams—analysand and analyst were gratified, their self-esteem rose, transference love induced countertransference love, a warm glow hovered over the treatment room.

The analyst's practice grew until he had no hours open. There was a waiting list. His refusal to publish papers only enhanced his aura. Of course, the real reason he hadn't published was that he had nothing to say, but his colleagues thought that he was reluctant to share his breakthroughs in analytic technique. As the years went on, he became a legendary figure in New York analytic circles. Other analysts despaired, and many gave up. The ravages of managed care were killing the profession. Worst yet, the climate of opinion had changed. To admit to being a practitioner of Freud's profession, let alone a Freudian, was to be perceived as a practitioner of an expensive, useless, misogynistic, pseudoscience. Empirically verified short-term solution-oriented therapy was in. There were surprisingly few suicides in the profession, but in any case, our analyst was protected from all that. His cache, his long waiting list and the deep pleasure, the self-satisfaction, the feeling of being perhaps a genius that the efficacy of his "Um-hums" and his almost infallible knack of calling out just the right one of an admittedly limited repertoire of interpretations protected him from both managed care and the trashing of analysis. The deafer he became, the stronger his self-love became until now he basked in the warmth of adulation of profession, patients, and self. Never had his self-regard been so high—or his income. For the first time in his life he didn't have to think about money. He could spend freely and buy what he wished. And what he wished to buy was heroin—pure heroin, the best, the good stuff. Now at long last he could afford all the heroin he craved.

Dr. Emanuel Sonnenshein said quietly but firmly, "That's enough, Mr. Dunkelfarb. You're in negative transference again. Your fantasy is entirely about your feelings about me. Your hatred for me knows no bounds. But it isn't really about me. We're going to have to end now, but in our coming sessions we're going to need to analyze your fantasy in as much detail as possible." Dr. Sonnenshein made a secret vow to never take a writer like Dunkelfarb as a patient again, especially one who obsessively reads psychoanalytic literature. He was angry with himself for letting his annoyance come through in his remark about negative transference, but this patient was impossible.

At the next session Dunkelfarb staved off Sonnenshein's desire to analyze his fantasy by saying, "Dr. Sonnenshein, you know it's poor analytic technique to interfere with the patient's free flow of thoughts.

Trying out my plot lines and characterizations on you frees me up to write my short stories and novels. That's what I'm paying you for, and don't forget it—so get out of my way!"

Dunkelfarb fell silent but not for very long and then continued: "The analyst needed the heroin not only because he was addicted and feared the anguish of withdrawal, but far more saliently to silence the voices arising from the depths within that threatened to puncture and destroy his euphoria. Dim as they were, they had to be silenced. Even with heroin, the analyst couldn't totally stifle the voice that was no less insistent than it was low. It endlessly reiterated, 'You're not in a state of grace. You have done awful things. You are a fraud. You don't listen to your patients even when you have the capacity to. No wonder you can't hear the unconscious—there's no music in you, no poetry in you, you can't dance. You're superficial, conventional, self-absorbed; a narcissist who will never be a flower, a travesty of a lover—between poor performance and your perverse preoccupations you are an effront to Eros. Even worse, you're a coward.' But most of the time, heroin assured the analyst that if waiting list, fortune, and reputation didn't stifle the voice, then something could and would."

Dr. Sonnenshein interrupted, "Mr. Dunkelfarb, you entered analysis because your drug use was getting out of control and that frightened you. Don't you think that has something to do with your attributing heroin addiction to me?" "I'm not attributing it to you, dummkopf! I've been sharing my latest story with you. Aren't you supposed to support my creativity?" Sonnenshein ran out of patience, "Come now, be serious. The analyst in your story certainly isn't Sigmund Freud. Of course, it's me." Dunkelfarb shot back, "You mean you're another fraud!" Sonnenshein lost control shouting, "Stop this nonsense! How can I help you if you won't be serious! Our work together is a series of put-ons, just like your life!" Dunkelfarb wet his pants. The urine soaked through to stain Sonnenshein's immaculate couch. Sonnenshein almost terminated the analysis but restraining himself said, "Mr. Dunkelfarb, that wasn't anxiety—that was hostility."

Dr. Sonnenshein was deeply troubled with the session. He was retaliating and it showed in his interpretations of his patient's associations, in his lecturing, his ridiculing, his moralizing. He had missed a golden opportunity to get to the core of Dunkelfarb's pathology. Why hadn't he asked the patient to elaborate on the "analyst's sexual inadequacy" and "perverse preoccupations?" They were assuredly anal in nature but they needed exploration.

Sonnenshein knew that he just wasn't doing the work that he was capable of. Why was he reacting so powerfully and inappropriately to Dunkelfarb's provocations? Was there a grain of truth in them? More than a grain? Was it all his countertransference? Dunkelfarb did remind him of his wiseguy brother the Seventh Avenue multi-millionaire who he could barely stand. Or was Dunkelfarb inducing in him a rage similar to his own as a form of communication—a way of making Sonnenshein know how it felt to be Dunkelfarb. Hadn't Dunkelfarb's ridiculing such an interpretation in his fantasy made it likely that it was true? Sonnenshein read up on projective identification, as the dynamic by which the patient induces emotion in the analyst is called. That helped, as did his self-analysis of his counter-transference. He regained mastery of his professional self and started doing first-rate work with Dunkelfarb. Once again, the distinctions between projection and projective identification, between transfer-ence and countertransference, became clear and Sonnenshein was able to give nuanced, well-timed, nonretaliatory interpretations that Dunkelfarb was able to hear. Dunkelfarb's self-revelations in his fan-tasy were illuminated. His use of mockery, sarcasm, and devaluation as defenses against feeling, memory, and intimacy was made mani-fest by Sonnenshein's interpretations of the fantasy. Dunkelfarb's use of the fantasy to emasculate Sonnenshein and render him helpless, his terror at learning the intensity of his self-hatred, his homosexual panic, lest Sonnenshein get close to him, and the yawning chasm—the abyss—threatening should his creativity fail were all made con-scious. Sonnenshein was particularly ingenious—even elegant—in the way he used Dunkelfarb's myth of the deaf analyst in a many-lay-ered simultaneous and successive interpretation. Delivered over many weeks, always at moments when the interpretation resonated to help Dunkelfarb realize—not only cognitively, but powerfully affectively—that what he feared more than anything else was his muse dying, and the hope/dread that he could salvage something, even if not his integrity, by writing pulp fiction was at the core of his desperate need to defend.

Further, Dunkelfarb was able to hear, however tremulously, that his fear of the failure of his powers was, at bottom, fear of castration—that devaluing and castrating the analyst in his fantasy was his way of projecting the dreaded threat onto someone else, while simultaneously his mockery held Sonnenshein at such a distance that he couldn't possibly touch Dunkelfarb emotionally or communicate any painful truths to him. Dunkelfarb's fantasy was pure transference attributing to the nameless "analyst" the very woodenness, lack of caring, and emotional blindness and deafness of his father, and Sonnenshein was able to communicate this, too. One of the high points of Sonnenshein's analytic efficacy was his artistry in putting Dunkelfarb in touch with bottomless shame, rage, and feelings of impotence that his father's emotional blindness and deafness had induced. To be neither seen nor heard was not to exist. To be treated as a nonentity was to be a non-entity. It was indeed true that just as Dr. Sonnenshein said, the best moments in his relationship with his father had been those in which he had been treated like a piece of shit. That, at least, was to be acknowledged as existing. Sonnenshein suggested that Dunkelfarb's anal obsessions were existential in origin, that they sprang from his only being recognized as existing when he was regarded as shit.

The searing pain of these realizations freed Dunkelfarb of illusion, of the need for denial, rationalization, intellectualization, mockery, and obsessional thinking. Over the ensuing months layer upon layer of defense was stripped away. Dunkelfarb came to know when he was projecting, when he was getting rid of intolerable feelings by inducing them in the other, when he was misperceiving the present as an almost exact replication of the past. The working-through phase of the analysis had aesthetic value—the Sonnenshein-Dunkelfarb dialogue became strangely beautiful, a give and take of great subtlety, penetration, and emotional truthfulness. Such dialogue is part of the work of art co-authored by analyst and analysand. After his early fall into the pits of a hateful and rejecting countertransference, Sonnenshein had become masterly in the ingenuity and not infrequently kindness with which he conveyed the most unwelcome and painful truths. Dunkelfarb's artistry consisted in the grace, even courage, with which he was able to take in such unwelcome communications from Sonnenshein.

Yet, for all of this, the alliance between patient and therapist remained fragile. Dunkelfarb became melancholic and was more and more silent during the sessions. His mood darkened ever more. Gone were his wild sadistic fantasies, the energizing battle with Sonnenshein, the pure pleasure of intellectual play. A newly won adherent to the reality principle, he was no longer a myth-maker. Melancholy became depression. Sonnenshein wasn't altogether surprised. He interpreted Dunkelfarb's depression as mourning for a lost self, a lost persona, a lost set of defenses, and a lost illusion. Analysis ineluctably entailed grief. He offered encouragement. A new, more real self would arise phoenix-like out of the ashes. The old had to die to make room for the new. Transition was always painful. Sonnenshein was aware that he felt guilt and offered more solace than good analytic technique would recommend. He knew he shouldn't feel guilty; he had merely done his job. Yet he did. He became less supportive, and Dunkelfarb came alive raging at him with open fury. Sonnenshein was relieved. He thought, "We are on our way to a 'cure,' whatever that might mean." But that wasn't to be. At least not yet. Dunkelfarb's rages became uncontrollable; he threatened violence, even murder; his reality testing failed and Sonnenshein and his father became one. He fell into a psychotic transference—you are my father—rather than a neurotic transference—you remind me of my father. Then Dunkelfarb lost it and totally decompensated. Sonnenshein hospitalized him. The analyst felt greatly relieved. Brief psychotic episodes weren't all that unusual in true analytic work. Just as he had predicted, hospitalization provided the structure that allowed Dunkelfarb to reorganize and he left the hospital greatly improved after the second week.

Sonnenshein was confident that the analytic work would soon be brought to a satisfactory conclusion. The crisis was over and Dunkelfarb had the resources to stabilize at a higher level of adaptation than his addicted, pathological old self had been capable of. Sonnenshein was looking forward to their session the following day when the phone rang, "Dr. Sonnenshein?" "Yes." "This is Detective O'Henry. You have a patient named Dunkelfarb?" "Yes." "Hate to be the one to tell you, doc, but your patient checked out last night. Craziest way of doing it I ever saw. He choked himself by swallowing an enema nozzle. The coroner might have labeled it as some weirdo stuff resulting in an accidental death, except your loony bird left a note. I'll read it. 'I'm going to reclaim my creative power by making my death a work of art. I'm going to do the impossible by condensing the oral and the anal—not symbolically, but concretely. It will be as great an achievement as squaring a circle. Give my love to Dr. Sonnenshein, signed Jeffrey Dunkelfarb.' Any thoughts doc?" Dr. Sonnenshein didn't answer, he couldn't. He had fainted.

Dr. Sonnenshein behaved oddly at the funeral. He stood looking at Dunkelfarb's body in the open casket for a long time. Then he starting speaking—not loudly, yet shockingly audibly, "Mr. Dunkelfarb, you did it to deprive me of a successful analysis. Your envy killed you. You had to make a mockery of our work together, to degrade and debase me. It was pure hatred that killed you. Transferential hatred of me. Really, your hatred of your father displaced onto me. You thought you were triumphing over me—over him—but no, you haven't. It's so sad. All you did was grotesquely destroy yourself." One of Dunkelfarb's relatives, fearing a madman had come to the funeral said, "Please." Sonnenshein starting sobbing hysterically before he screamed, "Fuck you, you bastard. You did it to me," as he ran out of the funeral parlor. When he got to the street, Sonnenshein realized that just as Dunkelfarb had provoked him to lose his analytic perspective in life, Dunkelfarb had provoked him to lose it in death. He was back where he was at the beginning of the analysis where he had cut off Dunkelfarb and been sarcastic with him and had retaliated for Dunkelfarb's aggression against him. The analysis had been useless, worse than useless. Not only had Dunkelfarb regressed further than he ever had, so had Dunkelfarb's analyst. Sonnenshein became aware of two mourners leaving the funeral parlor staring at him. Continuing to stare, one said to the other, "Jeffrey sure had some oddball friends." Dr. Sonnenshein's decline began that day.

He found that his concentration, which, if the truth be known, had been spotty for years, grew even worse. He was preoccupied, distracted, losing the thread of his patients' associations. He thought of the joke about the old friends who met on the street after a lapse of many years, "Hymie, I haven't seen you for years. What are you doing these days?" "Abie, I became a psychiatrist, a psychoanalyst." "*Oy vay iz mir*! How can you listen to people's *tsouris* all day long?" "Who listens?" It was true, he no longer listened, at least not consistently, and when he did, he couldn't hear. "Oh, God—Dunkelfarb's words again! Shit! I just can't get him out of my mind. I'm becoming like the analyst in Dunkelfarb's fantasy. Like him, it's not the deafness that bothers me. I've been doing analysis so long, I don't need to attend to what patients say.That's like Dunkelfarb's analyst, too! Oh, for Christ's sake, stop this! This way lies madness! No, it isn't not listening, not hearing. It's not being able to hear with the third ear that devastates me. I'm losing contact with the unconscious. It grows dim, opaque, beneath my threshold of reception."

Dr. Sonnenshein continued to decline. His hearing did actually begin to fail. Deafness was no longer a metaphor. He became more and more obsessive, more and more deeply depressed. He realized the good work with Dunkelfarb had been an aberration. The truth was that he had never been much of an analyst. Besides, analysis itself was suspect. Maybe even the managed care people and the critics were right. Freud was no longer a "climate of opinion." And the present climate of opinion was too much for Sonnenshein. Inner doubt and public skepticism were too much. Sonnenshein fell even further apart—and always it was thoughts of Dunkelfarb. He began to neglect his appearance. His golden blond hair became disheveled. Streaks of gray gave way to solid gray. Everything about him grew shabby and disarrayed. Yet, just as with Dunkelfarb's fictional analyst, his practice grew. He prospered as he became known as the "bohemian analyst," attracting artists and writers whose narcissism and self-absorption appalled him. Yet his own absence during analytic sessions only increased the demand for his services among this clientele. An occasional "Um hum" was all he could still manage. There wasn't much left of the renowned resourcefulness of Dr. Sonnenshein. He began drinking, stopping for a Seagram's Royal Crown on his way home from the office. Soon he was closing the bar. He told himself since he drank only the best it couldn't get him in trouble. He was shocked to find a bottle in his filing cabinet and another in one of his folders behind his notes—not that he took many notes these days.

Yet nothing stopped the obsessing. Now his anality, long relegated to manageable portions in his psychic life by his training analysis, flourished once again. He fantasized his patients in the throes of explosive diarrhea. He ruminated on his past sins, his acts of disintegrity, the earlier suicides in his practice, his clumsiness in bed, his inability to be heroic even on the rare occasions when he could have been. He ruminated that the deafness of his third ear was more an ethical than an intellectual or aesthetic failing.

Sonnenshein tried to reestablish his equilibrium by self-analysis, by reassertion of his professional identity. Always he came back to Dunkelfarb's fantasy. Was Dunkelfarb's fantasy transference, as Sonnenshein had thought? Was it a projection of Dunkelfarb's stuff onto him? Or was it a projective identification—Dunkelfarb inducing his mental states in Sonnenshein? Or was it possession? Had Dunkelfarb taken possession of him like some sort of dybbuk? After all, was projective identification so very different than possession?

Sonnenshein's professional self reasserted itself. That was superstitious nonsense. Possession indeed! Then, with blinding conviction the truth dawned on Sonnenshein. It was none of the above! No, it was reality! Dunkelfarb had seen through his disguises, his persona, his defenses, and had seen him as he really was—a worthless fake. From then on, Sonnenshein's depression was unremitting. Sonnenshein read and reread the American Psychiatric Association's *Diagnostic and Statistical Manual*, fourth edition—that doomsday book, that compilation of every possible mental and emotional disorder. What he read was the symptoms of depression, especially the self-accusations of the patient, the self-recrimination, the unrealistic self-evaluation, the self-hatred. Sonnenshein's professional self told him that his identification with Dunkelfarb's analyst was his depression talking, even if Dunkelfarb had seen something true, it was a partial picture, a distortion. He couldn't possibly be so awful! But reading the symptoms of depression in the diagnostic manual was of no avail. Sonnenshein's feeling self dismissed his professional self. "Dunkelfarb was right; he had my number to the most minute detail." Moving as if in a dream, Sonnenshein once more reached for the diagnostic manual and flipped through the index under "P" looking for possession, but there was no entry.

Sonnenshein considered antidepressants. He had had a patient recently who seemed to be doing better on Prozac. Dr. Sonnenshein had inquired, "Do you think the Prozac is helping?" The patient replied, "Who knows? The stock market went up!" Sonnenshein's stock assuredly wasn't rising. No, an analyst couldn't be on Prozac. Return to analysis? That was hardly possible. Sonnenshein's opinion of his colleagues was even more disparaging than his opinion of himself. No, the best thing was whiskey. His bohemian clientele approved of his drinking, and as bad as his hangovers were, his drinking gave him some relief. At least he knew what Chivas Regal and Crown Royal did, but who knew what another analysis or psychopharmacology might do? Sonnenshein's drinking reached a steady state, and his mood—although blacker than black—felt a little less black after the third drink.

Things went along in pretty much the same way until one afternoon Sonnenshein realized that he hadn't heard a word of his patients' discourses the entire day. His mind was exclusively on Dunkelfarb. Dunkelfarb's voice had to be silenced. His usual six drinks didn't even lower the volume. He could tolerate no more.

The obituaries didn't mention Sonnenshein's blood alcohol level. Nor did they quote the passers-by who had heard the disheveled man crying, "Fuck you, Dunkelfarb!" as he stumbled in front of the truck. Rather they spoke of Emanuel Sonnenshein's many publications, distinguished teaching posts, and prominent patients. The funeral was so well attended that hardly anyone noticed the absence of Sonnenshein's wife and children. On the other hand, Dunkelfarb's demonically grieving widow beat upon the coffin in hysterical grief, crying out, "He restored my husband to sanity!" How much of her hysteria was aggressive hatred of Sonnenshein, and how much bereavement for the death of the only man who had been able to return her husband—for however brief a period—from his manic world of illusion to reality was impossible to determine. She, herself, would not have known, and the attempt to disentangle the conflicting strands of her feelings for Sonnenshein so dramatically expressed at his funeral were to be the subject of her analysis for many years.

Interior Monologues
of Substance Abusers

There are four factors driving any addiction: the pharmacology of the drug (in the case of behavioral addictions the drug is a neurotransmitter released in the brain); constitutional predisposition sometimes denoted by genetics; personality; and the environment. Although personality usually refers to enduring patterns of observable behaviors I subsume psychodynamics under personality which I regard as not only behavioral but as including inner world, conscious and unconscious. If you prefer, you can think of psychodynamics as a fifth factor. The five factors are both etiological and perpetuating, that is, they not only bring about addiction, they maintain it. In principle, if we had complete knowledge of the role of the five factors in any particular case of addiction, we would have an exhaustive etiological explanation of that case of substance abuse disorder.

It is useful for the therapist to analyze addictions in terms of the respective saliencies of the four (or five) factors and then to make therapeutic use of that analysis. Therapeutic use here denotes both treatment planning, since the therapist would ideally do different things with the patient whose drug use was principally determined by avoidance of withdrawal symptoms than he or she would do with the patient whose drug use was a self-medication used to prevent a powerfully painful unconscious conflict from coming to awareness, and assisting the therapist in crafting effective interpretations and educational interventions. For example, a therapist aware of the virtual ubiquity of addiction in a patient's family might say, "With your family history your chances of becoming a social drinker are nil," while with a teenager who wants to get clean but is unwilling to stop hanging out with her heavy pot-smoking crowd the therapist might say, "I know how much you value your friends and how much you would miss them if you stopped seeing them, but you'll never get clean if everyone you spend time with is using," or in the case of a hard-wired sensation seeker the therapist might say, "Mr. Smith, you'll live longer if you give up injecting speedballs (a mixture of heroin and cocaine) and take up bungee jumping. You'll enjoy it just as much," or with a patient whose addiction is primarily driven by a need to keep shame and guilt from consciousness the therapist might interpret, "Every time you start to feel so horrible about abandoning your children you get stoned."

In the material that follows you will hear a group of alcohol addicts, some of whom use other drugs as well, who are musing about their drinking and why they do it, and who tentatively fantasize stopping. They are in what Prochaska and DiClemente (1992) call the "contemplative stage" in their work on the stages of change people go through when they move toward sobriety. All of our contemplators are ambivalent. Following each interior monologue I analyze the contribution of the four factors to the etiology and maintenance of that person's drinking and suggest how that analysis can be used therapeutically. I make a distinction between problem drinking and alcoholism. Controlled drinking is a possible treatment goal with problematics, but not with alcoholics.

ANDY, A DAILY DRINKER

Andy, our first ruminator, is a pretty average guy. He doesn't have unusual emotional problems, nor does he have a family history of alcoholism.

"Am I drinking too much?" The thought comes and goes. I put it out of my mind. I enjoy drinking. Those beers after work with the boys are relaxing, convivial; they don't hurt anybody. So why worry about it? And I really like wine with dinner; it enhances life and makes coming home festive. And parties. Well, parties are fun. So why do I sometimes wonder "Do I drink too much?" . . . The kids bring home all that health stuff from school, but kids are like that—rigid and all too ready to judge, especially their parents. It really hurt when Kathy said, "The dog asks to go out when you get home. You're so loud and harsh. You always sound angry." How does she expect a Daddy to sound, like a choir boy? Then there was that big fight with Ann. But she hardly drinks. A toast at weddings, a half a glass of wine with dinner and not even that a lot of nights. Oh, women, they're all New Years's Eve drinkers like Mother. Well not all. I got upset when Ann said, "The part of you I like hard isn't your head." That was clever, but hell, everyone has trouble getting it up once in a while. She shouldn't have said that. "Give me another beer, bartender." I have to stop this brooding. There's nothing wrong with my drinking.

Andy is a decent sort of fellow; he cares about his family; he has done reasonably well in his career. He didn't use to be troubled by feelings of inferiority, didn't have unusually low self-esteem, and didn't suffer crippling anxiety or depression. Yet he developed into a heavy hitter and he is worried about it. Andy appears to be a guy who developed a drinking problem by drinking. There is no alcoholism in his family and he probably doesn't have any of the varieties of genetically transmitted susceptibility to alcoholism. Perhaps some aspect of his personality attracted him to alcohol. It seems to be a social facilitator for him. Perhaps he was shy as a young man and drifted into daily drinking as a way of overcoming his shyness. In a sense, it doesn't really matter whether it was shyness or some other trait he didn't like that Andy tried, consciously or unconsciously, to overcome with alcohol. Whatever it was, it started him drinking on a regular basis. He drank, then he drank more, and now he is starting to suffer because of alcohol. He has become psychologically dependent on alcohol, and its addictive properties are likely to lead him to drink even more. If your patient, like Andy, is a daily drinker who is starting to run into flak about his drinking, try not to make him defensive. Tell him he's reacting that way because he's scared—something very important to him is threatened.

Andy drinks too much. He is certainly a problem drinker. There are worse problems associated with drinking but his are bad enough. One way in which drinkers defend is to compare instead of identifying with other people who have trouble with alcohol. In this way their drinking is not threatened. But as AA says, the key word is "yet." I haven't "lost a job," "been in jail," "destroyed a marriage" . . . yet. Although these dreadful things haven't happened to Andy—yet—he is already suffering plenty. By his own admission he has family problems, he has sexual problems, and he is beset by anxious worry.

Andy is drinking too much in several senses. Although I agree with AA that "it isn't how much you drink, but what it does to you that counts," Andy is drinking too much just in terms of quantity. He drinks every day. He drinks before he comes home and after he gets home. He is almost certainly underestimating how much he drinks. Most people do. When patients estimate how much they drink assume that they are counting low, since they almost certainly are. Andy's drinking too much is not drinking to drunkenness. He doesn't do that. Yet, his drinking is drinking too much in the sense that it makes him unhappy in a variety of ways. That's problem drinking. Andy is definitely at risk for alcoholism. He may or may not have crossed what AA calls the invisible line into overt alcoholism. Hundreds of thousands of folks are just like Andy, otherwise normal guys or gals who have become dependent on alcohol for whatever reason and who are now moving toward alcoholism. Could your patient be one of them? If so, use educational interventions. They reduce shame and demonstrate how easily people like your patient can get into difficulties.

MURIEL, A RELIEF DRINKER

Muriel drinks to raise a little hell and to deal with frustration. She enjoys tying one on. Does she drink too much?

What a hangover. Am I glad Jim drove home. It's bad enough for a guy to get a DWI—for a woman, it's the pits. I really wanted to tie one on last night. The headache is worth it. It's a great release. I don't do it very often. Do I do it too often? . . . There's so much stuff on TV about alcoholism . . . I don't think so. Five or six times a year. Sometimes I just want to raise hell. Flirt a little, dance dances I wouldn't dance sober. Jim almost killed me the time I stripped at the New Year's Eve party. I'm glad I did that. We still laugh about it. I'm uptight and letting my hair down felt great. Jim said, "Can't you let your hair down without letting your pants down?" I still wake up laughing about that. Another time we charged a flight to Bermuda and called his mother to take care of the kids. I only missed one day's work. Jim likes to get high too. Life's just too damn dull when we're sober. Getting high is great. Last night was too much, though. It's kind of blurred. It takes more to let go now. Still, life is so short I don't want to miss anything . . . the other kind of drinking I don't like. The kind when I say, "Screw it, I'll tie one on tonight." I do that when I'm frustrated or fed up, or disgusted, or really angry. Jim does that too. Well, what's sauce for the goose is sauce for the gander. If guys can get away with it why not women? Last Saturday was one of those. Job was a horror, Jim was uptight, and my mother was on the warpath so I said, "Baby, tie one on." I did, too.

How's that total up? Six or seven hell-raisers and three or four screw-its a year with an occasional drink in between. Seems all right. Should I cut back? Never had a problem with booze that a couple of aspirins couldn't cure, so why should I? Still, I must be worried. Otherwise I wouldn't be thinking all this . . . I know what I'm going to do—strip at this New Year's Eve party stone cold sober. Wish I could, but I couldn't do that if my life depended on it . . . Well, I'll just watch it. I'm going to stop for a while and when I go back it won't be so often or so much. Time to wake Jim and get ready for tennis.

Muriel is an occasional, or maybe not so occasional, relief drinker. She drinks to get relief from frustration and tension. She calls this screw-it drinking. Muriel also drinks recreationally, using alcohol for its disinhibiting effect. She calls this hell-raising drinking. Muriel is not yet in serious difficulty because of her drinking. She is not drinking alcoholically and it is questionable whether she is a problem drinker. Possibly she can cut back and avoid becoming a problem drinker. Of the three ways of drinking too much, Muriel is not drinking alcoholically, may be drinking problematically, and is drinking too much in the sense of getting drunk. There is no way to know if her borderline drinking problem will progress into full-scale problem drinking or alcoholism. If there is alcoholism in her family, she is on a slippery path. Muriel needs to look at the cost/benefit ratio and see if she is getting more pleasure than pain out of her drinking.

Since Muriel is drinking too much in the sense of getting drunk and having miserable hangovers, she could try not to drink to drunkenness. But that would be a problem for her since she often wants to get blasted. What she doesn't want is to feel godawful in the morning. There are more Muriels than Andys, literally millions of them.

Of the four factors—heredity, environment, pharmacology, and personality—that contribute to drinking too much, it is Muriel's personality that most puts her at risk for trouble with alcohol. I am going to assume that there is no alcoholism in her family.

She lives in an environment where heavy drinking is an accepted way of life and that is certainly a risk factor. She must also contend with alcohol's habituating and addicting properties, but it is her personality that puts her in danger of problem drinking.

Muriel is high-spirited, outgoing, and vivacious. She is a risk taker and on the rebellious side. She has a good relationship with her husband and holds a responsible job. She is in touch with her anger and isn't excessively anxious. If she is masking a depression, she is doing a very good job of it. Muriel is an extrovert and has lots of energy; she plays tennis with a hangover. Her major emotional problems are lack of a better way than drinking to handle frustration, and experiencing herself as sexually inhibited. She feels overcontrolled although most people would judge her undercontrolled. She very much wants to let go and raise hell but feels that she can't do so without alcohol. This is a highly doubtful proposition. "You can do anything sober you can do drunk" is a powerful intervention with patients like Muriel. I have seen people do all sorts of things sober that they thought they couldn't do without some "liquid courage," and I tell patients that.

Muriel has many personality traits that show up in children and adolescents who later become alcoholic. Social scientists like to follow a population from childhood through adulthood so they can determine what people were like before they developed conditions such as alcoholism. Methodological difficulties and high cost result in there being only a handful of studies that cast light on what people are like before they become alcoholic. These longitudinal studies uniformly show that pre-alcoholics on the average are outwardly confident, even overconfident, undercontrolled, devil-may-care, unbridled by convention, and prone to acting out their conflicts. This is interesting, since people say they drink to feel uninhibited. It appears that the uninhibited drink to feel uninhibited. That seems strange, but it makes sense. The people who get in trouble with alcohol are the ones for whom being and feeling unrestrained is most important. Drinking too much is a form of unrestrained behavior to begin with, one that permits yet more and even wilder unrestrained behavior. Muriel is like that—she enjoys letting loose; it is one of her most cherished values. Muriel has more than a little of the stuff that shows up in the longitudinal studies. If a person whose personality is as attractive as Muriel's is at risk for trouble with alcohol then "who shall 'scape whipping," you say, echoing Hamlet. "If you're depressed, watch it; if you're not depressed, watch it. It seems that nobody is safe." Since anyone, regardless of personality, can run into difficulties with alcohol, I have to agree with that. However, people who are at the extremes are the ones who are the most prone to problem drinking: the uptight, hold-it-all-in depressives and the hell-with-the-consequences, let-it-all-hang-out rebels. Underneath, the two types may share more than meets the eye. However that may be, it is important for therapists to know that people like Muriel who are gregarious, outgoing, basically emotionally healthy, have a strong need to disinhibit, and are more or less socially defiant are at considerable risk of developing problems with alcohol or other drugs especially if they run with a heavy-drinking, pot-smoking, or cocaine-using crowd.

Muriel needs to cut back on her drinking. At least she says so, and who am I to disagree? She can easily move from having fun with alcohol to suffering because of her drinking. That cost/benefit ratio can easily flip to the deficit side. A drinking pattern such as Muriel's does not necessarily lead to alcoholism, but there is definitely a risk. If Muriel tries to cut back and cannot she is in trouble and such a failure would be diagnostic of alcoholism.

WARREN, A DEPRESSED DRINKER

Warren retired a few years ago. Like many retirees, he isn't having much fun, and like many retirees, he is drinking far more than he ever thought he would.

It's funny, but I never drank much. Never really cared for it. Mary and I would have a cocktail before dinner if we went out, but half the time I didn't even finish it. It was more the idea of it—seemed festive, and sure, I'd have a drink or two at a party, but it never was very important—wasn't my thing. Sometimes months would go by without my even thinking of a drink let alone taking one. It's different now. Ever since I left Zander Manufacturing I've been stopping at Pete's Tavern in the afternoon. Never though I'd have any problem with retirement. I couldn't wait to get out of there. The last five years I was counting the hours. Golf, bridge, travel, more time with Mary, no schedules, no boss—no more pencils, no more books, no more teachers' dirty looks. Ha! Ha! You never do grow up. I have enough money. There's lots of things I like to do, so why do I sit here every afternoon drinking beer? No harm in it I suppose—something I never did before. What is retirement for if not to try something new? Wonder if I'm depressed. But why should I be depressed? I'm free now—money, time, no real problems. I suppose I do miss some of the boys . . . and Ralph. Losing Ralph, that was hard—so hard for Mary. Just like that—one slick in the road and it was all over at 24. I always hated that motorcycle. But that was ten years ago; I'm over that. The other kids are doing great and the grandchildren . . . well, I guess I'm as much of a fool as the other grandfathers, but they're the best. "Pete, give me another beer." Nice sitting here looking out at the rain and sipping beer. Pete's a great guy and there's the TV and the regulars. I like most of them. Never feel lonely here. Funny though, I'd probably be sitting here if it was beautiful out. Maybe not, might be at the club playing golf. Don't play as much as I thought I would. I always hated the drinking in the clubhouse. People acted so stupid after a while. They used to laugh at me when I ordered chocolate milk. But that was good-natured. People liked me. It's different now. I can't wait to get to the clubhouse and sock down a beer. Maybe I was missing something all those years. Drinking is fun. Relaxes you. Mary never says anything when I drink at home, but I know she doesn't like it—I can see it in her eyes. Good sport though, even says, "Can I get you another beer, dear?" I'm glad I got into beer. Cheers you up. I guess I need cheering up now. Damned if I know why. Never felt the same about the job after I was passed over for V.P. seven years ago. Those bastards might have made some allowances for the fact that I was down over Ralph. I was just a time server after that. Glad I'm out.

"Pete, I think I'll have one more—can't play golf on a day like this." Cheers you up but it does make you tired. Maybe I'll try to cut down. "Pete, did I ever tell you about the time I took the kids fishing in the Rockies and we got caught in a snowstorm in July? Sure, take care of that customer, I'll tell you about it later." Better watch it, I have to drive home in the rain, but what the hell, I'll have a last one. Damn Doc Fisher and his liver enzymes; he put these thoughts in my mind. Why shouldn't I drink a little now that I have the time? Well, maybe I should cut down a bit, it does make you tired.

When it comes to their relationship to alcohol, Warren, Muriel, and Andy are quite different. Warren, unlike Andy, was never much of a drinker. It is highly doubtful that genetic factors play a significant role in his present drinking behavior. There is no problem drinking in his family. Warren is drinking too much because he is having difficulty negotiating a new life stage and can't adjust to the changes attendant upon it. Warren mistakenly believes that alcohol will facilitate the adjustment. Alcohol, seemingly coming out of left field, is now a major or even dominant factor in his life. Warren is having difficulty adjusting to retirement but retirement isn't the only transition that can shake people up, sometimes to the point where they drink to cope, or seemingly cope, with that transition. Graduation, marriage, becoming a parent, promotion or success in a business or profession, divorce, job loss, and relocation are transitions that are sometimes extremely stressful. Success as a stresser may seem odd, but any change in fortune, for better or worse, can be highly stressful. If that stress is self-medicated with alcohol or drugs it is inevitably exacerbated and this can be interpreted and talked about with the patient.

DEPRESSION, LOSS AND DRINKING

Warren is not only having an adjustment problem, he is also depressed. Depression does not cause problem drinking, but using alcohol to self-medicate depression does frequently result in problem drinking and sometimes leads to alcoholism. Warren is dangerously close to late-onset alcoholism and is clearly already a problem drinker. He sort of knows this, but won't allow himself to fully know it—that would threaten the drinking now so dear to him.

Depression has many causes, both psychological and somatic. Drinking doesn't help relieve any form of depression, be it caused by a problem in the chemistry of the nervous system or by a disappointing love affair. On the contrary, it makes it worse. Warren was depressed before he started drinking heavily. Far more frequently, people become depressed because of their drinking. Both patterns exist. Warren had suffered a terrible loss, the tragic death of his son Ralph. He never really got over it. However, he fooled himself, not deliberately or even consciously, into thinking that he had put his loss behind him. Ralph's death was a long time ago and "that was over." It isn't. Unresolved mourning inevitably leads to depression. In fact depression is often a direct consequence of the failure to mourn. Because alcohol anesthetizes feelings, a person can't mourn if he or she is drinking excessively. Therapists need to tell their patients this.

Depression is often masked and not directly experienced. Instead there is a loss of zest for life and beloved activities—like Warren's golf—feelings of boredom and vague dissatisfaction. Difficulty in sleeping, especially early-morning awakening, loss of appetite, and loss of sexual desire are also symptoms of depression. Prolonged feelings of sadness, as well as feelings of helplessness and hopelessness are additional signs of depression. Look for a masked depression before your patient's drinking escalated. If so, he or she is drinking to treat that depression, although patients may not be aware that they are doing so. The therapist needs to interpret this and say "It won't work. Alcohol doesn't alleviate depression; it exacerbates it." Drinking to medicate a depression is always drinking too much.

DRINKING AND BLOWS TO SELF-ESTEEM

Warren suffered a terrible blow to his self-esteem when he was passed over for promotion. It was a narcissistic wound. Narcissistic wounds are injuries experienced very deeply, down where people live. They are injuries to the core self. Vocational roles are central to self-concepts; they are a vital part of the core self. If career disappointment and hurt go too deep, they lacerate to the core. Such was the case with Warren. One response to narcissistic injury is narcissistic rage— anger of monumental proportions. That feeling may be so frightening that it is repressed. But unconscious rage does not go away. It is turned against the self and causes depression.

Narcissistic rage is murderous. It is a response to a threat to the core self. Since it feels like someone is trying to kill a vital part of the self, it makes perfect sense to want to kill that person. An eye for an eye, says the primeval moral code. If one can't allow oneself to experience rage because to do so is too dangerous, or can't express it, as Warren couldn't to his employer, then that rage goes underground. Now without being aware of it the patient is murderously angry at himself. Rage against the self may be so intense that suicide results. Alcoholic drinking has been called a form of chronic suicide. Such drinking is an expression of self-hatred based on internalization of rage. This is usefully interpretable. Warren became depressed in this way and started to use alcohol to anesthetize his pain. His drinking was both an expression of his self-hatred and a passive, indirect expression of his hatred for the Zander Corporation and the people who screwed him there.

I sometimes say something like the following to patients, "We have mental images of ourselves and others. Sometimes we are aware of these self and object representations, as they are called, and sometimes we are not. They may be conscious or they may be unconscious. Normally, your mental image of yourself is distinct from your images of other people. As psychologists say, you have firm boundaries. However, when you are very upset—overwhelmed by strong feelings—your mental images of yourself and others become confused. Your boundaries blur. If you are very angry at somebody, and your internal representation, your mental image of him, is blurred and confused with your internal representation of yourself, then you will be angry at yourself. This is different than turning anger against yourself, but the result is the same."

Warren was confused in this way, and it worsened his depression. This, in turn, resulted in his drinking more. Unfortunately, alcohol blurs boundaries, so once again the attempted cure, drinking, made the problem worse. In fact this cure is worse than the disease. And therapists need to say that too.

Warren might have handled one blow, the death of his son. He might have handled two blows, the death of his son and being passed over, but he couldn't handle three blows. The emptiness, the loneliness, and loss of purpose in retirement did him in. Alcohol will complete the job if he doesn't stop. Narcissistic blows are often dismissed. The hurt and rage go underground and fester. Most people don't like to think of themselves as so vulnerable to hurt, and, of course, being excessively vulnerable is a problem. There are people who are grievance collectors and who nurse resentments. Such grievances and resentments can then be used to justify and rationalize their drinking. Some problem drinkers are grand masters at finding such seemingly rational reasons for drinking. Warren is not a grievance collector. Warren is sensitive all right, but he certainly has been injured. His problem lies in how he handles his hurt, not in excessive touchiness. When his promotion was denied he didn't let himself feel hurt, just as he couldn't endure fully feeling his son's loss. Then, *totally without*

conscious awareness of the connection, he turned to drink to anesthetize and indirectly express those feelings. Now he has a drinking problem of increasingly serious proportions in addition to his other difficulties. He needs to know all of this and therapy can provide that
knowledge.

DRINKING BECAUSE OF NOT HAVING
THE CAPACITY TO BE ALONE

There is another reason Warren drinks too much. Warren is lonely.
Loneliness is a universal human problem. The questions is, how is it
handled? Drinking is one way. People often go to bars looking for
companionship. They seldom find it. There is a sort of pseudointimacy
in a tavern—occasionally even some real intimacy. For Warren the
promise of companionship was not fulfilled. The bartender rebuffed
him. Feeling even lonelier he ordered another drink. That happens
to people all the time. Feeling rebuffed or just plain lonely, it is so
easy to turn to alcohol for companionship. At least the drink is reliably there and always available. Alcohol seems to alleviate loneliness.
Alcohol becomes a best friend. AA knows this. There is an AA rubric, HALT, which means don't get too *h*ungry, *a*ngry, *l*onely, or *t*ired.
AA members escape loneliness by attending AA meetings, where
there are always plenty of people. There is a very real need for companionship, for human contact and relationship. When this need isn't
met, people feel lonely. But the only cure for this kind of loneliness
is people. Alcohol won't fill the bill. Aloneness is a part of the human condition. It can't be avoided. Unendurable loneliness can result from an inability to be alone peacefully, rather than from lack of
companionship.

Donald Winnicott, who was first a pediatrician and later a psychiatrist and psychoanalyst, understood one cause of intolerable loneliness. One of his most beautiful papers is called "The Capacity to Be
Alone" (1958). In it he postulated that the ability to be alone is a
developmental achievement based on a paradox. It develops from the
experience of the small child being alone in the presence of another.

If one has been fortunate enough to have had the experience of being alone joyfully self-involved in play in the presence of a loving, supportive, but nonintrusive parent, one can enjoy being alone. The nonintrusion, the letting alone, or to use Winnicott's language, the "not impinging" is just as important as the "being with." Being alone under such circumstances is a good experience. If one has enough of it, the other person slowly becomes a part of the self, becomes internalized. Then you can be alone without being lonely because you carry your mother or grandmother, or father or grandfather, or whoever loved you with you in you. If, on the contrary, you either didn't have such a person to spend time with you, or to put it differently, you were pushed to a premature independence, *or* mother or her substitute couldn't let you be, was too anxious or too uptight to let you alone, then you will have been unable to develop the capacity to be alone to its fullest. Being alone will be painful and difficult, an experience to be shunned, perhaps by drinking. This is a common dynamic in addiction (see Chapter 8).

Being alone in Winnicott's sense is not isolating oneself; it is not an avoidance of people. It is something positive. It is not hiding, or hiding out because of fear. Avoiding people because you are afraid is defensive isolation. That is not what I am talking about. Being alone in Winnicott's sense is a vital human capacity. It is necessary for growth, for self-actualization, for creativity, and for a sense of completeness as a separate person. Being alone is so much a part of life that we usually take the capacity to be alone for granted. But it is far from being a given; it is something acquired only slowly and only if our early experience is "good enough."

Warren either hadn't developed or had lost this capacity to be joyfully alone. Something was missing inside. One way to make up for something missing on the inside is to supply it from the outside. Warren's beer drinking was, in part, just such an attempt at self-cure. Beer was not only a substitute for human companionship; drinking it was an attempt to internalize a loving presence. This too can be interpreted.

Such a deficiency is a "failure of internalization"—it means something that should have become a part of the self has not done so.

Unfortunately, the attempt to fill an inner emptiness with alcohol never works. It is like trying to self-medicate depression. In one case, the drinker gets more depressed, in the other the drinker becomes ever emptier. The reason this happens is that problem drinking inevitably impoverishes rather than enriches and one is left with an empty bottle, an empty world, and an empty self. Trying to fill an inner emptiness with alcohol is like trying to heal a gastric fistula by eating. It is an exercise in futility.

Warren drinks to alleviate a barely conscious or all-too-conscious depression, to express rage passively and indirectly, and to be companioned. The therapist needs to bring all of this to Warren's attention.

VICKY, A "MAD HOUSEWIFE"

Vicky is a closet drinker. She never goes to bars. She just stays home and sips a little wine. She could hardly get in difficulties that way, could she?

Those kids are driving me out of my mind. I'm going to have a glass of wine while I'm making dinner. I lost it yesterday. I never spanked Susie that hard before; her backside was purple. I get so angry I want to scream. A little Chianti will do me good. I shouldn't have hit her that hard; I don't want to do that again. This wine is great. "Shut up you kids, or I'll give it to you again." Nancy told me that she takes a glass of wine or two when she feels like she's going to lose it. It does mellow you out. Tomorrow I'll have Nancy over and we'll have wine and cheese together. I'll have another glass. "Yeah, do whatever you want. It's okay. Mommie won't get mad." I don't like feeling sorry for myself, but kids aren't people—not really. I need people to talk to. Tom's gone all day and I don't see Nancy often. They're really good kids, just a little naughty now and then. I feel awful about what I did yesterday. Am I turning into a child abuser? When I have the wine I don't get so worked up. Tom doesn't like it though. He says he can't stand coming home to a sloppy wife. I just sip wine while I'm making dinner. What's wrong with that? . . . Mother never drank around the house. Mom would be wild if she knew I hit Susie. She wouldn't like the wine either. Maybe the Valium is better. It doesn't smell. Come to think of it, I'm using a lot of Valium. Tom doesn't like that either, but he isn't home alone in this hot house all day. I'm getting a little . . . confused. I'm starting to feel high. A little too high. Maybe I shouldn't have had the Valium on top of the wine, I mean the wine on top of the Valium. I wish Nancy was here or Tom would come home. I don't like the way I feel. I feel like crying. I love those kids so much, why am I such a bitch to them sometimes? I don't want to be. I'm so moody. It must be awful for them. I'm so angry and anxious most of the time. The Valium stops that for a while. It helps, but not like wine. I get so sad when I drink wine. I can't cry in front of the kids; I'll go into the bathroom. I don't like the way I feel. Oh shit, the stew is burning. Tom will kill me. I better hide the wine and brush my teeth. I'll take an extra Valium. I'm not going to drink alone anymore. Only when I have Nancy over. Tom doesn't mind that so much. If only I wasn't so angry and resentful I wouldn't sip so much Chianti. It is good, though. Okay, I'll drink, but not alone, and I'll hold the Valium down. Oh hell, here's Tom and there'll be another fight.

Drinking to numb or *anesthetize rage* is extremely popular. Vicky, the "mad housewife," does just that. Lots of other folks do it too. Very few people are comfortable with anger. They were told at an early age that it isn't nice to boil over with rage. Women have even more trouble dealing with anger than men. They are more likely than men to have been taught that expressing anger is "bad." They hold it in, or try to, like Vicky. Sooner or later it gets away from them and they hit the kids, scream at the repairman, kick the cat, or just cry with rage. Vicky is an *extremely* angry lady. She hates herself for being so angry. She has no idea why she is so angry. The only thing she knows is that she can't stand it. Since she can't stand it, Vicky has to do something to stop it, and she only knows two ways to do that: mellowing out with Chianti or taking a Valium. Vicky does one or the other, and sometimes she does both. They give her some relief, but unfortunately it soon wears off, leaving her feeling even worse.

Drinking to quell rage is drinking too much. An occasional "fuck you" martini may not be the best way to express anger, but it has its uses. The same cannot be said for the routine use of alcohol to express/repress anger. Routine numbing of rage with alcohol or tranquilizing drugs has nothing to recommend it. Although it masks it, alcohol fuels rage. Then one has to drink more to quell the rage induced by the last drink, and before she knows it, the drinker is on a merry-go-round.

Drinking and "Losing It" with the Kids

Vicky hits her kids. If she is not a child abuser, she is getting close to it. She knows this and hates herself for it. One reason she drinks is to tranquilize herself enough not to react to the kids. Usually it works the opposite way: the kids get beaten when their parents are drunk or hung over. Child abuse and problem drinking are highly correlated. Although Vicky hits her kids when she is sober, she does so because her nerves are raw from the previous day's drinking. Although drinkers don't believe it, children are actually easier to handle sober. Children of recovering alcoholics who were abused when their parents were drinking almost never report being mistreated after their parents get sober.

Vicky also drinks because she's lonely. It isn't primarily that she lacks the capacity to be alone, although this too may be a problem for her. Rather, the problem is that she simply doesn't have enough human contact. One reason she is so angry with her kids is that they can't give her the kind of companionship she craves. Loneliness is painful. It can be intolerable. Many, many people drink to assuage loneliness. I'm not talking about feeling empty inside, just feeling plain lonely. So lonely one can't stand it. Many things make Vicky angry, but nothing angers her more than not having people to talk to. She blames her husband for her loneliness, but she has never told him so. Chianti has become her friend. It's so easy to wind up lonely because you're home drinking instead of out with people. Of course, such drinkers are drinking in the first place because they're lonely. Using alcohol as a friend easily leads to yet another vicious circle, another version of the merry-go-round.

That happened to Vicky. She really doesn't have enough stimulation and she makes sure that she doesn't find any by staying home and drinking. Circumstances are against her, but she makes things worse with the wine and the pills. She needs to be told this.

Vicky, like most problem drinkers, bargains. She doesn't want to give up drinking so she makes deals with herself. She sets limits, conditions for her drinking. She won't drink alone; she'll take less Valium. Social drinkers don't have to make deals with themselves about the conditions of their drinking. They just drink and enjoy it. Setting conditions—not before five, only wine, not with pot, no more gin, and so forth—are signs that something is wrong. It is virtually diagnostic of alcoholism.

Alcohol and Tranquilizers

Vicky takes Valium, a "minor tranquilizer." There are many other minor tranquilizers including Librium, Miltown, Ativan, and Xanax. They are all anxiolytics, antianxiety drugs; they make people more tranquil. Some of them are also muscle relaxants. Chemically they are benzodiazephines. "Major" tranquilizers are not really tranquilizers at all. They are antipsychotic drugs, not antianxiety drugs. They are properly called neuroleptics. Thorazine and Mellaril are examples. They are almost never used for recreational purposes; there is no high and people don't get hooked on them. Not so for the minor tranquilizers. They are all addictive. One needs more and more to get the same effect; that is, they build tolerance, and there is a definite withdrawal. Valium and the other minor tranquilizers are "downers." They are also called sedative-hypnotics. Pharmacologically Valium, Librium, ethyl alcohol, phenobarbital, and the other barbiturates are in the same category—they all sedate and as the dosage goes up they hypnotize; that is, induce sleep.

AA says of these tranquilizers that they are martinis in powdered form. AA calls their misuse "sedativism"—addiction to downers of whatever sort. Sedativism is a disease just like alcoholism is a disease. Cross-addiction to alcohol and minor tranquilizers is extremely common. Vicky is cross-addicted. Her nervous system is constantly being depressed, if not by alcohol, then by prescription drugs. Alcohol and tranquilizers are a dangerous combination. It is far easier to get hooked on the combination than on alcohol alone. Minor tranquilizers are medicines; they have many legitimate medical uses. Staying calm between drinks isn't one of them. They used to be prescribed indiscriminately. This is less true now, but it still happens.

Vicky started drinking too much because she felt trapped and didn't know how to get out of it. Now she's hooked, although she doesn't know it. All she knows is that she's miserable, guilty toward her children, filled with self-hate, and in conflict with her husband. She can't rationally express her dissatisfaction or do anything about it because the very solution she chooses, wine and tranquilizers, prevents her from doing so.

Vicky had one problem. She couldn't deal with her feelings of rage, sadness, and despair. She didn't know how to improve her situation. Now she has two problems: sedativism and not knowing how to express her feelings. There is no alcoholism in her immediate family and genetic factors probably play a minor role in her drinking too much. Her personality, her emotional inhibition, and her fear of confronting her husband with the seriousness of her isolation are the major factors that drove her to the sauce. She drinks too much largely because she can't express her feelings, especially her angry ones. The rest is circumstantial. Her only friend is a heavy wine drinker who serves as a model for sipping away the day; her doctor is an ass who prescribes Valium to shut up complaining women, and her husband is the kind of guy who doesn't want to see anything wrong. He prefers to look the other way—unless dinner is burned. The sheer pharmacological power of alcohol and Valium in combination closed the door on Vicky, leaving her addicted.

Vicky's story is extremely common. Hundreds of thousands of women have lived it. It seems so easy for Vicky to rationalize her drinking. But her rationalizations don't really work for her. She doesn't quite believe them. She is a mass of quivering guilt, conjuring up her mother's disapproval as a stick to beat herself with. Vicky justifies her drinking, "I'm lonely"; "It makes me feel better"; "I don't want to yell at the kids"; "I can't stand the anger, the sadness, the pain." Her justifications should be confronted. Her denial is brittle and properly approached can be penetrated by the therapist.

PEGGY, A BLACKOUT DRINKER

Peggy, our next ruminator, is on the fast track. She's young, bright, well educated, and in the right place at the right time. Opportunity knocks, yet she is miserable. Alcohol and drugs play an all-too-important role in her life.

Who's this guy? Jesus, it's the third time this has happened. Well, they do it pretty much the same way so what difference does it make? I feel awful. Went to Smith for this? Shit, I'll have to do something to change my life. I'm really out of it. Never got that smashed before. Have to stop using grass when I drink, or maybe it's the coke— coke sucks. I'll stick to margaritas and this won't happen. He's really out. Jesus, he isn't even circumcised. Never had one of those before. I wonder what it felt like. Probably real primitive. I must have loved it. Maybe he'll wake up and we'll go around again. Not with this headache. I think I'm going to puke. One more night like this one and I think I might pack it in. Oh hell, I'm too young to check out. Maybe some coke will straighten me out. No, I'm not doing any more of that. Just clean up and get dressed, kid. There's some beer in the fridge. I'll have a bottle—just like a Hemingway character. Beer in the morning; death in the afternoon. Stop this melodrama. So you slept with some hunk in a blackout. Who hasn't? I'll douche when I get home. Just get the hell out of here, okay? Jesus, I'm scared. I don't like what's happening to me. I have a great opportunity at Wallace Publishing and act like a slut. Only when I drink, though. Sex isn't all that great, especially if you don't even remember it. Could screw up my job, too. Feeling better now. That beer really helped. Well, I am having a hell of a good time. I'll cut the coke and either drink or smoke but not both. A little lipstick sure makes a difference. "Oh, hello there, I was just leaving." Nothing like being young and carefree. Why don't I stop for a margarita on the way home? Never hate myself after a few of them. Stop this doom and gloom guilt shit. It's still the weekend, isn't it? Weekends are to have fun. No coke or grass today, though. Everything will be all right. I know it. Maybe I should lay off the booze too. Naw, leave that for Mother Theresa. "So long, fellow. I'll be down at Tony's if you want to join me later. I like the margaritas there."

Peggy had a whopper of a blackout, as alcohol-induced memory lapses are called. The drinker doesn't have to wake up in bed with a stranger or find the police at his door investigating a hit-and-run to have had an episode of *alcoholic amnesia*. Patients say, "Forgetting the end of a party. That's not serious is it?" But amnesia is amnesia and not remembering what one did or said is *always* deeply disturbing. People joke about it, laugh about it, dismiss it as part of the "game," but underneath the jocosity is anxiety or even terror. So upsetting is the experience that people drink to blot it out, which may very well lead to another blackout. Peggy did that. She was so upset by what she woke up to that she assumed a cynical, hard-boiled attitude, far from her true feelings, and picked up a drink. Peggy dismisses anything she had apparently done while under the influence with cynicism, black humor, and an assumed hardness.

Peggy is on the coke, pot, booze merry-go-round, but booze is her real love. She tries to protect her drinking by putting the blame for her difficulties on other drugs. "If only I don't smoke pot or snort coke or use acid, then I can drink without worrying about it." Looking at her behavior from the outside this seems like blatant nonsense, but to a person like Peggy caught up in the fast lane it is a common defense of drinkers. Peggy is certainly drinking too much. If she hasn't crossed the line from problem drinking to alcoholism she is perilously close to it. "Better things for better living through chemistry," said the old DuPont ad. Peggy could subscribe to this slogan wholeheartedly. She is chemically dependent. If it's not alcohol, it's pot or coke. Such polydrug use is more the rule than the exception these days. She still values alcohol the most. It's her drug of choice. The other stuff is ancillary. Blackouts need not be total. They can be partial—grayouts—the sort of foggy, soupy, hazy recollection in which one is not too sure what really happened. Grayouts are *not* a normal response to drinking. Therapists need to educate about blackouts and grayouts and to confront their minimalization.

Drinking to Feel Together

One reason blackouts or grayouts are frightening is that they are interruptions in the experience of self. First you are there, then you aren't there, and finally you are there again. That's weird stuff and can be more upsetting than not knowing what you did or didn't do the night before. Paradoxically, people drink because drinking is integrative, makes them feel more together, more cohesive. Sometimes it also helps people feel more connected, better integrated with their fellows. So the very stuff that they sometimes use to confirm their "togetherness," their experience of themselves as cohesive and enduring, leads to the very opposite experience. Now, far from feeling together, they reach for more cement (booze) in a futile attempt to feel together again. Eugene O'Neill (1929), who was an alcoholic, wrote, "Man is born broken. He lives by mending. The grace of God is glue." For O'Neill's tormented protagonists, as for so many drinkers, the glue was "God's good creature rum."

Drinking to feel more connected is exactly like drinking to alleviate depression, becoming more depressed from the drinking itself, and then drinking yet more to alleviate the depression caused by the drinking. Vicious circles are characteristic of problem drinking; we have encountered them time and time again in our examination of drinking behavior. In each case there is an attempt at self-cure . . . of anxiety, of depression, of the lack of capacity to be alone, of not feeling together, and in each case the attempt is futile. The cure makes the problem worse. Drinking too much isn't a form of depravity, of badness, or a moral lapse. Rather, it is a mistake, almost like a mistake in arithmetic. It's bad logic, not badness that's causing the problem. Drinking too much is often based on a mistake—the mistaken belief that alcohol will heal or cure some inner deficiency or conflict. It never does. All of this is grist for the therapeutic mill and it needs to be discussed by the therapist.

Why Peggy Drinks

Peer Pressure and Drinking

Peggy drinks for many reasons. One of the most powerful is peer pressure. Adults tend to think of peer pressure as something that influences teenagers. The kid got into drugs because he traveled with the wrong crowd. It has nothing to do with us adults. But that's plain untrue. We are all deeply influenced by our fellows. Peers profoundly affect behavior. They are models and to a greater or lesser degree people want their approval.

Peggy runs with a crowd that drinks and drugs one hell of a lot. It is a lifestyle that works for some people; it is not working for Peggy. Peggy had fallen in with a literary Bohemian crowd in college. Typically they were ambitious, convinced that they would write great novels and profound poetry. Some of them may, but for the most part they were dreaming the dreams of youth. They tended to be arrogant, unconventional, and contemptuous of ordinary folks. They spent a lot of time telling each other how great they were. Peggy desperately wanted to be one of them. She identified with their values and with their lifestyle. They drank a great deal of wine, and not a little bit of the hard stuff. Peggy joined right in. She loved drinking and what it did for and to her from the first sip. It was love at first taste. It took away her insecurity and bought her acceptance in the aspiring poets clique. Her new friends served as models for heavy drinking. They gave her permission to drink as much as she wished and rewarded her for doing so. Since Peggy liked to drink anyway, she took full advantage of that permission. The feeling of belonging, of being part of an elite club, which went with her drinking, strongly reinforced it. Pot smoking was just as much a badge of membership as wine drinking in her literary circle. Although she didn't like it as much, Peggy was soon drawing on a joint with as much relish as the single published member of the clique. Peggy's friends romanticized drinking and drugging. She came to share in this romanticization. As she says, she's "just like a Hemingway character." She forgets, or unconsciously identifies with, Hemingway's suicide, a suicide intimately connected with his alcoholism.

Of course Peggy selected her friends, chose a peer group that drank heavily. But that's not the whole story. She went to college at a time when pot smoking was virtually a graduation requirement and shortly afterward entered a viciously competitive profession just as coke came in. Almost all of the young people she was thrown with drank and drugged. So once again her peers expected her to act in a way she wanted to anyway. But Peggy would never have found cocaine on her own. By now she was often depressed. Coke took care of that and it was the in thing to do. She did it, early and often, as Tammany Hall is said to have recommended to its voters on Election Day. Environment played a crucial role in Peggy's early entry into the fast lane. Everybody she associated with was into alcohol and drugs. For all her bravado, Peggy badly needed approval. Outwardly brash, inwardly she was jelly. Taking a drink or smoking a joint was an easy way to get that approval. Insecurity plus peer pressure is powerful stuff. The rest was pharmacological. She drank more, smoked more, and before she knew it, needed it. Throw in some coke and she was in real trouble.

Peggy also drinks to assuage guilt. She is a "closet puritan." She talks like a streetwalker, but the truth is that she is very uncomfortable with her sexuality. She has never had sex cold sober. I have had many patients who had never had sex sober, who were unaware that they needed to drink to go to bed until I drew their attention to it. They were closet puritans without knowing it. Peggy drank in order to have sex and she didn't know it, at least not consciously. She had gotten high in order to lose her virginity and she continued to have a drink or smoke pot to go to bed with her college boyfriend. There were other relationships, all tinged with fear and then she found anonymous sex. Leaving college and moving into the adult world was overwhelming for Peggy. The real literary world, the publishing game, wasn't like her college lit crowd. It was faster, tougher, smarter. If she barely felt safe in college, she now felt terrified. Again, she didn't let herself know it. Instead, she drank and drugged and before long started taking men home with her. Her conquests were reassuring. They were more about being with somebody and being wanted than about sensual pleasure. In the short run they shored up her tenuous self-esteem, but she was never really comfortable with any of it. Her guilt became unmanageable and she picked up a drink, a joint, or a line of coke to escape that guilt. Before she came down, more likely than not she was in bed with someone else, only to awake even more guilt-ridden. What could she do at that point? Drink, of course, and the merry-go-round would start again. Driving ambition; deep-seated insecurity, masked and denied; relentless, repressed feelings of guilt; and a peer group that's heavy into the sauce and other stuff—what else did she need to get hooked? Nothing except the addicting power of alcohol and the other drugs. Peggy's behavior is extreme, but her pattern is quite common.

Peggy's drinking and drugging is driven by yet another fear, a sadly contemporary one, the fear of AIDS. So terrifying is this possibility that Peggy dare not let her fear come anywhere near the surface. It is erased with margaritas and joints. In this case, burying her head in the sand may literally be fatal. The very ways in which she avoids her terror result in more unsafe sex, and her unconscious terror intensifies. The therapist should be on the lookout for this common behavior. When it is present confrontation is called for.

Peggy differs from Andy and Warren in an important way. She is far more insecure, lacking self-esteem, and driven to prove her worth, in short, far more emotionally troubled than either of them. She was a troubled young lady to begin with, and she has no chance at all to deal with her emotional problems unless she gets sober. Neither does anybody else. In a sense, it doesn't matter whether or not emotional difficulties existed before drinking heavily started. In either case one can't effectively work to overcome them while continuing to drink. Peggy's personality didn't cause her alcoholism, but it was an important factor in her getting hooked. Personality, environment, and the pharmacology of alcohol—that's what it did to Peggy.

Peggy's drinking and drugging was also motivated by rebellion. It was compensatory for feelings of low self-esteem and it was a way of thumbing her nose at the "straight" world. This can be interpreted

MAX, A PRIMARY ALCOHOLIC

Max has lots of alcoholism in his family. He thought it could never happen to him.

I never thought I would drink like my father. I hated him when he was drunk. I felt so ashamed when he made a fool out of himself. Who wants an asshole for a father? I was sure I'd never do that to my kids and damn, I'm doing it. Dad could get mean when he drank. I hated all the fighting and screaming and cursing and Mother crying, though she could get pretty mean too. I guess she just couldn't stand Daddy drinking. I don't get mean, I just act like an asshole. Why the hell do I do it? I never had any trouble with booze when I was young. Got drunk Saturday night at the fraternity when I was in college, but everybody did that. After I left the service and married Helen, it really leveled off. I guess it's just since I turned forty I started forgetting, and getting sloppy, and acting foolish. Hardly drank at all in law school, with what the G.I. bill gave to live on I couldn't. Well I'm a member of the bar now—sure am. I don't want to stop drinking; it's too big a part of my life. Sober as a judge, they say—well, I haven't seen too many sober judges and even fewer sober lawyers. Everybody drinks. I just have to learn to drink better. To hold my liquor like a man. Why couldn't Dad do that? He was great when he wasn't drinking. That early stroke must have had something to do with his boozing. As the years went on, he drank more and more. Didn't his Dad die of liver trouble? Someone on Mom's side, too. A lot of booze in the family. God damn it, I'm not going to stop drinking. How could I practice law? Half my business is conducted over martinis. What I have to do is set limits. No more than one at lunch. That was Dad's trouble—he drank before five. No more of that for me. As soon as I feel it hitting I'm going to stop. They all drink wine these days. I'll switch to wine coolers. That's the answer. Boy, do I feel better, no reason to have to go down the tube like Dad. All I have to do is stay away from the hard stuff.

Max is denial incarnate. He is full of rationalizations and strategies for drinking safely. Alas, none of them are going to work because Max is an alcoholic. He has the disease of alcoholism. His alcoholism is not advanced, but it isn't exactly a light case either. His disease will progress if he continues to drink. Unless arrested it will eventuate in premature death. Max's form of alcoholism is powerfully mediated by his genetic endowment. He came into the world with a predisposition to develop alcoholism. Either Max metabolizes alcohol differently from normal drinkers or it affect his nervous system differently or both. This cannot be changed; it is a biological given.

C. Robert Cloninger (1983) studied the heritability of alcoholism by tracing the drinking histories of children of alcoholics who were adopted by nonalcoholics shortly after birth. He found that these adoptees developed alcoholism at a much higher rate than the general population and concluded that there was something genetic that predisposed them to alcoholism. Cloninger found that there are two ways in which a predisposition to alcoholism can be inherited. One is called male-limited susceptibility to alcoholism. It occurs only in males and is highly heritable. It is characterized by early onset, severity, and antisocial behavior. Max does not suffer from male-limited susceptibility to alcoholism. The other is called milieu-limited susceptibility to alcoholism and affects both men and women. It is less heritable and requires environmental provocation to become expressed in alcoholism. That is, people with this kind of predisposition develop alcoholism only if they live in a heavy drinking environment. It develops slowly and is not associated with antisocial behavior. Max has this type of milieu-limited susceptibility to alcoholism. Regardless of whether the factor that led to it becoming manifest was growing up with an alcoholic father or the heavy drinking in his professional circle, he has it now. Although biological factors play less of a role in milieu-limited than in male-limited susceptibility to alcoholism, they are there. There is something biologically amiss in Max's reaction to alcohol. Max is a primary alcoholic.

Researchers have used the term *primary alcoholism* in a variety of ways. I am using it to mean that the alcoholism comes first and is not secondary to some other condition such as major depression. If someone is suffering from major depression and tries to self-medicate it with alcohol, the depression will get worse and the self-medicator runs the risk of developing *secondary alcoholism*.

In the literature the term primary alcoholism usually implies that the alcoholism is genetically transmitted, heritable, and has a biological basis in liver metabolism and/or neurochemistry. So used, primary means not only first, but also caused in a particular way. Cloninger's male-limited susceptible alcoholics are clearly primary in that sense. Their alcoholism is partly heritable and has something to do with aberrant enzyme systems or the like. I do not wish to convey any special theory about causes of alcoholism when I say primary. I only mean to say that drinking is the primary problem. Max, who is a Cloninger milieu-limited alcoholic, is also a primary alcoholic in the sense that I am using the term. His susceptibility to alcoholism has a genetic base, but that is not the whole story. Environmental factors and the way he handles his emotional conflicts play an important role in Max's drinking too much.

Max grew up in an alcoholic household. No child grows up in an alcoholic home without being scarred. Some alcohologists argue that parental alcoholism does not contribute to alcoholism in any way other than the transmission of genetic susceptibility. They cite research evidence and give elaborate statistical rationales to support their point of view. I don't find this believable. I have worked with hundreds of adult children of alcoholics and I have never met one who has not been emotionally damaged by his or her parents' alcoholism. Like Max, they often become alcoholic themselves. Like Max, they "never thought that they would drink like their fathers"—or their mothers. Yet . . . they do.

Part of the reason children of alcoholics are prone to alcoholism is genetic, but only a part. The rest is unconscious identification. One of the most powerful and pernicious defense mechanisms is identification with the aggressor. It was first described by Anna Freud (1938). Identification with the aggressor plays a large role in human life, as witness the ways in which oppressed peoples identify with their oppressors. To grow up in an alcoholic home is to grow up with chaos, unpredictability, and often violence. Identification with the aggressor is an attempt to feel some sense of control in a situation in which one is powerless. If you can't beat them, join them. The process can be conscious, but usually it isn't; it is something done without any awareness. Interpretation makes the drinker conscious of this identification and frees the patient from one shackle tying him to the bottle.

AA believes that "Alcoholism is the disease that tells you that you don't have it," and AA also maintains that "Alcoholism is a self-diagnosed disease." Both statements are integral parts of AA's folk wisdom, yet they are contradictory. As in so much of AA's folk wisdom, polar opposite perceptions and insights are expressed by a pair of mutually contradictory slogans. This seems to make no sense. If I combined the two slogans, the result would read, "Alcoholism is self-diagnosed by people who know that they don't have it." If that were the case, alcoholism would be a rare disease indeed; in fact, it would never be diagnosed. You ask, "A highly prevalent disease which is never diagnosed—isn't there something wrong there?" Yes, there sure is, but as with so many of AA's contradictory pairs of slogans, the paradox is more apparent than real. At a deeper level the paradox disappears and the two statements reconcile.

Hegel (1807) understood this reconciliation of paired opposites very well. He taught that in any attempt to elucidate the truth about anything, one first arrives at a partial truth, which he called the *thesis*. Being limited, an expression of only one aspect of reality, the thesis generates its opposite or *antithesis*. Thesis and antithesis then interact to generate a more comprehensive truth, the *synthesis*. Thesis-antithesis-synthesis. In our case, "alcoholism is the disease that tells you that you don't have it" is the thesis, while "alcoholism is a self-diagnosed disease" is the antithesis. What then is the synthesis? It would go something like this: "It is only when denial is overcome and the sufferer admits to himself or herself that he or she is suffering from alcoholism (self-diagnosis) that the cure becomes possible." In other words, denial is very much there, but it is only when denial breaks down sufficiently for self-diagnosis to occur that anything helpful can happen. If one's alcoholism is diagnosed by somebody else, this in itself is futile since the "cure" involves self-care, and the self-care necessitates awareness of one's alcoholism. So at a deeper level, AA's seemingly contradictory statements about the diagnosis of alcoholism are reconciled in such a way that the insight contained in both contribute to the possibility of successful treatment.

Alcoholism is frightening. Mere mention of the word sends chills up people's spines. Don't let the word alcoholism stand in your patients' way. There is no need to use the word. Rather, try to get them to examine their drinking, to look at their drinking patterns as dispassionately and objectively as possible. Max's pattern—youthful drunkenness minimized in memory, a period of trouble-free social drinking that gave pleasure, membership in a professional circle where heavy drinking was the norm, and finally, growing problems with alcohol—is common. Max misperceives how much his associates drink; heavy drinkers usually do. It is helpful for the therapist to ask, "Is it possible that you overestimate how much the people around you drink?" Max is also highly selective in choosing only the heavy drinkers in his professional circle to socialize with. That's exactly what heavy drinkers do. Ask patients if it's possible that they minimize their own drinking, assume incorrectly that others drink at least as much as they do, and avoid those who do not. This pattern is well-nigh universal among problem drinkers.

How about Max's symptoms? Does your patient have any of them, such as the forgetting, the change in the effect alcohol has on him, the emergence of behavior he regrets the next day? How about the rationalizations? *Everybody drinks . . . I can't be in business if I don't drink . . . It's okay as long as I don't drink before five . . . No more hard stuff, I'll stick to wine coolers . . . Only one at lunch.* All of this is an attempt to control what is not in control: his drinking. Social drinkers don't have to control their drinking. The therapist can and should point out all of this if he or she sees it.

LARRY, A NEUROTIC DRINKER

Larry drinks like a fish. He is Jewish and he believes that Jews are immune from alcoholism. Of course, they aren't. Larry is a tormented man, guilt-ridden and torn by conflict.

My grandfather was a religious fanatic—I once dreamed I told him to shove the Torah up his ass. Good thing it was a dream. My mother would have gone crazy if I ever said that to him. Sure liked his schnapps, though. He could kill a bottle of slivovitz without batting an eye. It didn't seem to bother him, he lived to 90. Zayde was the only one in the family who drank at all. Mom and Dad and the rest hardly ever drank except for bar mitzvahs and weddings. None of them understands drinking. That's why they're always harping on my drinking. "*Shicker iz a goy,*" so a nice Jewish boy like me shouldn't drink. They should only know what I *really* do. Suck cocks, pick up men and have every kind of sex with them. Lots of them. Wherever I can find them and that's usually in a bar. Everybody is coming out—if I came out it would probably kill my parents, so let them harp on my drinking, it's a lot better than, God forbid, they should know I'm gay. Didn't Maimonides prescribe stoning for homosexuals? Everybody else is marching in gay rights parades and proud of it. I'm not; for me it's a dirty secret. My boss doesn't know; investment bankers in pin-striped three-piece suits are supposed to have a wife, kids, dog, and picket fence. I have a dog. I'm not high enough up to be one of the decadent rich, then it would be okay, but I'm not exactly invisible either, so I have to hide my private life, not that there's much of that since AIDS. Oh God, what a horror! No wonder I drink so much. I used to drink to score, now I drink because I don't dare cruise. Life stinks. It's a cheat. At least I can drink and I only drink the best stuff. I can afford that. Rare vintages, aged brandies—even that isn't much fun anymore, but I still do it. It's all I have except for the dubious pleasures of my job. Well, Jews don't become alcoholic, so I'm not going to deny myself the only pleasure I have. But I sure wish I didn't feel so damned awful the next day.

Larry is another closet puritan, although his puritanism isn't the only thing in the closet. Closet puritans abound in our "liberated" age and come from all sorts of religious backgrounds, including the secular. Peggy, who woke up with a man she didn't know, belongs to the Protestant branch of closet Puritanism; Larry belongs to the Jewish branch. There isn't much difference. Guilt is pretty much guilt, although its manifestations vary somewhat from culture to culture. Alcohol can be used to quell any painful feelings. Guilt is extremely painful; it can be intolerable. Alcoholics and problem drinkers are often accused of being without a conscience, of lacking a moral sense. From this point of view, the problem is that drinkers don't feel enough guilt. Drinking behavior *is* self-centered, which seems to confirm this, but I have found, quite to the contrary, that alcohol abusers tend to have overly strict and punitive consciences. They are harshly self-punitive. Whatever else it may be, their drinking is a way of punishing themselves. This is true for Larry and for Peggy. This dynamic needs to be confronted and interpreted.

Guilt and Drinking

Guilt is tormenting, but it doesn't necessarily lead to treating others better. People are often treated abysmally by those who are feeling guilt toward them. They need to be angry with those they have hurt so they can feel less guilty, since the recipient of their aggression deserves it. Then they need not feel guilty. Drinkers often hurt those they love by their drinking, and then find reasons to hate those people so they no longer need to feel guilty. This too can be interpreted.

Now let me turn the screw a bit. Suppose the drinker feels guilty about something he has done to himself, drinking self-destructively, for instance. Then the drinker treating himself especially well to compensate for the self-inflicted damage would be a rational response. Unfortunately, what usually happens is that such drinkers treat themselves even more abominably to justify the damage they have already inflicted on the self. "You really deserved it, you bastard," is the unconscious thought. "In fact, you deserve yet more punishment." Additional self-punishment takes the form of drinking more. This accomplishes several things: the alcohol anesthetizes the guilt as it does all feelings and sensations and at the same time it punishes yet more. Perhaps the patient knows that he is doing this, but far more likely it is an unconscious process. One can feel guilt about damage inflicted on the self, and patients punish themselves consciously or unconsciously as a consequence of guilt, which itself is either conscious or unconscious, and which arises out of earlier self-inflicted damage.

Some of the guilt may be rational, make some sort of sense in relation to the sin or other transgression, real or imagined, that it's atoning for; or it may be irrational and totally disproportionate to the alleged offense, which may be a forbidden thought rather than an action, or even a childhood wish. The therapist needs to make it conscious. Drinking too much simultaneously to obliviate guilt, punish the self, and punish those toward whom one feels guilty is extremely common.

Larry is wracked by guilt. He not only punishes himself; he enlists his mother, his father, a medieval Jewish sage, a punitive God, and his boss to help him beat himself. Ostensibly he repudiates each of these figures and consciously he is at war with each of them. But he keeps calling them to mind as potential tormentors. He is enraged at each and every one of them. In fact, he feels rage of murderous proportions. Murderous? Yes. Well, what happens to murderers? They are almost as bad as homosexuals and we know what Larry thinks is recommended for them. Larry feels such rage that he wants to murder. He then equates the wish with the act and feels that he is a murderer as well as a sodomite, and that he deserves whatever punishment is meted out to him. At the same time he rebels, but he is a failed rebel. He can't break with his family, his tradition, or his society. On the contrary, they constantly haunt him. Their values are too strongly internalized that the war between Larry and the world around him has also become a war within him. Larry is a neurotic drinker trying to self-medicate a neurotic conflict. This is hard to see since one or both sides of the conflict are outside of awareness, and Larry doesn't know about the war within. Instead of being aware of conflict, he feels anxious, depressed, guilty, and just plain awful and doesn't know why. He drinks in a futile attempt to manage his neurosis without even knowing that he's doing so.

Larry is bitter; he is also pathetic. His blasphemies are childish, his anger is ineffectual and largely turned against himself, he is tormented by guilt and shame, and he lives in constant fear. His homosexuality has a good deal to do with this, but it is really his attitude toward his homosexuality and his way of handling it that is the problem. That is not to say that society's attitudes toward homosexuality don't powerfully affect him. Gays are prone to alcohol abuse. There are several reasons for this. One is guilt—identification with the aggressor, with all those who disapprove of homosexuality: parents, family, church, society. Another is the cruising scene, which is largely a bar scene. Anonymous sex is certainly not the only form of gay sex, but it is common among gay men, and most of us, gay or not, are uncomfortable with anonymous sex and that's where the booze comes in. A few drinks and the uncomfortable becomes comfortable. With the AIDS epidemic, anonymous sex has become dangerous and homosexual men are fearful. One way, albeit not a very good one, of dealing with fear is to drink. Guilt, shame, fear, and a social life set in bars certainly make one vulnerable to alcoholism.

Spirits and Spirituality

Larry is preoccupied with religion. He obsesses about it. He can neither let it go—be a comfortable nonbeliever—nor practice his religion. His dilemma is a common one. He is enormously rageful at his religious grandfather and at Judaism. He dreams that he tells his grandfather to shove Judaism's most sacred symbol. Deep religious conflict characterizes many alcoholics. Larry has a love–hate relationship with his religion. He can neither renounce it nor enjoy it. His very hatred constitutes a bond that he cannot sever. Many problem drinkers are in a similar bind. They are at war with a punitive God. More Catholics than Jews have this conflict, but that doesn't matter. The inner experience is the same. As Buck Mulligan says of Stephen Daedalus in James Joyce's novel *Ulysses*, these drinkers "have the Jesuitical streak injected backwards" (1914, p. 7). Alcohol makes one high—it transports the drinker out of self, as does intense religious experience. Larry uses alcohol to repudiate a religious identity— "*Shicker iz a goy*," drunks are gentiles—and simultaneously as a religious equivalent, a form of spiritual fulfillment. Drinking is the only fulfilling experience he has left and it is rapidly failing for him. He drinks to repudiate an identity, to rebel, or to mock the values of his parents, of his religion, and his society.

There are many aspects of Larry's drinking too much that a therapist could interpret and/or comment on: his bitterness and futile attempt to assuage it with alcohol, his unsuccessful rebellion enacted in his drinking that simultaneously punishes him for that rebellion, his use of alcohol as a sexual substitute now that AIDS has radically restricted his sex life, his use of alcohol to quell guilt and shame, his use of alcohol to resolve a neurotic conflict, and his use of alcohol to still a fear that will not stay quiet. Larry drinks for about every reason except to relax and have a good time now and then as normal drinkers do. He needs to know this.

I want to point out yet another aspect of Larry's drinking and the way he thinks about it, namely, that he uses his membership in a minority group not known for alcoholism in the service of denial. This is all too easy to do. "I don't drink too much, at least not in an alcoholic way, because I am Chinese, a woman, too young, from a good family, too old, Jewish, small-town, Italian, well-educated, left-handed, or what-have-you." The therapist needs to call such rationalizers' bluffs.

ROSE, A SUICIDE RISK

Rose is self-deluded. Her despair is bottomless, yet she denies it, just as she denies that she drinks too much.

Why is it that in moments of quiet contemplation my thoughts turn with a certain inevitability to the consumption of spirits either in the contemplation of the not-to-be-long-delayed consumption thereof, or to obsessional rumination over the frequency and quantity of that consumption and its effects on my productivity and sense of well-being? There can be no real question but that which has been fermented inspires and vivifies me. It adds a certain excitement to my life and what, after all, can be the harm in an afternoon glass of what my colleagues and I have taken to denoting "faculty sherry?" The English department practically runs on sherry. After all, what is poetry other than intoxication? Intoxication of the spirit—chills running down my back as Blake's lines run through my head. A sip or so of wine intensifies that. There can be no question of Dionysian abandon in my case. In fact, the penultimate occurrence of a somewhat excessive consumption was on the occasion of my presentation of my paper "Covert Eroticism in *Beowulf* with Particular Reference to the Relation between Grendel and His Mother." Odd that I should have been nervous at that meeting. I am, after all, a professional orator. I usually drink only wine at the Language Association meetings; however, at this the most recent occurrence of, perhaps I do have to so admit, overdrinking, martinis played their role. Ah, martinis—divine magic, so slightly green reflected clarity, penetrating the gleaming stemware. Yet, at the same time so much more scintillating than sherry or claret, or the dry, dry Mosel I so covet—covet? Yes, I must admit covet—during languorous summer afternoons. In winter there is the martini at lunch in the Faculty Club, the afternoon sherry, the martini before dinner, the red or white with dinner, and the brandy postprandially. I have to concede a certain constancy in my consumption, but in total it is not so very much. Is not so much too much? I do not believe so. Paper after paper written in the warm afterglow of sips and scents and through an almost subliminal fascination with glass and ice, tray and shaker. It is part of my lifestyle, which is, after all, sedate, academic, productive, satisfying. Lonely though. There have been a few, but never one, but love is an experience that I have not really needed and so, except in moments of slightly tipsy melancholy, I have not regretted not having it.

I must concede that things have changed. My productivity wanes, my moments of melancholy intensify and deliquesce through my already damp soul and, in short, I am no longer happy. Do I drink a bit more to recover my former state of inner peace? Or do I drink in an attempt to transcend known states and discover an as yet undiscovered bliss? Or is my increased consumption an attempt to compensate for a diminution in the intensity of my life? I do not know. Perhaps happiness is over for me. Whichever of these contingencies, if any, is in fact the case, dinner without wine is not civilized and I am, whatever else I may be, civilized. So I pour another sherry and turn my thoughts outward to my lecture on the influence of Anglo-Saxon poetry on the romantics.

Rose is a bullshit artist. Her self-deception is so total that it endangers her life. Her life is a secret from herself. She drinks around the clock, has long since ceased to be productive, and is increasingly melancholy—depressed. She can rationalize anything in service of her denial. "Faculty sherry," which she seems to think is in some miraculous way different from ordinary sherry, is certainly harmless. Martinis could be part of the problem, but they are practically works of art, so there can't be anything wrong there, the English department runs on alcohol, and it isn't civilized to have dinner without wine. What a con job. So easy for the therapist to see, but not for her. Rose truly believes that her drinking starting at lunch and ending with her passing out after dinner is not heavy, although she does have some instantly repudiated doubts. People who drink far too much commonly deny it and assume that everybody drinks more or less as they do. They need to believe this. Rose needs to be confronted, but with consummate tact. She is fragile; nevertheless she must be handled firmly, but in such a way that her minimal self-esteem is preserved.

Rose is a schizoid personality. She is so vulnerable and so afraid of people that she can't let them get close to her. She copes with this in two ways, one adaptive and one self-destructive. Her relationship to literature, which in her early years was imaginative and insightful, is the adaptive one, and her relationship to alcohol is the self-destructive one. Creativity is, after all, a lonely business, and many loners turn to alcohol for warmth and closeness. This is a mistake, although a very understandable one. Alcohol is a very unreliable friend, one not worthy of devotion. John Barleycorn turns on his friends.

Rose is tragic. A brilliant woman who has become vain, pretentious, and empty with the progressive inner impoverishment that inevitably occurs as an alcoholic career progresses. She has no meaningful human relationships; she must drink to give papers, whose quality is far below what she is capable of; her teaching, once enlivened by her passion for literature, now limps along; and she is sitting on an abyss of despair. Rose is the kind of person who is found dead one day, to the shocked amazement of colleagues, who say, "How could she have done it? I never knew she was so unhappy. The last few years she drank too much, but nobody thought very much about it—she was so witty and creative. I guess nobody was close to her, but everybody liked her. There will be a lot of tears at the memorial service."

Rose should not be treated as an outpatient. The risk is too great. The goal of therapy should be to have her agree to enter a rehab or perhaps a good psychiatric hospital.

Rose brings to mind Bill, another alcoholic English professor, who was every bit as pretentious and grandiose as Rose. In working with him I frequently thought of "Just My Bill" from Jerome Kern and P. G. Wodehouse's great song "Bill" written earlier but used in *Show Boat*. I would think that if only my patient could be "just Bill" he would be cured. Unfortunately, there was no way I could say that to him without deeply hurting him; but years later after, he was long sober, I did share my old rumination about him and he instantly understood that if only he had been able to put aside his defensive grandiosity and be "just Bill" he might have recovered much earlier. Defensive grandiosity covering abysmally low self-esteem is always an issue in substance abuse treatment and must be dealt with by the therapist with gentle confrontation.

HANK, A GUY WHO JUST CAN'T DRINK "NORMALLY"

Hank is preprogrammed to self-destruct when he drinks. He knows this, but he can't stop trying to drink like everyone else. He isn't having much success in that endeavor.

What happened last night? I took the crew out for drinks and that's as far as I can take it. How did I get this black eye? The first time I got high, way back in tenth grade, it was a disaster. Wrecked Jim's house and his parents went bananas. I'm not a kid anymore. I can't get away with this shit. Why? Why can't I drink like other people? I'm general manager on a million-dollar construction project and I act like a drunken sailor. Nothing like this ever happens when I don't drink. I like my life. I'm good at what I do. You can't work construction without drinking. Especially if you're the boss. The men expect you to set them up. But they don't expect you to brawl. That's for kids. It's outrageous. Everybody can drink but me. Car accidents, fights, in jail twice, lost a couple of jobs and I don't know how many girls. I didn't have a drink for two months and then last night I did it again. Am I nuts? I can just see this crew if they thought I was seeing a shrink.

Dad had the same problem, but he stopped when he was young. I hardly remember him drinking. But he was in the clothing business. Who cares if a shopkeeper drinks or not? Nobody. It's not like that for me. My crew expects it. What the hell am I supposed to do, put soda pop in my beer bottle? . . . I wonder who I hit? This can't go on. I guess I don't have to drink until the Christmas party. That gives me six weeks to cool out. No reason I can't nurse a beer all night. Nobody will notice. Figured it out, didn't I? No different from a problem on the site, all I have to do is think it out. Hell-raising makes sense for a kid; it doesn't for a thirty-five-year-old. It's not fun anymore. I wonder if it ever was. Sometimes I wonder if I go crazy because I'm a pussycat sober. Some pussycat, I can put a guy through the wall cold sober, so that's not it . . . I'm smarter than I thought. I doped it out. All I have to do is nurse the same drink all night. I can't wait for that Christmas party. I'll show them that I can drink like a gentleman.

Hank drinks too much because he has the type of alcoholism that is most preprogrammed. He is wired to self-destruct if he drinks, yet drinking is irresistibly attractive to him. He reacts to alcohol differently than other people. It does strange things to him. Hank's problem lies in his genes. He handles alcohol differently from normal drinkers and problem drinkers whose drinking isn't biologically based. Of all the drinkers whose thoughts we have eavesdropped on, Hank's drinking too much is the most biologically determined. He suffers from male-limited susceptibility to alcoholism. There is something about his liver or his nervous system or both that does something different with alcohol. Most male-limited susceptibles are in much worse shape than Hank. They quickly get into serious difficulty, often with the law, and have an awful time getting out of it. Their prognosis is not good. Hank's way of reacting to alcohol used to be called pathological intoxication, which is an accurate description of what happens to him when he drinks.

Hank is a periodic drinker. Unlike Warren, Max, Vicky, and Rose, Hank is not a daily drinker. In fact, considerable periods of time elapse between his benders. Unfortunately, it doesn't matter how long the gaps between his drinking episodes are, try as he will, Hank can't drink like other people. Oh, he may on occasion, but usually it's the same shit over and over again—blackouts, fights, God knows what.

What characterizes Hank's pattern? Its most salient feature is *trouble with alcohol from the start*. Hank first drank in tenth grade and went on a rampage. A drinker's experience doesn't have to be so extreme for him to have Hank's problem, but some sort of going wild, of losing control, characterizing his early drinking is necessary to make a diagnosis of male-limited alcoholism. Pay special attention to fights, destructiveness, drunk driving, and memory lapses. If these characterized the early drinking, and it hasn't gotten much better, the patient is suffering from the most biological of alcoholisms. Adolescent drinkers raise all sorts of hell, but they stop behaving that way by their mid-twenties. If the patient did not, that is ominous.

This business of going out of control is the crux of the matter. Everybody drinks to loosen control, to disinhibit, but they don't drink to lose control totally. Emil Jellinek (1960), who established the disease concept of alcoholism, cited loss of control as the single most significant defining characteristic of what he called *gamma alcoholism*. Gamma alcoholism is chronic and progressive. Loss of control means that the drinker who has lost control of his drinking cannot predict what will happen once he or she picks up a drink. Social drinkers sometimes drink to get drunk and that is a choice; gamma alcoholics try not to get drunk and get drunk anyway—that is not a choice.

Hank is definitely drinking alcoholically. He would not accept this diagnosis, but almost anybody, professional or nonprofessional, would conclude that there is something radically wrong with Hank's drinking. I would characterize it as episodic—periodic, male-limited susceptible alcoholism. Jellinek labeled episodic drinking to oblivion *epsilon alcoholism*, to distinguish such drinking from the more constant and progressively deteriorating drinking characteristic of gamma alcoholism. Classification schemes are abstractions; people don't neatly fit into pigeonholes. For instance, Hank has some Jellinek epsilon traits as well as the Cloninger biological susceptibility. Classification schemes help sort out the very complex phenomenon of drinking too much, but none of them is definitive or universally accepted. Jellinek's scheme emphasizes the loss of control issue. It is important for the therapist to know that that loss of control, early or late, is a sign of something very seriously wrong and that drinking episodically or periodically rather than continuously is perfectly consistent with drinking alcoholically. Episodic drinking to drunkenness, especially if it involves loss of control, is very serious. It always means that the patient is in trouble.

Hank has tried, and continues to try, to control his drinking. He tries to control the frequency of his drinking, the speed of his drinking, what he drinks, and the amount of his drinking. He will not succeed. Most people learn to drink more or less well, so a common problem-drinking pattern is to have early trouble with alcohol, learn to handle it, and then lose control again. Hank has spent his life trying to drink well, but he simply cannot. He does not have the right neurochemistry to do so. Most male-limited susceptibles quickly move from periodic drinking to daily drinking, thereby becoming gamma alcoholics. Hank is an exception, having so far avoided the progression to daily drinking. He is obviously an exceptionally capable and determined person who is risking everything he has achieved by continuing to drink.

Hank doesn't so much want to drink, as to not *not* be able to drink. Not to be able to drink would be a terrible blow to his pride. "Real men" drink. He rationalizes continuing to drink. Therapy must center on this issue. It is the key to helping Hank. He knows that being able to drink is important to him. His profession requires it; it is part of his public image; his father could stop because he did different type work. Hank is defiant. "I'll show them." Hank wants to and doesn't want to drink. "I can't wait for the Christmas party." The therapist needs to work with his ambivalence, amplifying both sides of it.

Hank even prefers being crazy to being alcoholic, although he doesn't like that idea either. Many drinkers prefer to believe that they are crazy rather than consider that they might be drinking alcoholically. Patients should be told, "You can't tell whether or not you're crazy unless you stop drinking. You don't know what's underneath your booze-induced irrationality. The chances are excellent that you aren't crazy." Alternately, "You think that you drink because you're crazy; did it ever occur to you that you're crazy because you drink?"

Hank also wonders if he isn't too passive, a pussycat when sober, and speculates that he drinks to vent his rage. Well, he may be too passive, although I doubt it, but passive or not, he isn't one of those people who drinks to vent his rage. What happens with Hank is that the alcohol causes his fury and mediates his unrestrained expression of it. Hank is something of a tough guy sober or drunk, but he is only violent when he's drunk. Hank's is a retrospective justification. He is trying to find a psychological reason why he gets in trouble when he drinks and there isn't any. The real problem is biological. Hank doesn't even know if he's angry. He may or may not be, but that's beside the point. Even Hank doesn't believe the justification he spins for himself. Many people try to rationalize or justify their drinking in just this way. "I can't express myself sober." . . . "I can't express my rage without drinking," are some of the rationalizations they use. Sometimes something very strange then happens: people stop drinking, and lo and behold they have very little rage to express. Their rage was caused by their drinking. This seems to contradict what I said earlier, but it doesn't. There are people who drink because they can't express anger in any other way, and there are people like Hank who are angry because they drink, and there are people for whom it works both ways. The therapist needs to very carefully tease out the components of alcoholic rage and give each one its due, both in his or her own mind, and in interaction with the patient. It makes a real difference in treatment outcome if the therapist understands the relationship between the patient's drinking and the patient's rage and uses that understanding therapeutically.

Just as we analyzed our ruminators' drinking in terms of the four or five etiological factors driving it, you will find that it facilitates treatment if you similarly analyze your patient's drinking or other substance abuse, and modify your interventions accordingly.

Spinoza's "Cognitive Therapy" of Addiction

"Philosophical therapy" has a long and distinguished history. Although contemporary academic philosophy, at least in the United States and the United Kingdom, tends to concern itself with language analysis and the elucidation of arcane technical questions, the Western philosophical tradition has always had a therapeutic purpose. That is, it has sought to discover and elucidate the good life and to demonstrate how one may live it. Most of the great philosophers have also taught ways to remove impediments to traveling the road to the good life; that is, in our terms, they have recognized and tried to deal with resistance. This is nowhere more true than in the case of Spinoza, whose entire work, for all of its technical brilliance on its epistemological and metaphysical sides, is about freeing men from bondage and leading them to what he calls "blessedness."

The work of Plato, the father of Western philosophy, is explicitly therapeutic, both insofar as it adumbrates a therapeutic technique, which he calls dialectic, the search for truth through dialogue and mutual questioning—the famous Socratic method—and insofar as it establishes a value system. It is an ontological/ethical vision that is intended to serve as a guide to entering into a journey toward insight and fulfillment.

The neo-Platonists such as Plotinus were even more explicitly therapeutic and this therapeutic aim of philosophy becomes overt in the
works of the stoics and the Epicureans. Albert Ellis credits the Greek
stoic philosopher Epictetus with being the spiritual father of his rational emotive therapy (RET). Non-Western philosophical traditions,
including the Indian and the Chinese, have also been therapeutic in
aim, intent, and technique. In the past few years, professional philosophers have started to practice psychotherapy, drawing both on
contemporary philosophical analysis and on the tradition from Plato
on down. It is unclear how successful, economically or therapeutically, philosophical therapy has been, but it has received a good deal
of attention, including coverage in the *New York Times*.

Thus, we come to Spinoza. I've long admired the man, and have
found his metaphysical vision both beautiful and plausible. I have been
fascinated by his life and its cultural/historical context. I've also long
pondered how, if at all, his insights into human nature and the nature of reality could be used in, or incorporated into, psychotherapy,
particularly the psychotherapy of addiction. Since his theme is escape from bondage, he seems a fitting therapist for the addicted.

From the beginning Spinoza has been a controversial figure. Many
have hated him and he has been denounced by a large variety of enemies. He has driven dogmatists and authoritarians of all stripes up
the wall. That, too, has recommended him to me. His admirers have
included Bertrand Russell and Sigmund Freud, which are equally
strong recommendations.

Spinoza lived in a violent and intellectually revolutionary time. He,
himself, both in his person and his thought, was part of that revolution.
His thought cannot be separated from his life. As I see that life it was
a struggle for liberation, for freedom, which was only partly successful.
His blind spots and sexual repression prevented the man who wrote
so movingly "Of Human Bondage" and its escape from becoming fully
liberated. He was not quite free himself. I see him as a deeply conflicted
human being. Stephen Nadler (1999), his most recent biographer,
disagrees with me on this. His Spinoza is far more placid than mine.

I have decided to use a dramatic format to acquaint the reader with
the man and his thought. After this, perhaps histrionic, exposition

of his philosophy, I will try to show how at least some of his ideas can be adapted to the treatment of addiction. I have used the device of a Chorus as an interlocutor to give voice to Spinoza's unconscious thoughts and feelings, as well as a commentator to give historical background and context. He was suggested by Shakespeare's Chorus in *Henry V* and by Thorton Wilder's Stage Manager in *Our Town*, although he most certainly doesn't exist at their aesthetic level. The Chorus is also a psychotherapist in a sense, in fact Spinoza's therapist. Unfortunately, he suffers from unanalyzed countertransference, which manifests, among other ways, in lack of therapeutic tact. The Chorus's intense emotional involvement with Spinoza is, in its own way, another entrapment. Therapists, too, become enslaved—to emotions if not to drugs. In addition to the Chorus, I have assumed dramatic license for the introduction of anachronistic characters including Nietzsche, William James, and Freud, who question, interact with, and disagree with Spinoza.

SPINOZA

Act One, Scene 1

(Interior of the synagogue in Amsterdam. On the dais sit Rabbis Morteira and Aboab. There are black candles on either side of the rabbis, and down the aisles. Rabbi Isaac Aboab rises and speaks.)

ABOAB: The chiefs of the counsel do you to wit that having long known the evil opinions and works of Baruch De Espinoza, they have endeavored by diverse ways and promises to withdraw him from his evil ways, and are unable to find a remedy, but on the contrary, they have had every day more knowledge of the abominable heresies practiced and taught by him, and of other awful deeds he performed, and have of this many trustworthy witnesses who have disposed and borne witness in the presence of the said Espinoza, and by whom he stood convicted, and all of this having been examined in the presence of the Gentlemen Elders of this community, they resolved with the rabbi's consent, that the said Espinoza be put to the *herem*, and banished from the nation of Israel, as indeed they proclaim the following *herem* on him:

(Morteira blows the shofar—its mournful sounds fade slowly as Aboab continues to speak.)

By the decree of the Angels and the words of the Saints, we ban, cut off, curse, and anathematize Baruch De Espinoza, with the anathema wherewith Joshua anathematized Jericho, with the curse which Elisha laid upon the children, with all the curses written in the Torah:

Cursed be he by day, cursed be he by night; cursed be he when he lieth down, and cursed be he when he riseth up; cursed be he when he goeth out, and cursed be he when he cometh in; the Lord shall not pardon him; the wrath and fury of the Lord will be kindled against this man, and bring down upon him all the curses which are written in the Book of the Law; and the Lord will destroy his name from under the heavens, and, to his undoing, the Lord will cut him off from all the tribes of Israel, with all the curses of the firmament which are written in the Book of Law; but ye who cleave unto the Lord God, love all of you this day!

CONGREGATION: Amen.

(Shofar is blown again.)

ABOAB: We ordain that no one may communicate with him verbally or in writing, nor show him any favor, nor stay under the same roof with him, nor be within four cubits of him, nor read anything composed or written by him.

(Shofar sounds once more mournfully. Spinoza appears as the synagogue fades. He tries to appear nonchalant, yet is clearly profoundly disturbed. He struggles to deny this.)

SPINOZA: This does not force me to do anything I would not have done of my own accord, had I not been afraid of the scandal. Fools! They should know they cannot cajole or bribe me into accepting superstition. Rabbi Manasseh might have persuaded me with his critical mind and broadness of thought, but he has left for England on his mad project to convince Cromwell to readmit the Jews. Absurd! As for the two who pronounced the ban, they are fools; I no longer respect them. In any case, I must needs have gone my own way quietly among my people if they had allowed it, but since they haven't, I will do quite well without them.

CHORUS: Things haven't changed very much. This could be Salman Rushdie and the mullahs. Baruch De Espinoza, age 24, has just been excommunicated by the Jewish congregation of Amsterdam, this Amsterdam congregation of Marranos and children of Marranos, Spanish and Portuguese forced converts to Catholicism, many of whom were secret Jews. The Iberian Peninsula remains ruled by absolute monarchy and lies in the icy cruel hands of the Inquisition. Spinoza's father fled to the United Provinces of the Netherlands, themselves formerly subject to the Spanish king. The Jewish congregation and the Dutch burghers are united by a memory of persecution by the hated Spanish. The United Provinces have become a republic, the freest state in Europe. The province of Holland, with its capital city of Amsterdam, offers more freedom of conscience, of speech, of religion than has hitherto been known in Christendom. Yet that freedom of conscience is far from absolute. The Calvinist orthodoxy is as oppressive, repressive, and benighted as their former rulers. They are locked in a bitter struggle with the liberal Republican government of Holland. The Republic attracts all sorts of refugees from persecution: Quakers, Levelers, Ranters, Seekers, Mennonites, Anabaptists, and God knows who else. The commercial oligarchy that rules the Jewish community is paradoxically allied with the most reactionary forces in Holland. These former New Christians, now become New Jews, are a highly educated bunch, professionals and merchants, important members of the Dutch East Indies Company. No longer Christians, they are not really Jews either; their spiritual leaders are obsessed with re-Judaizing them. Aboab, Morteira, and the Elders fear the widespread religious doubt, the freethinking, the skepticism, and the secularism that pervade so much of their congregation. Its long experience as a clandestine secret society has perhaps made them pseudo-Jews, as once they were pseudo-Christians. The rabbis must be vigilant. Those who have not become skeptics have become fanatics. Like their former persecutors, they persecute that which they do not understand and that which seems to threaten their sacred heritage—a heritage so many have died for in Spain and Portugal. The royal powers of Spain and Portugal continue to support the Inquisition, which continues its bloody work unabated. As if that horror is not enough, the Thirty Years War has just ended, leaving vast stretches of Europe devastated and decimated. Across the Channel, the English have revolted, killed their king, established a republic, and seen it degenerate into a dictatorship. The center does not hold, the certainties—spiritual, metaphysical, ecclesiastical, intellectual, political, and economic—of a thousand years crumble, and extraordinary vistas open, engendering overpowering fear. Ideologies that have given men security and meaning are assaulted, and that assault is defended against with murderous rage. It won't be long until the witch trials start. Such is the world in which Baruch De Espinoza has been excommunicated.

(Spinoza is once again seen walking away from the Amsterdam synagogue. Again, he looks back.)

CHORUS: You're afraid, aren't you?

SPINOZA: No.

CHORUS: Pissing in your pants.

SPINOZA: No.

CHORUS: Cut off forever from friends and family, from community, forever to be an exile, a pariah, a vile object of contempt. (Spinoza shakes his head and frowns.) Oh, those goyim! Your new friends. You can't trust 'em.

SPINOZA: You see how I can trust the Jews.

CHORUS: Look at me. Tell me you're not afraid.

SPINOZA: I'm not.

CHORUS: Look at yourself. Tell yourself you're not . . . afraid? Forever sundered from your roots, your people, your . . .

SPINOZA: Shut up! No! I'm going to the destiny I have chosen. (Runs offstage.)

Scene 2

MANASSEH: These are exciting times. Men are full of discovery. The New Science illuminates all of nature. The artists, like my friend Rembrandt, have learned to show what the new thinkers have discovered—a world luminous with the possibility of rational knowledge. Spain is in eclipse. We need not be so fearful, for Judaism is a rational religion—it too illuminates and casts light, not mystical but cognitive. We must not be afraid of change. The world, especially here in the United Provinces of the Netherlands, grows gentler. Our heritage has nothing to fear from the new knowledge or from the innovators. I have friends among the Cartesians. There is nothing in the Cartesian doctrine that threatens or contradicts anything in Judaism. The new science enriches us. As does Dutch tolerance. Even the sects have things they can teach us. We are too afraid. We have business relations with the Dutch, with the whole world, and that doesn't frighten us. Why do we hold back when it comes to their philosophers and their scientists?

MORTEIRA: You don't hold back. You have become more Gentile than Jewish. You talk rubbish with fools and endanger yourself, our Commandments, and our youth. Ugh! (Spits) Stay with the Torah and the Commandments. All of truth is therein. Philosophers breed apostasy. The Jewish philosophers are no better than your Descartes. Our educated ones are swollen with pride. We have already put you to the ban once; use your mind in defense of our sacred heritage. You are corrupting your most brilliant pupil.

MANASSEH: Give up your dark vision, your medievalism, your blindness. Torah is truth and truth is one, you have naught to fear from my worldliness. Our congregation is of the world and not frightened by it, only you. Do not reject the new knowledge.

ABOAB: Caution, you go too far! You allegorize dangerously. You cite pagans, Christian philosophers, dissolute poets showing off your knowledge of all that corrupts. Guard the truth that was revealed at Sinai; you need but follow the Law of Moses. Salvation lies in following the Law of Moses. Many have died for it.

(Lights dim, a projection shows an auto-da-fé. A crowd of well-dressed Spanish men and women are in a grandstand. Stakes piled high with wood are visible in front of the grandstand. In the second projection, bound men and women are surrounded by Dominican friars in black hoods and robes, holding crosses. In the third projection, the heretics and Judaizers are bound to the stakes. Some are weeping, and all are transfixed with terror. Christian prayers are sung. In the next projection, the flames burn, and we hear prolonged screaming. The audience nibbles candy as the screaming continues. In the final projection flames have consumed almost all.)

CHORUS: An act of faith—auto-da-fé—isn't piety wonderful? The sanctity of the faith has been preserved. Salvation in Christ shall not be threatened by salvation through the Law of Moses. Burning flesh—we've had a lot of that. Babies burned alive at Auschwitz, not to mention the smell of the crematoriums. Purity of the blood—it wasn't enough to convert if your grandmother's grandfather had Jewish blood—the Spanish came up with that. Goebbels couldn't do much better. After the expulsion of 1492, many converted and distinguished themselves as Spanish Catholics. They became physicians, cardinals, lawyers, professors, businessmen. They were too successful. Were they sincere? Some, some not. In any case, the purges of the secret Judaizers began. The Inquisition relied on torture, spies, false witnesses, terror to destroy the Marranos. The Inquisition burned them, pious Christians and secret Judaizers alike for the glory of God and the love of Christ— acts of faiths indeed.

(Scene returns to the synagogue where the three rabbis are once again talking.)

ABOAB: Juan Prado wants us to lift his *herem*. He is willing to do penance. His opposition is not as perverse as Baruch's; he wants to return to the community. What shall we make of his skeptical doubts? He studies too much philosophy and shows off his knowledge. We shall humble him and he will return to the Torah and the Law of Moses.

MORTEIRA: Not so with Baruch; he has ceased to observe the 613 commandments. His father conformed outwardly but disrespected the rabbinate. I do not say the father deserves the son but I fear for his salvation.

MANASSEH: (Interrupting) Michael Spinoza was a leader of this community and a pious Jew. To you, all who are not fanatical are suspect. I have always taught the Law of Moses, yet you doubt me.

MORTEIRA: As is written, one lives by the Torah or one does not.

CHORUS: (Offstage left) Much bullshit is written.

ABOAB: Many have died for the Law of Moses. (Angrily) I will tolerate no deviation.

CHORUS: (To audience) Aboab knows of what he speaks. He has just returned from Brazil where the Portuguese are assuring doctrinal purity.

(Projection of the Jewish street in the Dutch Brazilian colony of Pernambuco. It fades. Second slide shows Portuguese troops and revolting black slaves, killing, burning, and pillaging. Aboab speaks as the slides of the destruction of Pernambuco are on the scrim.)

ABOAB: Volumes would not suffice to relate our miseries. The enemy spread over the field and wood seeking here for booty and there for life. Many of us died, sword in hand, others from want. They now rest in the cold earth. We survivors were exposed to death in every form; those accustomed to luxuries were glad to seize moldy bread to stay their hunger.

CHORUS: The rabbi didn't make out so well in Brazil. Once the Portuguese defeated the Dutch, it was all over for the Jews.

ABOAB: (Turning toward Morteira) Even you don't know the Inquisition at first hand. You grew up in Venice, lived in the Medici court, and then came here to lead the congregation. You do not know how precious and precarious the treasure you defend is.

MORTEIRA: Nonsense. I didn't need to be in Pernambuco, or to be attacked by the Portuguese to understand my task here. The Spanish have forgotten how to be Jews. They are full of skepticism and doubt. They have become too worldly. They believe neither Judaism nor Christianity. They know too much Latin. They should emulate my pupil who fasted forty days so that he would forget his Latin. I know enough.

MANASSEH: Yet they risked their lives to return to Judaism.

MORTEIRA: We must allow no deviation. To open the door but a little is to see the entire structure defiled. Baruch has begun to speak openly. He denies the immortality of the soul. He mocks the Jews and denies that we are the chosen people. He maintains that the Law applies only to the ancient commonwealth. It is time to act.

ABOAB: Bring him in. (Servant leads Spinoza in.) Baruch, we are told that you teach abominations.

SPINOZA: I've done nothing to affront the community.

MORTEIRA: You have left your business and spend your time studying with the atheist Van dan Ende.

ABOAB: Your friends are unbelievers. You are absent from synagogue and seldom seen in the community.

MANASSEH: We have decided to stipend you so that you may return to your talmudic studies at which you so excel.

ABOAB: (To Manasseh) You are responsible for this—your associates are not much better than his. Cajole your errant pupil back to sanity.

MANASSEH: My Gentile friends do no harm. They have the best minds (Aboab spits) of our time. My friendships with them strengthen my Judaism. Read my books. You will see the strength of my commitment.

SPINOZA: (Aside) Not very good books—fuzzy allegorical interpretations of Scripture.

MORTEIRA: Let us not quarrel among ourselves. We are here to deal with Baruch.

SPINOZA: Why did you set an assailant on me who tried to stab me as I left the theater?

MORTEIRA: (Shocked) That's an outrageous accusation. You are the one inquested here. There is naught we can do to prevent reaction to your odious behavior and repellent teachings.

SPINOZA: And you set spies on me! Your witnesses pretended to be my friends, and wheedled statements out of me. I do not proselytize. These are my private thoughts; I attend the synagogue; I pay my communal taxes and poor dues. You have no right to demand more of me.

MORTEIRA: Take care—you are close to having the ban pronounced upon you.

SPINOZA: (Sarcastically) I will teach you the form of excommunication, and all rites of the *herem* in repayment for your kindness in having taught me Hebrew.

MORTEIRA: (Furious) You are outrageous! You have no respect. This is your final opportunity to recant.

ABOAB: Do you deny that you are seldom to be seen in the synagogue?

SPINOZA: My affairs take me elsewhere.

ABOAB: Two witnesses have testified that you deny the immortality of the soul, deny the chosenness of the Jewish people, deny that the Law of Moses is binding on us, maintaining instead that it is but the civil law of the ancient Hebrew commonwealth.

MORTEIRA: (Angrily) And mock the Creator who you say is no creator, but simply the totality of things.

SPINOZA: You understand my thoughts but poorly.

MORTEIRA: Do you or do you not teach these things?

SPINOZA: Scripture itself demonstrates that the Law is but the laws of the ancient commonwealth, which no longer exists. It makes no sense to obey the laws of a state that has perished. The Bible teaches no theoretical postulates. The prophets were not philosophers. They spoke to simple men—the multitude— in the language of their time and place. Scripture was written by men like us at diverse times and places. If we are to understand it, we must understand their personality, their historical situation, their language, and the audience to which they spoke. They used images, metaphors, illustrations that appealed to the imagination, not to reason. They were not philosophers! They were moral teachers with exceptionally vivid imaginations.

MORTEIRA: Vivid imaginations! They speak for God.

MANASSEH: There is no heresy in this. (The other rabbis stare angrily at him.) Judaism does not dictate belief, only practice. Baruch, will you not conform? Practice the rites of your people?

ABOAB: (to Manasseh) You are a menace; yet if you can persuade him, we will be grateful.

MORTEIRA: (to Spinoza) You maintain that even Moses was but a man of vivid imagination?

SPINOZA: All the prophets teach but one simple thing, that men should be just and charitable and that acting so constitutes the true worship of God. Rites are indifferent. Each man should practice those that render him more just and more charitable. Interpret Scripture in terms of itself, look at what it says in context, and you will have to agree with me.

ABOAB: (Angrily) What arrogance! You know more than the rabbis who wrote the Talmud?

SPINOZA: Yes.

MORTEIRA: Incredible! (Sputters) You are beyond . . . (Morteira is so upset that he is unable to continue speaking. He stammers several times and then recovers.) And the Zohar? You disavow it also?

SPINOZA: Superstitious rubbish!

MANASSEH: How do you explain the survival of the Jewish people?

SPINOZA: Gentile hatred has preserved the Jews. Our hatred of the Gentiles and our exclusiveness have made them hate us. The Hebrew Nation has lost all its grace and beauty . . .

RABBIS: (All three interrupting) Outrageous!

SPINOZA: . . . as one would expect after the defeats and persecutions it has gone through.

MANASSEH: Baruch, I cannot defend this. Be reasonable, forbear these insane teachings and return to us.

MORTEIRA: It is of lesser import, but you also teach that property should be held in common, which would destroy us.

ABOAB: Let us stick to his heresies, they are dreadful enough. (To Spinoza) You deny the immortality of the soul?

SPINOZA: The mind is the idea of the body; without the body there can be no mind. They are two sides of the same coin.

ABOAB: You equivocate.

MORTEIRA: Baruch De Espinoza, I give you a last chance to avoid the *herem*. If you must, you can continue to attend Van dan Ende's school.

MANASSEH: Even our most pious leaders send their children there to learn Latin.

MORTEIRA: We abjure you, return to your Judaic studies, write commentaries for scholars that can do no harm. You have turned away from worldly pursuits, given up your business interests. Use your mind in the service of Judaism, honor our martyrs, obey the Commandments, help others to find salvation through the Law of Moses . . .

SPINOZA: (interrupting) Salvation lies neither in following the Law of Moses nor the Law of Jesus; it lies solely in Reason—in the quest for adequate ideas that do not partake of the realm of the imagination. I realize that the multitude cannot be guided by reason alone. They are dominated by passion, and need rites and ceremonies that will externally shape them so that they will follow the path of Reason that is open but to a few.

ABOAB: (furious) This insanity is reason?

MANASSEH: Baruch, you did love me. Will you not . . . ?

SPINOZA: I must be true to myself. I must espouse what the inner light of reason shows to be clear and distinct.

MANASSEH: I cannot support you in this.

MORTEIRA: We have offered to stipend you in a life of scholarship if you but abjure your abominations. Have you no heart? How can you slander your own people who have suffered so deeply for God, for Torah, for the Law of Moses. You are a monster.

SPINOZA: I do what I must. (Exits.)

ABOAB: (to Morteira) It is agreed; he will be placed under the *herem*. (Morteira nods agreement, vehemently) Prepare the black candles.

(The lights dim on the rabbis, who fade. The CHORUS is again visible.)

CHORUS: It was a kind of cognitive dissonant phenomenon. You know, the severity of initiation theory—the tougher it is the more you value it. Go through Parris Island and you consider the Marines the greatest. It was the same for the rebs and their congregation. So many had died so horribly for it, the Law of Moses must be of transcendent value. And Spinoza—crazy kid—brilliant recruit to the Amsterdam counterculture—rebelled against the materialism of the Elders, driving them up the wall. He knows better than to suck back up to the rabbis like that Juan Prado they were talking about. He saw what happened to Uriel da Costa.

(Lights fade.)

Scene 3

(Synagogue is again filled with worshipers. A man stripped to the waist is tied to a pillar and is being whipped. The congregation sings psalms. As he is released he speaks.)

DA COSTA: When I came to Amsterdam from Portugal and became a Jew again, I was disappointed. These Jews were not at all like the Hebrews of the Bible. I started to question and soon doubted my new faith. They drove me out. At first I was glad, but then I couldn't stand the loneliness, so I returned. After I recanted my heresies, the Verger came to me, and with a scourge of leather thongs, gave me nine and thirty stripes. During the time of my whipping, they sang a psalm. After this I prostrated myself, the doorkeeper holding up my head, whilst all, old and young, passed over me, stepping with one foot on the lower part of my legs. (Da Costa picks himself up, leaves the stage, and the congregation resumes singing until a shot is heard. Chorus enters.)

CHORUS: That was Uriel da Costa shooting himself. Uriel was a weak-willed ass, unable to endure excommunication, but he hardly deserved what he got from the multitude. I guess I haven't told you about the multitude. That is one of our hero's favorite words. It is the multitude who burn the heretics and Judaizers, the multitude who drove Aboab out of Pernambuco, the multitude who savaged Europe for thirty years for the greater glory of God. The multitude of popes and cardinals, rabbis and generals, bourgeoisie and peasants, all who are incapable of philosophical insight. Our friend never did figure out how to deal with the multitude, though he thought he did. Uriel da Costa, vacillating rebel, subjecting himself to humiliation to regain membership in the synagogue, is our hero's model of what not to be.

Scene 4

(Spinoza and his half-sister Rebekeh enter.)

SPINOZA: Take the inheritance. I want only a bed. I give you what I couldn't let you steal from me. Here is my judgment against you. (Hands her legal papers.) Enjoy the goods I have given you.

REBEKEH: You are crazy. You will end like da Costa. You threw away Father's business, spend all your time with that atheistic ex-priest, Van dan Ende, and his revolutionary friends. You despise and revile your own people. I hate you. You love Gentile heretics more than you love us.

SPINOZA: I freely give you what you try to steal from me. Why do you hate me? (Exit Rebekeh.) She is like all the rest. They think the only thing they can lose is money. The elders, the rabbis, Father, my sister, my brother-in-law, my brother can think of nothing but money. It was the same for me when I ran the business. Then I perceived that I pursued a phantom and turned elsewhere to find a cure for my disease.

(Chorus enters.)

CHORUS: Hated your father, didn't you? You're really socking it to him, telling him to shove it, rotate it, cram it. You hate

Rebekeh, too—dragged her through the courts and then threw your victory in her face. I could go on. You despise your brother-in-law even more, and I'm not so sure you don't detest your brother.

SPINOZA: (Shocked) I do not hate my father, but I do not wish to live the life he lived. My sister and brother-in-law are not likable, but I do not hate them.

CHORUS: No? Actions speak louder than words. You are motivated by hate, not love. (Spinoza looks confused.) Your father married that bitch, didn't he, after your mother died. The bitch died too, but not soon enough for you. Your father pushed you into the business and then he died leaving you high and dry.

SPINOZA: Hate my father? No. No, my father was my friend. He sent me to Van dan Ende's school to study Latin as well as to the synagogue school. He was always loving toward me.

CHORUS: That's a lie. He loved your brothers more. He rejected you when you took his anticlericism and skepticism about ritual too far, didn't he?

SPINOZA: No.

CHORUS: How about the psycho-bitch from hell?

SPINOZA: You mean my stepmother? Father had a right to marry whomever he pleased.

CHORUS: You are the world's leading expert on unrequited love, all prettied up to be sure—in fact, presented as the highest form of love—but it is all bullshit. Your father was your first experience of unrequited love.

SPINOZA: (Angrily) No! My father's religion, his devotion to charity and justice, is his heritage to me.

CHORUS: He didn't reject you in the end?

SPINOZA: Perhaps a little. He had mixed feelings. It was okay.

CHORUS: Oh, now that I think about it, he wasn't your first unrequited love. That was your mother. She abandoned you, didn't she? Died, leaving you a devastated 6-year-old with a busy, emotionally distant, uninvolved, only abstractly caring father. (Nastily) You haven't got over that, have you?

SPINOZA: Shut up, you bastard. Shut up. (Puts his hands over his ears and runs off.)

(Projection onto the scrim. Slide of the Jewish cemetery at Ouderkerk showing the tombstone of Spinoza's mother. Spinoza stands before the tombstone weeping.)

CHORUS: Why are you weeping, you who say a free man feels only joy? It's interesting that after your excommunication, you came here and lived as close to your mother's grave as you possibly could. Was your mother's death so traumatic that you can never again risk loving and losing a woman?

SPINOZA: You're despicable.

Scene 5

(Van dan Ende's school.)

VAN DAN ENDE: Descartes has undone scholasticism, old forms crumble. Take nothing on faith, question all, question the sacred books, doubt, doubt, doubt, doubt all that can be doubted.

STUDENT 1: This is a Latin lesson? My father would withdraw me if he knew what you teach here.

STUDENT 2: Don't tell your father, you ass. The professor is the best teacher in Amsterdam. There is no place more exciting than this school.

VAN DAN ENDE: The Calvinists are trying to silence me—to silence all free thought. Dutch freedom is in danger. (Projection shows Van dan Ende on the gallows.)

CHORUS: Radicalism, involvement in hare-brained revolutionary schemes, systematic doubt of everything, even atheism—no wonder Van dan Ende ended on the gallows. Quixotic to the last, he joined a rebellion against the French king after having been driven from Holland. The rest were beheaded. He wasn't deemed worthy of that honor, so he was hanged.

VAN DAN ENDE: Property should be held in common. Kings should be driven from their thrones. The people should rule. Descartes hasn't gone far enough. He upholds the Church. I have been a priest, and believe me, the Church is always in the service of the crown. It is all benighted ignorance, justification of the powers that be, using people's fears to enslave them.

STUDENT 3: Should I join a communistic community?

VAN DAN ENDE: I have many friends among the Mennonites, Remonstrants, and the Collegiants. You meet them here, and through your acquaintance with them, you will find the proper path.

STUDENT 4: When are we going to go over the accusative? I have it confused with the dative.

SPINOZA: Do you doubt all religions?

VAN DAN ENDE: Religious doctrines are all foolishness. Their purpose is to keep men enslaved, yet there is a common ethical core, honored more in the breach than in the observance, that I respect. Property should be equally distributed; my Leveler friends are trying to end the exploitation of the poor. I hate all forms of mystification. Men are blinded by holy water so they may be stolen from. (To Spinoza) Baruch, you don't look yourself today.

SPINOZA: I am no longer a Baruch. Henceforth, I am Benedict—Benedictus.

VAN DAN ENDE: You are equally blessed in Latin or in Hebrew. Your mastery of Latin has progressed so far that you wish to translate your name into Latin?

SPINOZA: I am no longer a member of the Jewish congregation of Amsterdam, so it is not fitting that I be called Baruch.

CHORUS: They didn't take your name away. They can't deprive you of that.

SPINOZA: I no longer wish to be Baruch. I am no longer a Jew.

CHORUS: Are you then a Christian?

SPINOZA: No.

CHORUS: What are you then?

SPINOZA: (Frightened) Nothing. Nobody. I don't know.

VAN DAN ENDE: Latin is equally the language of the old scholastic philosophy and of the new science. Whoever would be a member of the community of scholars must learn Latin. Rabbi

Manasseh has written books in Latin; it is fitting that you have adapted a Latin name.

SPINOZA: Manasseh opens his home to the best minds; the most advanced thinkers congregate there; he writes Latin works, yet he opens no doors. All his learning is for naught, an empty show of quotes from Lucretius and Virgil, Dante and Aquinas.

CHORUS: You hate 'em all. A subtle mind like yours making no distinctions? Your hate blinds you, drives you. Dropping Baruch and becoming—what was it? Benedictus?—is saying "Fuck you! Fuck you to 'em all!"

SPINOZA: I can no longer be Baruch. There is no Jew named Baruch, so I must be Benedict. Further, I choose to be. I do not wish to pursue wealth, fame, or lust. I seek a tranquil soul.

CHORUS: Tranquil, my ass! Can't you feel the rage within you? You denigrate the Jews, take away their uniqueness, their chosenness, mock their rituals, ridicule their law.

SPINOZA: They are not chosen. That is the truth, and that is the only reason I say it. I am not motivated by spite.

CHORUS: I am not convinced. (All exit except Spinoza.)

(Enter Clara Maria Van dan Ende, age 13.)

CLARA: I have been giving Latin lessons in father's stead.

SPINOZA: I have never known a woman like you. Jewish women are uneducated. I want to marry you.

CLARA: You will have to become a Catholic.

SPINOZA: I can't.

CLARA: Besides, I do not love you. (Exits. Chorus reenters.)

CHORUS: A safe choice. A child. Besides, you knew there was no way that she could marry you.

SPINOZA: I have wished to marry Clara for a long time. She too seeks salvation through knowledge.

CHORUS: Cute ass, too.

SPINOZA: Go away, you nauseate me.

CHORUS: How do you get your rocks off?

SPINOZA: Rocks off?

CHORUS: Go back to your Torah school. You really belong there.

SPINOZA: (Looks perplexed.)

CHORUS: Man, you're 24! You must get horny, get the itch, feel it running out of your ears—what do you do when your cock gets hard?

SPINOZA: Lust is a passive affect, an inadequate idea of a state of my body. I strive to make it an active affect by understanding through reason the infinite concatenation of causes and effects that give me that inadequate idea. Only then can I have an adequate idea, a true understanding, of the bodily state to which you refer.

CHORUS: Oh, brother.

SPINOZA: Enough gutter talk from you.

CHORUS: You write that a man endangers himself in sexual love because he risks his beloved being unfaithful to him, which not only deprives him of the sexual pleasure he seeks but inflicts pain by putting another man's degraded parts and excrementa next to the beloved. Baruch, you have a rich fantasy life, not surprising given your lack of experience of the real thing. This particular fantasy is a regression to anality as a defense against your forbidden oedipal wish. That is, you imagine that your father shits on your mother during intercourse, which disgusts you so that you don't have to feel the pain of his exclusive possession of her.

(Spinoza begins to be ill.)

You write garbage. "A man's degraded parts and excrementa next to the beloved." Baruch, that's sick! You have a sick view of sex. (Pauses) Don't you ever want to get laid? (Spinoza vomits.) Hopeless. Why do you hate your body so?

SPINOZA: I don't hate my body. I don't hate anything.

CHORUS: Ha! Are you revolted by women? Ever see your mother bleeding? (Spinoza pukes again.) Or do you really want a man to stick his dick up your ass—guess not. That must be a passive affect, too. Perhaps you would rather stick yours in his— that would be an active affect. (Laughs) Or maybe you just want to kiss him. All your friends are men. Do you have a secret lust for them?

SPINOZA: I hate no man, but it would not be hard to hate you. Leave me alone.

CHORUS: (To the audience) Was he gay? Probably not. Was he a misogynist? (Pause) Well, let me ask him. (To Spinoza) Do you hate women? Miriam, your mother, abandoned you. (Spinoza shakes his head.) Don't shake your head. In dying, she abandoned you. And Esther, your psychobitch-from-hell stepmother, you hate her for taking your father away from you. Then your sister Rebekeh tried to steal your inheritance. And now, Clara scorns and rejects you. You don't hate them? They are all whores—excuse me, harlots—aren't they? They are filthy, unclean, terrifying. (Spinoza goes after him, trying to grab him by the throat. As he runs, the Chorus says:) In the grip of a passive affect again, I see. (Chorus continues to run around Spinoza, eluding him, as Spinoza continues to chase him.) Contemptuous and phobic of women, unable to feel sexual love for men, ashamed of your own body—what can you do but sublimate, you poor bastard.
(Stage darkens.)

Scene 6

(Spinoza is now a close associate of the radical, communitarian sect of the Collegiants. Scene is set in a Collegiant commune.)

SPINOZA: Now that I have left the commercial life, I need a way to make a living. You, friends, have also abandoned your businesses to seek the highest good—the union of the mind with all of nature.

COLLEGIANT 1: By nature, you mean God?

SPINOZA: I have not yet worked out all of my thoughts on this matter. I only know that I, like you, must seek truth with the guidance of the inner light.

COLLEGIANT 2: What brought you to us after your expulsion by the Jews?

SPINOZA: Experience taught me that all the usual strivings of social life are vain and futile, and I saw that all the things that were the cause or object of my fears had nothing of good or bad in themselves, except insofar as my mind was moved by them. So I resolved at last to try and find out whether there was anything that would be the true good, capable of communicating itself, and that would alone affect my mind, all others being rejected—whether there was something that once found and acquired would continually give me the greatest joy, to eternity. I say I resolved at last, for at first glance it seemed ill-advised to be willing to lose something certain for something that was uncertain. I saw, of course, the advantages that honor and wealth bring, and that I would be forced to abstain from seeking them if I wished to devote myself seriously to something new and different. And if by chance the greatest happiness lay in them, I saw I should have to do without it. But if it did not lie in them and I devoted my energies only to acquiring them, then I would equally go without it. So I wondered whether perhaps it might be possible to reach my new goal or at least the certainty of attaining it without changing the conduct and plan of life that I shared with other men. Often I tried this, but in vain. For most things that present themselves in life, and that, to judge by their actions, men think to be the highest good, may be reduced to these three: wealth, honor, and sensual pleasure. For as far as sensual pleasure is concerned, the mind is so caught up with it that it is quite prevented from thinking of anything else. But after the enjoyment of sensual pleasure is past, the greatest sadness follows. The mind is also distracted not a little by the pursuit of honor and wealth. Honor and wealth do not have, as sensual pleasure does, repentance as a natural consequence. The more each is possessed, the more joy is increased. And hence, the more we are spurred on to increase them. But if our hopes should by chance be frustrated, we experience the greatest sadness. I saw I was in greatest danger, and that I was forced to seek a remedy with all my strength, however uncertain it might be—like a man suffering a fatal illness, who, foreseeing certain death unless he employs a remedy, is forced to seek it, however uncertain, with all his strength. For all of my hope lies here. All those things that men ordinarily strive for not only provide no remedy but in fact hinder, often causing the destruction of those who possess them and always cause the destruction of those possessed by them. These evils seem to arise from the fact that all happiness or unhappiness is placed in the quality of the object to which we cling with love. Indeed, all these things happen only in the love of those things which can perish, as all the things I have spoken of can do. But love toward the eternal and infinite feeds the mind with a joy entirely exempt from sadness. This is greatly to be desired, and to be sought with all of our strength. I have come here because I feel that you, my friends, share my goals, that you too seek to find an object worthy of your love. I embrace your fellowship, and in our fellowship, we shall find fulfillment. Here I hope that my quest and your companionship will enable me to enjoy continual, supreme, and unending happiness. If I had not met you, I would have found it necessary to form a social order, such as would be conducive to the attainment of bliss by the greatest number with the least difficulty and danger. It is part of my happiness to lend a helping hand, as you do, that many others may understand even as I do.

CHORUS: (To audience) Now that he has left Jewish Amsterdam, he is living in the closest approximation to the East Village that seventeenth-century Holland has to offer. Living with but not a member of the Collegiants—those Cartesians of the Left, believers of property in common and followers of the inner light. (To Spinoza) Why don't you join them instead of remaining a fellow traveler? Always an egalitarian from above, aren't you? Never quite a member of anything. Just can't commit yourself to anything but your theories, eh?

SPINOZA: (To Chorus) I must retain my freedom, my freedom to think my way to blessedness, freedom even from as gentle and good a company of men as these.

CHORUS: Another defense against your homoerotic feelings? Or is it part of your defense against closeness to anybody?

SPINOZA: (To Chorus) Fool! Don't you see that I must preserve my independence? There is no other way I can be true to my mission.

CHORUS: Mission? Grandiose, aren't you?

SPINOZA: I wish to show men the path I seek but have not yet found to bliss, insofar as they are capable of it. In the pursuit of that goal, I renounced my people, exiled myself before they exiled me. I will not compromise now, neither will I cut myself off from men.

CHORUS: You're a snob. Many of these Collegiants have scant education, others aren't bright enough for you, so you keep your distance.

SPINOZA: I don't keep my distance. There is love between us. You fool, what I keep is my independence.

(Exit Chorus.)

SPINOZA: (Spinoza and his friends light pipes and sip wine. Conversation buzzes on as a rap session ensues. Spinoza's voice emerges from the general buzz.) I must have a way of making a living. I renounced my inheritance; I will learn to grind lenses for telescopes and microscopes. I can thus provide for my material needs, even as I forge the tools that enable men to investigate nature—to peer into the magnificent structures that manifest God's eternal law.

COLLEGIANT 3: I can help you financially. I can afford it, and I will be honored if you will permit me.

SPINOZA: No, I will grind lenses. (Chorus reenters.)

CHORUS: Another part of your masochism and martyrdom. You don't have to grind lenses.

SPINOZA: I wish to. It is part of my identity as a free man and an aid to my scientific researches.

CHORUS: Accept the pension. (Spinoza shakes his head. Chorus continues.) In the coming years, you will be forced to accept it, as your lungs deteriorate as glass dust accumulates in them from your stupid, prideful insistence on grinding lenses. Why be proud? Take the pension now.

SPINOZA: He who pays the piper calls the tune. I haven't gone the lengths I have to establish my independence to compromise it now. You do not know me. I put no value on asceticism—the free man seeks joy. Joy can never be excessive.

CHORUS: The glass dust will kill you.

SPINOZA: The relationship between inhaling pollutants and lung disease has not been established. As a free man, I would not choose to endanger myself should research show that connection to pertain. But I will die young in any case. My lung disease will progress even if the glass particles are not the cause of it.

COLLEGIANT 1: Benedict, you must help us understand Descartes' philosophy more clearly. He like us rejects dogma and authority, founding his thought on the certainty of clear and distinct ideas, ideas whose clearness and distinction can be affirmed by all men using the light within. His thought gives a rational foundation to our way of life, yet we but confusedly comprehend it. It is too complex.

COLLEGIANT 2: Could you demonstrate Descartes' system mathematically, derive it from definitions and axioms as Euclid does his geometry?

COLLEGIANT 3: Yes, give us a geometrical demonstration of Descartes.

CHORUS: (To audience) That Descartes again? You would think he was the Marx of the seventeenth century. He wasn't. A timid rabbit. Radical thinker, my ass! His doubt was purely theoretical. Follow the customs of your time and place, wrote he. Be a conformist, is what he meant. A believer in Catholicism, no less. Like I say, not much of a radical. His politics—who knows? He had royal patrons. Yet there was such excitement around him, the most diverse people thrilled to his partial, limited, hedged-in challenge to received wisdom. Clear and distinct. If it's not clear and distinct, then throw it out. But what's clear and distinct? As subjective a criterion of truth as can be imagined. My clear and distinct clearly and distinctly isn't Hitler's clear and distinct. Radical subjectivism is dangerous. Yet this Descartes must be counted as one of the liberators, one of the dark enlighteners, one of those who moved us along the painful path to enlightenment.

SPINOZA: (speaking to Collegiants) I don't have the literary skill.

CHORUS: (Returning to his mocking attitude) No doubts about your philosophical skill though. Let's have no false modesty.

COLLEGIANT 3: I will edit it and write a preface.

COLLEGIANT 4: I will publish it.

SPINOZA: I will do it. I will derive Descartes' metaphysics geometrically.

CHORUS: And it will be the only book you dare publish under your own name in your lifetime, my cautious one. (To audience) Descartes' metaphysics—that's different from his method of radical doubt. A whole megillah about two substances—extension and thought. Benedict—Baruch—will have none of that. There is only one substance, albeit two names, for him.

Scene 7

(Jan de Witt, Grand Pensioner of the Netherlands, is a vigorous intellectual in his mid-forties. He is self-assured, even arrogant. He is a great man, one of the first to espouse freedom of thought and religion, yet blind to his faults. He does not relate to other people, does nothing to please. He lacks charisma, and wouldn't use it if he had it. Spinoza is now in his mid-thirties. He is cheerful, having come to terms with his exile and having found a place for himself in the Christian world of which he is a part yet apart. Jan de Witt is with his brother, Cornelius. The Chorus is off to the side with Sigmund Freud.)

DE WITT: I rule by social mathematics. The edicts of the state are derivable. Statistical science determines our economic policy. A republican state is a rational state. Our government here in the Netherlands is a model of the social arrangements that optimize the self-realization of the free men of whom you write. Reason teaches that provision of security and the maintenance of peace are the proper functions of the state. Each man pursues his self-interest. Enlightened self-interest, self-interest when informed by reason, teaches that cooperation with other men maximizes reward and is to be avidly pursued. My policy is to bring all this to pass. Mathematical science rules the state. My brother Cornelius co-calculates policy.

CHORUS: And your cousin, and your cousin's cousins, not to mention your nieces and nephews, aunts and uncles, friends and friends' friends. And of course, your father. You run a connection-archy, all of course in the service of reason.

DE WITT: (Who hasn't heard the Chorus) Reason teaches that thought must be free, that religion should play no role in determining a man's place within the state, and that each shall be free to worship as he will, that theology and philosophy shall not trample on each other's domains so that professors may profess as they will in the universities, and that peace, if ever it be possible, shall be the goal of our foreign policy. Prosperity, the flourishing of our commerce, dictates that we pursue peace and maximization of profit through trade. This is clearly shown to be desirable through the application of social mathematics. Peace, freedom, prosperity—the goals of my, our, liberal Republic—are rational goals, goals sought by men's self-interest, yet many oppose them. The clergy and the common people hate me. (Emphatically) The state must rule the church and be the only sovereign. The multitude must not be allowed a say, nor granted the franchise. In our Republic, rule and office go to the man of virtue.

CHORUS: Especially if he is a relative.

DE WITT: Virtue is not the exclusive possession of the nobility. It is found in all ranks, and is accordingly awarded by us.

CHORUS: (Turns away from De Witt and addresses the audience.) The classical dilemma of the liberal. The masses crave authority and must be forced to be free. (Turning to Freud.) The liberals in your Austria restricted the franchise. They too were afraid of the masses, of the multitude. (Projection of Storm Troopers and of a Viennese crowd giving the Fascist salute. The sounds of shouts of "Sig Heil!") They had their reasons, didn't they? (Freud shakes his head.)

FREUD: It's the multitude. Men are controlled by their instincts. Reason is too thin a reed—the ego is too weak.

CHORUS: (To audience) Liberalism is everywhere deconstructed these days. The self-serving pecuniary motives behind its rationalizations exposed for the ideology of the commercial oligarchy that it is. The career open the talents—to virtue, as you put it (pointing to De Witt). It has been an empty promise, an illusion for most men, not to mention women. Actually these quibbles about liberalism don't matter much. The lust for submission, the desire to be ruled, fury, bloodthirstiness, the craving for war—these and not rational self-interest are what motivate men. (To De Witt) You and all of your successor liberals are not merely hypocritical; you are naive, though not naive enough to give the vote to the multitude.

DE WITT: (To Spinoza) The Calvinist clergy are fanatical. They whip the commoners to frenzy. They want power—power to control thought, ban books, run the universities, drive the Cartesians out, put the Prince of Orange back on the throne and end the Republic. They would replace a Catholic inquisition with a Protestant one. I understand the commoners' love for Orange, but their time has passed. The Prince would lead us into foolish wars, wars not dictated by rational calculation, by mathematical reasoning, as was our struggle against the Spanish throne. The Jews, too, back the House of Orange. It is irrational of them to support the Prince now. My government represents their economic interests and defends their religious freedom. Benedict, tell me, why are the Jews against me? You are a Jew. Why this opposition to the Republic?

SPINOZA: I am no longer a Jew.

DE WITT: Nor a Christian. You write a pamphlet defending my government allegorically. I need your support. Write and I will covertly defend and encourage you. I cannot do so openly as long as the multitude perceives and reviles you as an atheist Jew.

SPINOZA: I am neither atheist nor Jew.

DE WITT: You write convincingly of the wisdom and rationality of the republican form of government, of my government, of the necessity of all sovereignty residing in the state, of the clergy being kept in their place, and of the justification of tolerance and freedom of thought.

SPINOZA: Yes, I write even now of these matters. I write a theo-logical-political treatise in which I consider human actions and appetites just as if it were a question of lines, planes, and bodies. In the theological part, I treat the biblical text as an historical document like any other written by diverse men in diverse places and times, and use the biblical text itself, the science of grammar, the analysis of the Hebrew language, and of the circumstances and goals and personalities of its writers to explicate its meaning, not allegorically, but to show that the sacred text teaches no science, no philosophy, no theoretical beliefs, but merely, simply and consistently, that the practice of justice and charity are the only true worship, while rite and ritual, myth and doctrine are indifferent—no part of true religion but mere embellishments, and at their best, incitements to justice and charity. Further, I show that the ancient Hebrew state fell when the priests gained secular power, and that Jewish religious law was but part of the secular law of the ancient Hebrew state. To uphold and practice the ancient laws now is absurd.

CHORUS: As they did in excommunicating you.

SPINOZA: There is nothing special about the Jews. Their vanity maintains their uniqueness. They are not chosen any more than other men. That, too, I have shown in my treatise.

DE WITT: And how do you account for their survival during the centuries after which their state ceased to exist?

SPINOZA: The persecution of the Gentiles has preserved the Jews, as has their contempt for other men and their hatred of them, which has reinforced Gentile hatred. Further, circumcision is their sign of specialness, and it, like the Chinese pigtail, preserves them in the degraded state in which they now exist. Considering how they have been assaulted, hounded, and persecuted, it is not surprising that they are no longer beautiful.

CHORUS: (To audience) A little Jewish self-hatred here—or just plain hatred—has overcome our apostle of love. So anti-Semitism is caused by Jewish contempt and hatred, a useful text for the authors of *The Protocols of the Elders of Zion* and of the Nuremberg laws. (To Spinoza) Watch how you avenge yourself in your writings, Baruch.

DE WITT: And the political part?

SPINOZA: Therein I shall demonstrate how the state must have all power, how the clergy must be subordinate, how democracy is the best government, how state power does not extend to control of thought, how religion must be free insofar as rites are concerned, but that the state religion must induce the multitude to act as if they were wise and guided by reason, by inculcating the desire for charity and justice through rewards and punishments, through hope and fear. I will show how the multitude who are not themselves wise can be so led as to live wisely through the rule of the wise—by men of virtue such as yourself. Further, I shall show how the self-interest that rules men dictates that they cooperate with each other and seek peace.

DE WITT: My policy and your theory are akin. We are one. I need your justifications in my battle against the darkness. Write quickly and well, my friend. You have my love, even if I dare not publicly express it.

SPINOZA: And you have my love. In you, reason rules, and men in spite of themselves may come to see where their true blessedness lies. (Spinoza and De Witt embrace.)

CHORUS: (To Spinoza) You could publish neither quickly nor openly. It took you five years away from your philosophical work to defend the Republic, and even then you had to publish under a pseudonym with a phony imprint. But you didn't succeed in fooling anyone. Since publication you experience hatred like you have never known. Already anathematized by the Jews, now the massed hatred of the Gentile world assails you—vile atheist Jew, corrupter of piety. Stick by your motto *caute*, caution, and deny authorship, or you surely will die on the rack, Jan's protection not withstanding.

(Projection of Spinoza's ring with the word *caute* on the scrim. Spinoza and De Witt walk off, arms around each other's shoulders, talking animatedly, as the stage grows dark.)

Scene 8

(Spinoza is sitting quietly, writing contentedly, smoking his pipe. In the background is his worktable, many books, and apparatus for grinding lenses. Chorus sits to the side.)

SPINOZA: The city of Amsterdam reaps the fruits of this freedom in its own great prosperity and the admiration of all other people. For in this most flourishing state, and most splendid city, men of every nation and religion live together in the greatest harmony, and ask no questions before trading their goods to their fellow citizen, save whether he be rich or poor, and whether he generally acts honestly, or the reverse. His religion and sect are considered of no importance, for they have no effect before the judges in gaining or losing a case, and there is no sect so despised that its followers, provided they harm no one, pay every man his due, and live uprightly, are deprived of the protection of the magisterial authority.

CHORUS: (To audience) Written in the floodtide of liberalism, the apogee of the De Witts.

(Enter Adrian Koerbagh, a middle-aged businessman.)

KOERBAGH: I avidly read your writings, discuss and promulgate them. You have justified the Republic, shown the way to godliness, yet you are considered an atheist. How do you understand this?

(They are interrupted as several of Spinoza's Collegiant friends run in.)

COLLEGIANT 1: *The Theological Political Treatise* has been condemned by the Synod. It has been banned! You are in danger. It is widely believed that you are the author. De Witt cannot protect you. Adrian, you are in danger, too. If they can't get to Benedict, they will settle for you.

(Armed men enter and grab Adrian and take him off. Projection of a man on the rack. Screams. Center stage darkens.)

CHORUS: (At stage left) That's more like it. The multitude at work again. The freedom of De Witt's Republic is far from absolute.

(Center stage is again lit. Three Judges dressed as Calvinist clergy are sitting at a table. Adrian Koerbagh is dragged in. He has been tortured.)

    JUDGE 1: You uphold Spinoza's philosophy. Your ideas are his. He wrote the *Treatise*, didn't he?

    ADRIAN: No, your Worships. My ideas are my own.

    JUDGE 2: You know him.

    ADRIAN: We are friends, but he doesn't influence me.

    JUDGE 2: (Spits) Blasphemy, atheism, blasphemy!

    JUDGE 1: You talk of the "indwelling spirit of the immanent God" in your book. That is but the Hebrew doctrine of the Shechinah—it must come from the atheist Jew, not you.

    ADRIAN: My thoughts are my own.

    CHORUS: He is being accused of un-Dutch activities.

(Judges confer.)

    JUDGE 1: We sentence you to ten years in prison, to be followed by exile.

    JUDGE 2: You are not severe enough; his right thumb should be cut off, his tongue bored through with a red-hot iron, and he should be jailed for thirty years.

(Spinoza and the Chorus return. Koerbagh and Judges fade into darkness.)

    CHORUS: (To Spinoza) They were after you. (Projection of Koerbagh's body being removed from prison.)

    CHORUS: He did not live long in prison.

    SPINOZA: (Passionately) He who knows himself to be upright does not fear the death of a criminal, and shrinks from no punishment; his mind is not wrung with remorse for any disgraceful deed. He holds that death in a good cause is no punishment, but an honor, and that death for freedom is glory.

Scene 9

(Spinoza sits quietly, surrounded by books and lens-grinding equipment. He is subdued and has aged. He occasionally coughs. Glass dust is seen rising from his workbench. He takes out a sketchbook and pen and begins drawing. Chorus enters.)

CHORUS: I see that you participate in the drawing mania.

SPINOZA: Drawing mania?

CHORUS: All of Holland draws. You have the bug, too.

SPINOZA: Bug? You distract me. It is the part of the wise man, I say, to refresh and invigorate himself with moderate and pleasant eating and drinking, with sweet scents and the beauty of green plants, with ornament, with music, with sports, with the theater, and with all things of this kind that one may enjoy without hurting another. For the human body is composed of a great number of parts of diverse nature, which constantly need new and varied nourishment, in order that the whole of the body may be equally fit for everything that can follow from its nature. My beer drinking and drawing are of that sort. Why should I not enjoy them? Nothing but a gloomy and sad superstition forbids enjoyment. For why is it more seemly to extinguish hunger and thirst than to drive away melancholy? My reasons and my conclusions are these: No God, no human being, except an envious one, is delighted by my impotence or my trouble, or esteems as any virtue in us tears, sighs, fears, and other things of this kind, which are signs of mental impotence. On the contrary: the greater the joy with which we are affected, the greater the perfection to which we pass thereby, that is to say, the more do we necessarily partake of the divine nature.

CHORUS: Really? A lot of rhetoric to justify playing with your sketchpad. And you are sure it's only an innocent amusement? Nothing more? (Pauses.)

SPINOZA: (Sips at his beer.) Some beer, friend?

CHORUS: No thanks. I'm in recovery.

SPINOZA: Recovery?

CHORUS: The gloomy superstition of my time. I'm only kidding. Let me have a beer. (They sip together.) What do you draw?

SPINOZA: What I will.

CHORUS: Less evasion. (Takes the drawing and stares at it.) Not a bad self-portrait. It's your face but not your body, which is dressed like Masaniello, leader of the Naples rebellion. Identifying with a proletarian rebel, after teaching that rebellion is always wrong and that a wise man's duty is obedience? A bit inconsistent, no?

SPINOZA: He led a rebellion against the Spanish oppressor.

CHORUS: Of the Dutch or of the Jews?

SPINOZA: Of the Neapolitans.

CHORUS: You know what I mean.

SPINOZA: I am confused about this. Rebellion is futile; witness the tragedy in England in which a king was killed to be replaced by another in all but name who was far worse. Yet I admire Masaniello. He died for freedom. Here I cannot reconcile my thought and my feeling. When I draw myself as him, I am in the grip of imagination, not of reason, dominated by inadequate ideas and passive affects. My reason tells me that Masaniello's rebellion was as futile as the English one, and that I must not think of myself as him. (Tears up the picture.)

CHORUS: You do violence to the best part of yourself. Your reason is unreason, a voice of repression that enslaves you.

SPINOZA: (Obviously pained) No! Reason is our one hope. I must not give in to the passive affects of the imagination that but feed ambition.

CHORUS: Afraid of your grandiosity? You're very grandiose, you know. (Screams) Drop this passive affect shit, and take a stand for real freedom, political freedom.

SPINOZA: My identification with Masaniello is the product of false pride. (Thinks) Here in Holland, the rebels are the enemies of freedom; thus, I must deny the right of rebellion. You are a hopeless romantic; I am a realist. Be gone!

(Chorus exits. Spinoza picks up the pieces of his self-portrait as Masaniello and weeps. After a time, he dries his tears, and takes out a jar with insects. He takes another jar, also containing insects, and introduces them into the first jar. They battle. Spinoza starts to laugh. A projection shows the insects tearing each other apart as Spinoza continues to laugh. He opens the jar and takes an insect out. He pulls the wings off and laughs again. Chorus reenters with Freud.)

FREUD: (To Spinoza) As you were the first to see, morality is a reaction-formation, a turning into its opposite—of sadism.

However, not all of your sadism has undergone conversion. You are taking a delight in cruelty, a God-given, as the pastors might say, constitutional propensity. Sadism is innate. One of the components of the sexual instinct I have postulated.

CHORUS: You mean he's getting his rocks off. Come, let Baruch, I mean Benedict, alone. (To Spinoza) You're getting pretty worked up over there. (Spinoza giggles as he tears more wings off.) (To Freud) He's close to climax. (To Spinoza) Pretty sadistic, aren't you, considering you teach that philosophy leads us to hate, envy, and harm no one, and to offer mutual benevolence, justice, and charity. Bunk! Look at yourself. Filled with hatred and enjoying every second of it. (Shouts) Sadist!

SPINOZA: You are a bigger fool than I thought. I said no man, not no animal. I owe allegiance only to man, to my own kind.

CHORUS: Kind of biblical, eh? He created the beasts of the field, the fowl of the air, the fishes of the sea for your pleasure. Your sadism denied and repressed trips you up. For all your struggle against the old anthropomorphic God in your attitude toward animals, you fall into the old ways. Your sadism has to come out somehow. Laugh away, my politically incorrect pervert. (Spinoza continues to torture the insects, taking obvious pleasure in it.)

CHORUS: (Sardonically) The wise man seeks joy. (Spinoza puts his insects away and falls into a deep sleep.)

FREUD: Perhaps he will dream and we will learn more.

CHORUS: I already have his number. (Spinoza half awakes.)

SPINOZA: I see a black scaly Brazilian. (Rubs his eyes.) I can't get rid of the image. (Looks at his books.) It is gone. (Looks away.) It is back. (Rubs his eyes.) Stop tormenting me. Go away!

CHORUS: Hallucinating again?

FREUD: What does the scary black Brazilian bring to mind?

CHORUS: It brings to mind the blacks of Pernambuco who with Portuguese help killed so many of Aboab's compatriots, and almost got the old reb himself. The dream is a hidden wish fulfillment. Spinoza identifies with the black invaders and wishes to kill Aboab. The dream makes him anxious because his

repudiated death wish breaks through—the return of the repressed, as you would say.

FREUD: Not bad, but what about the father behind the rabbi. He
wishes to kill his father.

CHORUS: You're the analyst.

FREUD: The insects he tortures are his siblings, toward whom he
also has death wishes. The open expression of his sadism trig-
gered the dream of death to Aboab and to his father, while the
avenging black man punishes him for his forbidden wishes as
well as being a self-representation. An artful compromise formation. The mind works beautifully and lawfully, does it not?
(Frenzied shouting is heard offstage.)

SPINOZA: Yes, the mind is lawful. Even as we study the causes of
hatred, greed, envy, anger, and similar things, we acknowledge
that they have certain causes, through which they are understood, and have certain properties, as worthy of our knowledge
as the properties of every other thing, by the mere contemplation of which we are pleased. Understanding brings pleasure.

CHORUS: Oh God, if you'll pardon the expression, what an intellectualizer! My task may be hopeless. I cannot get you to
feel anything.

FREUD: Yet he is right. Intellectual understanding transforms.

CHORUS: (shouts at Spinoza) Did you wish to kill your father or
not? You still want to kill Aboab, don't you?

FREUD: There is no time in the unconscious.

CHORUS: (To Freud) You're just as bad. Another one locked
inside of his head. Lose your mind and come to your senses.
(Sounds from the street grow louder. Chorus and Freud exit.
Friends of Spinoza rush in. Projection of the mutilated bodies
of Jan and Cornelius de Witt hanging from a lamppost. Projections show the mob carving bits of flesh from the mutilated
bodies as souvenirs as it screams invectives. Spinoza's landlord
rushes in.)

LANDLORD: Benedict, horrible news. The mob, frenzied by our
war losses, broke into the prison where Cornelius, falsely accused, had been racked even as Jan was endeavoring to com-

fort him, and murdered them both. They were thrown down the steps, trampled, mutilated, and hung from the lamppost but a block from here. The mob even now cuts their bodies to shreds. The Republic has fallen, darkness descends on the Netherlands. (Landlord runs out. Spinoza goes into a paroxysm of rage. He screams.)

SPINOZA: Lowest barbarians! (Writes "lowest barbarians" on a large poster and starts out the door. Landlord reenters and wrestles the poster away.)

LANDLORD: No, Benedict. They will kill you, too.

SPINOZA: (Screaming) Lowest barbarians! (Landlord pushes him back shutting and locking the door.)

Act II, Scene 1

(Spinoza is once more in his room. He is in his early forties and sick. He coughs frequently. Glass dust rises from the bench, and his cough worsens.)

SPINOZA: De Witt failed. The Republic is no more. Scum. They murdered the greatest statesman in Europe. He alone ruled by reason, calculating policy as he would solve a mathematical problem. He never flattered the multitude or used cheap rhetoric to persuade. He never appealed to their passions.

(Chorus enters and remains apart at the side of the stage.)

CHORUS: (To audience) He was too arrogant. (To Spinoza) You are just as arrogant. You conceal it better.

SPINOZA: (Has not heard the Chorus) So they killed him and his brother. (Shudders) The times darken. I, too, am in danger. I have no taste for martyrdom. I do not understand it. Every creature seeks to preserve himself—strives, endeavors, to continue to exist. All of our actions are motivated by self-preservation and the need to increase our power so we may endure. I do not understand suicide.

(Freud enters.)

FREUD: I, too, sought to explain human behavior in terms of the pleasure principle. I gave it up. Analysis shows self-destructive-

ness to be a basic datum—a primordial fact. Only when I postulated the death instinct could I make sense of men's behavior.
You were on the wrong track with your one instinct—*conatus*—
self-preservation, the endless striving to go on existing, but your
obsession with unity, with oneness, blocked your development.
Only by postulating two instincts—Eros and Thanatos—the
desire for love and for death, can an adequate account be given.

SPINOZA: The free man thinks of nothing less than of death; his
wisdom is not a meditation upon death but upon life.

CHORUS: You think of nothing but death—the death of your
mother, of your brothers, of your father, of Koerbagh, of the
De Witts, of Van dan Ende, even perhaps of the Marrano
martyrs who you say you can't understand. (Aboab appears.)

ABOAB: There was and is a sublimity in their death—can you not
understand it? (Exits.)

CHORUS: You are dying. Your lungs are gone and soon so will
you be (hesitates) gone.

FREUD: (To Chorus) It's denial. His anxiety would overwhelm
him if he allowed himself to feel his terror and rage.

CHORUS: (To Freud) I thought there was no concept of death in
the unconscious.

FREUD: True. Fear of death is a derivative of fear of castration by
the father.

SPINOZA: To be obsessed with death is to be controlled by a passive affect. I would be a free man—active, expressing my essence, by maximizing my power.

FREUD: I hate helplessness more than all else. You are right to be
active, to understand, to insist that we use our minds. I create
a self out of the chaos of inchoate blind instinct. No longer
driven by my instincts, my fears, my passions, I achieve mastery—reclaim as much territory for the ego as I am able, even
as your countrymen reclaim the land from the sea.

SPINOZA: Given their miscalculation of the multitude, Jan and
Cornelius's murder were inevitable, yet I cannot accept it and
remain in the grip of passive affect.

CHORUS: (Scolding, wagging his finger at Spinoza) Freedom lies in choosing what is necessary, no?

SPINOZA: That is so. At this moment, I am not free. (In sudden fury, turns on the CHORUS.) Fucking bastard!

FREUD: We are threatened with suffering from three directions: from our own body, which is doomed to decay and dissolution and which cannot even do without pain and anxiety as warning signals; from the external world, which may rage against us with overwhelming and merciless forces of destruction; and finally, from our relations with other men. The suffering that comes from this last source is perhaps more painful to us than any other. We tend to regard it as a kind of gratuitous addition, although it cannot be any less faithfully inevitable than the suffering that comes from elsewhere.

SPINOZA: Thank you. You are quite right. You bring me back to myself.

FREUD: You are a seeker after consolation—a consolation that doesn't exist. Like the theologians, you are looking for a black cat in a coal bin at midnight, which does not exist, and you find it. My courage sinks to stand up before you as a prophet, and I bow to your reproaches, but I do not know how to bring you consolation, for that is fundamentally what you all demand, the wildest revolutionaries no less than the most conformist, pious believers. (Pauses) You are mourning. At the same time, you resist mourning. You cannot mourn without meditating on the death of your beloved.

CHORUS: (To Freud) He was in love with De Witt?

SPINOZA: To think of death is to let them win, to let the barbarians determine me. I will not do it. (Breaks down and weeps.)

FREUD: I, too, have experienced loss. As a confirmed unbeliever, I have no one to accuse, and realize there is no place where I can lodge a complaint. Where are we to look for justice? No one inquires after our wishes, our merits, or our claims. (Voice trails off.)

SPINOZA: God's decrees are the eternal laws of nature. He loves himself with a perfect love, but He does not love us, or make exceptions for us.

CHORUS: There is no less pleasure in intellectual understanding of the infinite causal sequence determinant of the most murderous passion than comes from understanding anything else. Or so you say. Where is your pleasure in this? Surely you can come to understand the causes of the mob's fury and come to appreciate the beauty of its causal nexus. Or can you? Philosopher, your philosophy deserts you.

SPINOZA: (Recovering himself) I shall come to understand it, for as Freud says, the pain inflicted by men on other men is no less inevitable than anything else. (Wipes away his tears as he begins coughing.) If only I can come to love the necessity of things, I will be free.

CHORUS: How does it help to understand the inevitability, the necessity of Koerbagh's torture and death, of the burning of the Marrano martyrs, of the savage murder of the De Witts? It is all whistling in the dark—it is all bullshit. Tell me, Benedictus, how does your knowing the causes of your being tortured by man or by nature, by cruel instruments or by disease, how does that understanding help you in your pain? It helps to know that you must be tortured? I don't think so. Do you really believe this?

Scene 2

(Spinoza is in his room. He looks worse than ever. He is writing a letter. Enter William James, about 30, looking depressed. Freud and Chorus are at stage left.)

JAMES: Benedict, you drove me to despair. I suffer the worst type of melancholia, panic fear. If all is determined, if I have no free will, my life is meaningless and there is no sense in my continuing to live.

SPINOZA: On the contrary, if all is grounded in the Divine necessity, then all is intelligible, luminous, comprehensible by the mind—contingency is not freedom. Nor is it meaningful. Freedom of the will is an illusion; men believe themselves to be free only because they do not know the causes of their actions. The more we understand the less free—you have an absurd inadequate notion of freedom—men are shown to be. Your alleged freedom of the will is only ignorance.

JAMES: Your philosophy drives me to thoughts of the pistol, the dagger, and the razor. You are an apostle of a closed universe. I seek an open universe, a multiverse in which creativity and novelty are possible.

SPINOZA: You are deluded.

JAMES: I do not say that freedom is causelessness. On the contrary, it is me as the cause—as an initiator, as the source of my beliefs, my actions, my feelings.

SPINOZA: You wish to be the cause of yourself. Absurd! As I have demonstrated, there can be but one substance that is the cause of itself. The infinite, eternal substance that I call God, or Nature. You are but a finite mode, and as such can be the cause of nothing.

JAMES: Then why live?

SPINOZA: Knowing that we are necessarily caused brings joy not sorrow.

JAMES: Not to me. I rebel. I cannot accept your philosophy. I do not find your proofs convincing. The existence of free will or its contrary can be neither proved nor disproved. Therefore, I can rationally believe what I wish in this matter. I ask, What is the cash value of my belief? Belief in freedom of the will lifts my depression. Therefore, (defiantly) my first act of free will shall be to believe in free will. My belief, to be sure, can't be optimistic, but I will posit life—affirm the self-governing resistance of the ego to the world. (Exits.)

SPINOZA: A madman. He thinks of suicide. Clearly he is in the grip of passive affects.

FREUD: He also rejects my insights into the determination of our mental life by the unconscious. He can't stand the idea that his thoughts, like everything else, have causes.

(Freud and Chorus exit. A Collegiant friend enters.)

    FRIEND: Benedictus, you must accept the offer of a professorship at Heidelberg. Your health is poor. You can no longer grind lenses and it is dangerous here. You may be arrested at any moment.

    SPINOZA: If I cast my accounts carefully, I have just enough from my pension to live from quarter to quarter. I need not grind lenses. Are there conditions to the appointment?

    FRIEND: You must not disturb the established religion.

    SPINOZA: I do not know within what limits my freedom to philosophize will be confined in order to avoid the appearance of disturbing the publicly established religion. For schisms arise not so much from an ardent love of religion as from men's various dispositions, by their love of contradiction, for which they are wont to distort and condemn all things, even those that have been correctly stated. I have already experienced these things while leading a private and solitary life; much more, then, are they to be feared after I shall have risen to this degree of dignity. I must decline. I must decline because of my love of peace, which I believe I can obtain to a certain extent, merely by refraining from public lectures. (Coughs.)

    FRIEND: You are rarely seen about, you grow more solitary.

    SPINOZA: I have little time left to finish my work.

    FRIEND: Yet you endangered yourself by going behind the French lines. The populace thinks that you are up to something traitorous. They rage and accuse you of having illicit intercourse with the enemy. Some believe that you sold your country out for a pension from the French king.

    SPINOZA: That is absurd. I am no sycophant.

(Landlord runs in.)

    LANDLORD: The mob looks at you as a spy. I fear that they will break into my home and plunder it as they drag you out. (Sound of raging mob is heard outside.)

    SPINOZA: Fear nothing upon my account. I can easily justify myself; there are people enough, even some of the most considerable persons of the state, who know very well what put me upon that journey. But, however, as soon as the mob makes the least noise at your door, I'll go and meet them, though they were to treat me as they treated the poor Messieurs De Witt. I am a good republican, and I have always aimed at the glory and welfare of the state.

LANDLORD: I do not believe you are a spy, yet I fear you will be killed nevertheless. But please not in my house. (Exits.)

FRIEND: You were on a peace mission? If so, they will kill you anyway.

SPINOZA: All my work aims at peace. Peace is the true aim of the state as well as of the philosopher.

FRIEND: We haven't seen much of it. The Synods justify censorship and torture in the name of winning the war and repress dissent. The war with France diverts the people's anger.

SPINOZA: Of the commonwealth, whose subjects are but hindered by terror from taking arms against it, it should rather be said that it is free of war than that it has peace. For peace is not mere absence of war, but is a virtue that springs from character. Besides, that commonwealth, whose peace depends on the sluggishness of its subjects, may more properly be called a desert than a commonwealth. For a free multitude is guided more by hope than by fear; a conquered one, more by fear than by hope.

MOB: Death to the atheist, communist Jew. Death to Spinoza! Death to the traitor! Kill the bastard!

(Spinoza goes out. Mob gradually quiets and he returns.)

FRIEND: All is well?

SPINOZA: I spoke to them. They saw the steel in my eyes. The danger is past.

FRIEND: When do you publish your *Ethics Demonstrated in Geometrical Order*? Do you sign it?

SPINOZA: Be cautious is not my motto for nothing. I put a Hamburg imprint on my political book. Nevertheless, the Synods condemned it and my authorship is widely known.

FRIEND: Yet you have never publicly acknowledged it.

SPINOZA: It endangers me. The multitude must read me as an atheist and would kill me. If I had not spoken so forcefully moments ago, I would be dead even now.

FRIEND: But your *Ethics*? That you must publish.

SPINOZA: I set out to Amsterdam with the intention of printing it. While I was engaged in this matter, a rumor was spread everywhere that a book of mine about God was in press, and in it I endeavored to show that there is no God. The rumor was believed by many. Certain theologians seized the opportunity of bringing complaints against me before the Prince, and the magistrates even now denounce my opinions and writings everywhere. When I heard all this from certain trustworthy men, I decided to postpone the publication I was preparing until I saw how the matter turned out, and I also intended to inform you what plan I would then follow. But the business seems to have grown daily worse, so I have decided not to publish now. Friend, when I die, it must be published!

FRIEND: Copies already circulate.

SPINOZA: My papers are in this desk. The landlord knows where to send them. (Friend exits.)

(Spinoza coughs frequently. He writes and paces then writes more.)

SPINOZA: I must be clear. There can be no doubt. My demonstrations must have certainty. They must convince intellectually, with no admixture of myth, rhetoric, or fantasy, no embellishment, no appeal to the imagination—only to the intellect. My *Ethics* must be demonstrated infallibly in geometrical order. Only then will my ideas be adequate. I will teach men how they may move from the confused realm of the imagination into the realm of reason where affect becomes active and we express ourselves, not another. My presentation must be as clear and distinct, going from definitions not of words but of things themselves and self-evident axioms to certain inferences. Men cannot reach blessedness before they become reasonable. I must write for the few, for those able to philosophize. The others, the multitude, must be led to a simulacrum of reason by external means, by the edicts of the state and the emotional appeal of rites and ceremonies, by the judicious appeal to hope and fear. Else the multitude will destroy us—murder the philosophers like they did Jan and Cornelius.

Enough about the multitude. Try as I may to understand the cause of, the inevitability of their behavior, they nauseate me. My book is not for them; it is for the few. All things excellent are as difficult as they are rare. Yet even in philosophers, only a stronger affect can transform an existing affect. So I struggle with a dilemma—to appeal to the emotions contradicts that which I demonstrate; yet without profound emotional realignment, blessedness cannot be achieved. It is only by virtue of the emotional transformation induced by the third kind of knowledge, intuitive knowledge, that blessedness becomes possible.

Oh, I see! I see! I do not need to use rhetoric, persuasion, embellishment, or appeals to beauty in my text. If I can but show the way from imagination to reason to intuition, then affective transformation will come from within, and the necessity for all things will become apparent in such a way that that necessity is loved. The eternal laws of nature are what Scripture calls the decrees of God. Nature, or God, is all there is. If men can but come to love—an intellectual, disinterested love—Nature's laws, then they are transformed and become blessed, not in eternity but in time, not then but now. Their lives become timelessly different and they partake of the eternal—not of everlastingness, for they must die. They would see things under the aspect of eternity. Their minds, here in this world, which is the one and only reality that exists, would be transformed.

As they continue to love in the full knowledge that their love is not returned, that God's will is but a metaphor, since His laws could not be otherwise, that God loves only Himself with perfect love, loves only the perfection of His own nature that is manifest in all that is—as they continue to love, they not only reach the blessedness of inner peace, of acceptance, of ravishment before the necessity of all that is, however indifferent to our desires and purposes it may be, but reach the blessedness of a new relationship to other men. A realization that hate can never be good, that benevolence is rational, that my freedom depends on the freedom of others, that only through allegiance with them is the good life possible, that the friendship of other free men is the best that I can hope for, and that charity and justice are the only rational attitudes I can have toward all. The fulfillment of my *conatus*—my indwelling striving, my endeavor to endure—to preserve my being and to increase my power— a desire I share with all individual things, with every finite mode, every particular thing that depends for its existence on other things—is maximized by entering into friendly union with other men.

Joy is rational. There can never be too much joy. A free man is joyful in his intellectual love of God, of Nature, of the universe, of all that is. Joy is the affect that intuitive knowledge engenders that transforms. I must convey this. I cannot keep it for myself. I must show those who can follow the way. Intuition is not possible without rationality. I left my family, such as it is, my religion, superstitious as it is, my community, greedy as it is, so I might find blessedness for myself. I have done that but it is not enough. I need share my joy, my liberation, and teach others how to be free. So I must finish my *Ethics*, and it must be published. Even those who do not reach the third kind of knowledge will benefit from becoming more reasonable. I am solitary, yet I am a communitarian. Only in community is freedom possible.

I ramble. I am confused. Let me return to my proofs. (Tries to concentrate. Pained.) So many say I am an atheist while all my thought leads to God—not to the god of superstition, not to the children's God who rewards and punishes, not to the god of miracles. No! To the one God who is eternal, who is all of what is, and never created it. That's why they persecute me. God, or Nature—they can't stand that idea. No, their God must be transcendent, above and outside of this universe. He is not so; He is immanent, indwelling in all that exists. His will manifest in the eternal laws, which are immutable and not in miracles. Scientific study is His worship, as is the ethical fruit of the third kind of knowledge.

CHORUS: God, or Nature. Equivocating again, aren't you? Yours is a strange nature, not at all like my nature. I remember climbing a mountain and looking out over an endless vista of magnificence. I felt such awe, wonder, and gratitude that I toasted the trailmaker with my canteen. My participation in such beauty was a validation of the worthwhileness of life, but that is not your nature. Your nature has nothing to do with mountains, or seas, or sunsets, or snowflakes. No, your nature is the ground, the logical necessity of those mountains, seas, sunsets, and snowflakes—the mathematical laws of the physicist. So when you say Nature, you are thinking of equations and relationships of equations. Your nature is of the mind, not the senses. Baruch, it is too abstract, your need to distance, idealize, desexualize, avoid the personal, which leads you to mistake abstractions for reality, to eat the menu instead of the steak.

SPINOZA: (Ignoring the Chorus) I'll go over the structure again. I start with definitions. (Rises and paces.) Definition one: By cause of itself, I understand that whose essence involved existence. Definition two. (Spinoza continues pacing and reciting his definitions. Only an occasional word is audible.) . . . conceived through itself . . . by attribute, I understand . . . that thing is called "free." . . . by mode, I understand . . . by eternity, I understand . . . Yes. Yes. Each of these definitions is a real definition, it tells of the thing, not of the words. None can rationally refute them. And my axioms? Are they really clear and distinct? I must make them so. Axiom one: Whatever is is either in itself or in another. Axiom two: From a given determinant comes the effect necessarily.

(Enter Chorus, Freud and Nietzsche.)

CHORUS: Oh, brother!

SPINOZA: (Mutters) Axiom six: A true idea must agree with its object.

NIETZSCHE: Someone who clothes his thoughts in the armor of a geometrical order must have enormous fear.

FREUD: His obsessive-compulsive defenses mask anal eroticism.

CHORUS: He wants to roll in shit?

FREUD: His philosophy is a defense against the forbidden pleasures of the anal mucosa induced equally by expulsion and retention. Such a need for control as exhibited by this deductive
system is derivative of a profound unconscious wish to relinquish sphincter control.

CHORUS: Ah! He wants to shit on the world. I knew he harbored
enormous hostility underneath that "Hate is always wrong
because it reduces our power to act" shtick.

NIETZSCHE: Fear—a defense against fear!

FREUD: Against anality.

CHORUS: Against hate and rage.

SPINOZA: Proposition one: A substance is prior in nature to its
affectations. This is evident from definitions three and five.
QED. (Continues to pace and mumble proofs. As the scene
goes on, Spinoza becomes more and more frantic and the
QEDs and "It is absurds" follow more and more rapidly and
insistently.) Proposition five: In nature, there cannot be two
or more substances of the same nature, therefore, QED, it is
absurd, QED, it is absurd, QED. There is only one substance
that necessarily exists, and it is necessarily infinite. QED.
Except God, no substance can be conceived, and God acts
from the laws of His nature alone. He has no human properties—neither loves nor hates. God is the immanent, not the
transcendent, cause of all things; His existence and His essence are one and the same. QED. So there is nothing but
God. And He is a substance, of which there can only be one,
which has infinite attributes of which we can know only two—
thought and extension. QED. (Spinoza breathes a sigh of
relief.)

I have done it! I have shown that God is one. All arguments
for a plurality of substances are absurd. Absurd! Absurd! Absurd! Yes, my opponents' arguments lead to absurdity. Yes,
there is but one substance, one God, one Nature, and we along
with all other particular things are modes—modifications of
that one substance. Finite modes depend on other finite modes,
but He is dependent on nothing.

CHORUS: Why do you call it God? It has nothing to do with God. You appeal to the imagination in your use of language. You are playing to the gallery when you speak of God. You are dishonest. You wear a mask and dissemble, and those who revile you for your atheism are far from wrong.

NIETZSCHE: When I first discovered you, I was utterly amazed, utterly enchanted. I realized that I had a precursor, and what a precursor! Not only did it seem that your overall tendency was like mine—making knowledge the most powerful affect— but in five main points of your doctrine, I recognized myself. You were closest to me precisely in these matters. You deny the freedom of will, the existence of final causes, of a moral world order, of anything that is not egotistic, and of evil. My solitude, which, as on very high mountains, has often made it hard for me to breathe and made my blood rush out, I discovered to be at least a dualitude. It was only later that I realized how you had seduced me, and how false your teaching is, how driven it is by your weakness and hidden pity.

CHORUS: Hate is love grown angry.

NIETZSCHE: (To Spinoza) Why call it He? You speak of brute facticity—the givenness of the universe. Call it It, for It is as it is. Why do you deify Nature?

CHORUS: *Shema Yisroel Adonoy Elohenu Adonoy Echod.* Hear, O Israel, the Lord our God, the Lord is one. Baruch, you went through all you did—your life of exile, your lonely years writing an unpublished book—only to arrive at the fundamental prayer of Judaism you heard all your life? You didn't need to go through all that to come to monotheism.

SPINOZA: An immanent is not a transcendent cause. Indwelling— in the world, not above it, not a cause of its coming into being, not apart from it.

CHORUS: That's still Judaism, albeit shorn of some of its dross.

SPINOZA: (Sticks out his tongue at the Chorus) That's the point— without the dross. My God is not the God of Scripture.

FREUD: I ended my life writing *Moses and Monotheism.* In it, I showed that Moses was a goy who sold the Israelites on his one

God without physical representation, and in their acceptance of this goyish notion there was an increase in intellectualization, in spirituality. It was a great step forward in human evolution.

CHORUS: (Pointing at Freud) His biblical scholarship is hardly scientific; it is distorted by his . . .

FREUD: (Interrupts) I too incurred wrath for refusing to flatter the Jews. My therapy is about oneness, the integration of split-off, repressed parts of self. Where it was, I shall be—I will reclaim my passive affects, as you call them, and their unconscious determinant instinct, and out of this create a self. In understanding, I am transformed into nothing as exalted as your blessedness, but into something like your active affects. My power is increased. If polytheism is a projection of the unintegrated parts of our selves—Mars, our warlikeness, Venus our libido—then monotheism is a projection of the human project of integrating drives and desires, consciousness and unconsciousness, into a whole. My therapy is about that integration, about the healing of the splits in the self through knowledge and acceptance.

CHORUS: That's your *shema*, your monotheism. I wonder though, what's so great about monotheism? There's a lot to be said for polytheism, for paganism—less fanaticism, less intolerance, more fun. As for your integration of the self, I wonder about that, too. I know a woman who is a multiple personality. She says she feels sorry for "singles." Their lives are so impoverished. Maybe she has a point. You guys are so obsessed with oneness because you are so divided, so split inside. Spinoza, you're split between Baruch and Benedict, between your first twenty-four years and the rest of your life, between your public persona and your secret thoughts, between Jewishness and universalism, between conscious love and unconscious hate, between repudiated passions and the reality within, between spirituality and atheism. You have to insist on one substance; it is your way of denying the divisions within you; thoughts of a unifying underlying reality keep you from exploding into a thousand pieces. (Looking at Freud.) You didn't change your name, but you have all the same stuff.

FREUD: I am an unbeliever—an atheist Jew.

CHORUS: But a Jew nevertheless.

FREUD: I have never denied that. (To Spinoza) You aim too high. You live beyond your emotional means. Forget blessedness. You are right about the necessity for strong emotion for there to be change. Patients only change because they love their analysts. Your intellectual love of God is a transference acting out. Your unrequited love is your experience with your parents projected onto the universe. You need to fall in love with your analyst and work it through. But you can't. You are too afraid of human love. You are a narcissist, unable to love anyone except your fantasy of an unloving beloved.

CHORUS: (To Freud) You go too far. Schizoid, perhaps, but not narcissistic.

FREUD: He doesn't transfer. If he doesn't transfer, he is narcissistic.

CHORUS: But he doesn't have an analyst. There aren't any.

FREUD: It doesn't matter; if he did have one, he wouldn't transfer.

CHORUS: Forget it.

SPINOZA: Having demonstrated in geometrical order the identity of nature and God, I will go on to demonstrate the nature and origin of the mind and of the passions by demonstrating their power to hold men in bondage. Finally, I will demonstrate the power of the intellect and show how its proper use leads to freedom.

FREUD: Grandiose—too systematic.

CHORUS: Reluctantly, I must admire your architecture. You have come up with a beautiful system. But you knew from your first definition exactly where you were going, and how you would conclude. Isn't there something wrong here? Is this really a deductive system? Isn't it more like an artistic vision, a product of your imagination—not of your intellect. But the aesthetic and the ethical are disjunctive. The SS enjoyed Beethoven and had slave orchestras play his music. There is no reason to believe that their aesthetic pleasure was any different from yours and mine. So the good and the beautiful are different things. Be that as it may, all your reasons are rationalizations for what you already believe. You hoodwink us with your geometrical derivation.

FREUD: Rationalization is one of the ego defenses.

NIETZSCHE: The hocus pocus of mathematical form with which you clad your philosophy—really, the love of *your* wisdom, in chain mail and mask, to strike terror at the very outset into the heart of any assailant who should dare to glance at that invisible maiden and Pallas Athena—how much personal timidity and vulnerability this masquerade of a sick hermit betrays!

FREUD: I told you it was a narcissistic system.

SPINOZA: I am not a hermit.

NIETZSCHE: You are a compulsory recluse. Under your most spiritual masquerade, perhaps without being aware of it yourself, you are a sophisticated vengeance seeker and poison brewer. Let me lay bare the foundations of your *Ethics*—thereby even you will see yourself as a poison brewer.

SPINOZA: I seek only to lead men to blessedness because I myself cannot find blessedness otherwise. I help them understand their affects.

NIETZSCHE: Your laugh no more, weep no more destruction of the affects through analysis and vivisection is hopelessly naive.

SPINOZA: I have seen too much to be naive.

FREUD: I have found that men have little to recommend them.

CHORUS: (To Freud) You are even more of an elitist. At least he has a (ironically) "treatment" for the multitude. You treat only the "deserving."

FREUD: Patients are mostly scum.

SPINOZA: (Starts pacing up and down, muttering to himself increasingly frantic QEDs) God or Nature has two aspects. Nature naturing and Nature natured. Nature naturing is in itself and conceived through itself—the attributes of substance as expression of an eternal and infinite essence. Nature natured follows from the necessity of God's nature; that is, all the modes of God's attributes insofar as they are considered as things and can neither be nor be conceived without God. The ground of all contingent things is their timeless necessity, the logical inevitability of the totality of all things.

CHORUS: (Laughing and undulating his hips, as if copulating) Nature naturing—ah, ah, ah, uh, uh, uh—(sounds of sexual climax.) Nature natured—plowed but good. You're projecting again. You are talking about your father fucking your mother, and projecting your repressed vision onto the big screen. (Continues to copulate noisily.)

FREUD: Obscurity indicates conflict.

SPINOZA: It's not obscure.

CHORUS: (Screaming) That's why it doesn't love you back! It's the primal scene. Old dad and your mom, Miriam, humping away. Or maybe your father shtooping that bitch Esther. Either way, you weren't part of it. You took your primal scene jealousy and hatred and converted it into love by reaction formation. This way, you get to contemplate them forever as they grind it out—the mastery of a trauma by repetition. You recreate the primal scene and its most painful part, your exclusion—no love for you. Only now you choose it, create it. That should be right up your alley—active affect. You do it to yourself—instead of passive affect—watching them bang away while your heart is breaking. The really crazy part lies in convincing yourself that the third kind of knowledge makes you love watching them do it eternally—outside of time, because you first saw them doing it before you had a conception of time. There is no time in the unconscious. (Turning to Freud) How am I doing?

FREUD: You have talent. You should go to analytic school.

NIETZSCHE: (To Spinoza) Nature naturing, Nature natured. These gentlemen are right. You're absurdly spiritualized conception is driven by unconscious motivation. It isn't even adequate technically. You are trying to deal with the relationship between the One and the Many. Nature naturing as the One, and Nature natured as the Many won't do it. The trouble is, there is no One. There is only blind striving, the will to power, repeating itself endlessly. Embrace your fate. Love your destiny—irrational, meaningless, as it is. (Sadly) Benedict, you came so close, so close to my joyful wisdom, joy in the knowledge that what you call rational is but brute fact. Don't love, intellectually or any other way, God. Love your fate. That's as much blessedness as men are capable of. (Pointing to Freud.) He's right. You love beyond your emotional means and beyond your philosophical resources. We are really brothers in unbelief, but you must pretty up your vision by calling it a vision of God. The truth is your vision is of a universe without divinity, meaning, significance. It simply is. God is dead. You are trying to resurrect him, and you leave us with the shadows of the dead God. You know that God is dead, but you run from your knowledge; therefore, you deify Nature. Give it up, Benedictus. Allow yourself to despair and you, too, will find the joyful wisdom you look for in the wrong place.

SPINOZA: Knowledge of God is the mind's greatest good; its greatest virtue is to know God.

NIETZSCHE: You are no better than Wagner. You write your own *Parsifal*. You both betray me.

SPINOZA: The intellectual love of God transforms.

CHORUS: Why do you cling to this delusion?

FREUD: We must love or grow ill. Since he is incapable of human love, he has no choice but to love his unloving God. Otherwise his libido remains within, becomes toxic, and poisons him.

SPINOZA: You are all fools. I go on to my theory of the affects. Each man seeks his own advantage. Reason asks nothing contrary to self-interest. There is no singular thing in Nature that is more useful to man than a man who lives according to the guidance of reason. When each man most seeks his own advantage for himself, then men are most useful to one another.

FREUD: More denial and foolishness.

SPINOZA: The greatest good of those who seek virtue is common to all, and can be enjoyed by all equally. (Freud, Nietzsche, and the Chorus shake their heads. Spinoza paces, mumbling more QEDs.) Joy is not directly evil, but good. Sadness, on the other hand, is directly evil. Cheerfulness cannot be excessive; it is always good. Melancholy, on the other hand, is always evil. Pleasure can be excessive. It is a titillation if it affects only one part of the body to the neglect of the rest.

CHORUS: You were starting to make sense until you started lamenting your throbbing cock—pleasure can be excessive if it influences only a part. Why don't you get real? Don't you ever get hard?

SPINOZA: Love and desire can be excessive.

CHORUS: Titillate me. You can titillate me any time. You're not my type, but I'll give you a hand job just to show you how good excitation of a part can be.

SPINOZA: Hate can never be good. Envy, mockery, disdain, anger, vengeance—all affects arising from hate are evil.

CHORUS: There are no bad orgasms.

FREUD: If there is love, there is hate. The two instincts are primordial.

SPINOZA: He who lives according to the guidance of reason strives, as far as he can, to repay the other's hate, anger, and disdain toward him, with love or nobility. (Freud, Nietzsche, and the Chorus scream at once:)

FREUD: Beyond your emotional means.

NIETZSCHE: A slave morality!

CHORUS: Too much!

SPINOZA: (More QEDs) Self-esteem can arise from reason, and only that self-esteem that does arise from reason can be the greatest there can be. Self-esteem is the highest thing we can hope for. Pity is not a virtue. Humility is not a virtue. He who repents what he has done is twice wretched. He who is guided by fear, and does good to avoid evil, is not guided by reason.

NIETZSCHE: You almost have it. Forget the geometry and let passion guide you.

FREUD: This has less of the unconscious driving it.

CHORUS: (To Spinoza) True, but you're getting to sound like a self-help book.

SPINOZA: You fight me because what I propose is too difficult for you. Blessedness consists in love of God, a love that arises from the third kind of knowledge—intuition. Blessedness is not the reward of virtue, but virtue itself. The free man is hardly troubled in spirit, but being, by a certain eternal necessity, conscious of himself, and of God, and of things, always possesses true peace of mind. If the way I have shown that can lead to these things now seems very hard, still, it can be found. And of course, what is found so rarely must be hard. For if salvation were at hand, and could be found without great effort, how could nearly everyone neglect it? All things excellent are as difficult as they are rare.

(End scene. Darkness.)

Scene 3

(Spinoza's room.)

CHORUS: (To Freud) It's all personal, isn't it—these theoretical systems. They all come down to disguised expression of forbidden wishes and desires and defenses against those wishes and desires.

FREUD: For the most part, yes.

CHORUS: So ideologies aren't what they seem, aren't about what they purport to be about.

FREUD: The manifest content isn't worth much. It is their latent meaning that is of interest. It always concerns the disguised expression of a repressed childhood wish.

CHORUS: It's true of psychoanalysis, of course?

FREUD: Your negative transference to me is manifesting in your resistance to the truth of analytic theory.

CHORUS: I thought ideologies weren't about what they are about. If their manifest meaning has no truth value, then its real meaning is the latent emotional one.

FREUD: (Coldly) Psychoanalysis isn't an ideology. It has no Weltanschauung, except for the scientific one. (Freud pauses, stares at the CHORUS.) What are you thinking about me?

CHORUS: I'm not thinking about you. I'm thinking about psychoanalysis.

FREUD: I am psychoanalysis.

CHORUS: (Shrugs his shoulders) Another narcissist.

FREUD: Come—tell me what are your thoughts about me. Perhaps you struggle against a sexual current, and denigrate analysis in the service of repudiating your homosexual transference to me.

CHORUS: You don't turn me on.

FREUD: According to my theory of negation, to negate a proposition is to affirm it, so I do turn you on.

CHORUS: Do you know the story of the two friends who meet on a train? The first says, "Moshe, tell me where you're going." "I'm going to Pinsk, Abe." "Moshe, you told me you are going to Pinsk because you knew I would think that you were really going to Minsk, while you are really going to Pinsk. So tell me why are you lying to me?"

FREUD: You stole that story from my joke book.

CHORUS: True.

SPINOZA: My ethical theory, my demonstration of the path to blessedness derived from my theory of the emotions, which in turn is derived from my theory of mind, which in turn is based on my metaphysical doctrines, which are demonstrated geometrically is not a disguised wish fulfillment. It is truth.

CHORUS: You are right. The wish fulfillment is not very disguised.

SPINOZA: Your ad hominem attack does nothing to invalidate my conclusions. You must argue on my turf, philosophical discourse. My motivation is irrelevant. You commit the genetic fallacy, equating the origin of my ideas with their truth value. If you wish to dispute me, challenge my proofs, and demonstrate their invalidity, show the error in my reasoning.

CHORUS: I refuse to get caught up in the hocus pocus of the geometrical method. Besides, no one will buy it; it is far too obtuse. You won't make two guilders on it.

SPINOZA: I renounced the pursuit of wealth.

FREUD: Few are rational about money. Your renunciation goes too far. It is tinged with masochism and is contaminated by your hatred of your money-grubbing family. Nonetheless, you are on the right track. Your renunciation costs you little because money rarely brings happiness. Wealth is not a childhood wish.

CHORUS: (To Freud) You equate money and feces, don't you? And the retention of feces is a childhood wish.

FREUD: Hence, hoarding brings satisfaction while acquisitiveness does not.

SPINOZA: You are right. The pursuit of wealth is as mad as the pursuit of excrement. Avarice is a disease.

CHORUS: Even if your *Ethics* is a product of unconscious wishes and its abracadabra of geometric proof an irrelevancy, it is still beautiful—the architecture, the way in which you structure it, the proofs themselves, the movement from metaphysics to psychology to ethics. It is magnificent as an aesthetic object. It gives pleasure in the way a fugue gives pleasure, so that it is actually about beauty, not about truth.

SPINOZA: (Exasperated) On that again!

FREUD: My critics say I am a poet, not a scientist. It is their way of dismissing truths they cannot face.

SPINOZA: My philosophy enjoins the enjoyment of the beautiful, taking joy in theatrical amusements and the like, but (loses control, pounds his fist and shouts) that is not what the *Ethics* is about! On the contrary, it is a demonstration from definitions of real things, and from self-evident, self-validating axioms whose clarity and distinctness is totally transparent, of the necessary existence of one eternal and infinite system, which I call God or Nature, having infinite and eternal attributes of which we know only two—mind and body, thought and extension—which manifest themselves in infinite modes, the laws of mathematical physics, of which I demonstrate but one, the proportion of motion and rest, and in the finite modes—particular things, including ourselves, which cannot subsist by themselves but which rest logically and for their very existence on the infinite substance. That substance, the ground of things, necessarily exists and can be comprehended in two ways—as the eternal ground of particular things, as Nature naturing, and as the totality of particular things, Nature natured. The human mind is the idea of the human body, mind and body being two attributes of the same finite mode. Further, mind, insofar as it thinks rationally and thinks adequate ideas, thinks the idea of God, which exists eternally, and thus sees things under the aspect of eternity and becomes itself eternal, although this in no way confers immortality. Men and their minds live in duration, not eternity, as is true for all finite modes, which must pass away so that the eternal part of the human mind exists insofar as it attains rationality. Further, having demonstrated these diverse truths about the human mind and its nature, I show the nature of the affects and demonstrate that an affect can only be modified by a stronger affect, and that like all finite modes, man's essence consists in his endeavoring to continue existing and to increase his power. Rationality dictates that we do nothing against Nature, and continue to strive to maximize our power, pleasure consisting in the increase of our perfection, in our activity, while displeasure consists of a lessening of our power, perfection, and ability to act. All my insights into affect and into our emotional life is based on this. Further, I demonstrate how enthrallment to the passive affects, to drivenness without understanding, leads to human bondage, while active understanding transforms the givenness and necessity of our lives into freedom when at the end of the long process of deductive reasoning, of seeing the causes of things, our vision moves from the exterior to the interior, from the outside to the inside, and we see that the necessity of events is but the necessity of our own essence, and in that synoptic vision of the whole and of the interiority of necessity, which I call intuitive knowledge, or the third kind of knowledge, I am transformed, and feel that disinterested love of that which is, of reality itself, which I metaphorically and inconsistently rhetorically call God, in such a way and with such power that my adoration of what is and my understanding of why it is and why it must be as it must be, engenders in me an intellectual love that transforms all my affects, being that more powerful affect of which I write, so that I come to experience peace and in that peace, cease to hate, envy, pity, and regret, and accepting all that must be, come to love it. As a result of this transformation, I continue to try to understand, blaming nobody. So following from the very first axiom, I demonstrate how men can find peace within and be at peace with one another. That, my friend, is not, or is not merely, an aesthetic structure, or a personal ax to grind, or an unconscious wish fulfillment. It is a roadmap for the few who can follow it to blessedness.

CHORUS: And so in the end, to accept the one and only life that has been possible.

(End of scene.)

Scene 4

(Spinoza's room some months later in 1677. Spinoza is now dying. He is turning the pages of a manuscript.)

CHORUS: What are you doing?

SPINOZA: Burning my Dutch translation of the Old Testament.

CHORUS: Your Dutch isn't all that good.

SPINOZA: That's not why I burn it.

CHORUS: Forget that the free man thinks about nothing less than of death, his meditation being a meditation on life.

SPINOZA: It is true that I shall die soon and do what I must before I do. But I do not think of death.

CHORUS: I don't believe you.

SPINOZA: A part of the mind is eternal.

CHORUS: You don't believe that.

SPINOZA: I'm not sure. But my demonstration of the path to wisdom and salvation is valid regardless.

CHORUS: And the book burning?

SPINOZA: It is unfinished, and I have become unsure of whether the multitude reading Scripture is a good idea. It results in even more superstition.

CHORUS: I thought you believed in freedom of thought.

SPINOZA: That doesn't mean I have to contribute to error.

CHORUS: You have another manuscript there.

SPINOZA: My new book on politics.

CHORUS: Oh, the one where you demonstrate that a commercial aristocracy is the best government, that the state should be ruled exactly the way the Jewish community of Amsterdam is ruled—by a merchant oligarchy, like the one that excommunicated you.

SPINOZA: I wasn't thinking of them. I had Venice in mind.

CHORUS: Doesn't matter. Benedict, what's with you? You really have become an ass-kisser. Your God, whom you love with an intellectual love, who loves you not, is bad enough—masochistic submission to father, rabbis, mob, synod. But not this, this direct justification of the bastards who threw you out. You swore that you would never follow the path of da Costa, yet in this book you all but prostate yourself on the steps of the synagogue to be stepped on and spat upon. Why recommend rule by the few? What happened to your faith in democracy?

SPINOZA: After the De Witts? Surely you jest. But I haven't written the part on democracy yet.

CHORUS: You never see the personal behind the theoretical.

SPINOZA: I see more than you credit me with. (Feeds the rest of his translation into the flames.) It makes me sad to destroy this. I would have liked to finish it. My health doesn't permit it. (Weeps.)

CHORUS: The philosopher weeps.

SPINOZA: My not being able to finish it is as necessary as all else. When I see that from the inside, see its inner necessity, then I freely choose that which must be and my sadness evaporates. (Music is heard.) What's that?

CHORUS: Bach's Cantata, *Ich Habe Genug, I Have Enough*, actually written a few years after your death. Can't you hear the world-weariness, the resignation, the wish to leave this earth? *"Ich freue mich auf meinen Tod,"* "I take joy in my death." I've had enough—take my soul.

SPINOZA: You know that's not my style of religiosity.

CHORUS: I thought you were a God-intoxicated man.

SPINOZA: I am, but not in that way. I don't yearn for heaven. My salvation is here, in the eternity of my thoughts. I have found an object worthy of my love. My love doesn't exhaust me. I am weary because I am sick; still my meditation is on this life. There is no other. But I listen. It is very beautiful. It seduces me, but I will not give in to its mood of melancholy.

CHORUS: I know, melancholy is a passive affect. I guess Bach is too Christian for you. Maybe this is more to your taste. (Hebrew song, *Dayeinu*, is heard.) "*Dayeinu*," "It would have been enough." It would have been enough if you had parted the Red Sea, it would have been enough if . . (Breaks off.) More life-affirming. You should like that better than the Bach.

SPINOZA: That too is superstition—it tells of miracles that never happened. The glory of God is manifested in the uniformity of Nature, not in the violation of its eternal laws.

CHORUS: Superstition, perhaps, but at least it's Jewish superstition. You prefer Jewish superstition to Christian superstition in spite of yourself.

SPINOZA: The song does bring back a few happy moments from my childhood.

CHORUS: I'm surprised you allow yourself such an emotion.

SPINOZA: It's not a matter of allowing myself. (Several of Spinoza's friends and his landlord burst in.)

FRIEND 1: The Jews say the Messiah has come.

FRIEND 2: They say Shabbatai Zvi, a strange man from the East, is the Messiah. He has proclaimed himself the messiah. They believe it. (Jews of Amsterdam enter and mill about talking excitedly about the Messiah from the East.)

JEW 1: Yes, but he can't be the Messiah. He is converted to Islam.

JEW 2: That merely proves his divinity, that he works so cleverly that he fools people by pretending to convert.

FRIEND 2: Even the sanest, the best educated, the most rational are caught up in the madness. They truly believe that Shabbatai Zvi is the Messiah.

FRIEND 3: Aboab and Morteira are in ecstasy. Even Manasseh is swept up in the mania.

CHORUS: Shabbatai Zvi easily persuades the credulous, ignorant Eastern masses of his Messiahhood. It isn't long since Chmielnicki's Cossacks swept through the Ukraine, murdering and raping, sewing cats into the bellies of pregnant women. So it is not surprising that the survivors fall for Shabbatai's nonsense. But that the highly educated Jews of Amsterdam do, that I find unbelievable. I am amazed.

SPINOZA: I am not. They too are of the multitude.

FRIEND 2: They say that he is converted to Islam, yet they believe in him all the more.

SPINOZA: Men are ruled by hope and fear. This strengthens my resolve that the manuscript of the *Ethics* must remain hidden until my death. (To Landlord) You know what to do. (All exit but Spinoza who lights a pipe and sips a beer.) I have finished all the things I wished to demonstrate concerning the mind's power over the affects and its freedom. I die a free man. (Dies. Landlord enters, takes the manuscript of the *Ethics* and runs out. Curtain.)

It is difficult to know what a philosophical therapy would look like. Aside from the recent move of some academic philosophers to reposition themselves as purveyors of psychotherapy, the only model we have is existential psychotherapy, which frankly bases itself on a philosophical school. The existentialists all play down technique and explicitly state that there is no existential technique and that even if such an oxymoron existed, they would not avail themselves of it. On the contrary, the genuineness they seek and the I–Thou encounter of therapist and patient would be vitiated by in any way routinizing, protocoling, or mechanizing existential psychotherapy. Rather than technique, the essence of existential psychotherapy is thematic and attitudinal. This stance and understanding of what existential therapy is and does has been consistently held by thinkers and practitioners as varied as Freud's friend, Ludwig Binswanger; the theologically influenced Rollo May; and the Stanford professor Irvin Yalom. Thematically the existentialists emphasize such ultimates as aloneness, responsibility, limitation, meaning or the absence thereof, relatedness, and mortality. Attitudinally they emphasize openness to the mystery and unpredictability of the therapeutic process. In looking for what must be characteristic of a Spinozaistic theory of addiction, I take my clue from the existentialists and mostly ignore whatever implications for technique his work might have, instead concentrating on the themes and to a lesser extent the attitudes that his work implies.

What is it that we can learn from Spinoza's life and work that can be adapted for therapeutic work in general and substance abuse work in particular? To start with the life, two things jump out as having therapeutic import. First, as the Chorus never tires of pointing out, repression does not work. The patient, here Spinoza, must get in contact with his or her repudiated, projected, split-off or repressed sexual, dependent, and aggressive drives, wishes, and fantasies. If he does not, his logic will be contaminated, his emotional life constricted, and his very self impoverished. In the case of the substance abuser or behavioral addict there is enhanced risk of relapse or acting out. The instinctual life cannot be denied.

But there is another side, too, or at least another way of looking at Spinoza's impulse life, namely, as one that was successfully sublimated. That is the view of Bertrand Russell (1945) and of Steven Nadler (1999), so the addiction therapist must not only look to de-repress and to de-project; he must also be attuned to successful sublimation and alert to possibilities for sublimation in the patient's life. He should point out such possibilities and do what he can to facilitate their actualization. It is of some interest that George Vaillant, author of *The Natural History of Alcoholism* (1983), found in his study of the relationship between psychological defenses and life outcomes in *Adaptation of Life* (1977) that those who used sublimation and altruism as primary defenses were the happiest, healthiest, and most successful participants in this longitudinal study. Here is empirical support for one of Spinoza's major theses about the good life; he would be pleased. So the therapist needs to be simultaneously alert for maladaptive repression *and* for successful sublimation, confronting the one while supporting the other.

The next therapeutic lesson of Spinoza's life is that the therapist must be alert to the patient's conflicts with family, community, and larger world. Especially in addiction work our focus tends to be too narrow, ignoring the surround unless it too is addicted. This is a mistake. No patient can be understood without probing for clashes of values, beliefs, and conduct between the patient and his or her environment, both familial and cultural. Spinoza's clash with the Jewish community of Amsterdam gets replayed in many guises in contemporary America. All conflict between patient and family does not derive from the parents' alcoholism or drug addiction. The therapist needs to look for more subtle conflicts, particularly between discordant value systems. Such discord is often intensely painful, and that pain can be an etiological factor in addiction. It can also maintain it and/or trigger relapse.

What about Spinoza's philosophy? What can that contribute to addiction treatment? I think the key factor in Spinoza's work applicable to therapy is the dialectical tension between cognition and affect. In Spinoza's epistemology there is a hierarchy of stages of knowing, starting with the imagination, progressing to reason, and culminating in intuition. For Spinoza *imagination* is not an honorific term. The imagination gives us only confused, muddy, inadequate ideas. It is a result of forces acting on us; or in his terms, we are passive when we use images as our primary source of knowledge. Even when imagination gives veridical knowledge, it does so without imparting understanding. The active addict lives and knows at the level of images and the imagination. By definition his or her knowledge is inadequate. The therapeutic corollary of this is that the therapist must be active in confronting the addict's inadequate, that is, fuzzy, distorted, or plain wrong, ideas.

The case is better with reason, the next stage in the ladder of insight. Here there is the possibility not only of knowing, but of understanding. Insight becomes possible. The therapeutic import of this is that insight is intrinsic to cure. For the patient to develop adequate ideas about his addiction, that is, to come to understand not only that he is addicted, but also what brought about that state of being and what maintains it, the patient must be capable of reason. Does the patient have an adequate idea of what the addiction is doing to her? If not, what can the therapist do to enable that knowledge? Cognition is crucial. Without knowledge, stable recovery is impossible.

But then there is the other side of Spinoza's dialectic of knowledge encapsulated in his aphorism, "Only a stronger affect can change an affect." So as important as knowledge, cognition, is, it is not enough. Emotion is needed as well. But Spinoza's theory is never simple. Knowledge itself can engender powerful emotion. We therapists, especially in the substance abuse field, who are so wary of intellectualization tend to forget that the mind has its passions just as much as the heart. In fact, in recovery it is the affect released by the insight that it is the alcohol or the gambling or the cocaine that is the cause of the trouble that transforms, as does the insight that one has lost control over substance use or compulsive behavior. Knowledge is emotional, and it is emotion that brings about change.

For Spinoza, intuition is the highest form of cognition. Here there is true insight into the nature of things and the internal necessity of them. Intuition in this sense plays its role in recovery when patients who have come to see the biopsychosocial determinants of their illness in the rational stage of knowing, now have a more total view of their place in family, culture, history, and circumstance, and reach an acceptance of the unalterable nature of that causal nexus. They also come to some comprehension of their place in the universe and their relationship to it. AA's serenity prayer, "God grant me the serenity to accept the things I cannot change, the courage to change the things I can, and the wisdom to know the difference," is profoundly Spinozaistic. Being more deterministic than the Program, Spinoza put it somewhat differently: "Freedom is the acceptance of necessity." But acceptance is key—accepting the reality of addiction, accepting limitation, accepting the inevitability of, in Erik Erikson's words, "the one and only life that is possible." But this acceptance must not be facile or cheap. It cannot be achieved by repressing the emotions of hatred, rage, and shame, particularly if their object is abusing, possibly substance-involved parents. Only after these emotions are worked through is true acceptance possible.

That brings us to the centrality of love in Spinoza's philosophy. It is love, intellectual love, that is, love that comes from knowledge that transforms and makes change and growth possible. Spinoza is absolutely right here. It is the user's love for substance or compulsion that keeps him in bondage and it is only a stronger, more powerful love that can free him. Only a more powerful affect can release him from bondage and move him toward freedom. The nature of that love will differ from patient to patient. For some it will be love of the Twelve-Step program, for some love of the Higher Power, for some love of truth or beauty or children, or an idea, or a quest. But love there must be. Freud knew that, too, when he said, "Love is a great teacher," and put transference love at the center of his therapy.

The episode of Shabbatai Zvi is also instructive. Countertransferential incomprehension of the shear irrationality of addiction is disabling of its treatment. It may help to remember that both the traumatized, downtrodden (the victims of Chmielnicki's massacre) and the highly educated, affluent, who may have been traumatized themselves (the Jews of Amsterdam), are easily bewitched by false messiahs, and there are no falser messiahs than drugs and compulsive behavior. Spinoza was right not to be surprised. The multitude, those not anchored to reality, regardless of their level of achievement, are highly vulnerable to belief in false-messiahs, and action on that belief is all too common. Seeing addiction in this way reduces or eliminates countertransferential feelings of rage, bewilderment, frustration, and the desire to retaliate.

There are two other aspects of Spinoza's teaching that are crucial for addiction therapy. The first is his emphasis on community, on the necessity of sharing one's quest for blessedness with other men. That is what happens in the Twelve-Step program or in a successful therapy group. Addiction therapists must do all they can to help patients reintegrate into community, whatever community may mean for a particular patient. The second is his emphasis on the irrationality of guilt, self-recrimination, and remorse. The corollary to this is his endorsement of moderation and legitimizing of pleasures of all sorts, as long as they harm neither self nor others. In short, Spinoza is no fan of the superego. Addiction therapists can usefully emulate Spinoza here, dispute their patients' irrational guilt, and endorse their right to pleasures.

Most addicts, appearances to the contrary, are gloomy ascetics and they need an anodyne for this. They need to learn, as Spinoza did, that there can never be enough joy.

To end on a less exalted level, Spinoza was a realist. He knew that all men were not capable of blessedness, so he devised a "therapy" for the multitude based on incentives of hope and fear administered by the wise, by those capable of philosophizing. We in our allegiance to an egalitarian ethos tend to find this too elitist. But Spinoza's social analysis is worth keeping in mind. There are patients who are not capable of insight, let alone intellectual love, who are best helped to sobriety and recovery by behavioral interventions, by the use of carrot and stick, or of hope and fear. And there are patients who are capable of insight who require a more dynamic approach. And there are patients who are capable of transformation and transcendence fueled by love. It behooves the therapist to make distinctions and to adopt different tactics with patients at different levels even while keeping in mind that it may be the same patient at different levels of development who receives each of these therapies.

It may seem impossible for the addictions therapist to de-repress, help sublimate, elucidate conflict with family and community, move the patient from imagination to rationality to intuitive knowledge, find the balance between cognition and affect, help the patient work through pain to a state of acceptance, put the patient in contact with the love that transforms, reconnect the patient with community, and evaluate the patient's level of understanding in order to tailor the treatment to reach a particular patient. But as Spinoza said, "All things excellent are as difficult as they are rare," and the goals of Spinozaistic therapy are ideals to be striven for, not demands that increase burdens on therapists practicing one of the most difficult of specialties.

A CASE ILLUSTRATION

Steven's was in a sense a Spinozaistic therapy. A brilliant man who started out as an engineer and ended up as a poet, he had been bedeviled all his adult life by problematic drinking. His alcoholism had cost him a marriage, had been a main cause of his failure to complete his dissertation, and had played a major role in his being denied tenure as an English professor. Additionally, his recent relapse, after a period of sobriety, has led to his current girlfriend breaking off with him, an event that brought him into therapy.

Steven's life has many parallels to Spinoza's. He'd been brought up a Catholic in an overwhelmingly Protestant environment, having the same sort of equivocal relationship to the majority culture that Spinoza did. Of course, it was different. Steven's Catholicism, unlike Spinoza's Judaism, posed no danger of outright persecution, but it did make him an outsider. Further, his widowed mother (Steven's father died when he was 2), emotionally distant, beleaguered, and almost totally preoccupied with the struggle for existence, pushed her gifted son toward the Church and ordination. Perhaps he might even rise to bishop and free her from a life of grinding labor. The priest he served as an altarboy also recognized his talent and tried to recruit him for the Church. The fatherless boy bonded with his spiritual fathers and was soon studying Aquinas and Augustine, just as the adolescent Spinoza had studied Maimonides and Rashi.

But Steven's skeptical and inquiring mind was filled with doubt. Temporizing with the support of his "fathers" who recognized the scientific bent of his mind, he postponed a decision about entering the priesthood and in a masterful compromise between his rational and his mystical sides studied engineering in a Jesuit college. But it was a compromise that was not to endure. By the time he graduated, he had rejected Catholicism and left the Church. He told me he did so because it was the only intellectually honest thing he could do, and intellectual honesty was his highest value.

It was a decision that cost him dearly. This virtually loveless boy turned his back on the institution and people who had given him whatever love he had known. His Jesuit sponsors lost interest in him and his mother became colder than ever. Not surprisingly, he was impelled to find a replacement, and the replacement was alcohol. When I met him thirty years later, he had spent at least ten years trying to stop, alternating periods of abstinence with binge drinking. One of the major impediments to his recovery was his angry, ambivalent, disdainful, and frequently hateful relationship with AA. He became enraged with AA, which he saw, not quite consciously making the connection, as manifesting everything he hated about the Catholic Church: an irrational belief system, hypocrisy, a vacuous and false spirituality, and an optimistic take on life incongruent with his experience. The ambivalence that brought him back time and time again was a manifestation of his unconscious longing for that which he had rejected.

I would like to highlight a few ways in which Spinozaistic therapeutic elements played a role in what was ultimately a successful therapy, one that was failing until this element became incorporated into the treatment.

The first was the way in which I handled Steven's intellectualizations. This was a patient who had read everything and remembered it. His discourse was both philosophical and metaphorical. At times it was beautiful, but it served as a distancing device and was clearly in the service of his addiction. Accordingly, I confronted this defense and tried to get him out of his head and into his gut. My efforts backfired and I almost lost him. My interventions merely made him argumentative. Then I had an "Aha!" experience—his head was his gut, or better, his heart. Steven was in love with ideas and with language and this was the basic datum, not his defensive and avoidant use of that love. His was literally an intellectual love, and as soon as I recognized and acknowledged this, things opened up. By going to where Eros was, emotion entered the room. I joined the resistance, so to speak. But I wasn't merely doing that. If I had been, he would have smelled a rat. Rather, I really felt his love of the intellectual and aesthetic and genuinely valued it. It was only after this that its defensive aspect could be analyzed and gotten out of Steven's way.

The rapport that resulted from my change of approach, however fraught with danger of too much countertransferential enjoyment of the sheer exhilaration of seeing a first-rate mind at work, gave me an opening to interpret his alcoholism as a substitute religion. This resonated and reverberated. We worked on this for a while before I appealed to his rationality, suggesting that worship of Dionysus was just as irrational as worship of the Trinity. When I reminded him that his intellectual honesty had led him to relinquish the latter belief, he finished my sentence by saying, "So intellectual honesty compels me to relinquish Dionysus." I said, "So it seems."

Amazingly, Steven stopped drinking, this time without returning to AA. I was worried about his isolation. He was a freelance translator who worked and lived alone, and I was his only connection to the world. He went into a deep depression. I interpreted, "You're feeling what you felt when you left the Church, and what you felt when your mother ignored you after your father 'left.' Now, unlike when you relinquished Catholicism, you don't have alcohol to mask and anesthetize your sorrow." This opened up a flood of pain and the following months were spent working through his now de-repressed rage, hurt, shame, guilt, and longing.

It took almost a year before Steven finished mourning, mourning for many things—father, mother's love, spoiled career, failed marriage, Church as institution and as belief system, and alcohol as ritual, rite, source of hope and comfort, and chemical solace. By then, somewhat parallel to the Chorus, I had come to admire my intellectualizing patient. Toward the end of this mourning period Steven discovered SOS (Secular Organization for Sobriety), a self-help group for those addicts who cannot in good faith (no pun intended) subscribe to the tenets of the Twelve-Step movement. Further, since it has far fewer members and meetings than AA, most of its activity is on the Internet and via e-mail. Both its belief system and its structure were a perfect fit for Steven's value system and personality structure. In a short time he became an avid participant in SOS. In fact he came to love SOS with something like the intellectual love recommended by Spinoza. It gave him an understanding of who he was and of his relationship to the cosmos, including the role that alcohol had played in his life, that was indeed transforming, and unlike AA did not elicit rebellion and skepticism in him. He had finally found something he could give his allegiance to and that brought him into community as he began to spend long hours composing e-mail to follow SOSers in need of support, guidance, and love. SOS allowed Steven to remain alone, satisfying the schizoid side of him that was so afraid of abandonment by people, and simultaneously satisfied the part of him that longed for symbiosis and community.

So Spinozaistic therapeutic insight guided a successful therapy by helping the therapist to see that ideas can be loved, that conflict between value systems can lead to psychopathology, that de-repression (as vital as it is) can only occur in the context of rapport, and that the patient must find his own way to an object worthy of his love, in this case love of SOS with its ethos of mutual self-help in the context of immanence, not transcendence, and the realization that the cure necessarily entails reconnection with community on whatever terms work for the patient.

It is important to note that Steven didn't merely come to love ideas; he had always done that, and loving ideas is not intrinsically different from loving, let us say, horseracing. As Freud pointed out, "We must love or grow ill," so it's better to love something than to not love at all. But this is not yet anything like Spinoza's intellectual love, which transforms. Steven did come to experience something like intellectual love when he came to understand his addiction and its ineluctable determinants, those manifestations of the eternal laws of nature that made it impossible for him to drink safely. With that understanding came a deeper understanding of himself and his relationship to the universe. This synoptic vision, and his deeply affective acceptance of it is what was mutative, what allowed him to move from depressed addict to reasonably happy recovering person. This change in intellectual stance is both the same as and different from what alcoholics and other addicts experience when they "hit bottom," to use the Twelve-Step phrase. Both involve the relinquishing of denial, but the move toward intellectual love involves a far broader insight and a different type of emotional realignment. It is not the path for all, but it is vital that the therapist travel that road with those patients who are capable of such insight.

I'm going to end Steven's story on what sounds like a literary flourish, but it is not. It is true. Almost a year after Steven became involved in SOS, he started an e-mail correspondence with a woman in China struggling to maintain her sobriety. Steven was able to help her and they fell in love. He is now living in China with his beloved, the two of them sober and content. Although a nonbeliever, she is a practicing Buddhist, which Steven first saw as an impediment to their relationship. But borrowing a slogan from the Program he rejected, he decided to "Live and let live," and it has worked.

❖ CHAPTER 12 ❖

Family Therapy with an Addicted Adolescent

Substance abuse is said to be a family disease. What is meant by this? On the surface it seems absurd. Surely substance abuse is about a particular person and his or her use of substances. It isn't a family disease, it's a person disease. This is of course true, yet it is also untrue. In physics there is the principle of complementarity. When the physicist is explaining the effects of electromagnetic energy he sometimes regards it as a particle and sometimes as a wave. Similarly, in substance abuse it is sometimes most useful to look at things from the perspective of the user and sometimes from the perspective of the family (or society). The family perspective enriches understanding and gives us a new way of seeing things.

To return to our question: In what sense is addiction a family disease? To start, it runs in families. Of this there is no doubt. The empirical evidence is overwhelming. This running in families can mean many things. Perhaps addiction is a genetically transmitted disease, or at least the vulnerability to it is genetically transmitted, and addiction runs in families because the predisposition to it is inherited. Perhaps addiction runs in families because it is learned. The familial transmission of addiction has nothing to do with genes; rather it has everything to do with modeling and the transmission of values.

Or, perhaps addiction runs in families because of defensive identification with the aggressor. That is, the children in addicted families can't cope with their parents' dysfunction and the pain that dysfunction inflicts on them in any other way than becoming like the substance abusing parents. If you can't beat them, join them. Or perhaps, growing up in an addictive family is so painful and leaves such emotional scars that substances come to be used as anesthetics and self-medication. Or perhaps all of these play a role in the familial confluence of substance abuse. Regardless of the relative strengths of these factors, substance abuse does run in families and the odds of a family member being addicted are proportional to the number of other addicts in the family and to their closeness. That is, if the parents are substance abusers, the odds are highest that at least one of the children will be. The odds are somewhat less if a sibling is, and even less if the addiction is in the grandparent, uncle, or aunt. In the case of alcoholism we have highly robust and consistent evidence for this (Bleuler 1955, Goodwin 1988, Goodwin et al. 1973 and many others). In the case of other drugs of abuse, the evidence is weaker but clinical experience is highly congruent with the hypothesis that addiction runs in families.

The second meaning of "alcoholism [or addiction] is a family disease" takes the focus off the identified patient and looks at addiction as a symptom of dysfunction in the family. The addict may be seen as a scapegoat; as a deviant necessary to strengthen family cohesiveness, delineate family boundaries, and clarify "mainstream" values; as a target and focus of family aggression; as necessary to the maintenance of homeostasis, that is, stability of the family; as a distraction and defense against facing other conflicts.

The third sense in which addiction is a family disease is the least controversial of its meanings. Few in the recovery, professional, or scientific communities doubt that the presence of an addicted family member has profound effects on all the other family members, particularly when the addict is a parent and the family member is a child. Therefore every rehab has a family therapy program (or did until the current emphasis on cost containment under managed care). The vast and growing popular and professional literature on ACOAs

(Adult Children of Alcoholics) as well as the ACOA and codependency movements attest to the saliency of this meaning of the family as the seat of addiction.

MAJOR FAMILY THERAPY APPROACHES

The major theories of family dynamics and systems of family therapy are: the family as group—Freud and Bion; strategic family therapy—Haley; structural family therapy—Minuchin; experiential family therapy—Whitaker; intergenerational systems therapy—Bowen; and psychodynamic family therapy—Ackerman and Scharff.

FAMILY AS A GROUP

One of the most obvious things about the family is that it is a group. As such, it can be treated by group therapy just as any other group. But there are important differences. In constituting a therapy group, the therapist is able to select the members. The family therapist has no such freedom; he or she has to take the family or couple as they come. Most groups are not multigenerational; families are. Nevertheless, the fact remains a family is a group.

SIGMUND FREUD

Almost all of Freud's work is about individual psychology; he was very well aware of the effects people have on one another. In 1921, approaching 70, he published *Group Psychology and the Analysis of the Ego*, in which he analyzed group behavior. Freud concluded that men in groups undergo *regression* and *de-individuation*. Starting as he often does with a selective review of the literature, Freud summarized the work of LeBon (1895) on crowds—short-lived, moblike aggregations of men. LeBon describes the crowd as fickle, intellectually regressed, primitive, and driven by emotion. Affectivity is heightened and rationality all but disappears in the group or crowd mind. Freud strongly endorses LeBon's definition, but finds it incomplete. Freud makes two points: LeBon's crowds are leaderless while most natural groups have leaders, and LeBon sees only the negative side of group consciousness. Freud, on the contrary, believing that the individual is always driven by self-interest, thinks that the highest moral achievements and acts of self-abnegation are group achievements, in contradistinction to intellectual achievements, which are solely the province of individuals.

LeBon's transient moblike crowds appear to have little to do with the dynamics of the family. And yet—yet—the heightened emotionality, diminished (or augmented) egoism, and lowering of intellectual level is certainly not unknown in the cauldron of family conflicts, especially when fueled by drugs or alcohol.

Freud goes on to look at McDougall's (1920) theory of the highly organized group, which seemingly is more like the family. Such groups are characterized by continuity; clear ideas about the nature, composition, function, and capabilities of the group; interactions with similar groups from which it is nevertheless differentiated; traditions, customs, and habits; and a definite structure that provides for specialization and differentiation of functions. Freud points out that McDougall's highly organized groups have many traits of the individual. They also have many parallels to the family. In fact, McDougall's descriptive analysis of group behavior could clearly be converted into a normative theory of the "healthy" family.

Freud then turns to Trotter (1916) and his theory of a "herd" instinct or innate gregariousness in man. He agrees with Trotter "that the tendency towards the formation of groups is biologically a continuation of the multicellular character of all higher organisms" (Freud 1921, p. 87).

McDougall's delineation of the qualities of the enduring group have clear implications for family therapy. Structure, boundaries, clearly defined roles, purposes, and expectations all contribute to "stability." Of course, as we have seen, the inertia of the system, the forces making for the maintenance of homeostasis, may ossify roles and structures into an all too stable stability characterized by pathology. Roles, purposes, and expectations may be all too clear, albeit "sick." Some addictive families may be too chaotic to be stable in McDougall's sense, while others may go on forever in the same ruts. Paradoxically, there can be *stable chaos*.

Trotter's "herd instinct" reminds Freud of Schopenhauer's parable of the freezing porcupines who cuddle together seeking warmth only to prick each other with their quills, then moving apart again and freezing once more until drawing close once again only to feel those quills and retreat. We are kind of like that, neither able to subsist without others nor to sufficiently blunt our quills to be comfortably close.

Having borrowed from LeBon, McDougall and Trotter, Freud develops his own theory of group psychology. In order to analyze what is unique about the psychology of enduring groups with structure and leaders, Freud examines two "artificial" groups: the church and the army. He concludes that they "work" because all of the members feel *equally loved* by the leader: Jesus Christ and the Commander-in-Chief, respectively. This condition of equality reduces *sibling rivalry* and makes possible strong feelings of solidarity with fellow congregants/soldiers. Egotism is forsworn and one "loves one's brother as oneself." Being (or feeling) equally loved by the "father" leader is the sine qua non of group cohesion. Cain and Jacob, who murder and swindle their brothers, respectively, and who are our mythic cases of sibling rivalry, did not feel equally loved by their father-leaders. The children in families with addiction rarely feel loved as much as the parent loves his substance and the conditions for group cohesion are absent. The success of Twelve-Step groups may have much to do with either inducing feelings of being equally loved by the Program or by the Higher Power.

The implications for family dynamics of Freud's group psychology are fairly obvious. "Leaderless" families will be more primitive, more emotional, less rational, and more erratic and unstable than those with a strong leader, and paradoxically the strongly led group, provided that the leader (parent) loves the followers (children) equally, will be more "democratic," or at least more egalitarian within the sibling system than one with diffuse leadership. Further, group cohesion is only possible through the relinquishing of self-love. The family will share an ego-ideal, which is an identification with the parent(s), and this shared ego-ideal facilitates their mutual identification. The conversion of the sexual into the affectionate is a necessary condition of group solidarity, so whatever else, incest and sexual abuse—both common in addicted families—does, it makes family solidarity and cohesion impossible.

WILFRED BION

One of the most clinically useful as well as conceptual powerful analyses of group behavior was made by Wilfred Bion, an English psychiatrist and analyst. In 1961, he published *Experiences in Groups*, a slim volume chock full of insight. Bion saw that every group operated on two levels simultaneously: a realistic task or *work level* and an unconscious or *basic assumption level*. There is a clear parallel here to the distinction between the conscious and the unconscious in individuals. Every group is a "work" or "task" group, including the family. Every group simultaneously pursues its "basic assumptions"—its unconscious aggressive, sexual, and dependency needs. Aggression is expressed by fight or flight fantasies and action, dependency needs by dependent fantasies and behavior, while sexual needs are met by pairing; the unconscious fantasy of both the group and couple doing the pairing is that they will conceive the Savior or Messiah. It is only because the group believes that the pair will conceive the Messiah that it tolerates pairing. David Scharff (1992) has added a fourth basic assumption: fusion-fission—the need to fuse (merge) and the need to isolate (fragment).

Families are very usefully viewed as simultaneously pursuing tasks—raising children, mourning losses, earning money—and pursuing the unconscious basic assumptions of fight/flight, dependency, pairing, and fusion/fission. The basic assumption may contribute to the "work" of the group or it may undermine it, but in either case, it is a mostly unconscious process. *Addicted families tend to do poorly as task groups and to be driven, more than most, by their unconscious basic assumptions.*

STRATEGIC FAMILY THERAPY

You will probably not be amazed to learn that strategic family therapy is about *strategies*. The strategic family therapist self-consciously tries to contrive a strategy to bring about change. Such strategies are by their very nature ad hoc, designed to fit a particular situation and in that sense, are spontaneous and creative. They also tend to be manipulative and gimmicky. The whole emphasis is on what, or perhaps how, rather than why whatever goes on goes on. Strategic therapy grew out of Gregory Bateson's work on the *double bind*. (Bateson et al. 1956).

Bateson's original interest in mental illness was in schizophrenia. What he came to see was that the families of schizophrenics drove them mad without the least awareness that they were doing so. They did this by a pattern of communication Bateson called the double bind. In a double bind, there is no way for the recipient of the communication to "win," no way to be "right." It is a damned if you do, damned if you don't trap. The double bind theory asserts that the continuous immersion in "damned if you do, damned if you don't" environments in which covert messages contradict overt ones leads to madness (schizophrenia), the only way out being to go "mad." Another way out is to drink or drug.

We all communicate in double binds on occasion, but what makes the schizophrenic family different is the pervasiveness and persistence of this mode of interaction. Bateson gives the example of the mother of a schizophrenic patient, who was doing rather well in the hospital, visiting her son. As she walked into the room the mother said, "Aren't you going to embrace your mother?" but when the "patient" embraced her, she said, "Stop smothering me." The "patient" immediately began acting "crazy." It is essential to the double bind that it not be commented upon; that is, there is a "rule" that specifies no communication about communication. In our example, if the "crazy" son could say, "Mother, you are telling me to get close and pushing me away at the same time," he would not have to "go crazy," but he cannot, either because he lacks the insight into the double bind in which he is trapped or because the "rules" of the family prohibit such an utterance. These possibilities are not mutually exclusive. Lack of insight and the prohibition reinforce each other. The therapist who does have insight into the double bind situation can comment on it, thereby breaking the double bind impasse. Such an interpretation is not usually well received and is often not heeded, illustrating the inertia of the "system;" its tendency to resist change, to maintain its homeostasis. Families with addiction demonstrate lots of double binding behavior and therapists need to comment on it.

Strategic therapy is largely the creation of Jay Haley (1976, 1984, 1990), who started by analyzing the communication patterns of families. Pathology was seen as garbled communication and the task of the therapist was to improve communication by making the covert overt, clarifying, disturbing double binds by commenting on them, pointing out various language games people play, and so on.

Improving communication is certainly work fit for the gods. Yet it has become a cliché. I haven't seen a couple in years in which at least the wife, and often both of them, didn't say, "We are having trouble communicating." Sometimes that is true, maybe even often, and the couple doesn't exist whose communication can't be improved, but very often communication *isn't* really the problem. "Communication" has become another place to hide, another defense. The real problem isn't *lack* of communication; it is the *content* of the communication, a content one or both of the partners doesn't wish to hear. A very effective, albeit painful, intervention is to point out that the problem isn't lack of communication but the content of the communication.

Watzlawick (1978) developed a technique or strategy of the therapeutic double bind that takes the form of prescribing the symptom. Bateson (1971), in his paper on addiction, alludes to AA members telling a recalcitrant drinker to "go out and tie one on." If the drinker follows the "prescription," John Barleycorn himself may convince the drinker the game isn't worth the candle and if he doesn't follow the prescription he gets a chance to try sobriety. Ideally the therapeutic double bind sets up a win-win situation. In "I want you to become 'more anxious,'" the anxious person may increase his anxiety only to discover that he can control his anxiety or he may refuse, similarly learning that he can control his anxiety, thereby changing if he does and changing if he doesn't. Strategists use the unconscious, rather than trying to understand it. Manipulating dragons is an inherently risky business, but the therapeutic double bind has its uses.

Another strategy is *reframing*, also called *relabeling* which usually means putting a positive spin on a symptom or symptomatic behavior. To the pot-smoking college student who angrily says to his mother, who is furious at his smoking, "You really don't want me to stop or you wouldn't have given me that bottle of whiskey for Christmas," the therapist says, "She was trying to save you money so you could put it toward tuition." An absurd example, although relabeling or reframing can be highly effective. A more dynamic take on reframing is to interpret the adaptive function of the symptom or behavior. "Your drug use is your way of asserting your identity" is both a reframing and an interpretation of the adaptive meaning of the patient's use.

Haley went on from the communication therapy approach he learned from Bateson to develop his own approach. His central insight is that all relationships including, in fact especially including, that between therapist and patient, are *power* relationships. Whether it's the way people use language, gestures, body postures, or behavior, they are always trying to establish dominance and control or being dominated and controlled. Of course people can control through weakness and no one is more attuned to the power of passive aggression than Haley. As an immediate corollary of the ubiquity of power in human relations, Haley stresses the absolute necessity of the therapist taking control and his entire thrust is directive. According to Haley all therapy is, in reality, directive, and there is always an enormous power differential between therapist and patient. Whether acknowledged or not, the therapist controls the patient and that is exactly the way it should be, only the control should be overt and self-conscious.

Haley's analysis of symptoms also centers on control. The purpose of a symptom is to *control others*. Further, the symptom may serve as a control device or power advantage for other members of the family. Thus a symptom cannot be understood as an intrapsychic (or biochemical) event but only as an interpersonal one.

The implications of this for drug addiction treatment are clear. Drug use being a symptom like any other, it must have some interpersonal significance, let us say to be taken care of by the other family members. Haley would not interpret as might a dynamic therapist, but would urge the family members to continue to caretake, on the assumption that they will resist him and cease caretaking, which will deny the drugger his or her payoff and presumably put an end to the symptom.

Haley makes an extreme statement with which I disagree, namely that the "patient" cannot get well unless the family does. Since the function of the symptom is to control the rest of the family it is logical that there would be absolutely no reason to change if the family continued to let itself be controlled, and conversely, if the family were threatened by the patient changing and their homeostasis put in jeopardy, they would undermine the patient to make sure no change occurred. From a systems viewpoint, Haley is right, but people flee systems and they change in spite of environmental resistance to that change. If they could not and did not there would be no hope for the myriad of addicts who live in dysfunctional, heavily drug or alcohol involved families.

Although Haley overstates his case, it is true that it is extraordinarily difficult to change when everyone around you is fighting that change, even as they loudly advocate it. If the patient is a child or otherwise totally dependent, the situation may indeed be hopeless unless the system can be broken up. For Haley, family therapy is the only way to go, since change is only possible if all change.

To summarize strategic therapy it (1) establishes the therapist's control; (2) is highly directive; (3) believes that the whole system needs to be changed; (4) devises strategies to bring about the required change; (5) relies heavily on reframing, paradoxical interventions, and prescribing the symptom; and (6) views symptoms as having covert, interpersonal purposes which are under the control of the patient.

STRUCTURAL FAMILY THERAPY

If the point of strategic therapy is the development of strategies to effectuate change, the point of structural therapy is to elucidate the structure of the family—its recurrent patterns of interaction, its hierarchies (or lack of them), its boundaries and their degree of rigidity or permeability, its subsystems, and its coalitions—and to use that knowledge of structure to change the structure. The structuralists largely agree with the strategists that no change is possible unless the structure is modified or it will fight any change.

As with so many of the schools, structural therapy is associated with a charismatic leader, in this case Salvador Minuchin. Minuchin is a genuinely colorful and interesting person. An Argentine who emigrated to Israel after medical school to fight in Israel's war of liberation as an army doctor; he later moved to the United States where he retrained as a child psychiatrist. Minuchin started psychoanalytic training but left to work with children who had survived the Holocaust. Returning once again to the United States, he entered into what was perhaps his most formative experience, his eight years as a psychiatrist in the Wiltwych School for Delinquent Adolescents. Wiltwych had an illustrious pedigree, having attracted the attention and support of such notables as Eleanor Roosevelt; it also had a treatment-resistant, highly recalcitrant population of largely black and Puerto Rican kids from the worst neighborhoods in New York. Most of what became structural therapy came out of Minuchin's Wiltwych experience. He found that the insight-oriented, dynamic approach he had been trained in simply didn't work. He found that individual therapy per se was ineffectual, since participation in the family structure quickly undid whatever gains came out of the milieu and individual therapy of the training school. Never one to be daunted or to let an opportunity pass him by, Minuchin started to work with the families as well as with the kids. His efforts culminated in a classic book, *Families of the Slums* (Minuchin et al. 1967).

Minuchin (1992) tells us that, "The therapeutic process will be that of changing family members' psychosocial position vis-à-vis each other" (p. 2). So the therapist is going to actively assert control to change the role relations within the system. The family structure is the sum total of the customary interactions within the system. They are relatively enduring, but in health not invariant or inflexible. Within that structure are subsystems—spousal, parental, sibling, and individual. In health the subsystems are organized hierarchically. They also stand in reciprocal, complementary relationship to one another. One cannot be a father without a child. *Boundaries* are of the essence. If boundaries between subsystems are too rigid, the result is *disengagement*, a family characterized by lack of cohesion, support and warmth; at the opposite pole is the *enmeshed* family, characterized by all-too permeable, diffuse boundaries, intrusions, and lack of differentiation. A healthy, nurturing environment both meets the needs of its members for affiliation and bonding, and provides the matrix out of which differentiation and individuation occur. As Minuchin (1992) puts it, "Dependency and autonomy are complementary, not conflicting, characteristics of the human condition" (p. 2). Paradoxically, the disengaged family disables the development of autonomy no less than the enmeshed one. Addicted families tend to be either enmeshed or disengaged.

Minuchin sees family pathology as rigidity, a rigidity that sets in if the stress is too great for the resources of the system. Pathology is a response to overload. Healthy families are basically open; they have conservation mechanisms that guarantee stability and ongoingness, but they are also flexible, protean, and responsive to internal and external change. The inherent homeostatic mechanisms do not ossify. But when the resources of the system are depleted and overloaded, as by the stress of alcoholism, a defensive rigidity sets in and the homeostatic mechanisms go into overdrive.

In trying to understand the family structure, Minuchin pays particular attention to alignments and coalitions. Is the son in alignment with the mother? Do the children form a coalition against the parents? Clearly related to concern with coalitions is making overt the power relationships in the family. For Minuchin as for Haley, power is primordial and ineluctable. Far from seeing power as malignant, Minuchin sees much pathology as flowing from weakness, from lack of power, particularly of parents.

Minuchin creates structural maps that make immediately clear the structural relations in the family—its hierarchies; subsystems; clear, diffuse, or rigid boundaries; its affiliations, conflicts, coalitions, enmeshments and detours. A structural map is illustrated in the Baker case below.

What is it the structuralist does? The structuralist is active, directive, and provocative, challenging frozen dysfunctional patterns, and insisting that parents exercise parental authority (use their power), and that subsystems be differentiated. One form of that challenge is a reframing, not in terms of putting a positive twist on the symptom, but rather by redefining the symptom as a systemic one. The identified patient ceases to be the patient and the "structure" is put on the couch. This in itself radically changes structure. There is no attempt at insight; action precedes understanding, but insight may follow the change. The switch is from an individual to a systems viewpoint. Change relationship patterns and the "cure" is here.

All this is very well; just get the parents to be parents, engage but unmesh, establish clear boundaries, and all will be well. Maybe, but how? Minuchin's method tells us the therapist must be a commanding presence. He gets to be that commanding presence by *joining* the family. He does this by adopting or accommodating to the family's style, imitating their speech patterns, pace, and idiosyncrasies. This is called *tracking*. The therapist must be a superb actor, because to do this poorly is to be perceived as mocking. Having joined the family, the therapist can now participate in and take a control stance toward the family interactional pattern, that is, toward its structure. But the therapist is not a family member, so he or she simultaneously is in and out of the family and as an out, can command. Minuchin does such things as making enmeshed members literally move away from each other by changing chairs, and by taking sides often with the weak against the strong. This is sometimes called *unbalancing*. The chair game in which the family relationships are seen as expressed in their physical deportment has been generalized into an important family therapy technique, *family sculpture*, in which the family is asked to represent their relationships by the placement of their bodies by one or more members of the family. The active form of this is called *family choreography*. This is a widely used technique in substance abuse treatment.

So the structuralist reframes the problem as a systemic one, "joins" the family, takes control, challenges pathological structure, uses directives to establish clear boundaries and hierarchical subsystems, and uses enactments to bring the problems into the treatment room. All of this is done with humor, warmth, and authority.

EXPERIENTIAL FAMILY THERAPY

If strategic therapy is about strategies of change, and structural therapy about the establishment of firmer structures, then experiential therapy is about experience. It is not the therapist as strategist or the family therapist's manipulation of structure that cures; rather it is the experience that the family has with the therapist that enables change. What is mutative is felt interaction in the here and now. Change isn't primarily something that occurs as a result of therapy; it is what happens during the therapy.

There is something quintessentially American about experiential family therapy. It is pragmatic, skeptical of theory and action-oriented. Its principal exponent is Carl Whitaker (Whitaker and Bumberry 1988).

Whitaker is a joiner with reservations. There and not there; in and out. Though he doesn't talk about resistance, he has two key technical means to deal with the resistance inherent in any family system. The first is the *struggle for structure*, the second, the *struggle for initiative*. In the struggle for structure, the therapist establishes control, but Whitaker's control looks different from Haley's. Its essence is Whitaker's insistence that all members of the family attend the first session. He refuses to deal if the family won't play by his rules. In the struggle for structure, Whitaker defines himself as parent, not peer. He also reframes the problem as systemic and interpersonal, not an individual one. He does this not by teaching; "Nothing worth knowing can be taught" (Whitaker and Bumberry 1988, p. 85), but by doing. The family having "learned" that the therapist is a parent who imposes the structure, it naturally looks to the therapist for answers, which occasions the struggle for initiative. The therapist must firmly put the ball in the family's court. He or she vigorously leaps from the pedestal, saying such things as, "I'm lucky if I can muddle through my own life, let alone live yours." He makes it clear that he has no "reality" answers. His function is to enable growth, not to tell anyone how to live. Whitaker uses all sorts of confrontation, humor, and absurdity to win the battle for initiative. There is a paradox here. The therapist is demanding that the patient—the family—be free and responsible. "I order you to be free" somehow doesn't work. Returning the ball does. Another kind of reframing goes on here: the problem is redefined during the struggle for initiative from symptom removal to growth. The therapist has no interest in symptom removal.

This raises real questions for the substance abuse or addictions therapist who does think that he or she knows a better way of living (sobriety), and does wish to alter the reality situation of patients in a determinate way. Perhaps there is no way out of this dilemma and substance abuse therapy is incompatible with experiential therapy.

As part of his insistence on spontaneity and aliveness, Whitaker abhors history taking, calling it voyeuristic "pornography." No psychosocials for him. For Whitaker, there is also no diagnosis. Try selling this one to your friendly managed care company.

The political struggle is over once the family accepts responsibility, and we are in the middle of the "journey of family therapy [which] begins with a blind date and ends with the empty nest" (1988, p. 53). Blind dates engender anxiety, and Whitaker makes it clear that anxiety is the motivating force for change. Accordingly, he does nothing to reduce the anxiety level; on the contrary, he makes moves to heighten it.

Whitaker also relishes his "toughness," comparing therapy to surgery. Like the surgeon, his business is to cut away diseased tissue, not to avoid bloodletting. Perhaps related to toughness is Whitaker's use of the *bataca* (pillow bat), which he instigates the family members to use on each other. This more direct variant on pounding the pillow both surfaces suppressed (or repressed) anger and aggression and demonstrates (gives the experience of) anger not destroying its object.

The middle phase of Whitakerian family therapy is characterized as symbolic therapy, which deals with unconscious process. "Just as water flows through pipes under our streets, impulses flow through our unconscious. . . . We all have these emotional infrastructures that ensure the flow of our impulse life" (Whitaker and Bumberry 1988,

p. 75). The themes of loneliness, rage, sexuality, and death are universal; they are particularized among other ways in family rituals. Whitaker does not interpret the unconscious; rather, he surfaces, largely through the use of his own associations. Since the themes are universal, the therapist's articulation of his thoughts and feelings frees up the family to surface their infrastructure. Whitaker also uses confrontation and reductio-ad-absurdum techniques. "My husband always runs away from me" is answered by "Why don't you shoot him?" "How could I?" His answer, "With a gun, or you might use a bow and arrow." Before long, the wife's murderous rage surfaces, having been tapped by Whitaker's literalism. Whitaker's whole technique has been called a "theater of the absurd." Particular emphasis is put on death and loss.

Whitaker advocates starting with the father, since he believes that gender differences are biological and that men are less in contact with feelings, symbols, and impulses. So go after Dad first and hard. Whitaker emphasizes the intergenerational transmission of patterns, shared symbols, and rituals. He believes that at least three generations are germane to the current family functioning, and he includes grandparents, if he possibly can, saying such things as, "We are stuck and need help. Would your parents (the grandparents) come and help us?"

Experiential family therapy would appear to have limited application to the treatment of substance abuse or the actively addicted family. Its stated indifference to symptom removal, its agnostic take on diagnosis, and its focus on the symbolic representation and enactment of the unconscious impulse life seem too removed from the usual stance of substance abuse therapy in which the therapist takes a strong stand for sobriety. I am fairly sure that Whitaker would disagree. He says, "Alcoholics drink because they're afraid of being afraid" (Whitaker and Bumberry 1988, p. 86). If that is the case, then experiential therapy would seem to be just the thing with its push toward experiencing the anxiety intrinsic to being fully alive and aware. The problem is that if the therapist ignores the pharmacological regression concomitant with addiction, the experiential approach may become irrelevant. Experiential family therapy appears to be much more suited for work with recovering families.

MULTIGENERATIONAL SYSTEMS FAMILY THERAPY

Multigenerational systems therapy is the creation of Murray Bowen (1978a, b). The cornerstone of Bowen's theory is *differentiation*, explicitly differentiation of the self. All development entails differentiation. In the embryo, undifferentiated cells differentiate into ectoderm, mesoderm, and endoderm, which in turn differentiate into even more specialized cells. It is only after differentiation that the integration necessary for the formation of tissues and organs can take place. All development involves differentiation and integration. Without differentiation, there can be no integration, and without integration, we have a colony instead of an organism. De-differentiation is always pathological.

So differentiation is a universal biological phenomenon (so is exact replication and homogeneity, the two forces being in dynamic equilibrium), which manifests itself in differentiation of the self from the *undifferentiated family ego mass.*

Over and over again, Bowen speaks of the undifferentiated being "stuck" in the family ego mass. There is a feeling of ensnarlment, stickiness, entrapment. Images of flies caught by flypaper or entangled in spider webs come to mind. Bowen would be an apt candidate for spiritual grandfather of the codependency movement. To be codependent is to be undifferentiated.

For Bowen, differentiation isn't only between or from people, it is importantly differentiation of thought and feeling. Differentiation entails being able to separate thought from feeling, and failure to be able to do so is the mark of ensnarlment in the family ego mass. Bowen has developed a scale to estimate the degree of differentiation and maintains that the relatively undifferentiated family can function well under conditions of low stress, but falls into dysfunction as stress escalates.

This brings us to another key Bowenian concept, *triangulation.* Bowen sees the family and indeed all human relations as systems of interlocking triangles. Triangles are essentially defenses against twoness, against pairing. Relationships are intrinsically stressful, conflict between people is inevitable, and people flee from the tension of dyadic relationships, of I–thou relating, of two-person intimacy, to triangular relationships. One or both members of the pair suck in another person to deflect, to support, to ally, to defend, to dilute.

Triangles, inevitable as they are, are the great danger. If the therapist is triangulated into the system, all is lost. The primary task of the therapist is to remain untriangulated so he or she can "coach" the patient on detriangulation. The only way the therapist can avoid countertransferential triangulation is to have worked through differentiation from his or her family of origin. The therapist is a calm, uninvolved, objective teacher explaining the triangulation process in the family and helping develop strategies for detriangulation.

Substance abusers are triangulators par excellence and the addictive family is one of triangular entanglements, so Bowen's analysis of triangulation is directly applicable to the treatment of addicted families. If Bowen's fear of being sucked in seems excessive, it is a real danger for the substance abuse family therapist, who needs to be aware of the contending forces trying to enlist him or her as an ally in the family struggle. This gets tricky when there is an active user. There, "joining" the triangle "against" the user is sometimes necessary. Bowen would not agree. He has written on alcoholism (1974) and sees the alcoholic as the least differentiated member of the family system. The "cure" is to enable differentiation rather than focus on the symptom— the drinking.

Undifferentiation is projected onto the dysfunctional symptomatic family member. The real problem is *family fusion*. In the fused family, members either have no-selves or pseudo-selves, never real-selves. There is often a pattern of overadequate-underadequate role assignment, the underadequate person being presented as the problem in what is clearly a relationship problem. This has direct relevance to substance abuse treatment. In his paper on alcoholism, Bowen presents the alcoholic as the overadequate partner who is in reality undifferentiated or defending against that undifferentiation by overcompensation. Alcohol enables the fusion that the overadequacy denies. This is a variation on the dependency-conflict theory of addiction, which states that those who are counterdependent; that is, phobic about intimacy and human relating and hence denying their need for it, covertly meet their dependency needs by the use of substances, particularly alcohol. This is usually a male dynamic, but need not be. The drinker/drugger maintains that he needs no one, is totally independent, while in reality is totally dependent. Returning to Bowen's theory, as the addiction progresses, roles reverse and the drinker becomes underadequate. The possibilities are legion, his point being that it isn't the drinking, it's the fusion and its byproduct that need to be addressed.

People tend to select spouses on the same level of differentiation (or undifferentiation) as themselves. They in turn project their undifferentiation onto and triangulate with their offspring, there usually being a favorite target who becomes the most fused family member. This sets up a *multigenerational transmission process* in which the less differentiated marry the undifferentiated who produce (and create) at least one even less differentiated child who marries the same, so that by the third generation, schizophrenia may appear, although this may take as much as ten generations. What is transmitted is not genetic in the sense of chromosomally encoded; rather it is relational. Yet the process seems to be natural selection reversed; it is survival (barely) of the least fit. The application of this to substance abuse makes sense. We frequently see families in which a parent (usually the father) is a "functional alcoholic," or, as one of my patients put it, "I want to be a successful alcoholic like my father," while one or more of the children are dysfunctional drinkers or druggers who are unable to make it in the world.

Another Bowenian concept highly applicable to substance abuse is the emotional cutoff. This is moving to northern Alaska and exchanging Christmas cards with the family in lieu of true differentiation. It is a defensive movement that is bound to fail (although it may be better than total submergence in the fused family), since the substance abuser's fused family remains in his head awaiting projection and re-enactment. We also see this in addicts who fuse with their substance of choice instead of with their families. Twelve-Step programs speak of this as *isolation*, which it sees as a characteristic character flaw of the addicted.

When a recovering person returns to his addicted family, the entire family may move from the fusion implicit in addiction and the games played around it to sobriety and greater differentiation. However, more often than not, that is not the outcome and the recovering person's hurt, disappointment, and rage may endanger that recovery. Bowen would say that the recovering addict lacked the calm and the ability to differentiate between thought and feeling characteristic of the true self and needed more therapy before attempting further differentiation through differentiation of the family. This seems rather utopian to me, but helping recovering people recognize and avoid enmeshment and triangulation in their still addicted families is highly therapeutic. Some degree of emotional cutoff may be adaptive and indeed necessary to continued recovery.

Bowen is greatly interested in genealogy, enjoining his patients to trace their families. He himself has gone back three hundred years. Closely related to this interest is his development of the *genogram*, probably his best known contribution. All patients, be they individuals, couples, or families, prepare with the aid of the therapist genograms as part of the evaluation process. The genogram is a pictorial representation of multigeneration family structures going back at least three generations. Bowen has a system of symbols for birth, death, divorce, and so forth, but the therapist can use any symbols that vivify relational patterns. The genogram is of particular relevance to substance abuse treatment where the family intergeneration pattern of use and abuse needs to be made manifest. This is illustrated below in the Baker case.

BEHAVIORAL FAMILY THERAPY

Behavioral family therapy works on extinguishing the effects of maladaptive past learning, changing present contingencies (that is, modifying reward patterns), and challenging the attitudinal components of dysfunction. Although most often used in individual therapy, these techniques can be adapted to couple and family work. Behavioral family therapy has many incarnations, but these days is strongly cognitively oriented. Behavioral family therapy uses homework, for example, say something positive to your partner every day; contingency contracts, for example, if you do your homework, you can watch TV; reinforcement; modeling by the therapist; and shaping, that is, reinforcing successive approximations to a desired behavior. Behavior therapy encourages self-monitoring, the keeping of diaries, and training in problem solving. The behavioral approach to family problems is most often used with families with recalcitrant teenagers. Generally speaking, the behaviorists focus on the individual patient, seeing the patient's problems as the cause of the difficulties in the family. This is the direct opposite of the systems approach, although behavioral family therapists recognize that the family members may be unwittingly reinforcing the aberrant behavior.

Two behavioral approaches that can be extremely helpful with recovering families are *parental skills training* and *conjoint sex therapy*. There are several varieties of parental skills training; all are essentially educational and all seek to help reduce family conflict. Parenting sober is very different from parenting while drug involved, and concrete, didactic training, advice, and guidance can sometimes substantially reduce anxiety and conflict in the recovering parent and his or her family and promote growth into a new role as a responsible, emotionally available father or mother. Sexual dysfunction in early sobriety is common and the anxiety it engenders threatens recovery. Conjoint sex therapy directly ameliorates this potential source of trouble.

Timothy O'Farrell (1993) has worked out a behavioral marital therapy for alcoholics and their families. It has a substantial success rate. He has the spouse administer Anabuse and directs the couple to work on their conflicts in the sessions, not in their lives. He also assigns a good deal of homework.

PSYCHODYNAMIC FAMILY THERAPY

If strategic family therapy develops strategies to enable change, structural therapy modifies structure, experiential therapy provides alternate experience, Bowenian therapy differentiates, behavioral therapy modifies behavior, psychodynamic family aims at *insight*—insight into overt behavioral patterns and interactions and into unconscious re-enactments, projections, and identifications. Psychodynamic family therapy uses all of the knowledge Bateson, Haley, Minuchin, Whitaker, Bowen, and the behaviorists have gleaned about systems, communication, power relations, boundaries, intergenerational transmission, positive and negative feedback loops, double binds, social learning, and contingencies of reinforcement in families, but it does so in a nondirective way in which that knowledge is instrumental, not determinative. What the psychodynamic family therapist is primarily interested in is increasing self-awareness, particularly awareness of unconscious process.

Nathan Ackerman

Ackerman's (1994) major theoretical contribution was to understand simultaneously psychopathology as intrapsychic (within the mind) and systemic (familial). Ackerman characterized family dysfunction as arising from roles and enactments becoming fixed, rigid, and dead. The family then deals with the unresolved conflict manifested in the stalemate by scapegoating, the scapegoat most usually being the identified patient. What makes Ackerman a psychodynamic family therapist is the unconscious nature of the unresolved conflict. Most of the failure to use the other to enact underdeveloped parts of the self in a flexible, fluid way, (which Ackerman calls *complementarity*) is between the parents. Scapegoating serves as a diversion and defense. This is an extremely common dynamic when the identified patient is an adolescent or young adult substance abuser. On a conscious level, the parents are passionately (and genuinely) invested in halting the adolescent's substance abuse; on an unconscious level they need the adolescent to continue to use and to be a problem so he or she can be available for scapegoating and the parents don't have to look at the disturbance in their own relationship. Inevitably the scapegoat is only too willing to continue in that role, and the drug use remains unabated. Ackerman would see this as a case of interlocking pathology.

Like the other founding fathers of family therapy, Ackerman was charismatic. Anything but neutral, he took sides, "unbalanced," particularly his siding with the scapegoat. Ackerman openly commented on his feelings. In part this was modeling: modeling openness about sex, dependence, aggression, and anxiety. Ackerman's aims were always to increase self-awareness of both repressed and projected aspects of self, including the enactment of interacting psychopathologies. He sees the therapist as a catalyst of change, all technique being subordinate to the catalytic role. There is a great deal in Ackerman's approach, particularly his understanding of the mutually interlocking psychopathologies, that readily lends itself to work with addicted and recovering families.

Jill and David Scharff

Another psychodynamic approach is *object relations family therapy* (Scharff and Scharff 1991), which relies heavily on transference interpretation, that is, on commenting on the projections that the family members make onto the therapist, and the therapist's use of his or her own feelings as a source of insight as to what's going on in the family.

Object relations therapy sees family interaction as projection of and enactment of the internal worlds of the family members, internal worlds that are mental representations of early relationships. The Scharffs use Ronald Fairbairn's (1952) conceptualization of the ego or self rather than Freud's structural model as their theoretical guide to understanding the internal world. This is illustrated in Figure 12–1. Such Fairbairnian notions as the libidinal and antilibidinal ego are alluded to in the discussion of the Baker case. Referring to the figure should clarify their meaning. The process of intergenerational internalization and projection casts much light on the pathology we see in alcoholic and substance abusing families. Object relations family therapists use dreams, drawings, and play as an integral part of their work.

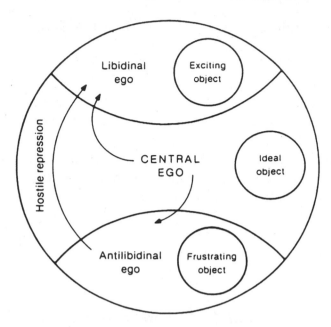

FIGURE 12-1. Fairbairn's model of psychic organization, by David E. Scharff, from *Refinding the Object and Reclaiming the Self.* The central ego in relation to the ideal object is in conscious interaction with the caretaker. The central ego represses the split-off libidinal and antilibidinal aspects of its experience along with corresponding parts of the ego that remain unconscious. The libidinal system is further repressed by the antilibidinal system. (Reprinted courtesy of David E. Scharff.)

THE BAKER FAMILY

In the clinical vignette that follows, I try to show how family therapists taking a communications approach, a strategic approach, a structural approach, an intergenerational systems approach, an object relations approach, an experiential approach, a behavioral approach, and a substance abuse approach might work with the Baker family. The first five therapists have been influenced by Bateson, Haley, Minuchin, Bowen, and the Scharffs, respectively. The experiential, behavioral, and substance abuse therapists have no one model, although Whitaker has clearly influenced our experientialist. The substance abuse therapist most clearly reflects the approach I used in treating the family that inspired these vignettes, although my usual approach would be more psychodynamic.

We see the Bakers in an opening session, greatly distressed by the return of their oldest son who has recently left a therapeutic community (TC) and returned to daily marijuana smoking. Tom is 16; his younger brother, Sam, is 12, almost 13. The parents, Rob and Harriet, are fortyish. They are neatly albeit informally dressed, the boys in age-appropriate jeans and T-shirts, Father in hard-pressed work pants and a short sleeve shirt, Mother in a bright, not quite loud cotton dress and heels. She wears slightly too much makeup (for my taste). Father is a muscular, powerful-looking man. Mother is plump, not quite fat.

The family enters the consulting room in single file, Mother first, followed by Father, Tom, and Sam. Tom is sullen, and mostly stares at the floor. Sam, although not sullen, seems distracted and not quite there. The substance abuse therapist wonders if Sam is the "lost child" in this family. Mother enters purposefully, almost marching, and proceeds to the most distant chair, followed by her husband, to whom she says, "I want the kids to sit next to me; you sit at the end." Tom raises his eyes from the floor and looks at her hatefully but sits next to her. Sammy and Father make up the rear, taking the remaining seats just as they were told to do. Mom is the one who contacted the therapist, telling of Tom's return to drugs, and of her anger and despair and her fear (possibly her wish) that Daddy will "beat the shit out of him." Although her focus was on Tom during the phone contact, she expressed the wish that the whole family be present at the first session. The systemic therapist wonders, "Is she an intuitive systems theorist or does she just want to set the stage and direct the play?" The substance abuse therapist thinks, "Perhaps both; from her entrance, it appears that she runs the show, but appearances aren't always reality and this may not be the case." All the therapists have the same information derived from Mother's call, and have observed the same behavior.

THE SESSION

Mother (pointing at Father): He was circumcised at age 26 for me. (Laughs) But that's not why we're here. I've been in love with Rob from the beginning, but I wouldn't have married him unless he had a *bris*. We did, and we've had a great time ever since. I'm in electronic parts and I make a helluva lot of money. I barely got out of high school, and I never expected to make so much money, but I turned out to be one helluva saleswoman. Rob's in the best construction union in the city, and he makes out like a bandit. Sam is a doll. He gets great grades, he's going to be Bar Mitzvah, and things are great—except for that fucking kid. Two months out of New Start and he's back at it. ("Fucking kid" seems discordant, and is said without visible anger in the same animated, pressured voice she's been using all along.)

Father (angrily): I'm going to break his fucking neck if he doesn't stop. (His biceps harden as he says this, and he looks like he's about to get up and do it.)

Mother: We're not putting up with this shit anymore.

Tom (mutters): Fuck you! (Father starts to go for him, thinks better of it, and sits back down.)

Communications Therapist (more to Mother, but to the entire family): You don't communicate directly. Tom's right here, but you talk about him instead of to him.

Father: Talking to him is like talking to the wall. What he needs is the strap, and he's not too big for it either.

Communications Therapist: You're still talking about him, not to him.

Father: If I talk to him, he's not going to like what I say. I want that fucking kid to go to college. I didn't go, and he's going to go even if I have to kill him.

Structuralist: Mr. Baker, I want you to sit next to your wife. Tom and Sam, you sit down at this end.

Strategist: I won't tolerate threats in the session. I want you to speak emotionally but civilly to one another. No threats.

Sam: (giggles).

Mother (starts giggling too; to Sam): Come sit next to me.

Structuralist: No, I want you to sit next to your husband.

Systemic Intergenerationalist: Let's back off and find out a little more about your family. (To the parents): I'd like to know more about your families of origin. I'd like all of you to help me draw a "genogram"—a picture of the relationships in your family.

Structuralist (to Mother): What did you do with the tip?

Sam (still giggling): The rabbi gets the salary; the *mohel* (ritual circumciser) gets the tip. (Mom puts her arm around Sam and seems to be flirting with him.)

Object Relations Therapist (to Father): How does it feel to have your wife tell us that you were circumcised for her?

Tom (trembling with fear but defiant): Daddy's a monk because Mom made him cut off a piece of his dick. (He runs out of the room.)

Father (Looking at Tom): He's a real asshole. (Shouts). Tom, come back in here! (Tom peeks in, realizes his father isn't really mad at him, and goes back to his place.)

Mother (to Tom): You should only be as much of a man as your father.

Father: (beams).

Behaviorist (unconsciously moves his hand to his crotch).

Dynamic Therapist (thinks to himself): *Mom reminds me of Judy, the lady I treated last year who couldn't understand why giving an enema to her 16-year-old son wasn't a good idea. This Mom's another phallic mother. If Tom relates to her as a phallic mother, that puts him way back developmentally—definitely preoedipal. So all the apparently oedipal stuff going on in this session isn't really oedipal. My association to the enema-giving mother makes me wonder if this isn't an anal family characterized by "messy" acting out. They need to "get their shit together." Is all their anger anal sadism and anal explosiveness? Should I say that and speak directly to their unconscious? That would also be tracking—using metaphors this family can understand.* (Speaking): You're here to get your shit together, but you can't seem to do it even here.

Mother (starts to cry): We can't get our shit together. This just goes on and on—therapists, getting thrown out of school, talking to him, beating him, the TC. Now he's smoking again. I can't stand it. I can't stand it. He's got everything. I was poor. My father was a shoemaker. Rob had it real rough. He ran in gangs, drank like a fish, went to reform school. I loved him from the first time I saw him, but I wouldn't go to bed with him unless he married me. Rob's a man, not like my father—or that damned kid. My father's a wimp. Never made much of a living and was pussy-whipped all his life. My kids love him, but they've known Grandma wears the pants almost since they were born. (To therapist): Yeah, that's the way we talk. We let it all hang out in *my* family. (All of the therapists wonder—is Rob pussy-whipped too, in spite of his supermasculinity and Mom's denial?)

Structuralist (mentally notes): *"My" rather than "our" family.*

Mother: My ignorant parents said they would sit *shivah* (observe the mourning period) if I married Rob. He was 25, tough as nails, and was he handsome! My mother said the tattoos made her sick. I love them. Anyway, Rob converted and we got married, and now my folks love him. Tom has had it good from the beginning. Everyone adored him. My parents really changed after he was born and accepted Rob. Rob stopped drinking—once in a while, he has a beer, but he doesn't even like that anymore.

Tom (mumbling): Yeah, Dad doesn't drink, so how can he understand why I smoke? Some macho! The only reason he doesn't drink is because my mom doesn't let him. (Starts to say, "He is a pussy," but looks at his dad and gets scared, so pussy doesn't quite sound.)

Mother: Then Rob got in the construction union. His family never did shit for him. His dad was a drunk; it killed him—shot his liver, and his mom's a doormat. She's got rosary beads up her ass. Always praying; never did a thing for the kids. Rob's lucky he's in the union; never graduated high school. He's done real good. Nobody works as hard as my Rob. The rest of his family is a total loss. All of his brothers drink and fight and are just horrible. We stay away from them. I'm really proud of Rob.

Intergenerational, Object Relational, Strategic, and Structural Thera-
pists All Think: *She regards him as a child—her child. What does*
that say to the kids? Can they be kids too? She presents Father
on one hand as both castrated and pussy-whipped like her father,
and on the other hand, as a "real" man. The boys must have a
very split image of Father and major difficulties in male identifi-
cation. There is also a historical split between Dad, the delin-
quent drunk, and Dad, the heroic success overcoming his back-
ground to become the hardworking provider. Sam, the good boy,
identifies with the hardworking father; Tom, the bad boy, with
the delinquent father.

Mother: Once the kids were in school, I got a job in the office of a
defense industry plant. After a few years, they realized I had the
gift of gab (all of the therapists think, *Yep, to the point where no*
one can get in a word edgewise), and gave me a crack at sales. Boy,
am I good at it! A woman too—the only one. So now we have
plenty of money, a lovely home, two dogs and a cat—they always had all the toys in the world and a great life. Sam appreci-
ates it—I don't know what went wrong with Tom. He was a good
kid. When he wasn't, Rob would take the strap to his bare backside and he would straighten out quick. My dad used a razor strap
on my brothers when my mother told him to. I think that's good
for boys. But now when they get into it, Rob punches him in
the head sometimes—and I hate that. Someone's going to get
hurt, and that's one reason I called you. You tell Rob to keep his
hands to himself.

Anyway, Tom's always had it real good. My mother still
spoils him rotten. All we ever asked of him was a little respect
and good grades. Sam's an honor student.

Father (with near rage and in a loud voice): And Tom flunks damn
near everything. You'd think he was a real dumb kid but he
ain't—just a fuckoff.

Tom (muttering, still looking at the floor): You can't even read.

Father: Like hell I can't.

Mother: Well, not too good, dear.

Father: (blushes).

Mother: The only thing we want from our kids is that they go to college. We never had a chance to go, and that's really important to us. They can study anything they want, do whatever they want, as long as they graduate. That's not much to ask. (Cries.)

Sam (giggles): Zero point zero averages don't graduate.

Mother: The trouble started around 8th grade. Tom never did too good in school, but he got through; then all of a sudden, he started cutting classes and Rob spanked him good and hard, but that didn't work, and his grades went to F's. Then he found the grass.

Father: It was his scumbag friends.

Mother: Rob's right—his friends get worse every year. Nobody but the scumbags want anything to do with him. Anyway, we tried therapy; he was in a special class—what do you call it, the resource room?—I was always in school. Rob wouldn't go after a while. We yelled, we hit, we begged, we bribed, we told him we'd do anything for him if he just stopped getting stoned. Nothing helped. The school sucks, too. They kept putting him into the next highest grade, even though he hadn't learned anything. Then he was even more lost. You don't know how many times I've said, "Tom, please tell me what's really bothering you," and all he says is, "Leave me alone." And I just wanted to slap him. Sometimes I did, other times I cried. Finally the guidance counselor said he should go to New Life. That was last year, after he got caught shoplifting. He fought us like hell, but Rob said it was the cops or the TC. So he went. It was like a miracle. When we got to visit him, or went to their family days, he was a different kid. There was one family session when he and Rob were crying and hugged each other, and told each other how much they loved each other, and then cried some more. Tom even told us that he knew how much he hurt us and felt really rotten about it.

Tom: I must have been out of my mind.

Mother (ignores him): It was wonderful. No chip on his shoulder, no sullen, miserable attitude. He went through their whole program—18 months to reentry. Now he's home and back in school, and the same rotten kid.

Father: And his scumbag friends are back.

Mother: We knew he was smoking before we found it. It's his attitude. As soon as he smokes.

Father (interrupting): He starts acting like an asshole. We even let him bring his girl to his room, and he fucks his brains out. What other parents would let him do that?

Structuralist, Intergenerationalist, Object Relations Theorist, and Addiction Therapist All Wonder: What kind of mixed message is being given here? It is also interesting to hear that Tom has a girl. All the therapists want to hear more about her. Is Tommy more together than we think?

Mother: You have to help us. I'm going to pull my hair out of my head.

Experientialist: You have the resources to help yourselves.

Mother: No, we don't. That's why we're here. What should we do?

Clearly the Bakers present us with a complex problem, or should I say problems? On the surface, there is only one problem—drug use by the identified patient. However, from both an intrapsychic psychodynamic and an interpersonal systemic viewpoint, a great deal more is going on and needs to be addressed. How can we understand the material presented by the Bakers? How would therapists from the various schools understand it? What would they do with it?

On one level, the system is unbalanced—skewed—by a domineering, perhaps castrating mother, and it is not unreasonable to think that her interaction with the family and their reaction to it may be a big piece of the action. Is Tom's drug use a maladaptive way of coping with Mother, of avoiding her, of ducking an adolescent second oedipal struggle, of rebelling, of expressing rage at her? As the communications therapist points out, the family members all too often talk about rather than to each other. Therapists of whatever school can't miss the lack of generational boundaries in this family. The parents' sex life is all over the room with Dad being simultaneously presented as a pussy-whipped castrato and as a hypermasculine stud. In either case, he seems to be defined by Mother. What sort of anxiety does this blatant and exhibitionistic sexuality stir up in the boys? To grow to manhood must simultaneously mean that one will be castrated and one can't possibly compete with a father with whom Mother is "madly in love" (or is she?), and who is not so implicitly presented as a great lover. Rather remain a helpless child, albeit a counterdependent, pseudoautonomous one by staying stoned, than be either castrated or inadequate.

The lack of, or at least seriously blurred, generational boundaries are in need of repair. Perhaps the reason this family is "stuck," unable to move to the next stage of its life cycle, is that the very absence of boundaries makes progression much too dangerous. Does the family need Tom to stay stoned so they can stay stuck? What about Dad's rage and his physicality with his children? After all, one of Mother's reasons for making the appointment is her fear that, "Dad will beat the shit out of him." What is Father so angry about? The wife's demeaning him (although she doesn't see it that way and maybe he doesn't either)? Her apparent dominance? His failure to be able to control his son? His envy of his son's "freedom" to act out after his renunciation of such freedom for family responsibility? Or is this historical anger? We know that his childhood was painful and deprived. What is his anger a defense against? Pain? Hurt? What sort of pain or hurt? Ancient wounds? Something about his marriage? The implicit rejection of his love in his son's disobedience? His renunciation of his youthful wildness? Pain experienced in the reformatory? I vote for all of the above, first and perhaps most significantly that his son apparently isn't going to vicariously fulfill his wish for literacy, for education, for entry into a middle class profession as opposed to a successful blue collar career. How much is his anger a defense against his feelings of shame, a shame accentuated by the contrast with his more educated or at least literate wife, over his own deficiencies? Does he need to undermine his son in some surely unconscious way to prevent that son from surpassing him? Indeed one wonders at how good an approximation Father is to the role of Freud's (1913b) primal father with his rage and violence. On the other hand, much of that rage is culturally syntonic, and for the most part, meets the approval of his wife.

Let's look at Father from Tom's side. Father was a drunk. Being a pothead is thus both an identification ("I get high like Dad did"), and a disidentification ("Dad never used grass"). He can be Father and feel close to him in what is perhaps the only way he can feel that closeness and simultaneously feel safely removed from him. My "hunch" (and I tend to trust my hunches, although I know they may be completely off base) is that one of the most powerful factors keeping Tom stoned is his most likely semiconscious, but perhaps completely unconscious, belief that he, like Father, can safely live a drug-dominated, acting-out adolescence and easily and painlessly emerge from it in his early twenties. That may be a dubious proposition, at best; we frequently see a generational cycle in which the children, usually of "functional" alcoholic fathers, go rapidly downhill as either their drug use or drinking progresses to dysfunction. Rob and Tom don't quite fit this pattern, but they are perhaps close to it. Rob was a tough, heavy-drinking kid, "who made it on his own," both as a street child and later on, as worker, husband, and father. Rob always functioned in his world, whatever that happened to be. Tom fails in his world. Father stopped drinking easily, but there is no certainty that Tom will stop smoking as easily, and the damage that he is inflicting on himself is cumulative. The further down he goes in his addictive fall, the harder it will be to come back. It is also clear that whatever the problems in their marriage, Harriet has had a stabilizing influence on Rob, providing him with something of the family support he apparently lacked as a child. In Kohut's (1971, 1977a) terms, she has served a selfobject function in his life, particularly in late adolescence and early adulthood, crucial times in an addictive career—nodal points in which an adolescent externalizing acting-out lifestyle either becomes the prelude to a full-blown addiction or is reined in and becomes a developmental episode in the life rather than the first stage of a progression toward death. There is no guarantee that Tom will turn the corner as Rob did, and I planned to tell him that at some point.

A related aspect of Tom's magic thinking that he doesn't need to get clean yet, which is perhaps a denial of the fact that he can't get clean ("I can stop whenever I want, but I don't want to just yet") emerged in a later session. I also wondered if Tom believes that he doesn't have to get clean and graduate from high school because Daddy can always get him into the union where he can "make out like a bandit." Subsequent sessions proved this to be the case, although Tom's belief was not fully a conscious one, or at least one that he could not articulate. Closeness to Father, if not complete identification with him (cf. Freud's [1917] comment on regression and object relations, "An object relation regresses to an identification") gave these quasi-conscious fantasies additional saliency and power. This too I planned to interpret, although the timing of that interpretation was open.

What about Sam, the "good boy"? I worried most about him. Given the amount of attention Tom gets from this family, it will be remarkable if Sam is not tempted to go in the same direction. "Good boy" is, to say the least, not the easiest of roles. He did indeed seem "lost" in the session, ignored by both Mother and Father and seemingly having no alliance with Tom. His occasional use of humor would be consistent with his being in the "mascot" role. For all this seeming isolation, one wonders about the sexualized teasing by Mother. What's that like for a pubescent boy? Again, the boundary problem in this family. Minuchin would almost surely address some of his first interventions to Sam. What is Sam's role in the family's dynamics? Is he ever allowed to be "bad"? Does he occupy all the good space, leaving no "good" space for Tom? Does the family put Tom in a kind of double bind, overtly enjoining him to be good while covertly telling him that his role is to be the bad boy? Perhaps Dad needs him to enact the self that he has relinquished. On the other hand, this is a session that has been convened to deal with Tom's drug addiction, and perhaps Sam's neglect by the family is atypical and his silence is atypical. We can't be sure. This needs exploration, but it is very odd that Mother doesn't, for all practical purposes, mention him in her long monologues.

What are the internal mechanisms and forces in this family? What is keeping them stuck? Mother tells us that in practical ways they are far from stuck, being ambitious, upwardly mobile people. Has there been a failure of selfobject relating here, leaving Tom to form his selfobject relations with marijuana and "scumbags"? In the Scharffs'

(1991) terms, there has been a failure of the contextual mutual transferences; the holding in this family is not strong enough to contain its centrifugal forces. This seems to be so. Yet this may not be the case. Both Mother and Father deny it, however defensively; they passionately believe that they are loving, supportive parents. So this could be, in Steinglass's (1987) terms, a family with addiction rather than an addicted family. We don't know enough yet to be sure.

Then there is the intergenerational. Is Tom the least differentiated of the family members, or, paradoxically, is it Sam, the good boy? Have Mom and Dad projected their undifferentiation from their respective families onto Tom? They don't come across as undifferentiated, so I don't think so; yet it is possible. The parents are people who struggled mightily to emerge from the pathology of their families of origin, and they have in some ways admirably succeeded; yet they may be unconsciously re-creating some of the undifferentiation in their own families. I wonder if some of Dad's rage at Tom is transferential as he sees his alcoholic father being re-created in his drug-addicted son. Is this interpretable to this unsophisticated, unpsychologically minded man? How can I track? Say this in a way that he can hear it, and how relevant is it anyway, given the strong here-and-now determinants of his rage? Who knows, but it's worth a try. This family is too angry and needs help chilling out. I also thought of Guntrip's (1968) "Hate is love made angry" in thinking of Father's rage at son. There is the hurt underlying the rage.

There is yet another aspect of the intergenerational drama. There is a significant amount of apparently exclusively male alcoholism in Father's family, and it sounds a helluva lot like Cloninger's (1983) male-limited alcoholism, which has a heavy genetic loading. Although the heritability of other chemical addiction is inferential, one wonders how much genetic loading predisposes Tom to addiction. Clearly he does not "smoke well." He is not a kid partying; he is an addict. How large a role does constitutional predisposition play in his addiction? Has he (and the family) been educated about his biological vulnerability in his previous therapy or at his TC? We don't know enough about this family, and regardless of school (experientialists and possibly behaviorists excepted), the therapist either needs to take a careful multigenerational history or to construct a genogram.

What are the existential issues here? What does Tom's addiction help him and his family avoid—separation, tension in the marriage, aging, the decline of the maternal grandparents who have become parents to both Harriet and Rob? Suspicion that their material success isn't enough and something—something in the realm of meaning or values—is missing? We don't know, and that is something we need to be on the lookout for. Struggling to care for a sick (i.e., addicted) kid gives meaning and purpose to one's life. Would Tom's cure leave this family at sea and directionless?

What about the object relations side of things? Tom is both an exciting and a rejecting object for each of the others. Mom is an exciting object, enticing and dangerous. Rob primarily plays the antilibidinal rejecting object, and Sam's role in object relations terms is less clear. Seen in this way, it becomes strikingly clear that there is no ideal object, and not a strong enough central ego anywhere to give this family the cohesion it needs to help Tom recover and to itself move on. That is why the family's holding, selfobject function, and contextual transference fail. It is an interlocking system of exciting and rejecting objects. I am speaking here of the family members as external objects for each other; they are, of course, also internal objects insofar as they are activating internal object relations, which are then projected onto them. The therapist is going to have to figure out (if he or she is working at all dynamically) what each is projecting on the others. What exciting and what rejecting objects are being projected on Mother by Father and Tom, by bad boy onto good boy and Mother and Father, by Father onto Mother and onto his sons? Who are the original objects and what are the splits in their respective selves? In short, what is the internal drama being played out in the external actions of this family?

Perhaps even more importantly, can the therapist provide the holding, build a strong enough contextual or selfobject transference to anchor this family and enable their growth? What can the therapist do to facilitate this, if anything? We know that Tom did well in the TC, which, if it was a good one, provided a powerful holding environment. This suggests that on the more behavioral level, Tom needs structure. One also wonders how much the TC functioned as a holding environment for the entire family. Mother talks of emotionally open family sessions there. This augurs well; if they could do it there, perhaps they can do it here.

Finally, what basic assumptions are being played out in this family? On the conscious level, this session is a task group working to help Tom get clean; at an unconscious level, there is a dependence of all on all and all on the whole, mostly unacknowledged or denied; fight and flight are all over the place; pairing is there, overtly between Mother and Father, Sam and Mother, and perhaps Tom and Mother or Tom and Father; and fusion/fission and defenses against them are readily apparent. All families work on both task and basic assumptions levels, but in this family, the basic assumptions group overwhelms the task group. This is a useful way of organizing the complex material of this session and of thinking of ways of working with it.

Similarly, Melanie Klein's (1921–1945, 1946–1963) developmental scheme throws light on this family's functioning. Rarely do they work from the depressive position of tolerance for ambivalence, mourning, and reparation for damage done; they readily regress to the paranoid-schizoid position, perhaps also to the autistic-contiguous position. Of course, all of human action is a complex dialectical interplay of the various Kleinian positions; however, in healthy maturity, the depressive position predominates. That is not the case with the Bakers. This means that the therapist must be alert to the projections and projective identifications rampant in the family's interactions. They may or may not be interpretable, but awareness of them strengthens the therapist as understanding reduces the disabling consequences of countertransference. Now let us go back to the session and look at how the various schools might work with this family.

STRATEGIC/COMMUNICATION

The strategic therapist would immediately search for strategies for engaging and changing this family. The strategist would be concerned with taking control of the therapeutic situation. Antecedent to strategy is the question of strategy for what, so the first task of the strategist is to figure out what problems this family has, and what sort of dysfunction. This is not a why inquiry but a what inquiry. What are the dysfunctional behaviors? In common with the other schools and lay opinion, Mother's dominance is seen to effectively blunt communication in the Baker family. So the first strategy will focus on containing Mother and correlatively bringing out the other family members. The second problem is the behavior of the identified patient. Whatever function his addiction serves for the other family members, Tom's drug use is unquestionably problematic. It requires immediate attention and a strategy must be devised for dealing with it. Antecedent, though not entirely distinct from containing Mother and sobering Tom, is the strategic therapist's taking control.

Let us look at the control issue from the point of view of a strategist. First, it is assumed that each and every member of the family is vying for control within the family and without it—here in relationship with the therapist. This is an a priori assumption, since the struggle for power in every human relationship is axiomatic for this school. This is an important point. The therapist's knowledge of the ongoing, here-and-now struggle for power is not empirical; it is something "known," even before the family has been met. This a priori knowledge does not tell the therapist how the power struggle will manifest itself, merely that it will be inexorably present. Like any theory, Haley's (1990) tells the therapist what to look for. It was once empirical, too. That is, Haley presumably arrived at his belief in the universality of the drive for power and dominance from experience (rather than from personal hang-ups or bias), and made an inductive leap from that experience to a "rule" or a scientific generalization or principle or law, here the law of the centrality of power in human relations. The generalization now directs our attention to a new particular—the family relations of the family at hand, in this case the Bakers. But Haley's generalization does more than direct our attention to the particular manifestations in the case we are treating. This is so because the generalization does more than state that power aspects of relations are universal; it states that they are the center and core of every human relationship. That they are the most salient thing happening. Further, there is a treatment corollary of this generaliza-tion. Haley's technique is directly derived from his theory. The im-plication of power for therapeutic technique is that the first task of the therapist is to gain control of the session and of the treatment. Concretely this means activity and directiveness on the part of the therapist.

Before saying how this might play out in an actual session, it will be useful to look at the Baker family through the prism of power-dominance-control, remembering that passivity can be extremely controlling and inactivity highly active. As the existential philosopher Martin Heidegger (1927) said in another context, *"Das Nicht nichts,"* "the nothing nothings." Let us look at how the Bakers dominate and nothing.

Mother's control is perhaps not only the easiest to see, but the easiest to deal with. She is up front, the boss, making the appoint-ment, presenting the problem, literally putting the family members in their place. An analytic or intergenerational therapist might won-der where she is coming from. Are her attempts to control an effort to reverse a position of powerlessness in her family of origin? Is she compensating for low self-esteem? Is she merely filling a void? The strategist is uninterested in all this. It is irrelevant. What counts is coming up with a strategy to defeat Mom at arm wrestling. Dad's style is physical intimidation. However much Mom appears to be boss, Dad may very well have the final say: "One reason I called is I was afraid that Dad would beat the shit out of Tom."

Haley doesn't much talk about it, but the strategist must be some-thing of an analyst, at least in the sense of analyzing the real power relations in the family. Be this as it may, Dad has his own strategies for dominance and control, and the therapist must settle his hash also. One wonders if Haley would duke it out with him. Tom is perhaps the most interesting power broker. As the "perp," as they say in po-lice circles, that is, the identified patient, Tom is at the center of things. That in itself gives him enormous power. In a very real sense, he, not Mother, controls the Baker family. This "secondary gain," to borrow a concept from another, the analytic, tradition, may very well be powerfully maintaining Tom's addiction. Getting the family's focus off Tom may be curative, although he presumably would fight such a loss of control by escalating his acting out. Humans don't relinquish power easily or gladly.

Here is one place where interpretation so foreign to the strategic school makes sense, even from the strategic perspective. The family needs to be told that the tail is wagging the dog, and Tom needs to know that he is getting off on the attention his drug use brings him. In strategic therapy we don't ask why, only what and how. Yet we cannot help but wonder why Tom meets his power needs in this way. Are Mother and Father simply too powerful in their respective styles for him to have a modicum of power in any other way? Or has he so undermined his opportunities for alternate satisfactions of his power needs that the interpersonal pull of his addiction is all that he has left?

Although the strategist isn't interested in, but does not deny, the reality of underlying process, Tom, in common with all addicts, knows and feels that he is out of control and powerless to control his addiction, making the "control" he exercises over his family and the feelings of empowerment he derives from it a stringent psychic necessity for him. The strategist may overtly ignore all of this, but whatever may be the case as far as Tom's conscious, semiconscious, and unconscious motivations are concerned, the strategist will rightly move in in some way on Tom's being the tail that wags the dog. Of course, Tom's drug use itself gives him the illusion of power and control. Again in common with all addicts, his chemical courage and his reactive grandiosity are camouflage for underlying feelings of worthlessness and powerlessness. This gives drugs an extraordinarily strong degree of power over him.

In their 1972 book, *The Drinking Man*, David McClelland and colleagues convincingly argue that men drink in order to feel (more) powerful. Their argument has strong empirical support from its analysis of folk tales of preliterate cultures where they found a significant correlation between cultures with a strong conflict between obedience and autonomy (which presumably left the obedient men feeling powerless, since to be autonomous, that is, powerful, brought them into intolerable conflict with authority) and drunkenness, a state in which they felt powerful. The stories these cultures told were about what McClelland and colleagues called "egoistic" power, that is, self-assertion, rather than "altruistic" power where the power is in the service of social goals. Drunkenness was depicted in their folk tales as a state in which men were powerful.

Interestingly, Child and colleagues (1965), studying the same cultures, found that societies that frustrated and/or punished the meeting of "male" dependency needs had the highest rates of drunkenness. One way to feel powerful is to "participate" in the power of others or of one's collective, so this study too supports McClelland and colleagues' assertion that "men drink to feel powerful."

Tom, of course, also fits the dependency conflict rubric, simultaneously asserting his "independence" and being totally dependent on family and on drugs. McClelland and colleagues present more direct evidence that men drink to feel egotistically powerful in a series of responses to Thematic Apperception Test (TAT) cards. In the TAT, subjects are shown situations that, unlike the Rorschach, are essentially realistic (the original set of cards had the look of old movie posters), and are instructed to tell what happened before the scene depicted, what is happening now, and what will happen. McClelland and colleagues conducted "cocktail parties" in which the subjects, Harvard graduate students, were told that they could drink all they wanted if they would tell some stories in "payment." The heavy drinkers told stories of egotistic power, and the more they drank, the more monothematic their stories became. Pot isn't booze, but it is not far-fetched to extrapolate from McClelland and colleagues' findings and to postulate that "men smoke pot in order to feel powerful."

The Twelve-Step Program makes the issue of power central to its ideology. The first of the twelve steps of spiritual (emotional) growth states, "We admitted we were *powerless* over alcohol—that our lives had become unmanageable" (Alcoholics Anonymous World Services 1955, p. 5). Of course, this admission of powerlessness has a paradoxical Zen-like twist to it: the act of admitting powerlessness empowers. Twelve-Step further teaches reliance on a *Higher Power*, which, theological implications apart, is a didactic or cognitive intervention intended to enjoin (or teach) a healthy form of dependency.

Bill Wilson is the AA co-founder and author of *Twelve-Steps and Twelve Traditions* (Alcoholics Anonymous World Services 1952), known as the "12 and 12," a guide to and interpretation of the twelve steps, which Wilson modified from a similar set of steps expounded by the Oxford Movement. This was a sort of upper-class revival movement originating at Oxford University that Wilson joined when he first became sober, but found wanting insofar as it preached and talked down to alcoholics rather than sharing with them. He made sharing the central tenet of AA ("AA is a fellowship of men and women who *share* their experience, strength and hope with each other" says the AA preamble, which is read at every meeting), and used the example of our dependence on electrical power as an example of healthy dependence.

Thus there is a reciprocal relationship between admitting dependency needs and relinquishing grandiose illusions of power. Instead of claiming power for self, the recovering Twelve–Step person "hits bottom," throws in the towel, admits powerlessness, and then meets his or her power needs relationally, in relationship with the group, with the program, with the sponsor, and for some with the Higher Power. This "epistemological shift," to use Bateson's (1971) categorization of it, can be conceptualized as a shift from a mirror to an idealizing transference. Interestingly, Twelve-Step literature mostly ignores the mirror and idealizing transference to the substance of abuse, although there are references in the Twelve-Step literature to "alcohol being the alcoholic's Higher Power," and to alcohol as the controller, with that control being the reality behind the alcoholic's insistence that he or she can control the controller.

Returning to the Bakers, it is clear that none of them has admitted powerlessness, whether that powerlessness be Tom's vis-à-vis pot or his parents' vis-à-vis Tom. A Twelve-Step approach would push for open recognition of what is clearly the case—Tom can't control his pot smoking and Mom and Dad can't control another human being, here their addicted son.

So the vicissitudes of power as central, salient, and determinative of behavior and dynamics of self and system, of addict and family, is not exclusively the insight of the strategist; in their respective ways, the social-psychological researcher McClelland, the alcoholic Wilson's self-help movement, and the Kohutian analyst subscribe to the same belief. The difference is not so much in the analysis of dynamics, as in what they do with that analysis. The strategist's form of "ego deflation" is direct, confrontational, and self-consciously aiming for control. The strategic school having grown out of the communication school of family therapy (founded by Bateson while Haley was part of Bateson's team), strategists still pay extremely careful attention to communication and its disturbances. They make extensive use of paradoxical interventions, including therapeutic double binds. How would that work in our first session with the Bakers?

In common with therapists of all schools, our strategist would start by listening and trying to figure out what's going on. One thing that's going on is that the family talks "about" and not "to."

> *Strategist*: Nobody in this family talks to anyone else. You talk about each other, but not to each other.
> *Mother*: Talking to him is useless.
> *Strategist*: I want you to pretend that he doesn't exist. (This is a paradoxical intervention.)
> *Tom:* She never listens to me.
> *Father*: Why should she? Your brain has turned to shit and you don't make sense. (Note that they are now talking to each other, and that the therapist has taken control of the session.)

What about a double bind? Are the Bakers telling Tom that if he continues to smoke, he is hateful and bad, yet telling him that if he quits, the family will suffer in some catastrophic way? There is certainly a subtext here, and some family needs are being met by Tom's continuing use—Mother's for power, Father's to stay angry and perhaps vicariously act out, Sam's to continue as good boy and favorite, and perhaps some avoidance of latent conflict, say between the parents as well, yet this family sincerely wants Tom to stop and this is not a classic double-bind situation. The Bakers' communications aren't that disturbed. So the therapist in this case isn't going to go after the double bind. What he will do is to formulate a plan, a strategy, to effectuate change and to take control by using directives, perhaps paradoxical directive.

> *Strategist*: I want you all to totally control Tom. Tell him how to run his life down to the last detail. Tell him when he's going to shit, when to get up, when to and what to eat, what programs to watch, what music to play.

This is a form of prescribing the symptom. The hoped-for result is for the family to realize that they can't control Tom. As they let go, he will cease to have a reason to rebel and insofar as his addiction is driven by rebellion, will smoke less or not at all.

> *Strategist* (to Sam): I want you to do everything you're told, to clean the house, to help Tom in any way you can, to help Dad and Mom. I want you to be so good that your brother will learn how he should act. I want you to study more and work harder at your Bar Mitzvah lessons. You shouldn't go out with your friends so you will have more time to be at home to help your parents.

Presumably, our good boy Sam will be unable to stand such an overdose of goodness and will rebel. In his rebellion, he will gain some freedom for himself, shake up the family system, relinquish his form of control—good boys are rewarded and loved and parents jump through hoops for them—and occupy some of the bad boy space now exclusively occupied by Tom, perhaps driving him out of it.

> *Strategist* (to Tom): I want you to smoke as much pot as you can. Light up a joint when you get out of bed. Have one with break-fast. Stay stoned all day and all night and make sure you have a joint before you go to bed.

Presumably having permission to get high will take some of the kick out of it for Tom. No more rebellion. If he follows the instruc-tion, he will be too stoned to get any pleasure out of it, and may voluntarily give it up—or he may rebel and be oppositional by not smoking—so if he follows the instruction he may get clean, and if he doesn't, he may get clean.

The strategist has now taken control. He is enacting his power in his paradoxical directives. He has a strategy. He may have laid the groundwork for his interventions by asking the family what they were prepared to do to solve the problem. If they say they will do anything, he has set them up and the Bakers are desperate enough to probably agree that they will do anything to get Tom clean. If the strategy works, things are certainly going to escalate in the Baker family. Things may become hellish, but the status quo—the homeostasis, which is also hellish—will be disturbed. All in all, it is not a bad strategy, but what about prescribing around-the-clock pot smoking for Tom? This has some support in the AA statement that, "John Barleycorn is the best convincer," and the not infrequent injunction to resistant members to "go out and tie one on." Nevertheless, I have my doubts. Tom's level of psychopathology is an unknown. He may be a borderline kid who could be driven across the border into a psychotic break by saturation cannabis intake. It is risky. But Tom has had a lot of treatment and nothing has worked. He is already in danger. Desperate situations sometimes call for desperate measures, and a case can be made for the strategist's paradoxical directives to the Bakers, including the one to Tom to smoke pot around the clock. Note that the strategist takes power, he does not discuss it or interpret it. The power relations in the family are disturbed by the paradoxical directives, but there is no attempt to increase insight. It is not my way of working, but I have seen therapists work with families with chronic teenage drug users in exactly the way our strategist did with success.

STRUCTURALIST

The structuralist is also interested in power and control, both between therapist and family and within the family. Generally speaking, the structuralist will work to strengthen the parental dyad. (I tremble for my soul when I use phrases like "parental dyad," but such is the state of the art.)

> *Structuralist* (Early on, when Mom has described Dad's circumcision; mostly to Mom but directed at all): What happened to the tip? Do you still have it?

This intervention does several things. As we saw earlier, when all the therapists were speaking together, it elicited some rebellion and humor on the part of Sam. More importantly, it takes power away from Mother, essentially neutralizing her. Although not altogether apparent in the segment of the session we have, openness about sex verging on crudeness, bantering, humor, and informality are part of this family's style, as is a certain degree of exhibitionism, and the structuralist here is "tracking," speaking in the family's style. The therapist takes control and at the same time "joins" the family, making a remark a family member might have made. This particular comment is closest to Sam's occasional near wisecracks. The castrating mother and presumably castrated father are recast as benign and intact, respectively—sort of.

From the structuralist's viewpoint, this is an enmeshed family. Differentiation is difficult, and one reason Tom may hold onto his addiction is to differentiate himself from the enmeshment and this may be true in spite of the strong element of identification with Father in Tom's drug usage. One way to demonstrate the enmeshment is to construct a structural map.

This family could be mapped in several ways using Minuchin's system of dashes for clear boundaries, dots for diffuse boundaries, one line for rigid boundary, two lines for affiliation, and three lines for overinvolvement. There are also symbols for conflict, coalition, and detouring (see Figure 12–2).

I have constructed the map (Figure 12–3) to demonstrate Sam's rigid boundary (apparent distance) from Tom and Father and his affiliation with Mother. One suspects that Sam is overinvolved with Mother and two parallel lines connecting Sam and Mom may change to three parallel lines in the structural map as we get more data.

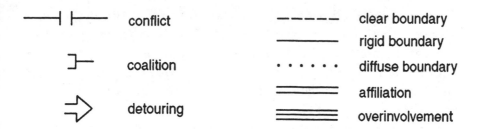

⊢ ⊢	conflict	– – – – –	clear boundary
		———	rigid boundary
⊐⊢	coalition	· · · · · ·	diffuse boundary
		═══	affiliation
⟹	detouring	≡≡≡	overinvolvement

FIGURE 12-2. Minuchin's Symbol System

Mother is overinvolved with Tom, although also in conflict with him, but I choose to highlight the overinvolvement in my structural map. Mother has an apparently diffuse boundary with Father in which she defines him and in some ways assimilates him. His fury directed at Tom may be partly coming from his struggle to differentiate from his wife. Her "castrating" stance toward her husband can also be seen as a kind of engulfment, manifested in such behavior as speaking for him. Father seems to have a rigid boundary with his younger son and little relationship with him, but this may be an artifact of Tom's being the center of the present crisis, so this mapping too may have to be revised as more data become available. Father has a diffuse boundary with his wife and is in intense conflict with his older son, with whom he is also overinvolved. In the map, I highlight the conflict.

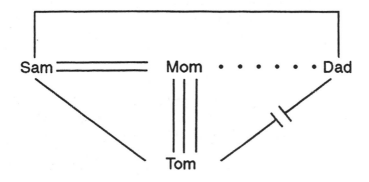

FIGURE 12-3. Structural map of the Baker family.

Tom, the identified patient (IP), is cut off from his brother, overinvolved with his mother, and in conflict with his father. Note the lack of clear hierarchy in the Baker family as here mapped. Contrast it with the Jones family (Figure 12–4), where Mother and Father have an alliance and each relates to, but has clear boundaries from each of their children, c_1 and c_2.

For didactic purposes, we have mapped the Bakers too early and are going to have to rework our map. Nevertheless, the usefulness of Minuchin's structural map is apparent. The aloofness of Sam, the lack of hierarchy, and the weakness and confusion of the parental alliance are very clear in the map. The device is limited insofar as it is difficult to depict complexity in relationships, but this is also advantageous in that it forces the therapist to choose the most salient relational characteristic of the various subsets of the family (a subset can be an individual). How would you map the Bakers?

The structuralist would move to strengthen the parents in their alliance and to help them "control" the "bad boy." Here we see an exactly opposite approach to that of the strategist.

> *Structuralist* (to parents): You have to stop Tom's drug use immediately.
> *Mom and Dad:* We'd love to but we can't.
> *Structuralist*: You support him, don't you?
> *Mom*: Of course.
> *Structuralist*: You'll support him into the grave. Tell him he can't live in *your* home if he smokes pot and that you won't give him a cent until he stops except for treatment.

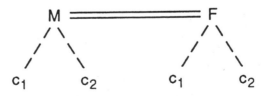

FIGURE 12–4. Structural map of the Jones family.

Here the structuralist is teaching "tough love." Note *"your* home," which simultaneously points to a source of parental power and speaks to parental alliance; they own their home together and have the power to decide who will live in it.

Mother: We can't just throw him out.
Father: Why not?
Mother: People will say we're monsters.
Structuralist: That's a cop-out.
Tom: You can shove your house up your ass.
Structuralist: If they do, you surely won't be able to live in it.
Tom (to structuralist): Fuck you.
Structuralist (to parents): Are you serious about wanting Tom to get clean? If you are, you have to be tough. Tell him he's out, and you won't do a thing for him if he uses.
Mother: Right now?
Structuralist: You bet.
Father (to Mother): Harriet, let's do it.
Mother (looking shaken): Okay.
Structuralist: Tell him.
Father: You're out of here if you use any more of that shit.
Structuralist: Mother?
Mother: I agree.
Structuralist (to Mother): Tell Tom, "Dad and I have decided no drugs in our house. And no users either."
Mother (weeping): Tom, the therapist is right. We'll worry about you, but Dad and I won't let you live with us if you keep smoking.
Structuralist (raising the ante): And you have to arrange urine monitoring. I'll tell you how.
Tom: A piss test too?
Structuralist: If you're taking piss tests, you can't get pissed.
Tom (to structuralist): Asshole. (But his bravado is crumbling. He is clearly upset.)
Structuralist (to Sam): Tell Tom you won't have anything to do with him if he uses.
Sam (gloating and joyful): I won't give you shit if you get stoned.

> *Structuralist* (to Sam): You're really getting off on this, but that's not important now. The important thing is to get Tom clean. (To Tom): You have no place to go, kid.
> *Tom:* (cries).

Our structuralist is every bit as directive as the strategist, but his direction takes a different tack. For the structuralist, some of the strategist's paradoxical directives were just too dangerous, although structuralists typically are willing to take risks to move families off ground zero. Our strategist assumes some degree of health in the parents' relationship and works to strengthen it and to establish or reestablish a hierarchical relationship between parents and children. Everything he does aims at establishing clear, but not overly rigid, boundaries and to unmesh the family. Here the unmeshing is unusually directive: sever your ties with the drug user if he won't stop. The Bakers didn't come to the session to conduct an "intervention," yet the structuralist has maneuvered them into (in effect) doing one. This structuralist approach would not have worked with a "sicker," that is, more enmeshed, family where the unconscious needs to keep Tom using were more powerful. It also assumes a certain degree of health in the parental relationship. Typically, the work a structuralist does needs some preliminaries, some loosening of Tom's symbiosis with Mother (however defended against) and some loosening of Father's projective identification with Tom. These are analytic terms, but they are perfectly applicable to the structuralist's analysis of enmeshment.

> *Structuralist* (to Tom): We will do anything to help you stop. Perhaps you can't stop—if you need detoxification you can have it; if you need medication, that can be arranged; if you need to go back into the TC or to a rehab, that's okay too; or you can keep coming here.

Here the structuralist is using a little paradox—"Perhaps you can't stop"—although that may be true, and he is being supportive. Structuralists often support or ally with the identified patient to "unbalance" the system. Another structuralist approach would do that.

Structuralist 2: Being high must be great. What's it like?
Or Structuralist 2 (to Tom): Your parents are really up your ass.

In both these interventions, the structuralist is tracking, joining the family, unbalancing, and forming an alliance with Tom all at once. Our first structuralist indirectly joined with Father in his question about the foreskin. A more direct approach would have been:

Structuralist (to Father, interrupting Mother): You don't get to say much, do you?

Or the first structural intervention could have been addressed to the "lost child" good boy:

Structuralist (to Sam): Do your parents ever pay any attention to you?

This also unbalances the family, disrupts their obsession with Tom, and shakes the homeostasis, making change at least possible. It may also serve to help the family member in the most long-term danger. Reframing is another typically structural intervention. If it were the case, the structuralist might say, "Tom stays stoned to keep the family together. If he gets clean, you two (indicating the parents) are going to have to talk to each other and deal with your problems. Tom is afraid you won't be able to do that and will divorce." There may indeed be some degree of this dynamic in the Baker family, but if present we do not have the evidence for it, and our structuralist wonders about this possibility, but goes to helping the parents put the screws on Tom. A more on-target reframing would be, "Tom uses because he thinks that's what everyone expects him to do, not only in the family, either, and he doesn't know how to fill any other role." This makes Tom less the "bad child," cuts down on the recrimination, and makes Tom's use a system problem, at least in part, which indeed it has to be, at least in part. It isn't used here because the structuralist chooses to address the "crisis," but that doesn't preclude its later use.

Our structuralist has done a good job. He has played to the strengths of the family, successfully joined them, made good use of tracking, clarified and strengthened boundaries, and given the family a means of dealing with their crisis. Tom is probably going to get clean. Would it be so easy! Usually it is not, but sometimes it is, and this sort of highly directive structural approach should be in the repertoire of the addiction family therapist.

INTERGENERATIONAL SYSTEMIC

The *genogram* is integral to the intergenerational approach, and the systemic therapist would make construction of the genogram one of his or her first therapeutic tasks. The Bakers spontaneously gave us a good deal of information about the family's antecedents and our systemic therapist would build on that information by asking questions to flesh out the genealogies. Bowen has a set of genogram symbols (Figure 12–5).

The genogram can be elaborated by indicating spouses of fathers and mothers, siblings and their children, and the IP's cousins as has been done in Figure 12–6. This was relevant in the Baker case, since two of Tom's cousins are drug-involved and he has a relationship with them. A systemic therapist will elicit as much information as possible to help in constructing the genogram.

> *Intergenerationalist* (successively to Dad and then to Mother, ignoring the children): Did anyone in your family of origin drink heavily? Who? Have there been any deaths associated with drinking or drugging? Divorces? (And so forth, going back at least to the parents' parents, and better, to the parents' grandparents.)
>
> *Dad*: My Dad's liver went and it killed him. My brothers are heading in the same direction.

The genogram vividly depicts the multigenerational problem drinking in Father's family and the equally salient fact that Father is the

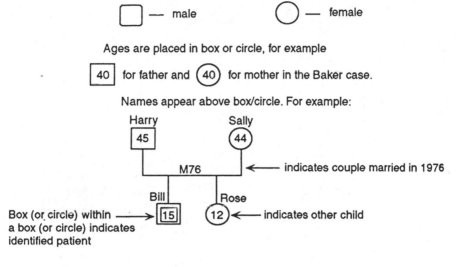

Names appear above box/circle. For example:

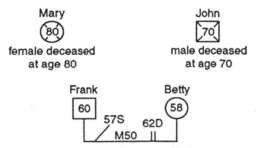

Other conventional symbols:

Mary — female deceased at age 80

John — male deceased at age 70

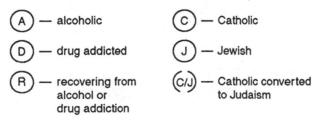

Slant line with date followed by S indicates date of separation. Parallel lines perpendicular to marriage line with date followed by D indicates date of divorce.

We will add symbols for substance abuse and religion.

(A) — alcoholic   (C) — Catholic

(D) — drug addicted   (J) — Jewish

(R) — recovering from   (C/J) — Catholic converted
      alcohol or   to Judaism
      drug addiction

FIGURE 12-5. Genogram symbols.

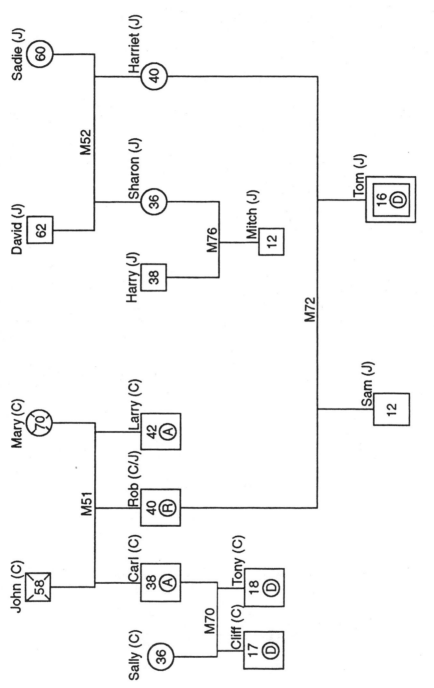

FIGURE 12–6. Baker family genogram.

only family member who has recovered (or at least stopped drinking, Twelve-Step making a distinction between being "dry" [merely abstaining] and being "sober" ["working the program" to enable growth]). Whether the transmission be genetic, cultural, learned, psychodynamic, or the result of Bowenian intergenerational undifferentiation, the males in the Baker family are at high risk for addiction.

The intergenerational therapist is definitely not a joiner, at least as incarnated by Bowen, yet like every other therapist, he needs to forge a therapeutic alliance. The construction of a genogram with the family enables this alliance. The therapist is definitely the expert here, yet is engaged in a cooperative venture with the family. Further, the construction of the genogram is not merely meaningful process, as important as that may be, to be left as therapy progresses. On the contrary, it is a tool that is repeatedly utilized. This is particularly so in substance abuse cases like the Bakers.' It can be used didactically to demonstrate the dim odds of Tom becoming an occasional pot smoker. Further, it is an objectification, an artifact that is hard to dispute and serves as a form of dispassionate evidence. In a family as volatile and as upset as the Bakers, this pacification function of the genogram may be important and powerful.

Since Rob's conversion is central to the Bakers' family dynamics, religion can be added to the genogram. The solidness of the Catholicism in the Baker family makes Father's conversion stand out. It clearly took courage—love, perhaps—for him to break with his family in this regard. Again, the genogram clarifies and vivifies the context of individual actions.

In the case of the Bakers, the information necessary for the construction of the genogram was easily elicited. The family's style of openness almost to the point of exhibitionism made the systematist's task easy. This is by no means always the case. Family secrets are not easily divulged, even within the family, let alone to strangers. This is particularly true of substance abusing families and, to a lesser extent, of families with a substance abuser, to again use Steinglass's differential. There is a Twelve–Step slogan, "You are as sick as your secrets," with which I agree. It isn't so much the content as the secretiveness itself that sometimes literally, and always figuratively, drives people crazy. Families that lie, distort, deceive, and withhold often make the construction of a meaningful genogram difficult, if not impossible. Substance abuse in significant others or even remote others and its frequent concomitants—spousal abuse, child abuse (physical and sexual), and suicide—are not readily shared. Additionally, secrecy within the family, particularly in earlier generations, may make the necessary information unavailable to the family in treatment. So ignorance, unconscious repressive processes, and conscious deception and denial all contribute to the genogrammer's woes.

The prevalence of conscious deception in substance-abusing families in treatment brings to mind Freud's (1905b) story of the Jewish man in Eastern Europe deeply into *yiches* (social status) who goes to the *shadchen* (marriage broker) to arrange a marriage with a woman of good pedigree. The marriage broker assures the prospective groom that all the candidate's relatives were upstanding and outstanding people, including the prospective bride's dead father. The deal is made and the wedding takes place. Several months later, the groom infuriatingly accosts the marriage broker, "You're a liar and a thief. You told me that my father-in-law was dead and I just found out he's alive and in jail." Nonplussed, the marriage broker replies, "You call that living?" Many families are just as honest as the marriage broker.

You don't have to be an intergenerationalist to love genograms. Therapists in many schools find them useful and incorporate their use into their technique. This is particularly true for substance abuse therapists who are rightfully interested in addiction in the family. A word of caution here. Overzealous addiction therapists press extraordinarily hard to unearth the family antecedents of addiction, searching out the alcoholic in grandparents or great-grandparents with the passion of a McCarthyite seeking out Communists in a government agency. Usually such therapists are committed to the heritability wing of the disease model contingent of therapists. If you look hard enough, you will find addiction or compulsion in any family, and the result is trivial. Not only is it trivial, but it blurs the differential, obscuring the saliency of familial, intergenerational addiction in the treatment of the family at hand. In the Bakers' case, that history is indeed salient.

Our systemic intergenerationalist would work in a dispassionate, researcherlike manner in eliciting the information needed to construct the genogram. Further, he or she would work individually, that is, question each family member individually rather than solicit a familial response. The intention here is to encourage individuation or, to use Bowen's word, *differentiation*, to sculpt individuals out of the family mass. (I always misread "family mass" as "family mess" and envision the differentiated ones as fecal dolls, but no doubt that's my problem.) From the systemic point of view, the therapist's stance and style are more important than the content of his/her interventions. Nothing is more relevant to the proper therapeutic stance than the therapist's own differentiation. In common with most other therapists, but more so, the intergenerationalist's goal in this first session is *evaluation*. Construction of the genogram is an essential part of this evaluation.

> *Intergenerationalist*: Mr. Baker, can we analyze the drinking in your family? If we do, we can clearly see that all of the men have trouble with alcohol. Your son's drugging is entirely consistent with your family history.
>
> *Mother* (humorously, to husband): I knew the problem was on your side. (To therapist): Okay, it runs on Dad's side. How does that help us?
>
> *Intergenerationalist* (refusing to be "triangulated"): Mrs. Baker, I'm talking to Mr. Baker about his family.
>
> *Mother* (to Tom): You see, you just can't get high; you have the addiction gene from Dad.
>
> *Intergenerationalist*: Mrs. Baker, you're bringing Tom into it because you don't want to deal with my saying to you that I was talking to your husband. First you broke up my dialogue with your husband, and now you're bringing in your son. It's hard for you to stay with or tolerate two-person relationships. You either become or bring in a third person.

Here the intergenerationalist interrupts the elucidation and elaboration of the intergenerational analysis to comment on and indeed arrest attempts at triangulation in the here and now of the family session. In his analysis, he sees triangulation rather than castration by Mrs. Baker. In her own undifferentiation, she has trouble allowing the differentiation of others. From this point of view, although her aggression appears to be in the service of separation, it is actually driven by the need for fusion, which is seen as central to the family dynamic. Tom is a clear case of "emotional cutoff," resulting in a false self or a pseudo–self-sufficiency. He is neither fused nor differentiated, and uses drugs to do both. He fuses with the drug and simultaneously isolates himself from his family. I would comment on this early in treatment, perhaps in this first session. I assume an intergenerationalist might say something like this:

> *Intergenerationalist* (to Tom): When you get high, you feel independent. You are able to get some distance from your family. But then, just as you're feeling like yourself, you lose yourself in the fog of your high.

But then again, he might not. More typical of the Bowenian approach would be to see Tom's drug problem as a correlative of his parents' relative undifferentiation and projection of undifferentiation onto him, this being so in spite of the relatively high degree of differentiation in the Baker family when compared to, let us say, a schizophrenic family. So the Bowenian therapist is much more likely to say:

> *Intergenerationalist*: In our session today, I have been able to see some patterns both in your immediate family and in your extended family. I would like to coach you in ways to change some of those patterns, the ones that are making it difficult for Tom to grow up. The best way I can do that is by meeting with Tom's parents. Mr. and Mrs. Baker, would you be willing to meet with me without the children?
>
> *Dad*: If you're trying to put it on us, you're crazy, doc.
>
> *Intergenerationalist*: Not at all. I always suggest meetings with the parents to help them help their children become independent.

Tom: If you want to cook up some scheme for my folks to run my
  life, go ahead. It ain't going to work.
Intergenerationalist: My meeting with your parents scares you, so
  you butt in.
Tom: Fuck you.
Dad: Let's do it.
Mom: What the hell, okay.

And the arrangement is made. Presumably the intergenerationalist
will coach the parents in differentiating themselves from their families of origin, thereby reducing or eliminating their need to triangulate Tom and to project undifferentiation onto him. Sam, who may
actually be the less differentiated child, although not caught up in
emotional cutoff, would also benefit from this strategy.

An alternative intergenerational strategy would be to "coach" Tom
individually, focusing not on his drug use but on his lack of differentiation. This has merit, but I have my doubts how well it would work
without Tom's abstinence.

Yet another intergenerational strategy would be to continue to work
with the genogram to increase the Bakers' awareness of, not the neurochemical genetic, but the intergenerational transmission patterns
culminating with Tom's addiction.

EXPERIENTIAL

Unlike the Bowenian intergenerationalist with his coolness and analytic detachment, an experientialist would wade right in, joining and
engaging in the "political battle."

Experientialist: Shit, I can't even control my own kids, how the hell
  do you think I'm going to control yours? Half the time, I can't
  even control myself.
Father: I can kick his ass the fuck out of the house.
Experientialist (Thinks, *I won that political battle. Dad's taking responsibility*; to Dad): That's not a bad idea.

Mom: We can't do that.

Experientialist (Thinks, *I should have known that was too easy*; to Mom): Well, if you don't want to exile the kid to Siberia, you could try to make things more peaceful at home.

Mom: How?

Experientialist: You could build him a greenhouse to grow pot in.

Father: You're nuts.

Experientialist: Dad, you could design it, and all of you could build it. It would bring the family together. You could all work on it. Mom could order the best seeds, Tijuana Gold. And Sam, you could water them every day. Dad, you could run in the electric power and pipe, and Tom, you could hoe. And it should have air conditioning and a state of the art stereo system.

Mother: We couldn't do that; we'd go to jail.

Experientialist: That's good. Tom's heading for jail, so that would help you understand him.

Tom: Assholes. He thinks you're helping me use by letting me live in the house, so he's making fun of you.

Experientialist (to Tom): Who, me?

Sam: I think we should build a tower on the greenhouse for Tom to hang himself from.

Experientialist: Maybe your parents could hang themselves too.

Mother (starts crying): I really do wish I was dead. I am so ashamed. I am so scared. I know Tom's going to die if he keeps this up and I can't live through that.

Experientialist (to Tom): What kind of funeral do you want? Shall we throw grass seeds on the grave?

Tom: Let me out of here. He is nuts.

Experientialist: Or maybe you'd like to go to Mom's funeral if they let you out of jail to attend.

Tom: Oh fuck.

Father (to therapist): He ain't no tough guy. I've been on the street and in the can. I know what it's like. It sucks, it really sucks.

Mother: Stop! I don't want to hear about it. Oh. Oh. Tom, you can't live in our house if you get high. You're out.

Experientialist: What would become of the greenhouse?

Tom: I can't stop. I feel like shit when I don't smoke. (Pauses). Just don't make me go back to that school and I'll try.

Father: Trying is bullshit. You can stop.

Mom (sobbing): Tom, just stay clean and I won't ask anything else.

Tom: Yeah, okay.

Mother (embraces Tom. He pulls away, then returns the embrace.)

Sam: Oh, shit.

Mother (pulls Sam into the embrace).

Father: Maybe it'll work this time.

Experientialist (to Dad, wiping away a tear): Maybe. (Looking at Mother and the boys.) I feel left out. How 'bout you and I hugging? (They do.)

Here our experiential therapist tries some theater of the absurd. Sensing that the family is enabling Tom in one way or another, he makes that enabling transparently clear, and that clarity shakes the family, moving them to remove their destructive support. The experientialist also intuits some of the subterranean themes in the Baker family: their fears (and perhaps wishes) that Tom would die, Dad's acquaintance with the night, Sam's hostility to Tom, and the desperate need of all four for love. A great deal of this surfaces in response to the experientialist's absurdity. This openness could be therapeutically exploited and expanded in a variety of ways, perhaps by probing for the parents' fears of death, which may be motivating their ambivalent enabling; for Tom to move toward adulthood underscores their own passage through time and the life cycle. There is some mourning work to be done before they can let Tom go.

Sam's comment brought to mind a particularly acrimonious divorce hearing in which I was an expert witness. Jane claimed Ken had put a quarter of a million dollars "up his nose" during his cocaine addiction. Ken was claiming disability and asking for support payments. Jane bitterly told the court that their assets were gone except for their condo, but that even that was virtually worthless because Ken had trashed it during one of his cocaine sprees. In the most innocent of little boy voices, Ken interrupted her to say, "The only damage I ever did to the apartment was to leave a hole in the ceiling when the hook pulled out when I tried to hang myself." The judge barely managed to restrain her laughter.

BEHAVIORAL

In contrast with the communication/strategic, structuralist, inter-generational, and experiential approaches, the behaviorist would focus on Tom's problem behavior. The IP is indeed the IP, although the family may be unwittingly reinforcing the objectionable behavior. So our behaviorist's work will be with the whole family and yet will focus on Tom. He will attempt to elicit drug signals, teach coping skills, and suggest ways the family can help Tom achieve abstinence. Constructing contingency schedules and the like are the essence of his approach. His role is teacherly.

> *Behaviorist*: There is an awful lot of anger directed at Tom. It's hard to stay clean when everyone is putting you down. I wonder if you would agree to say something positive to Tom three times each day until our next session.
> *Dad*: I've heard that positive reinforcement shit before. He never does anything right, so what could we reinforce?
> *Mom*: He's not that bad.
> *Sam*: (giggles).
> *Behaviorist*: Mr. Baker, I'm not asking you to reinforce behavior, just to say something positive. For example, "Thank you Tom for coming to therapy tonight." Or, "You look spiffy today."
> *Sam*: Spiffy?
> *Mom* (to Dad): You're too quick to hit. Why not try this? Do it for me.
> *Dad*: Well, he's handsome when he doesn't look strung out. That's not surprising since he looks like me. I'll tell him that.
> *Behaviorist*: Sam, what about you?
> *Sam*: Yeah?
> *Behaviorist* (Hands out forms): There are three blank spaces in each of the two columns on these forms. I want you to write down

your positive comments to Tom in the first column and we'll discuss them next week. (To Tom): Tom, I need you to do something, too. I want you to tell your parents and your brother that you appreciate their saying positive things. Just check it off each time you do that on this form. (Hands form to him.)

Tom: What if I don't feel it?

Behaviorist: Say it anyway.

Tom: That's like the NA (Narcotics Anonymous) slogan, "Bring the body and the mind will follow."

Behaviorist: Exactly. Will you do it?

Tom: Okay.

Our behaviorist approach and the NA slogan are interesting. If you want to get fancy, the social scientist Darryl Bem (1967) reports having empirical evidence that our attitudes are determined by our behavior as is our awareness of them in exactly the same way that we infer other people's attitudes from their behavior. I believe that similar work was cited in the Supreme Court desegregation decision or in the brief supporting it, the idea being that if you change the behavior—go to school with blacks—your attitude will be changed, too. This is classically behavioral stuff.

Notice how the behaviorist, somewhat like the intergenerationalist, cools the situation by being rational, calm, and reasonable, and ignores a lot of the emotion coming from the Bakers. He elicits cooperation by asking little, and his minimalist approach may open a door allowing broader change. He goes on to deal with drug signals.

Behaviorist (to Tom): You don't want to get high all the time, do you?

Sam: Yes, he does.

Tom: Shut up, creep. No, not all the time.

Behaviorist: So something must happen to make you want to smoke. We call that something a "trigger"; NA speaks of "places, people, and things" that make people want to use drugs. I would add "feelings" to that list. I want you to notice when you want to get high and write it down on this chart. (It may take a whole forest to provide the paper the behaviorist needs for his schedules, contingency charts, self-observational charts, and so forth.) As you can see, there's a place to write down the people, places, feelings, or things that precede or accompany your urge. For now, I am not asking you to stop getting high, only to record each urge, each usage, and what set you off. It's kind of like a scientific experiment. Are you game?

Tom: I don't have to stop using?

Behaviorist: Not this week.

Dad (to therapist): Are you sure you know what you're doing?

Behaviorist (to Dad): I'm sure.

Sam: Why don't you give me some pot and those forms, and I'll do the experiment too.

Behaviorist: Now Tom, I have one more chart for you. This one is to record how you feel after you use, if you do.

Mom: He'll be so busy writing it all down, he won't even get a chance to light it.

Behaviorist: Now Mr. and Mrs. Baker, you have to agree to let this run—not to yell at Tom if he smokes this week.

Mom and Dad: Okay.

Behaviorist: Now Sam, I have a chart for you, too. I want you to record Tom's behavior and moods before and after he smokes as you see them, if he does smoke grass. All you have to do is put a check mark next to the word that describes them best. See, column one, date and time, column two, before, column three, after.

Sam: Most of the time he gets high out of the house.

Behaviorist: But I'll bet you know when he does.

Sam: Yes.

Behaviorist: Then record as much as you see.

Sam: I love this.

Behaviorist: I think we have a deal. I call it a contract, and I want everyone to sign it. Mr. Baker, you agree to say three positive things to Tom each day, record them, and not interfere with Tom's use or nonuse this week. Sign here. Mrs. Baker, the same for you. (They sign.) And Sam, you're going to try and say one positive thing to Tom each day, record it, and if you see him high, check what you see. Okay? (Sam signs.) And Tom, your contract stipulates that you thank Sam and your parents for the positive things they say to you, and that you record your urges and usage just as I explained.

Tom: I'll sign.

Behaviorist: Great. I think we're on the right track. I'll see you all the same time next week.

Well, our behaviorist has laid it all out. Next week he can go on to contingency contracting—rewards for abstinence and sanctions for use—and start to teach coping behaviors, self-efficacy skills, and alternate (to drug use) behavior to Tom, and teach the family ways of helping Tom cope as well as going over their homework, both for its intrinsic value and as a way of building a we-ness in solving Tom's problem without undermining Tom's responsibility for his own behavior. Our behaviorist will also use Tom's self-observations and Sam's observations as feedback loops to make triggers that are presently automatic and out of awareness, self-conscious and in awareness. The next step is to work on alternate responses to those triggers. Notice that the family "craziness" is ignored, and the behaviorist focuses almost entirely on the IP's problem and the family's response to it. This elicits cooperation and lowers resistance by turning the whole thing into a kind of game. It is also "shaping," approximating the desired behavior—abstinence—rather than expecting it prematurely. In reality, things would rarely go so smoothly, yet our behaviorist's approach sometimes succeeds and is worth trying. At some point, there might be a contract in which Tom's attendance at NA's young people's meetings would be rewarded, say with a trip to a professional hockey or basketball game with Dad or with the whole family.

Twenty-five years ago, I attended a program called Smoke Enders. I was a three-pack-a-day Marlboro man when I entered the program, which consisted of eight sessions culminating in the dreaded "cutoff" (abstinence day) followed by five more reinforcement sessions. I was angry as hell because I knew that I would leave smokeless. Something was being taken away, albeit by me, and I didn't like it. Be that as it may, Smoke Enders worked for me, and with the exception of one cigarette the day after cutoff, I haven't smoked since. Smoke Enders was a kind of amalgamation of behavior therapy and borrowings from AA such as "sharing," "telephone therapy" with peers, and group support. One of the more behavioral techniques was a rather simple one of having people wrap a paper marker around their packs of cigarettes and having them record each cigarette smoked and whether or not smoking that cigarette was pleasurable. In common with my fellow Smoke Enders, I was amazed to discover how very few cigarettes I actually enjoyed. This simple self-observation device constituted an extremely powerful feedback loop. Smoke Enders also used shaping—successive approximations to a nicotine-free state (there were no patches then) engendered through switching to low nicotine cigarettes, progressively restricting times smoking was permitted, forbidding carrying matches or a lighter, carrying your cigarettes in a different place, smoking with the other hand, and so on. Some of this was done to break habit patterns, and some of it to sever the connection between stimulus and response—between trigger and cigarette. The contract was an agreement to abide by the progressive restrictions imposed by the leader each week until cutoff. A reward system was built into the sharing and mutual reinforcement of the group meetings. It worked for a good number of people. Having beaten an addiction through participation in a behaviorally oriented therapy, I can hardly devalue the behavioral approach, however uncongenial I may find it.

PSYCHODYNAMIC

The psychodynamic approach to the Bakers is here represented by an object relations therapist. It doesn't mean that our dynamic therapist will ignore drive, ego, and self understandings of the Bakers; on the contrary, he will integrate them into his object relations perspective. In general, dynamic therapists are not too active in an opening session, since interpretation requires knowledge of the family's dynamics and the acquisition of this knowledge is a time-bound process. Additionally, the creation of a holding environment and the unfolding of the transferences require time. Having said this, it is important to remember that the opposite of activity is not, in this case, passivity; rather, it is receptivity and therapeutically tactful interpretation. Typically, the dynamic family therapist provides drawing materials and if there are younger children, play materials. Our object relations therapist has done so, and Sam has been "doodling" during the session (Figure 12–7, parts I and II).

Object Relations Therapist: Would you share your drawing with us, Sam?

Sam (blushes but hands over the drawing. The therapist passes it around.)

Object Relations Therapist: Any thoughts about Sam's drawings?

Mom: I'm all teeth. Twice.

Dad (to Sam): You got Tom right with that smirk and that joint hanging out of his mouth.

Tom: You sure can't draw.

Fascinated by Sam's representation of his mother as a semihuman devouring beast, the object relations therapist's thoughts went to an early sexual encounter with an inexperienced partner who bit his penis as she attempted fellatio. He remembered his comment, "Teeth kitty" that later became a joke between them. Thinking along his countertransferential associations, he realized that he was condensing Mother's castrating tendencies, "He was circumcised for me" with her cannibalistic tendencies as experienced by her younger son. Going with his own unconscious process, which had associated a moment of personal sexual anxiety with Sam's drawing, he went with his intuitions and played a hunch that Tom was so afraid of his castrating, devouring Mother that he needed to get high in order to have intercourse. Mother's well-fanged mouth was also her vagina dentata. Having made this connection by assessing his own experience and actually feeling anxiety when he looked at the drawing, he recovered, moving back into a stance of professional neutrality and objectivity. Now working from a central ego rather than an antilibidinal ego stance, drawing more on consciousness rather than from the unconscious process, he debated whether or not to make a "wild" (Freud

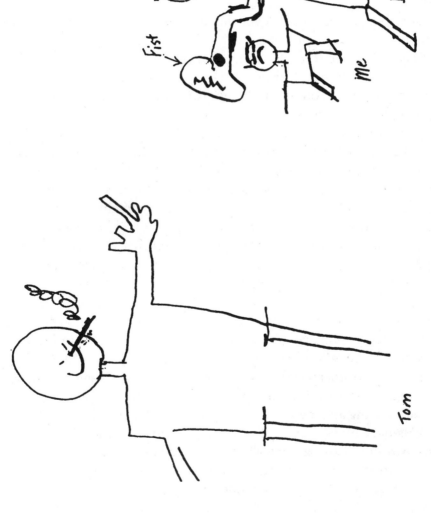

FIGURE 12–7. Sam's drawing Part I.

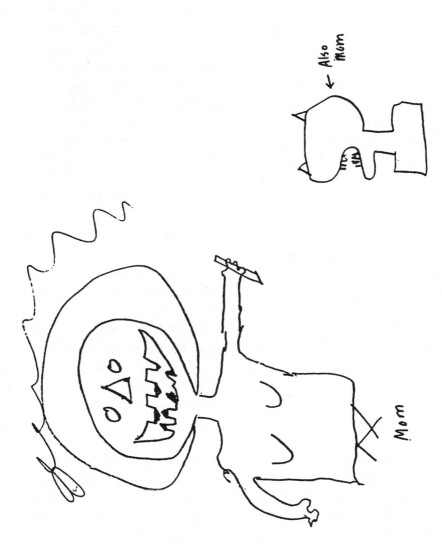

FIGURE 12-7. Sam's drawing Part II.

1910) interpretation. Knowing that creating a holding environment takes precedence and that interpretations require context, he at first decided to hold his insight, but reconsidered. Tom was so isolated both in the session and in the drawing that the object relationist decided that making contact with Tom was what most needed to be done, and that perhaps Sam's drawing and his own associations to it just might be the vehicle of such contact. He played his hunch.

> *Object Relationist*: Sam's drawing makes me anxious, and my anxiety must be mild compared to yours. Your whole family lives in a condition of high anxiety. Tom, I don't quite know why, but when I realized how anxious everyone is, I thought, "Tom smokes to control his anxiety," and I wondered if you are so anxious that you have to get high to have sex. Have you ever had intercourse straight?
>
> *Tom* (blushes beet red): No, I never got laid unless I was high. It makes it better. (Angrily.) You ought to try it, doc.
>
> *Object Relationist*: That's kind of sad, Tom, that you can't even enjoy your own body without getting high. Really sad.

Our object relationist has scored a bull's eye. Pot not only allows Tom to be sexual; smoking it is a sexual act. Smoking pot, like any inhalant, can be viewed as a form of respiratory eroticism. I have sometimes wondered if smokers—of crack, pot, tobacco—aren't unconsciously attempting to master the primal anxiety they felt when they first attempted to breathe on their own, surely a core component of the birth trauma, if there be one. In their anxious inhalation, they quell that anxiety through the physical act of inhaling and through the pharmacological effects of the inhalant. Smoking is also an oral act, both physically and symbolically, and it is interesting that Mother has something of the aspect of a smoking dragon in Sam's representation in which Tom also smokes. Is there some sort of identification here? Is Tom's smoking the turning of a passive experience into an active one, taking in the smoking dragon where she can be tamed and contained rather than being devoured by her? In all probability, some such dynamic is at work here. Of course, Sam's drawing is a representation of his internal object relations as well as his experience of the external objects constituting his family, and Tom, in his usual closed, defensive manner, has made a critical comment rather than associating to his brother's drawing. The avoidance is more salient than the hostility. Our object relationist is feeling guilty. This is really bad technique. Instead of providing a safe place for Tom, he has stirred up enormous anxiety. Yet he has made contact. Putting aside his self doubts, he continues.

> *Object Relations Therapist*: Tom, you haven't told us your thoughts about the drawing.
> *Mother*: The doctor is right. It really is sad that you can't get laid without getting high.
> *Father*: He can't do anything without getting high.
> *Object Relations Therapist* (again feeling guilty; to Father): Do you realize you are attacking Tom when he has made himself vulnerable? No wonder he closes down emotionally.
> *Tom*: He's like that. That's why Sam drew him with his fist cocked.
> *Object Relations Therapist* (thinks, *Mother's all sexual aggression; Dad, aggression aggression. If I were Tom, I'd be stoned all the time too*. Then catching himself, he thinks, *I'm overidentifying with Tom. Both of these parents are capable of loving concern and care of and for their children. That was amply demonstrated in the material emerging earlier in the session. My mother was sometimes seductive, and I wished my father was more aggressive. The Bakers really do make me anxious; too much id. Too little central ego. How can I use myself to understand and help, rather than act out? I think I do understand a piece of Tom anyway; if I don't lose my boundaries, I can exploit my identification with him therapeutically. Now I think I know what happens in this family that makes their holding not good enough. At their best, they can operate from the depressive position demonstrating Winnicott's capacity* (1963) *for concern, but when their anxiety gets too high or their rage too intense, they regress to the paranoid-schizoid position and attack and project their hostility and libido. Of course, we all do that and the dialectic between the depressive and paranoid-schizoid posi-*

tions enriches our experience [Gabbard 1996, Scharff 1992]. *But there is too much paranoid-schizoid functioning in the Baker family. At times they fragment and regress further to Ogden's* [1990] *autistic-contiguous position. The Bakers need help augmenting their capacity to function in the depressive position.*) (to Dad): Mr. Baker, any more thoughts about this drawing?

Father: I always said my wife had a big mouth. But it bothers me that Sam sees me as all fist. I got a heart too, you know. Hey, doc, what's the kid so anxious about? Like I told you, he's got it made except for the grass.

Mom: Sam, you drew yourself like a baby. You're kind of lost, too.

Sam: Who'd want to grow up in this family?

Object Relations Therapist: I don't understand that. Do you mean it feels better to be a baby?

Sam: Naw, I just meant I don't want to be like him (sticks his tongue out at Tom).

Object Relations Therapist: Tom, what's it like to have a dad with such big fists?

Tom: Scary, man, scary. He's violent.

Father: Don't scapegoat me, you asshole.

Object Relations Therapist: You need to be angry at each other.

Mom: Yeah, they're always fighting.

Object Relations Therapist (to Father): I think you see a part of yourself you don't like in Tom, and that infuriates you.

Father: Yeah, he's the asshole I used to be. I don't like to think about what a punk, total-loss kid I was.

Tom: Dad, I'm not you. I don't know how to be you. You make money. People respect you. You can go to a party and nurse a beer all night.

Object Relations Therapist (to Father): That punk kid's still a part of you. You must have had it pretty rough. Can you feel any compassion for him?

Father: No, he's just a loser.

Object Relations Therapist: Seeing him in Tom infuriates you.

Father: I get it. You want me to lay off him.

Object Relations Therapist: I wonder if you also see something of your drunken father in Tom and then you really hate him.

Father (looks shook, even shattered. His hands shake): Christ, you're right. I'm afraid of Tom when he's stoned out of his mind, and I ain't afraid of anything. I don't like admitting that.

Object Relations Therapist: So you're afraid of each other.

Tom: I'm not afraid. (Hesitates.) Shit, yes I am.

Object Relations Therapist (to Tom): I think you're sitting on so much rage you're afraid you're going to explode, so you tranquilize your rage with pot, run away from it, or put it on your dad. The way you do that is to provoke him until he is in a rage, which isn't too hard to do. And then your rage, which you can't handle, is in him and not you, and you can run away from it. You can't run away from the rage inside, but if you put it on him or in him, it's outside you and you can deal with it. Besides, having Dad foaming gives you a reason to get high and you want to do that for other reasons, including the fact that you're hooked. So each of you puts a part of yourself into the other because it's easier than having the rage inside for Tom and the hurt, confused, wild child within for Dad. Mr. Baker, in a funny way, except it isn't funny, you need Tom to stay a stoned, hurt, lost kid, although I know that another part of you really and sincerely wants him to get clean, to protect you from feeling the sorrow and pain inside you.

Tom: Dad, I need you. I know you love me, but I can't get close to you. You're too strong.

Object Relations Therapist: And frightening.

Tom: (weeps).

Mother (rises to comfort him).

Object Relations Therapist (gently): No, Mother, this is man's stuff. Don't get between them. You're afraid to let your husband be emotional, to be a wimp like your father. You need him to be "strong," so you rush in, and Tom and Dad never make contact.

Mother (sits on her hands): You're right. That's why I love Rob, he's
    so masculine. I'm the boss, but that doesn't make him a wimp.
Father and Tom (talk to each other intensely but not audibly).
Father (embraces Tom): So you have to stop. I don't want you to
    die like my Dad.

Once again, our object relations therapist interprets very early in
treatment, which is somewhat atypical for this school. His long interpretation to Tom and Dad is an interpretation of mutual projective identification. It results in a strengthening of the contextual transference, since both Tom and his father feel understood without being
judged in spite of the fact that the content of the interpretation is
painful and anxiety provoking. Following the interpretation, Tom and
Dad and later Mom move from a paranoid-schizoid stance to a depressive one. As the therapist "holds" the family, the family becomes
better able to hold Tom. There is little focal transference, that is,
unconscious re-enactment of early object relations in interaction with
the therapist, as we would expect in this first session, but there may
be intimations and precursors of it manifest in some of the comments
family members make to the object relationist. Note the extensive
use the object relations therapist makes of his countertransference.
He also wonders if he was somehow represented in Sam's drawing
or in the family's associations to it. Although nothing surfaced, he
wondered if the doubled maternal figure, which at a manifest level
served to make Mom a relatively benign mascot or pet, might also be
a representation of him, reflecting both Sam's fear of him as a toothed
beast and his mastery of that fear through the diminutive nature of
the representation. All of this is too speculative to be of any use, yet
at some level the therapist must be represented in the drawing.
    Our object relations therapist is pulling for more central ego func-
tioning so the family can get on with the task of helping Tom achieve
sobriety rather than functioning predominantly on the "basic assumption" level (Bion 1961). But that doesn't mean that split-off internal
objects and object relations are not constantly being enacted by the
Bakers. Sam's drawing makes crystal clear Mother's ready availability for projection of both rejecting and exciting objects by all of the

Bakers. Additionally, their antilibidinal egos suppress their libidinal egos' exciting objects. Another way of understanding this is to say that both boys repress their oedipal yearnings for Mother, and convert her into a witch-like rejecting object to avoid dealing with those yearnings. Given Father's rageful jealousy, which Mom continually provokes, the boys' avoidance/repression of oedipal yearnings is entirely rational. Her personality, style, and internal world make this easy. One wonders what Mother's early object relations were like and what sort of relationship she had with her infant sons.

Tom uses marijuana to augment the repression of his antilibidinal ego at the same time that it allows some expression of his libidinal wishes/fantasies/drives. Our object relations therapist has partially interpreted this to him. Pot is also an ideal exciting-rejecting object for him, ideal here used not in Fairbairn's sense but ironically. It tantalizes, excites, and then tranquilizes that excitement before it becomes too dangerous, giving marijuana a power and allure hard to find in this world. It has multiple hooks which fit all too well Tom's internal objects. Similarly, Tom's smoking pot expresses aggression and quells and quiets it at the same time. In the long run, and by now the long run is not very long for Tom, marijuana turns into the rejecting object, giving him a pseudo-opportunity to work through his relationship to his "bad" rejecting objects as his smoking punishes him in myriad ways, including the castration of not being able to function. Thus his marijuana smoking simultaneously permits some expression of forbidden libidinal and aggressive wishes, and punishes him for having those wishes. Such simultaneous gratification of id and superego, or in Fairbairn's terms of libidinal and antilibidinal aspects of ego, is hard to find in this world. It is all too good a deal. This makes it extraordinarily difficult for Tom to achieve abstinence.

Dynamic therapists of ego and self-psychological schools would understand Tom's relationship with pot as fusion with the symbiotic mother, and as a selfobject with which Tom has both mirror and idealizing transferences (see Chapter 3), and interpret it so. The rampant, multiple mirror transferences and the narcissistic rage consequent upon the failure to mirror adequately, so characteristic of this family, are also interpretable. Our object relations therapist, unless he is unusually doctrinaire, would have no difficulty with these alternate conceptualizations. Interpretation along ego and self-psychological lines might be quite useful, even mutative. Mutatis mutandis, Sam's drawing would be interpreted differently by these schools. The dragon, orally ingestive mother would be seen as a wish fantasy by an ego psychologist, and indeed the anger, the fighting, and Tom's substance abuse could all be accurately interpreted as a defense against active and passive oral incorporative wishes and perhaps more fundamentally, a defense against merger/symbiotic wishes, which are of course enacted even as they are defended against by Tom's pot smoking.

All of this will be fodder for the object relations therapist's interpretive mill in future sessions. He will also encourage participation in supportive and structuring therapeutic activities such as Twelve-Step meetings for both Tom and his family (Al-Anon for the parents, Al-Teen for Sam).

In this session, there was almost no interpretation or comment about the family's relationship to the therapist, although we have seen some of the therapist's thoughts about what might be going on in that area. We would anticipate such transference interpretation playing an increasing role as the object relations therapy proceeds.

The Bakers offered us no dreams. In dynamic family therapy, each of the family members associates to the dream and then associates to each of the others' associations. Generally speaking, dream interpretation is minimally useful in working with "actives," individually or in family sessions, however mutative it can be in working with the recovering. But there are exceptions.

Gary, a middle-aged safety engineer, came to therapy for depression. His presenting problem was writer's block. Since he was supposed to be writing safety reports for a nuclear facility, this was of some salience. Drinking was never mentioned. After several months, he reported the following dream.

"I was in my underpants. They were on backward and inside out. They had shit stains on them. I was afraid people would see me."

The patient, who had significant anal conflicts and who remembered excitedly showing his mother his feces appropriately evacuated into the potty and failing to elicit her interest, a traumatic disappointment, was certainly anally exhibitionistic. It was not without significance that he could not "produce" on the job. He associated desultorily and neither of us was able to "do" much with the dream. The session went elsewhere; then, just as we were about to "end," Gary suddenly snapped his fingers and said, "I know what that dream was about. I got shit-faced last night." In dreaming the dream and telling it, Gary "told" me about his alcoholism. More importantly, he told himself that he had a drinking problem.

Classical analysts spoke of regression to anality or orality as a defense against genital (oedipal) conflicts. We don't hear much about regression as a defense these days. Yet it is often a dynamic in addiction. Perhaps Twelve-Step intuitively speaks to the addict's developmental level in its injunction to "become clean and dry." Gary's interesting oral-anal condensation in being "shit-faced" presaged our understanding of his drinking as, among other things, a defense against oedipal conflict after he achieved sobriety. Similarly, Tom's pot addiction served as a regressive defense against genital conflict.

SUBSTANCE ABUSE APPROACH

The substance abuse therapist would be likely to incorporate elements of all of the schools in his/her treatment, yet would keep the focus on the substance abuse in a way none of the schools does. He or she might also wonder about Tom's using some of the object relations therapist's interpretations as rationalizations for his continual use in somewhat the same way as the kids in "Dear Officer Krupke" in *West Side Story* rationalized their delinquencies, in Tom's case, "I'm so anxious I have to get high." I think in a real session, the object relations therapist would have done all he could to prevent that by saying, "Tom, I know you smoke to control your anxiety, but there are other ways to reduce anxiety and I can help you learn them." That moves him away from the neutrality of the object relations school into a more active, didactic stance.

Although most dynamic therapists would modify their technique in a didactic direction if they are working with a teenage addict, there is some conflict here which would not exist for a substance abuse therapist. Tom and his family have had a great deal of treatment, including Tom's extended stay in a therapeutic community, which doesn't give our substance abuse therapist his usual scope. Such typical interventions as exposition of the disease model of addiction, explanation of and referral to Twelve-Step program meetings, making the family aware of their enabling, and giving the family members an opportunity to express and work through their feelings of shame, rage, and guilt, enlisted by and directed toward the substance abuser, have been repeatedly made. That doesn't mean that all of that doesn't need to be done again. Given the power of resistance and denial and of the need for working through, repetition is certainly in order, yet this family is not a "virgin" and none of this has worked before. Perhaps the substance abuse therapist needs to do something different or at least something additional. As with all of our therapists, the substance abuse therapist listens very carefully, and he asks some characteristic questions.

Substance Abuse Therapist: I need to know a lot more about Tom's treatment and your treatment as a family as well. (The Bakers detail the therapists, the programs, the experiences they have had.)

Substance Abuse Therapist: Did anything help?

Dad: Only the TC, but it didn't last.

Substance Abuse Therapist: Tom?

Tom: I hated the TC. They shaved my head and made me wear stupid signs.

Substance Abuse Therapist: They used shame as a therapeutic tool.

Tom: Well, I didn't feel shame. I felt rage.

Substance Abuse Therapist: And you started smoking again to get back at them.

Tom: You're damn right.

Substance Abuse Therapist: That's pretty stupid, isn't it?

Tom: Yeah. I know that.

Substance Abuse Therapist: And to get back at your parents for putting you there.

Tom: Yeah.

Substance Abuse Therapist (to all): Do you know addiction is a disease?

Bakers: Yeah.

Substance Abuse Therapist: Tell me what you know.

Bakers (demonstrate a good collective and individual understanding of the disease concept of addiction).

Substance Abuse Therapist: Tom, if you really believe addiction is a disease, then you know that you have lost control, and if you continue to smoke, you're going to go down the tubes.

Tom: Yeah, I know.

Substance Abuse Therapist: Your smoking is like getting back at somebody by giving yourself cancer.

The substance abuse therapist is concentrating on the identified patient, yet he involves the family. They are seen as part of the solution, not part of the problem. For the moment, their pain and rage are ignored or acknowledged but not dealt with. In this style of family therapy, they will have ample opportunity to deal with their issues after Tom gets "clean"; right now, those issues are put aside. Of course, enlisting them as helpers raises their self-esteem and generally strengthens them.

The substance abuse therapist takes Tom through his experience in the TC in considerable detail and elicits the information that it was not altogether a negative experience for Tom. In particular, Tom pleasurably bonded with some of his fellow TC-ers. To say that he made friends is perhaps saying too much, but his ties, however, transitory were important to him. It also became clear that Tom found the rigid structure of the TC helpful, however much he hated the highly questionable therapeutic methods of that TC. This argues that firmness would be helpful for him.

Substance Abuse Therapist: I want to hear from all of you and from Tom himself just how he got into drugs and what his relationship to drugs has been over the years.

The taking of a painstakingly detailed drug history, bolstered by many questions from the substance abuse therapist, constitutes both a cooperative effort of the family and therapist and a vital source of information. It differs from the detailed history-taking of the genogram drawing intergenerationalist in that it concentrates on Tom's drug history. As Tom's drug history unfolded, it became clear that Tom was enacting a dismally familiar story. The marginal kid, always the outsider, academically pushed by his upwardly mobile parents, yet with scant academic skills and limited potential. (The therapist wondered about learning disability and/or attention deficit disorder, even possibly hyperactivity-attention deficit disorder, common comorbidities with substance abuse and the possibility of remediating/treating them.) This marginal kid finds pot, acceptance, even leadership, and an easy escape from self-esteem–deflating activities all at once at age 13. It was love at first sight. Within a year, Tom was trapped, incorrigibly identified with what he and his parents call the "scumbag crowd," hopelessly behind in school, and completely scorned by the college-bound crowd. There was no way back. The rest followed as the night the day, three years of progressive decline, rageful arguments at home, trouble in school, eventuating in around-the-clock pot smoking, Tom's collapse, and his entry into the TC.

For all his hatred of it, the TC had possibly saved Tom's life. Whatever its merits, discharge planning doesn't seem to have been one of the TC's strengths. Tom's reentry into school with which he could not cope socially or academically left him with no place to go except back to the scumbag crowd and he quickly relapsed. Angry at his parents for putting him into an impossible situation, furious at being pressured into the TC, retaliating against the TC, finding acceptance and self-esteem in smoking and dealing (a further step down the addictive staircase), Tom was in deep shit, caught up in the addictive cycle and going nowhere but down. The family's intervention in bringing Tom to the session may be literally lifesaving for him, and from this substance abuse point of view, the family's dynamics are irrelevant, at least for now. As a committed subscriber to the disease model, our substance abuse therapist sees no possibility of Tom becoming a "social smoker." He is an addict, and according to the disease model, his disease will progress, or should I say retrogress, and he has lost control in the sense that he cannot regulate his substance use. His only option is abstinence. The fact that his father can sip an occasional beer in spite of his youthful history of alcohol abuse is a pernicious model for Tom. He clearly cannot do what his father has been able to do. In the course of this history-taking, it also became clear that Father is functionally illiterate and deeply ashamed of it, in spite of his financial success as a skilled craftsman.

Equipped with this knowledge, this detailed history of Tom's drug use and treatment, and remembering Tom's pleading to leave school early in the session, the substance abuse therapist made a dramatic, early move, intervening in a directive way with the Bakers. Further, sensing Tom's unconscious or barely conscious belief that he, like his father, could recover, join the union, and live happily ever after whenever he wanted to, so he didn't need to stop smoking pot, the substance abuse therapist wove a firm repudiation of this belief into his interventions.

Substance Abuse Therapist: Tom, I'll make a deal with you. You want to drop out of school but you can't without your parents' permission. I'll help you get that permission.

Mother/Father: Over my dead body.

Substance Abuse Therapist: If you agree to get a job, to go to Twelve–Step meetings, and to stop smoking grass.

Sam: He's too dumb for school anyway. I get A's.

Tom (to Sam): Shut up.

Substance Abuse Therapist: Will you do it?

Tom (remains silent).

Substance Abuse Therapist: You think you can do anything you want, stay stoned right around the clock, then get clean when you're ready, and your old man will get you a job in the union, and you'll be just fine. I think your family believes that at some level, too, though they don't know it. It isn't true. The longer you smoke, the sicker you will get, and there may be no turning back. Or you'll have so much catch-up to do that you'll be overwhelmed and really screwed. Each day you smoke, you get sicker. How about a deal? I'll help you get your father's permission. We can work together in therapy and you'll be out of an impossible situation.

Tom (screams): Okay! Okay! Just get them to agree.

Mother/Father: No!

Substance Abuse Therapist (to parents): I know it breaks your heart to have Tom drop out of school, but you *have* to let him. He just *can't* do it. He's too far behind academically. The straight kids won't accept him and he has no place to go except back to the scumbags, and that means being stoned. I know how much you love Tom, and I know you'll do this for him. He can get a high school equivalency (G.E.D.) at night when he's in stable recovery. I'll get him into the G.E.D. program when he's ready.

Mother (cries).

Father: Okay, but he's got to get a job.

Mother: I can get him a job in the warehouse where I work.

Tom: I'll take it.

Notice how strongly our substance abuse therapist speaks. "You *have* to let him," and how much responsibility he takes for Tom's life. Many, perhaps most, therapists wouldn't be comfortable with this or see their role as being directive in this way. The therapist may be wrong, dropping out could be a disaster for Tom, but the substance abuse therapist senses that the present situation is hopeless, and there is nothing to lose by taking such a bold step. It is highly doubtful that Tom would be allowed to continue in school for very long in any case. Notice also how direct he is with Tom, and simultaneously how unashamedly manipulative he is in forging an alliance with Tom. He is similarly manipulative with the parents, appealing to both their love and their guilt. All he needs now is closure.

Substance Abuse Therapist: I'll see Tom individually for two weeks and then we will have another family session. Okay, Tom? (Tom nods.) And we will keep that format—two sessions with Tom and then a family session. Tom has absolute confidentiality, unless his life is in danger, so he can be free to say anything here.

I find this format of several individual sessions alternating with a family session extremely useful in treating adolescent substance abusers.

Substance Abuse Therapist: I try to respect everyone else's confidentiality, but since we will be meeting as a family, it is less of an issue and Tom is the primary patient. I'll see you next week, Tom.

As therapy proceeds, the substance abuse therapist will engage the Bakers to give them an opportunity to express their feelings about Tom's addiction and to give them some support. The substance abuse therapist will probably be especially supportive of Sam, who, as a lost child, needs bringing out, but for now Tom is the primary patient and the family's role is ancillary to his recovery.

Each of the therapeutic approaches—communications/strategic, structural, intergenerational-systemic, experiential, behavioral, object relations/dynamic and substance abuse—has its place in working with addicted families and families with addiction. If I were not so fond of felines, I might say, "There is more than one way to skin a cat." Instead I will say, "There are more ways than one to dry out the besotted."

The Psycho Ward

In the old days, alcoholics and other addicts went to what AA calls the "flight deck," that is, the closed ward. Later on, substance abuse rehabilitation units came into being and psychiatric hospitalization became rare. Currently, the ravages of managed care health plans are closing one inpatient rehab after another, so we may see a return to treatment on the flight deck.

The experience of going through a psychiatric hospitalization is traumatic. For most addicts it is a profound narcissistic wound, cutting to the core of their being. It can serve as the "ego deflation in depth" necessary to penetrate grandiosity and denial, but that doesn't always happen. The experience of hospitalization may be so upsetting that the addict drowns his or her humiliation as soon as possible. There is a bar across from the Bellevue Hospital psychiatric ward that does a booming business serving the just-discharged. Any inpatient treatment—detox, rehab, psychiatric—is a crucial event in an addictive career. It can be a fulcrum around which recovery is organized, or it can fuel the feelings of rage, shame, hopelessness, and defiance that keep people drinking.

David is a retread. He had several years of sobriety before "slipping" and precipitously deteriorating. Skid row is called skid row for a reason, and David sure skidded. His bottom was a psychiatric hospitalization. Bottom is a state of being, an inner experience, so in saying that hospitalization was David's bottom I mean that it was the occasion for that experience, not the experience itself.

I met David some years after his hospitalization. He was a social worker who used a lot of psychiatric jargon as a defense against feelings. Intellectualization is an extremely popular defense among problem drinkers. It supports denial—"I'm so smart I can't be a drunk"—and it protects against feeling too much. Patients who drink too much intellectualize too much. Smarts can work against you if you use them to fool yourself. David is an intellectualizer who learned to feel. His bottom was dramatic, but his movement from defiance and denial to acceptance and serenity is something many substance abusers identify with. This is the story he told me:

> Doctor, I've come to you because I'm not enjoying my sobriety, although my present unhappiness is paradise compared to how I felt during my drinking. I've been thinking about my drinking. Four years ago I wound up on the flight deck—that's AA-ese for the psycho ward. Naturally, I didn't go to just any psycho ward, I went to the University Hospital Psychiatric Clinic. I'd been drinking since high school, except for a couple of years in AA. I didn't much like AA; I was so much smarter than most of the people there. I always thought that I would drink again, but I didn't until I broke up with my girlfriend. I used that as an excuse to pick up a drink. Doctor, I'm sure you've heard that alcoholism is a progressive disease—believe me, it is. It was sheer hell once I picked up that drink. I would go on a binge, not go to work, not go home, sleep in fleabag hotels, wake up shaking in the middle of the night and reach for the bottle or run past the other bums to find an open bar. Then I would go to a few AA meetings, get sober, and go back to work. But I couldn't sustain it. Before long I would pick up another drink and be off and running again. It, or maybe I should say, I, was crazy. Since I had been in AA I knew I had to stop drinking, but I wouldn't or couldn't do it. Things got worse. My sober periods became shorter, and when I drank I drank nonstop. I couldn't get my feet on the ground. Finally, I became so ill—physically and mentally—that

I went to my doctor and told him I was going mad. He suggested that I take a little rest. I got drunk and went to my job, where I resigned with a flourish. I drank some more and blacked out. The next thing I remember I was signing myself into the mental hospital. It hadn't taken me long to change from a dissatisfied, anxious, but functional human being into a stumbling zombie who couldn't even remember how he got to the funny farm.

By then I had found a new girlfriend. I had stayed away from her when I was drinking so she hadn't seen much of me. I started to call her, but two attendants interfered. I started shaking. What had I done? Signed away my freedom? I wanted a drink. I wanted a thousand drinks. I wanted to leave. Too late! The attendants led me to the elevator. I told them that I had permission to make a call. Permission to make a call? Jesus Christ, what had I gotten myself into? I called my girlfriend and told her I had signed myself into the bughouse. She said, "Good, you should have done that long ago." I gathered that she had been less than delighted with my condition and I had thought that she didn't know. In AA they say the drunk is the last to know he has a drinking problem. I found out that's true. I told Annie, "I love you," and stumbled to the elevator. The attendants looked like concentration camp guards. The clang of dungeon (elevator) doors closing resounded in my ears. You raised your eyebrows, Doctor? Think I'm overdramatizing, don't you? Of course, I threw away my freedom myself, but it felt like it was taken away from me. By then I was quaking inside and out.

The elevator door opened and I was in the "floor." It was dark and gloomy. I was locked in. For the next month I didn't leave there without an escort. Ever been locked up, Doctor? If you're writing that the patient suffered a blow to his self-esteem, you're right. I still shudder at those locked elevators. You can put down claustrophobia, too. I felt bewildered. I couldn't remember how I had gotten there or what I did that day. Now it was night and the place was deserted. There were bars on the windows. A shiver ran down my spine. I was told to take a shower—that made me feel dirty. I wondered if I smelled. My dread of being locked in faded some, but my blood alcohol level was falling and I was feeling more and more shaky. Every nerve was screaming for a drink. I barely managed to shower and put on a hospital gown. My arms and legs were rubbery and not working very well. Two very young residents arrived to examine me. They asked an endless series of stupid questions, which I resented. These "kids" weren't exactly great at establishing rapport, and I sure needed some rapport. I put them down because I was scared. I was in such bad shape that I had a hard time answering their questions. I thought, Oh shit! I really did it this time! I'm brain damaged! Mercifully, the residents switched to a medical mode and gave me a physical. I found this reassuring.

I had been drinking two quarts of rye a day for quite a while and you might say that I was more than a little worried about my health. You'd better get your eyebrows analyzed, Doctor, they're out of control. I can't be your only patient who drank two quarts a day. The examination ended and I fell into a stupor.

I woke feeling like death. A nurse told me to come to the dayroom. All I could think of was a drink and I made my way unsteadily down a seemingly endless corridor and found the dayroom. The people there didn't look like patients, however patients are supposed to look. I found this reassuring. Maybe this wasn't such a bad funny farm. I met my regular doctor, Dr. Kruse. I perceived him to be extremely authoritarian. He told me he was detoxifying me from alcohol and that I would be given decreasing dosages of medicine for five days and then nothing. He suggested I spend a few days in bed. I found Kruse so intimidating that I forced myself to enlighten him by telling him that alcohol strips the body of B vitamins and that I wanted vitamin therapy. I don't even know if that's true. Kruse prescribed the vitamins and I felt more in control. Pathetic isn't it, Doctor? Still, being able to ask for something and get it helped.

Then I panicked. Five more days and then no alcohol and no medicine. I literally didn't think I would survive. I didn't have to deal with a drugless state for five days, yet I was going up the walls. I turned to my AA experience and decided that this was going to be tough but that I could deal with it a day, an hour, a minute at a time. And I did. My years at AA were not entirely wasted. I used the program to get through the hospital experience and to get all that I could from it. I decided not to stay in bed and to participate in the hospital program from the start. My desperate attempt to retain a little dignity in front of Kruse and my decision to use AA's one day-at-a-time concept to do what I had to do to face drug-freeness were important events in my recovery. I know that sounds corny, Doctor, but it was at that point that I started to fight to get well and somehow, sick as I was, I knew it then. Knowing it was almost as important as doing it, because knowing it changed how I felt about myself. Nothing like an "observing ego," as you shrinks say, eh Doctor? Smiled that time didn't you? Seriously, as soon as I was capable of it, I tried to understand what was happening to me as it happened. Sure, this was a defense against feelings and I can intellectualize forever, but this trying to understand also helped me a great deal. If it did nothing else, even if all the insight was pseudo-insight, it increased my self-esteem. Interesting patient, aren't I, Doctor?

These vestigial feelings of self-worth and of having a coping strategy didn't last long. As I walked back to the dayroom, my skin crawled. My breath came hard, then seemed to come not at all. I started to hyperventilate. My palms dripped sweat; my heart pounded wildly; the vessels in my temples pulsed and felt like they would pop; my legs quivered; my hands shook; my vision blurred; the lights seemed to dim. Ever have a panic attack, Doctor? Do you know Edvard Munch's painting, *The Scream*? I see you do. Well, that's what it's like. Oh, why am I explaining—you're human aren't you? "Nothing human is alien to me," eh? I must stop mocking you. It's part of my cool, detached, arrogant yet proper and polite persona. In the hospital, I was super polite and very controlled—under the shaking, that is. I liked to look in control. I acted superintellectual. Technical terms poured from my lips like I had four Ph.D.s. It was a pathetic attempt to retain some dignity.

I was given my withdrawal medicine—pentobarbital. It felt wonderful like two triple whiskeys. Soon I felt drunk once again and loved it. This was only a reprieve, but I didn't care. It felt good.

I was soon staggering and slurring. Pat, the big, snappish, tough black nurse who had given me the medicine, tried to talk me into going to bed. I refused. She relented and I staggered from the nursing station to the dayroom, bouncing off the walls. I'm glad the hospital let me stagger around. I needed to be allowed to fight. The will to do so made the difference. It's a mystery, isn't it, Doctor. Why did I choose life instead of death? I don't know, but I did. God? The anabolic forces of the universe? A massive psychic reorganization? Who knows, but it happened. Somehow I was able to say to myself, "I fucked up but I'm going to do it differently this time. I'm going to build on bedrock instead of sand." Somehow I knew that I could do that, although I would forget and return to panic and despair. I decided to use everything the hospital had to offer and to get everything I could from the experience. Kind of goody goody, eh, Doctor? Of course I was casting myself in a heroic role and I enjoyed that. But so what. Why shouldn't I have enjoyed my private version of the myth of death and rebirth?

So I staggered into the dayroom. Sitting there were an angry-looking bear of a bearded middle-aged man and a seventyish, stylishly dressed woman. Bill was slapping down cards from a tarot deck with great force and looked every bit the conjurer. I wobbled across the room, introduced myself and said, "Will you overlook my ataxia and dysarthria? They're induced by the medication that I'm taking." Sadie looked blank. Bill said, "Sure, kid," and slammed down the tarot cards harder than ever. I lunged into a jargon-filled discussion of my condition. Bill said, "Sit down and let me get a reading." I continued to play the pleasantest of gracious intellectuals who knew more or less everything, and was willing to share it with all. As they say in AA, I was being a people pleaser. Bill and Sadie took it all in stride and again invited me to join them. This time I did.

I was slurring so badly that it would have been difficult to understand me even if I was making sense, which I wasn't. That didn't bother Bill or Sadie. As we say in AA, we ran our stories. Bill, a lecturer on communications, was manic-depressive. He was in the hospital because his wife was afraid of him. Looking into the deep pools of hatred and rage that were his eyes, I understood why. Sadie was 67 and in her third hospitalization for depression. She was very much the lady, and I thought it funny that her doctor had told her to buy a set of cheap dishes and smash them. I couldn't picture that. Internalized anger doesn't do much for people, does it, Doctor? It almost killed me. Just as we were getting acquainted, a chime rang. It rang for meals, for meds, for activities, for bedtime, for everything. Structure for the structureless, I suppose. Comfort in routine. I got to hate those chimes. The dayroom filled and we were lined up and marched to the locked elevators. The attendants were actually kind and friendly, but I still experienced them as prison guards. Being escorted everywhere through locked doors was humiliating. I staggered as the others walked. We were taken up to the top floor, which had a gym, game room, and a screened-in roof garden. The younger patients played volleyball while the older patients played board games. I didn't feel capable of doing anything so I went out on the roof garden and looked down at the traffic far below through the wire mesh. At least it's not barbed, I thought, as my depression rose like waves through the waning pentobarbital.

The next four or five days I followed the hospital routine as best I could. There was individual therapy, group therapy, recreational therapy, occupational therapy, dance therapy, and community meetings. As the withdrawal medication was reduced, my anxiety returned and once again moved toward panic proportions. The slurring and staggering gave way to a sort of spasticity. I should mention that I was withdrawing from Valium as well as alcohol. My arms and legs would jump up much as if I was a dancer in the dance of the toy soldiers. It was embarrassing, although it was hard to feel embarrassed in the totally accepting atmosphere of the floor. It was also disabling. Without warning, an arm or leg would fly up. I remember sitting, playing bridge with Bill, Sadie, and "the Princess," a wealthy, uptight woman who had gotten herself hooked on pills and had attempted suicide. I had had my last dose of pentobarbital. I could feel the drug losing its effect. I was excited about being drug-free and terrified at the same time. Suddenly, the dayroom grew bright and the objects in it sharply defined. It was as if the lights had gone on in a dark theater. I was fascinated. So this was what the world was supposed to look like. I was dealt a hand. As I picked it up my arm involuntarily snapped over my head and the cards flew across the room. The heightened illumination of the room now seemed sinister. My thoughts raced. I thought, I'm going mad. This is the madhouse. I'm losing my mind. I'll never get out of here. I felt sheer terror. Yet, I picked up those cards and bid one no-trump. Made the hand, too. I wanted to talk about what was going on inside of me but I was afraid to. My thoughts became more confused. I jumped up, ran to my room, and collapsed. Doctor, I know part of it was physiological, but I must have been close to madness that night.

I fell into a troubled sleep. After I don't know how long, I woke to one of the strangest sensations I have ever felt. Waves of force emanated from the center of my abdomen, traveled through my body, and smashed against my skin. Rhythmic and relentless, wave succeeded wave. It felt like I would shatter. The impact of the waves against the surface of my body was so strong that I feared I would fly off the bed. I reached up, grasped the bars of the bed, and held on for dear life. Smash, smash, smash, the waves kept coming relentlessly, inexorably. I thought of screaming out, but I didn't. Suddenly a thought occurred to me. "Good God! That's my anger—my rage—my, my, my anger coming out. This is not something happening *to* me; it *is* me. It's my rage!" I held on to that thought as my last tie to reality. I repeated to myself over and over again, "It's my anger and nothing else."

Doctor, it was sort of a Copernican revolution. It was my Copernican revolution. What I mean is that that thought changed the center of things for me like Copernicus changed the center of the solar system. It was I who was doing this thing, not some outside force. It took a long while for the waves of pressure to stop shattering themselves against my flesh, but the terror was gone. I fell into a deep sleep from which I awoke drained, yet somehow freer than I had been for a long time. Doctor, I suppose that you would classify what happened to me as a somatic delusion, but that doesn't matter. What does matter is that I was able to use it to "own" my anger.

The floor had two long arms connected to a body consisting of the dayroom, the nursing station, and the dining room. During the days following the anger waves, I paced those arms, the corridors, obsessively. You're probably thinking I was going in and out of Mother's arms to her breasts, the nursing station. Perhaps you're right on that, Doctor. It's probably of some significance that I forgot to mention that my mother was critically ill during my final binge. Responded to that one, didn't you Doctor? As it turned out, Mother survived, but her illness must have had something to do with my prolonged binge.

One of the things I am most grateful to AA for is that it taught me how to mourn. When I returned to AA, I was able to mourn my father. That was an old loss and I think that my failure to come to terms with my feelings about him and his death were connected to my slip.

Gratitude for being able to mourn. That's really crazy, isn't it, Doctor? I'm embarrassed by the depth of my feelings. AA puts a lot of emphasis on gratitude: gratitude for sobriety, gratitude for the program itself. Sure, sometimes that gratitude is defensive, another form of denial, but sometimes it's genuine. At least it has been for me, and that's really important. It may sound like I'm intellectualizing again, but I'm not. On the contrary, I'm choked up thinking of all I have to be grateful for.

As the days passed, the spastic jerking of my extremities became less frequent. I still paced, but the focus of my concern had shifted. I became hypochondriacal and drove Pat, the nurse, crazy. Pat did not take kindly to my pestering and I considered her the floor ogre. During my hypochondriacal phase, I was very aware of my anger. At times it was so intense that I thought it might break me in half, but never after the anger-wave hallucination did I experience it as external. It was an objectless anger—free-floating rage.

I was so overwhelmed by the intensity of my rage and fear that I self-consciously tried to constrict my experience to an instant at a time. My world became more and more constricted until I was living in a succession of infinitesimal discrete moments, an infinitesimal at a time, so to speak. I did not dare look even five minutes ahead or behind. To do so engendered too much fear. I similarly constricted my spatial world. I mean this quite literally. When my anxiety was high enough I could feel my world shrinking toward an instant and a point. It was as if there was a camera in my head being focused more and more narrowly. I remember being in the gym, totally overwhelmed by rage and fear and something like despair as I stared at the punching bag. Suddenly, my visual field narrowed to a patch of pebbly brown. I tried to expand it but I couldn't. I thought, "You really did it this time. All you can see are spots!" Then I thought, "So be it," and I started pounding that patch of pebbly brown with the pent-up rage of a lifetime. When I stopped, wringing wet and exhausted, my point-world gradually expanded to encompass the gym and my fellow patients. That was scope enough for me. I knew that something important had happened but I didn't understand what. I spent many hours punching that bag. It helped.

The hospital I was in did a terrific job of creating a sense of community. For all of the inevitable aloneness, there was a real feeling of shared adventure and closeness on the floor. I liked the hospital's emphasis on being honest about your feelings and expressing them. It wasn't AA, but its values were similar. I know that I also have a lot of negative feelings about the hospital and the way I was treated like a prisoner. But my positive feelings aren't all phony or a form of denial either.

Paradoxically, my period of being "stimulus bound," as I thought of it, coincided with my increasing involvement in the life of the floor. The way my perception of the world would expand and contract was almost cinematic. During my expansive periods, my relationships with Bill, Sadie, and the Princess, Jan, deepened. There was a real bond around the bridge table, a bond not without its conflicts and disturbances. I became increasingly afraid of Bill. He looked like he might kill everyone on the floor. Sitting across from him at the bridge table was no easy thing. He was threatening to sign himself out because his psychiatrist was insisting that he take an antipsychotic. I told him I thought he was dangerous and that he should take the medicine. Amazingly, he agreed. After that, we became closer and I was initiated into tarot card mystique. When I had a good reading, I felt elated. A recovery is made of many tiny steps, like those infinitesimals I spoke of, that accrete into something substantial and solid. Telling Bill he was dangerous was such a step for me. I'm preaching to you, aren't I, Doctor?

Sadie was a lovely person who had had a lot of loss. I wished she would break those dishes. The Princess could be arrogant, but she was bright and witty. I enjoyed her. She had been in the hospital for a long time and was scheduled for discharge. She went on pass and took an overdose. Her suicide gesture greatly upset me. I thought nobody gets out of here intact. I was surprised when the Princess was discharged anyway. She was replaced by an overtly psychotic patient. When I told him I was in for alcohol abuse, he said, "Oh, that! I stopped drinking years ago and joined AA. Look at me now!" This frightened and discouraged me more than the Princess's suicide attempt. About the same time, a late-middle-aged man was brought in on a stretcher. He was also an attempted suicide. He turned out to be a physician whose son had been killed in a South American political upheaval. He clearly did not want to live. The sadness in his eyes was as profound as the anger in Bill's. He was a charming and worldly man whose charm and worldliness were clearly automatic and emptily mechanical. He insisted on leaving the hospital. I was sure he was going to his death.

During my "social period," I felt a great need for approbation. After I confronted Bill, I seemed to regress. He improved on his medicine and was out on pass most of the time. The Princess was gone. Sadie offered little companionship. I felt isolated and alone. I became even more of a people pleaser. I felt that I needed the approval of every single person there. My facade turned people off, particularly Pat. Every night we had a community meeting. The night Jan left and Bill's discharge date was set I was particularly forlorn—left behind in the madhouse. At the community meeting some blowhard droned on, monopolizing the conversation. I was furious, but said nothing. I couldn't risk alienating anybody. I should tell you that a psychotic medical student had been brought in that day. Julie was a student at Einstein and kept repeating, "E equals MC squared." In the course of the day, she became more and more disorganized. They put her in the quiet room, an isolation cell used for out-of-control patients. The quiet room held a peculiar fascination for me. I was utterly and totally terrified by it. I was afraid of losing control—and I unconsciously wished to. Fear of confinement permeated every fiber of my being. The quiet room was a prison within a prison. I identified with Julie and her "E equals MC squared," and by that night all of my terrors were focused on the quiet room. At that community meeting I was not only desperately into people pleasing, I was in dread of losing control and being put in the quiet room.

So there I was, listening to a long-winded asshole ramble on. Suddenly I knew I had to say something. I was slumped down in a couch, almost buried in it. It took every bit of my strength to force myself to sit up. Sweating and shaking, I finally managed to say, "I don't like what you're doing. You're taking over this meeting. Sit down and shut up." My body almost convulsed, but I had done it! I sank back into the couch. That was one of the hardest things I have ever done. It took more courage to say those few words than to accomplish many of the more significant things I have done. At the end of the meeting, Pat came over and put her arm around me and said, "You did good." I won't forget that.

Speaking up at the community meeting opened things up for me. Julie grew increasingly agitated. I thought that she was reacting to being locked in the quiet room. Put in the quiet room because she was agitated—agitated because she was put in the quiet room. I would look hypnotically through the window of her locked door. She became more frantic. Finally they "snowed" her—put her out with massive doses of tranquilizers. Now she lay on the floor of the quiet room, unconscious, with her arm raised and splinted as an IV dripped into it. I thought, "They're killing her." I became totally absorbed in her fate. The quiet room became a symbol of all I feared and dreaded, yet perhaps secretly wanted. After all, hadn't I rendered myself unconscious with a drug—alcohol? Hadn't I sought death? That day in my session with Kruse, I said, "I'm afraid of you. You have too much power." The reference was to Julie, but I was thinking of myself. Making this comment to Dr. Kruse was difficult, but not as difficult as speaking at the community meeting. Courage is cumulative. Each instance of it makes the succeeding one easier.

Another way in which I opened up was by running my story. I had learned to do this in AA. I ran my story to everybody who would listen and to some who didn't. I did it in group therapy, at community meetings, with the staff, and with my fellow patients. Each time I told my story, I learned something new.

I also opened up physically. I had been involved in recreation therapy, playing volleyball with the greatest reluctance. I played fearfully, holding my body tight and closed. I was self-protective to an extreme. Naturally, my playing was awful. A few days after the community meeting, I was cajoled into playing. This time it was different. I could feel the energy flowing through my body. I became the game. I felt myself leaping into the air. I felt myself coming down hard. I felt myself taking risks. The closeness, the tightness, the self-protectiveness fell away. It was wonderful. They say that how you play the game is a picture of yourself. It's true. I was not self-conscious while it was happening, but afterward I processed what had occurred and that helped, too.

I had a similar experience in occupational therapy. At first I was reluctant to do anything. I looked upon arts and crafts—"basket weaving"—with contempt. But I thought to myself, I'll do this garbage anyway since I've decided to work the hospital for all it's worth. Commitment won over arrogance. I struggled for weeks to make a ceramic ashtray. At first it was almost impossible because my hands shook so much. Finally I finished the damned thing. I couldn't believe my reaction. I was ecstatic! I had proved that I could function in the face of anxiety. I told Pat that the ashtray was "an external and visible sign of an internal and invisible grace." She treated this bit of pretension with the contempt it deserved, but the idea behind it is valid enough. I think of that ashtray whenever I think I can't do something.

Julie stayed "snowed out," and I kept returning to her window to stare at her prostrate body much like a child compulsively putting his tongue to a sore loose tooth. One of the staff told me, "It's okay. She needs to regress." I oscillated between thinking that this was a bullshit rationalization for what they had done to her and that it reflected really deep empathy. I guess that reflected my ambivalence toward the hospital—mistreated and understood at the same time. A few days later Julie was released from the quiet room. She and a rough street kid named Ruth immediately became friends. I remember one exchange between them. Julie asked, "How is this nuthouse different from all other nuthouses?" Ruth answered, "It's the real McCoy." For some reason I loved the medical student and the street kid for this exchange.

I was getting better. I was given a pass to leave the hospital. As I walked out of the hospital and started to walk down the street, I felt a magnetic force drawing me back to the hospital. I don't mean this metaphorically. I mean I actually felt pulled back to the hospital. Another quasi-psychotic episode, I suppose. I said, "No, this can't be happening." But it was. It felt like the force would pull me back. I fought it and succeeded in breaking loose. No doubt a projection of my desire to cling to the mother, eh, Doctor? Or was it the regressive, seductive pull of addiction? Fortunately, I had had enough regression; I feared it more than I desired it. I started to run and didn't stop until the pull was gone.

I felt a surge of joy. I was free. I bounded toward the park. I felt as if I had springs in my heels. Looking back on it, I was more than a little manic. AA calls this the "pink cloud." I ran toward the polar bears at the zoo. They seemed glad to see me. We spoke for a while, at least I spoke to them. I felt a great sense of communion with the polar bears. A psychologist wrote of the toddler's "love affair with the world." My feelings in the park were like that. Later in the day, I stubbed my toe, so to speak, and ran crying back to my mother-hospital. You know, Doctor, AA's like that—a safe home base from which you can go into the world, take your lumps, and return to be comforted. We all need that, don't we?

After a while I left the park and went to my new girlfriend's. The hospital strictly regulated phone calls and visits. When she was finally allowed to visit, Ann had been very supportive. I shared as much of my hospital experience with her as I was able to. I had an overwhelming fear of being impotent sober. If you've been to AA meetings, Doctor, you know that that's a very common fear. At her last visit, I had spent an hour explaining to Ann that we couldn't make love for at least a year. I was perfectly serious. Five minutes after I arrived in her apartment, we were in bed. Everything went fine.

Several hours later, I left Ann to go to an AA meeting. I had come down off my "pink cloud," but I was still feeling good. That wasn't to last long. I was excited about going back to my old group. I had bounced in and out of that meeting during my nine months of drinking. Now I was sober and hopeful. I walked into the meeting and immediately felt estranged. I couldn't connect with anything or anybody. It was horrible. I sat through the meeting, but I really wasn't there. I felt very far away. It was as if a viscous fluid surrounded me and isolated me. Again, I do not speak metaphorically. I could feel that viscous medium intruding between me and the people in that room. It prevented me from making human contact. It was like being under water. I must have been doing the distancing, but I sure didn't know that I was doing it. I left in a state of deep despair. Whatever my ambivalence toward the hospital, I felt warmth and concern there. I had counted on finding that at my AA meeting. I didn't, or couldn't, or didn't want to, or something; but it surely didn't work. I have never felt as alone as I did on my return to the hospital. I felt defeated and profoundly depressed. I wanted to give up. I think that was my bottom. I knew that I couldn't drink anymore. It just wasn't going to work for me, but I wasn't at all sure that I wanted to live if sobriety was going to be like that.

During the following days I went through the hospital routine mechanically. My friends had been discharged, making me feel even more forlorn and abandoned. For some reason, I didn't talk about my experience at the AA meeting. Although Julie was out of solitary, I was still obsessed with the quiet room. Although I didn't know it, I had put myself into a quiet room by emotionally detaching at that AA meeting. My discharge was approaching. I thought that I would probably kill myself. I was given another pass. I didn't want to use it, but I did. With great reluctance, I decided to try a new AA group. This one met at the Church of the Epiphany, a few blocks from the hospital. I was very shaky as I walked into that meeting. I didn't really expect anything good to happen. The meeting started. The preamble was read: "Alcoholics Anonymous is a fellowship of men and women who share their experience, strength, and hope with each other. . . . " Something happened. Those words sounded like pure poetry.

The speaker was a beautiful young woman, intensely and vibrantly alive. Her vivacity and sparkle certainly facilitated what was about to happen. She spoke of her years of drugging and drinking, of her progressive spiritual and emotional death. Finally she said, "I got to the point that I couldn't feel anything. For no particular reason I went on a trip across the country with some drinking buddies. As we crossed the country, my feelings became more and more frozen. We arrived at the Grand Canyon. I looked at it and felt nothing. I knew that I should be responding with awe and wonder to the sight before me, but I couldn't. I had always loved nature, and now that love, like everything else about me, was dead. I decided to take a picture of the magnificence that spread before me so that if I ever unmelted I could look at the picture and feel what I couldn't feel then."

At that moment, something incredible happened to me. I completely identified with the speaker. I understood her frozen feelings; they were mine. I understood her wish to preserve a precious moment in the hope that someday she could adequately respond with feelings of awe and wonder to it. Something welled up in me. I began to sob, deep, strong, powerful sobs. They did not stop for the hour and a half that the meeting lasted. As the speaker told her story—how she managed to stop drugging and drinking and how her feelings had become unfrozen—my feelings became unfrozen. I was still crying when I shook her hand and thanked her. I walked out of the meeting feeling happy. *Happy*, Doctor! I couldn't even remember feeling happy.

As I walked down the street toward the hospital, the tears were still flowing. Now they were tears of happiness and gratitude. I who had been so formal and controlled and concerned to impress, walked past staring strollers with tears streaming down completely indifferent to, indeed oblivious of, their reactions. Doctor, do you know Edna St. Vincent Millay's poem 'Renascence'? It tells of a young woman who has been buried; then the rain comes, washing her grave away, returning her to life. She becomes aware of "A fragrance such as never clings/ To aught save happy living things. . . . " I had always loved that poem; now I truly understood it. My tears were like the rain in the poem. They, like the rain, washed me out of the grave I had dug for myself with alcohol and emotional repression. I, too, smelled the fragrance that never clings to aught save happy living things.

I walked into the floor feeling buoyant. As I joined the perpetual rap session in the dayroom, a thought came to me, "God is in the quiet room." I didn't know where it came from, or what I meant by it, but I vocalized it. I think it had something to do with feeling loved and connected and potentially capable of loving. It seemed that whatever I had experienced at that AA meeting was also present in the quiet room. That's as close as I can get to understanding what I was trying to express in that phrase. What happened at the meeting had something to do with receptivity, with being open and being able to hear. That part of it was a gift. From whom, I do not know.

Well, Doctor, I'm not much on theodicies, and I can't do much with a young girl going mad as a manifestation of divine grace. I don't know who or what, if anything, is out there and I haven't become religious in any formal sense. I don't belong to a church. So when I said, "God is in the quiet room," I must have meant it in some metaphorical sense. But I did mean it. There was certainly denial in that statement—denial of evil and pain and sorrow, denial of all I hated about the hospital, denial of my rage at the waste that my life had been. But there was something else in it too, something that liberated me to engage in the long, slow, up-and-down struggle for health. In AA we say that sobriety is an adventure—it certainly has been for me.

References

Abraham, K. (1908). The psychological relations between sexuality and alcoholism. In *Selected Papers on Psychoanalysis*, pp. 80–90. New York: Brunner/Mazel, 1979.

Ackerman, N. (1994). *The Psychodynamics of Family Life: Diagnosis and Treatment of Family Relationships*. Northvale, NJ: Jason Aronson.

Alcoholics Anonymous World Services. (1955). *Alcoholics Anonymous*, 1st ed. New York: World Services.

———. (1976). *Alcoholics Anonymous*, 3rd ed. New York: Author.

American Psychiatric Association (1994). *Diagnostic and Statistical Manual of Mental Disorders, Fourth Edition*, Washington DC: Author.

Aristotle (330 BC). Metaphysics. In *Introduction to Aristotle*, ed. R. McKeon, trans. W. D. Ross, pp. 243–297. New York: Modern Library, 1947.

Austin, J. L. (1961). Performative utterances. In *Philosophical Papers*, ed. J. O. Urmson and G. J. Warnock, pp. 220–240. London: Oxford University Press.

Bateson, G. (1971). The cybernetics of "self": a theory of alcoholism." *Psychiatry* 34:1–18.

Bateson, G., Jackson, D. D., Haley, J., and Weakland, J. (1956). Towards a theory of schizophrenia. *Behavioral Science* 1:251–264.

Beck, A. (1976). *Cognitive Therapy and Emotional Disorders*. New York: International Universities Press.

Bem, J. D. (1967). Self-perception: an alternate view of cognitive dissonance phenomena. *Psychological Review* 74:183–200.

Binswanger, L. von (1944). The case of Ellen West. In *Existence*, ed. R. May, E. Angel, and H. F. Ellenberger, trans. W. M. Mendel and J. Lyons, pp. 237–364. New York: Basic Books, 1958.

Bion, W. R. (1961). *Experiences in Groups*. New York: Basic Books.

Blane, H. T. (1968). *The Personality of the Alcoholic: Guises of Dependency*. New York: Harper & Row.

Bleuler, D. M. (1955). Familial and personal background of chronic alcoholics. In *Etiology of Chronic Alcoholism*, ed. O. Dretheim, pp. 110–166. Springfield, IL: Charles C Thomas.

Bowen, M. (1974). Alcoholism as viewed through family systems theory and family psychotherapy. *Annals of the New York Academy of Sciences* 233:115–122.

————. (1978a). *Family Therapy in Clinical Practice*. New York: Jason Aronson.

————. (1978b). On the differentiation of self. In *Family Therapy in Clinical Practice*, pp. 467–528. New York: Jason Aronson.

Brown, S. (1985). *Treating the Alcoholic: A Developmental Model of Recovery*. New York: Wiley.

Child, I., Bacon, M., and Barry, H. (1965). A cross-cultural study of drinking. *Quarterly Journal of Studies on Alcohol*, (Suppl. 3), 5–96.

Cloninger, C. R. (1983). Genetic and environmental factors in the development of alcoholism. *Journal of Psychiatric Treatment and Evaluation* 5:487–496.

Conners, R. (1962). The self-concepts of alcoholics. In *Society, Culture, and Drinking Patterns*, ed. D. Pittman and C. Snyder, pp. 455–467. Carbondale, IL: Southern Illinois University Press.

Dostoevsky, F. (1880). *The Brothers Karamazov*, trans. C. Garnett. New York: Random House.

Durkheim, E. (1897). *Suicide*. Glencoe, IL: Free Press.

Eissler, K. R. (1958). Remarks on some variations in psychoanalytic technique. *International Journal of Psycho-Analysis* 39:222–229.

Ellis, A. (1962). *Reason and Emotion in Psychotherapy*. New York: Lyle Stuart.

Erikson, E. (1950). *Childhood and Society*, 2nd ed. New York: Norton.

———. (1968). *Identity, Youth and Crisis*. New York: Norton.

Fairbairn, W. R. D. (1940). Schizoid factors in personality. In *Psychoanalytic Studies of the Personality*, pp. 3–27. London: Routledge & Kegan Paul, 1952.

———. (1952). *Psychoanalytic Studies of the Personality*. London: Routledge & Kegan Paul.

Fenichel, O. (1945). *The Psychoanalytic Theory of Neurosis*. New York: Norton.

Fitzgerald, F. S. (1933). *Tender Is the Night*. New York: Scribner.

Freud, A. (1938). *The Ego and the Mechanisms of Defense*, rev. ed. New York: International Universities Press, 1966.

Freud, S. (1897). *The Complete Letters of Sigmund Freud to Wilhelm Fliess*, trans. and ed. J. M. Masson. Cambridge, MA: Harvard University Press, 1985.

Freud, S. (1905a). Three essays on sexuality. *Standard Edition* 7:123–243.

———. (1905b). Jokes and their relation to the unconscious. *Standard Edition* 8:1–236.

———. (1910). "Wild" psychoanalysis. *Standard Edition* 11:219–230.

———. (1912a). The dynamics of transference. *Standard Edition* 12:97–108.

———. (1912b). Recommendations to physicians practicing psychoanalysis. *Standard Edition* 12:109–120.

———. (1913a). On beginning the treatment. *Standard Edition* 12:121–144.

———. (1913b). Totem and taboo. *Standard Edition* 13:1–161.

———. (1914a). On narcissism: an introduction. *Standard Edition* 14:67–104.

———. (1914b). Further recommendations on the technique of psychoanalysis: remembering, repeating, and working through. *Standard Edition* 12:145–156.

———. (1917). Mourning and melancholia. *Standard Edition* 14:237–258.

———. (1920). Beyond the pleasure principle. *Standard Edition* 18:1–64.

———. (1921). Group psychology and the analysis of the ego. *Standard Edition* 18:65–144.

———. (1923). The ego and the id. *Standard Edition* 19:44–50.

———. (1926). Inhibitions, symptoms, and anxiety. *Standard Edition* 20:77–178.

———. (1928). Dostoevsky and parricide. *Standard Edition* 21:173–194.

———. (1930). Civilization and its discontents. *Standard Edition* 21:64–148.

Freud, S., and Breuer, J. (1895). Studies on hysteria. *Standard Edition* 2:1–318.

Fromm, E. (1941). *Escape from Freedom*. New York: Rinehart.

Gabbard, G. O. (1996). *Love and Hate in the Analytic Setting*. Northvale, NJ: Jason Aronson.

Glasser, W. (1965). *Reality Therapy*. New York: Harper.

Glover, E. (1928). The aetiology of alcoholism. *Proceedings of the Royal Society of Medicine*. 21:1351–1355.

Goldstein, K. (1939). *The Organism*. New York: Schocken.

Goldstein, K., and Scheer, M. (1941). Abstract and concrete behavior: an experimental study with special tests. *Psychological Monographs* 53:1–231.

Goodwin, D. W., (1988). *Is Alcoholism Hereditary?* New York: Ballantine.

Goodwin, D. W., Schulsinger, F., Hermansen, L., et al. (1973). Alcohol problems in adoptees raised apart from alcoholic biological parents. *Archives of General Psychiatry* 28:283–343.

Guntrip, H. (1968). *Schizoid Problems, Object-Relations, and the Self*. New York: International Universities Press.

Haley, J. (1976). *Problem-Solving Therapy*. San Francisco: Jossey-Bass.

———. (1984). *Ordeal Therapy: Unusual Ways to Change Behavior*. San Francisco: Jossey-Bass.

———. (1990). *Strategies of Psychotherapy*, 2nd ed. Rockville, MD: Triangle.

H. D. (1956). Tribute to Freud, rev. ed. Manchester, England: Carcanet, 1985.

Hartocollis, P. (1968). A dynamic view of alcoholism: drinking in the service of denial. *Dynamic Psychiatry* 2:173–182.

Havens, L. (1986). *Making Contact: Uses of Language in Psychotherapy*. Cambridge, MA: Harvard University Press.

Hegel, G. W. F. (1807). *The Phenomenology of Mind*, trans. J. B. Baille. New York: Macmillan, 1931.

Heidegger, M. (1927). *Being and Time*, trans. J. Macquarrie and E. Robinson. London: SCM Press, 1962.

Horney, K. (1945). *On Inner Conflicts: A Constructive Theory of Neurosis*. New York: Norton.

Jacobson, E. (1938). *Progressive Relaxation*. Chicago: University of Chicago Press.

James, W. (1902). *The Varieties of Religious Experience*. New York: Longmans.

Janov, A. (1970). *The Primal Scream: Primal Therapy; The Cure for Neurosis*. New York: Putnam.

Jellinek, E. M. (1943). Heredity and premature weaning: a discussion of the work of Thomas Trotter, British Naval Physician. In *The Dynamics and Treatment of Alcoholism: Essential Papers*, ed. J. Levin and R. Weiss, pp. 28–34. Northvale, NJ: Jason Aronson, 1994.

———. (1960). *The Disease Concept of Alcoholism*. New Haven, CT: College and University Press.

Joyce, J. (1914). *Ulysses*. New York: Random House, 1934.

Jung, C. G. (1961). C. G. *Jung: Letters, vol. 2, 1951–1961*, pp. 623–625. Princeton, NJ: Princeton University Press, 1973.

Kant, I. (1781). *The Critique of Pure Reason*, 2nd ed., 1787, trans. M. K. Smith. London: Macmillan, 1929.

Kernberg, O. (1975). *Borderline Conditions and Pathological Narcissism*. New York: Jason Aronson.

Khan, M. (1974). The concept of cumulative trauma. In *The Privacy of the Self*, pp. 42–58. New York: International Universities Press.

Khantzian, E. J. (1981). Some treatment implications of ego and self-disturbances in alcoholism. In *Dynamic Approaches to the Understanding and Treatment of Alcoholism*, ed. M. H. Bean and N. E. Zimberg, pp. 163–188. New York: Free Press.

———. (1999). *Treating Addiction as a Human Process*. Northvale, NJ: Jason Aronson.

Khantzian, E. J., and Mack, J. E. (1989). Alcoholics Anonymous and contemporary psychodynamic theory. In *Recent Advances in Alcoholism*, ed. M. Galanter, pp. 67–89. New York: Plenum.

Kierkegaard, S. (1849). *The Concept of Dread*, trans. W. Lowie. Princeton, NJ: Princeton University Press, 1944.

Klein, M. (1921–1945). *Love, Guilt, and Reparation and Other Works, 1921–1945*. New York: Dell, 1975.

———. (1955). On identification. In *Envy and Gratitude and Other Works, 1946–1963*, pp. 141–175. New York: Dell, 1975.

———. (1946–1963). *Envy and Gratitude and Other Works, 1946–1963*. New York: Dell, 1975.

Knight, R. P. (1937). The dynamics and treatment of chronic alcohol addiction. *Bulletin of the Menninger Clinic* 1:233–250.

———. (1938). The psychoanalytic treatment in a sanatorium of chronic addiction to alcohol. *Journal of the American Medical Association* 111:1443–1448.

Kohut, H. (1971). *The Analysis of the Self: A Systematic Approach to the Psychoanalytic Treatment of Narcissistic Personality Disorders*. New York: International Universities Press.

———. (1972). Thoughts on narcissism and narcissistic rage. In *The Search for the Self*, ed. P. H. Ornstein, pp. 615–658. New York: International Universities Press, 1978.

———. (1977a). *The Restoration of the Self*. New York: International Universities Press.

———. (1977b). Preface to *Psychodynamics of Drug Dependence*. National Institute on Drug Abuse Research Monograph 12, pp. vii–ix. U.S. Department of Health, Education, and Welfare. Washington, DC: U.S. Government Printing Office.

———. (1984). *How Does Analysis Cure?* Chicago: University of Chicago Press.

Krystal, H., and Raskin, H. A. (1970). *Drug Dependence: Aspects of Ego Function*. Northvale, NJ: Jason Aronson, 1993.

LeBon, G. (1895). *Psychologie des Foules*. Paris: Alcan. [*The Crowd: A Study of the Popular Mind*. London: Unwin, trans. R. Meton, 1920.]

Levin, J. D. (1987). *Treatment of Alcoholism and Other Addictions: A Self-Psychology Approach*. Northvale, NJ: Jason Aronson.

———. (1991). *Recovery from Alcoholism: Beyond Your Wildest Dreams*. Northvale, NJ: Jason Aronson.

———. (1993). *Slings and Arrows: Narcissistic Injury and Its Treatment*. Northvale, NJ: Jason Aronson.

———. (1995). *Introduction to Alcoholism Counseling: A Bio-Psycho-Social Approach*, 2nd ed. Washington, DC: Taylor & Francis.

———. (1998a). *The Clinton Syndrome: The President and the Self-Destructive Nature of Sexual Addiction*. Rocklin, CA: Forum.

———. (1998b). *Couple and Family Therapy of Addiction*. Northvale, NJ: Jason Aronson.

———. (1999). *Primer of Treating Substance Abusers*. Northvale, NJ: Jason Aronson.

Lindner, R. (1954). *The Fifty-Minute Hour.* New York: Rinehardt.

Loper, R. G., Kammeier, M. L., and Hoffman, H. (1973). MMPI characteristics of college freshmen males who later became alcoholic. *Journal of Abnormal Psychology* 82:159–162.

MacAndrew, C. (1965). The differentiation of male alcoholic outpatients from non-alcoholic psychiatric outpatients by means of the MMPI. *Quarterly Journal of Studies on Alcohol* 26: 238–246.

Mack, J. G. (1981). Alcoholism, A.A. and the governance of the self. In *Dynamic Approaches to the Understanding and Treatment of Alcoholism,* ed. M. H. Bean and N. E. Zinberg, pp. 128–162. New York: Free Press.

Mahler, M., Pine, F., and Bergman, A. (1975). *The Psychological Birth of the Human Infant: Symbiosis and Individuation.* San Francisco: Jossey-Bass.

Maraniss, D. (1996). *First in His Class.* New York: Simon & Schuster.

Masterson, J. F. (1976). *Psychotherapy of the Borderline Adult: A Developmental Approach.* New York: Brunner/Mazel.

May, R. (1953). *Man's Search for Himself.* New York: Norton.

McClelland, D. C., Davis, W., Kalin, R., and Wanner, E. (1972). *The Drinking Man: Alcohol and Human Motivation.* New York: Free Press.

McDougall, W. (1920). *The Group Mind.* Cambridge, England: Cambridge University Press.

Menninger, K. (1938). *Man Against Himself.* New York: Harcourt, Brace.

Millay, E. St. V. (1917). Renascence. In *Collected Poems,* ed. N. Millay, pp. 3–13. New York: Harper & Row, 1956.

Miller, A. C. (1981). *Drama of the Gifted Child.* New York: Basic Books.

Minuchin, S. (1992). Constructing a therapeutic reality. In *Family Therapy of Drug and Alcohol Abuse,* 2nd ed., ed. E. Kaufman and P. Kaufmann, pp. 1–14. Boston: Allyn & Bacon.

Minuchin, S., Montalvo, B., Guerney, B. G., Jr., et al. (1967). *Families of the Slums: An Exploration of Their Structure and Treatment.* New York: Basic Books.

Myers, W. A. (1994). Addictive sexual behavior. *Journal of the American Psychoanalytic Association* 42:(4): 1159–1182.

Nadler, S. (1999). *Spinoza: A Life.* New York: Cambridge University Press.

O'Farrell, T. (1993). A behavioral marital therapy couples group program for alcoholics and their spouses. In *Treating Alcohol Problems: Marital and Family Interventions,* pp. 170–209. New York: Guilford.

Ogden, T. (1982). *Projective Identification and Psychotherapeutic Technique.* New York: Jason Aronson.

————. (1990). *The Matrix of the Mind.* Northvale, NJ: Jason Aronson.

O'Neill, E. (1929). *The Great God Brown.* In *The Plays of Eugene O'Neill.* New York: Random House, 1967.

————. (1946). *The Iceman Cometh.* New York: Random House.

Perls, F. S. (1969). *Ego, Hunger and Aggression.* New York: Vintage.

Plato (375 B.C.). Republic. Book VII. In *Plato: Collected Dialogues*, ed. E. Hamilton and H. Cairns, trans. P. Shoney, pp. 575–845. Princeton, NJ: Princeton University Press, 1961.

Prochaska, J., and DiClemente, C. C. (1984). *The Transtheoretical Approach: Crossing the Traditional Boundaries of Therapy.* Homewood, IL: Dow-Jones/Irwin.

Rado, S. (1933). The psychoanalysis of pharmacothymia. *Psychoanalytic Quarterly* 2: 2–23.

Rogers, C. (1961). *On Becoming a Person: A Therapist's View of Psychotherapy.* Boston: Houghton Mifflin.

Russell, B. (1945). *A History of Western Philosophy.* New York: Simon & Schuster.

Schachter, S., and Singer, J. (1962). Cognitive, social and physiological determinants of emotional state. *Psychological Review* 69:379–399.

Scharff, D. E. (1992). *Refinding the Object and Reclaiming the Self.* Northvale, NJ: Jason Aronson.

Scharff, D. E., and Scharff, J. S. (1991). *Object Relations Family Therapy.* Northvale, NJ: Jason Aronson.

Seligman, M. E. P. (1989). *Helplessness: On Depression, Development and Death.* San Francisco,. CA: Freeman.

Simmel, E. (1948). Alcoholism and addiction. *Psychoanalytic Quarterly* 17: 6–31.

Spinoza, B. (1677). *Ethics Demonstrated by the Geometric Method (Ethica Ordine Geometrio Demonstrata).* In *The Chief Works of Benedict De Spinoza*, trans. R. H. M. Elwes, vol. 2, pp. 44–272. New York: Dover, 1951.

Steinglass, P., with Bennett, L., Wolin, S., and Reiss, D. (1987). *The Alcoholic Family.* New York: Basic Books.

Stern, D. N. (1985). *The Interpersonal World of the Infant: A View from Psychoanalysis and Developmental Psychology.* New York: Basic Books.

Szasz, T. (1958). The role of the counterphobic mechanism in addiction. *Journal of the American Psychoanalytic Association* 6:309–325.

Tiebout, H. M. (1949). The act of surrender in the therapeutic process. *Quarterly Journal of Studies on Alcohol* 10:48–58.

———. (1957). The ego factor in surrender to alcoholism. *Quarterly Journal of Studies on Alcohol* 15:610–621.

Trotter, W. (1916). *Instincts of the Herd in Peace and War*. London: T. Fisher Unwin.

Vaillant, G. E. (1977). *Adaptation to Life*. Boston: Little, Brown.

———. (1983). *The Natural History of Alcoholism: Causes, Patterns and Paths to Recovery*. Cambridge, MA: Harvard University Press.

Wallace, J. (1995). Working with the preferred defense structure of alcoholics. In *Dynamics and Treatment of Alcoholism*, ed. J. Levin and R. Weiss, pp. 222–232. Northvale, NJ: Jason Aronson.

Walzer, M. (1985). *Exodus and Revolution*. New York: Basic Books.

Watts, T. D., and Wright, R., eds. (1983). *Black Alcoholism: Toward a Comprehensive Understanding*. Springfield, IL: Charles C Thomas.

Watzlawick, P. (1978). *The Language of Change*. New York: Basic Books.

Whitaker, C. A., and Bumberry, W. M. (1988). *Dancing with the Family: A Symbolic-Experiential Approach*. New York: Brunner/Mazel.

Winnicott, D. W. (1950). Aggression in relation to emotional development. In *Through Paediatrics to Psycho-Analysis*, pp. 204–218. London: Hogarth, 1958.

———. (1951). Transitional objects and transitional phenomena in *Through Paediatrics to Psycho-Analysis*, pp. 229–242. London: Hogarth, 1958.

———. (1956). Primary maternal preoccupation. In *Through Paediatrics to Psycho-Analysis*, pp. 300–305. London: Hogarth, 1958.

———. (1958). The capacity to be alone. In *The Maturational Processes and the Facilitating Environment*, pp. 29–36. New York: International Universities Press, 1965.

———. (1960). Ego distortion in terms of true and false self. In *The Maturational Processes and the Facilitating Environment*, pp. 140–152. New York: International Universities Press, 1965.

———. (1963). The development of the capacity for concern. In *The Maturational Processes and the Facilitating Environment*, pp. 73–83. New York: International Universities Press, 1965.

Witkin, H. A., Karp, S. A., and Goodenough, D. R. (1959). Dependence in alcoholics. *Quarterly Journal of Studies on Alcohol* 20:493–504.

Witkin, H. A., & Oltman, P.K. (1967). Cognitive style. *International Journal of Neurology* 6:119–137.

Wolpe, J. (1969). *The Practice of Behavior Therapy*. Oxford: Pergamon.

Wordsworth, W. (1850). The prelude. In *The Poetical Works of Wordsworth*. New York: Oxford University Press, 1910.

Wurmser, L. (1978). *The Hidden Dimension: Psychodynamics in Compulsive Drug Use*. New York: Jason Aronson.

Index